New Perspectives on

The Internet

7th Edition

Introductory

Gary P. Schneider

Jessica Evans

 **COURSE TECHNOLOGY**
CENGAGE Learning™

Australia • Brazil • Japan • Korea • Mexico • Singapore • Spain • United Kingdom • United States

COURSE TECHNOLOGY
CENGAGE Learning™

New Perspectives on The Internet, 7th Edition—Introductory

Executive Editor: Marie L. Lee

Senior Product Manager: Kathy Finnegan

Product Manager: Erik Herman

Associate Product Manager: Brandi Henson

Editorial Assistant: Leigh Robbins

Director of Marketing: Cheryl Costantini

Marketing Manager: Ryan DeGrote

Marketing Specialist: Jennifer Hankin

Developmental Editors: Amanda Brodkin, Kim T. M. Crowley

Senior Content Project Manager: Jennifer Goguen McGrail

Composition: GEX Publishing Services

Text Designer: Steve Deschene

Art Director: Marissa Falco

Cover Designer: Elizabeth Paquin

Cover Art: Bill Brown

For product information and technology assistance, contact us at **Cengage Learning Academic Resource Center, 1-800-423-0563**

For permission to use material from this text or product, submit all requests online at **cengage.com/permissions**
Further permissions questions can be emailed to **permissionrequest@cengage.com**

Some of the product names and company names used in this book have been used for identification purposes only and may be trademarks or registered trademarks of their respective manufacturers and sellers.

Microsoft and the Office logo are either registered trademarks or trademarks of Microsoft Corporation in the United States and/or other countries. Course Technology, Cengage Learning is an independent entity from the Microsoft Corporation, and not affiliated with Microsoft in any manner.

Disclaimer: Any fictional data related to persons or companies or URLs used throughout this book is intended for instructional purposes only. At the time this book was printed, any such data was fictional and not belonging to any real persons or companies.

ISBN-13: 978-1-4239-2507-1

ISBN-10: 1-4239-2507-6

Course Technology
25 Thomson Place
Boston, Massachusetts 02210
USA

Cengage Learning products are represented in Canada by Nelson Education, Ltd.

For your lifelong learning solutions, visit **course.cengage.com**

Visit our corporate website at **www.cengage.com**

Printed in the United States of America
1 2 3 4 5 6 7 8 9 12 11 10 09 08

Preface

The New Perspectives Series' critical-thinking, problem-solving approach is the ideal way to prepare students to transcend point-and-click skills and take advantage of all that the Internet has to offer.

Our goal in developing the New Perspectives Series was to create books that give students the software concepts and practical skills they need to succeed beyond the classroom. With this new edition, we've updated our proven case-based pedagogy with more practical content to make learning skills more meaningful to students.

With the New Perspectives Series, students understand *why* they are learning *what* they are learning, and are fully prepared to apply their skills to real-life situations.

"I really love the Margin Tips, which add 'tricks of the trade' to students' skills package. In addition, the Reality Check exercises provide for practical application of students' knowledge. I can't wait to use them in the classroom."

—Terry Morse Colucci
Institute of Technology, Inc.

About This Book

This book provides a thorough introduction to the Internet, and includes the following:
- Up-to-date coverage of the most popular browsers and email tools, highlighting new features such as tabbed browsing
- Instruction on how to use Microsoft Internet Explorer, Mozilla Firefox, Microsoft Outlook Express, Windows Mail, and Windows Live Hotmail
- Expanded and in-depth coverage of topics related to searching the Web and downloading data, including search engines, digital rights management, online storage providers, and Web-based collaboration services
- Interactive Student Edition Labs on using a browser, working with email, and protecting a computer from viruses
- An Online Companion, which is a centralized and constantly updated launching pad for students to find all the links they will use and explore in conjunction with this text
- Updated business case scenarios throughout, which provide a rich and realistic context for students to apply the concepts and skills presented

System Requirements

This book assumes that either Microsoft Internet Explorer 7.0 (or higher) or Mozilla Firefox 2.0 (or higher), and Windows XP or Windows Vista (or higher) are installed. Note that the figures and steps in this edition were written using Windows Vista; therefore, Windows XP users might notice minor differences in the figures and steps. This book assumes that students have a complete installation of the Web browser software and its components, an Internet connection, and the ability to create an email account. Because the Web browser or email client students use might be different from those used in the figures in this book, students' screens might differ slightly; this does not present any problems for students in completing the tutorials.

The New Perspectives Approach

Context

Each tutorial begins with a problem presented in a "real-world" case that is meaningful to students. The case sets the scene to help students understand what they will do in the tutorial.

Hands-on Approach

Each tutorial is divided into manageable sessions that combine reading and hands-on, step-by-step work. Colorful screenshots help guide students through the steps. **Trouble?** tips anticipate common mistakes or problems to help students stay on track and continue with the tutorial.

InSight

InSight Boxes

New for this edition! InSight boxes offer expert advice and best practices to help students better understand how to work with the Internet. With the information provided in the InSight boxes, students achieve a deeper understanding of the concepts behind the features and skills presented.

Tip

Margin Tips

New for this edition! Margin Tips provide helpful hints and shortcuts for more efficient use of the Internet. The Tips appear in the margin at key points throughout each tutorial, giving students extra information when and where they need it.

Reality Check

Reality Checks

New for this edition! Comprehensive, open-ended Reality Check exercises allow students to practice skills by completing practical, real-world tasks, such as hosting a Web site, evaluating Internet resources, and searching for information about a topic of personal interest.

Review

In New Perspectives, retention is a key component to learning. At the end of each session, a series of Quick Check questions helps students test their understanding of the concepts before moving on. Each tutorial also contains an end-of-tutorial summary and a list of key terms for further reinforcement.

Apply

Assessment

Engaging and challenging Review Assignments and Case Problems have always been a hallmark feature of the New Perspectives Series. Colorful icons and brief descriptions accompany the exercises, making it easy to understand, at a glance, both the goal and level of challenge a particular assignment holds.

Reference Window

Task Reference

Reference

While contextual learning is excellent for retention, there are times when students will want a high-level understanding of how to accomplish a task. Within each tutorial, Reference Windows appear before a set of steps to provide a succinct summary and preview of how to perform a task. In addition, a complete Task Reference at the back of the book provides quick access to information on how to carry out common tasks. Finally, each book includes a combination Glossary/Index to promote easy reference of material.

New Perspectives Series v

Brief
Introductory
Comprehensive

Our Complete System of Instruction

Coverage To Meet Your Needs

Whether you're looking for just a small amount of coverage or enough to fill a semester-long class, we can provide you with a textbook that meets your needs.

- Brief books typically cover the essential skills in just 2 to 4 tutorials.
- Introductory books build and expand on those skills and contain an average of 5 to 8 tutorials.
- Comprehensive books are great for a full-semester class, and contain 9 to 12+ tutorials.

So if the book you're holding does not provide the right amount of coverage for you, there's probably another offering available. Go to our Web site or contact your Course Technology sales representative to find out what else we offer.

Online Companion

This book has an accompanying Online Companion Web site designed to enhance learning. This Web site includes:

- All the links necessary for completing the tutorials and end-of-tutorial exercises
- Student Data Files
- Additional resources for topics in each tutorial
- Links to the Student Edition Labs for hands-on reinforcement of selected topics

Student Edition Labs

These interactive labs help students review and extend their knowledge of Internet concepts through observation, step-by-step practice, and review questions. The Student Edition Labs are tied to individual tutorials and cover various subject areas, such as using a browser, working with email, and protecting a computer from viruses.

CourseCasts – Learning on the Go. Always available…always relevant.

Want to keep up with the latest technology trends relevant to you? Visit our site to find a library of podcasts, CourseCasts, featuring a "CourseCast of the Week," and download them to your mp3 player at http://coursecasts.course.com.

Ken Baldauf, host of CourseCasts, is a faculty member of the Florida State University Computer Science Department where he is responsible for teaching technology classes to thousands of FSU students each year. Ken is an expert in the latest technology trends; he gathers and sorts through the most pertinent news and information for CourseCasts so your students can spend their time enjoying technology, rather than trying to figure it out. Open or close your lecture with a discussion based on the latest CourseCast.

Visit us at http://coursecasts.course.com to learn on the go!

Instructor Resources

We offer more than just a book. We have all the tools you need to enhance your lectures, check students' work, and generate exams in a new, easier-to-use and completely revised package. This book's Instructor's Manual, ExamView testbank, PowerPoint presentations, data files, solution files, figure files, and a sample syllabus are all available on a single CD-ROM or for downloading at www.course.com.

Skills Assessment and Training

SAM 2007 helps bridge the gap between the classroom and the real world by allowing students to train and test on important computer skills in an active, hands-on environment. SAM 2007's easy-to-use system includes powerful interactive exams, training or projects on critical applications such as Word, Excel, Access, PowerPoint, Outlook, Windows, the Internet, and much more. SAM simulates the application environment, allowing students to demonstrate their knowledge and think through the skills by performing real-world tasks. Powerful administrative options allow instructors to schedule exams and assignments, secure tests, and run reports with almost limitless flexibility.

Blackboard

Online Content

Blackboard is the leading distance learning solution provider and class-management platform today. Course Technology has partnered with Blackboard to bring you premium online content. Content for use with *New Perspectives on The Internet, 7th Edition, Introductory* is available in a Blackboard Course Cartridge and may include topic reviews, case projects, review questions, test banks, practice tests, custom syllabi, and more. Course Technology also has solutions for several other learning management systems. Please visit http://www.course.com today to see what's available for this title.

Acknowledgments

Creating a textbook is a collaborative effort in which authors and publisher work as a team to provide the highest quality book possible. We want to acknowledge the major contributions of the Course Technology editorial team members: Kathy Finnegan, Senior Product Manager; Brandi Henson, Associate Product Manager; Leigh Robbins, Editorial Assistant; and Jennifer Goguen McGrail, Senior Content Project Manager. We also appreciate the expert management of Karen McCutcheon and the Online Development Group for their creation of the Online Companion for this book. We thank Christian Kunciw and his team of Quality Assurance testers for their work as well. We offer our heartfelt thanks to the Course Technology organization as a whole. The people at Course Technology have been, by far, the best publishing team with which we have ever worked. We also thank our Developmental Editors, Kim Crowley and Amanda Brodkin. Their sharp eyes caught many mistakes and they contributed excellent ideas for making the manuscript more readable. We would also like to thank Katherine Pinard, who has not only contributed to this book as a Developmental Editor in the past, but who has also authored the book's adaptation for other markets.

We want to thank the following reviewers for their insightful comments and suggestions at various stages of the book's development: Brian Ameling, Limestone College; Frank Lucente, Westmoreland County Community College; and Mark Shellman, Gaston College.

Finally, we want to express our deep appreciation for the continuous support and encouragement of our spouses, Cathy Cosby and Richard Evans. They demonstrated remarkable patience as we worked to complete this book on a very tight schedule. We also thank our children for tolerating our absences while we were busy writing.

– Gary P. Schneider
– Jessica Evans

Dedication

To the memory of my brother, Bruce. – G.P.S.
To Hannah and Richard. – J.E.

Brief Contents

Internet

Table of Contents

Internet—Level II Tutorials

Credits

Tutorial 1

Figures 1-3 and 1-4: Courtesy of w3 Communications

Figure 1-7: Courtesy of Microsoft Corporation

Figure 1-9: Courtesy of Mozilla

Figure 1-10: Courtesy of Opera Software ASA

Figure 1-11: Courtesy of irider.com; Courtesy of amazon.com

Figures 1-12, 1-19, and 1-25: Courtesy of Microsoft Corporation

Figures 1-29, 1-30, 1-34 through 1-37, 1-39, and 1-40: Courtesy of Mozilla

Tutorial 2

Figures 2-1 through 2-4: Courtesy of Microsoft Corporation

Figures 2-5 through 2-11: Courtesy of Mozilla

Figures 2-12 through 2-15: Courtesy of Opera Software ASA

Figure 2-16: Courtesy of Public Storage – The Real Storage Experts

Figure 2-17: Courtesy of Google

Figures 2-19 through 2-66: Courtesy of Microsoft Corporation

Tutorial 3

Figures 3-4 and 3-7: Courtesy of Yahoo! Inc. ® 2007 by Yahoo! Inc. YAHOO! and the YAHOO! logo are trademarks of Yahoo! Inc.

Figures 3-5 and 3-6: Courtesy of Google

Figure 3-9: Courtesy of Ask.com, a division of IAC Search & Media, Inc.

Figures 3-10 and 3-12: Courtesy of Yahoo! Inc. ® 2007 by Yahoo! Inc. YAHOO! and the YAHOO! logo are trademarks of Yahoo! Inc.

Figure 3-11: Courtesy of © 2007 AOL LLC. All Rights Reserved; Copyright © 1998-2007 Netscape

Figure 3-13: Courtesy of Gigablast, Inc.

Figure 3-14: Courtesy of Copernic, Inc. - © Copernic, Inc. 2007 All Rights Reserved.

Figure 3-15: Courtesy of Kartoo.com

Figure 3-16: Courtesy of Google

Figure 3-19: Courtesy of Yahoo! Inc. ® 2007 by Yahoo! Inc. YAHOO! and the YAHOO! logo are trademarks of Yahoo! Inc.

Figures 3-20 and 3-21: Courtesy of Ask.com, a division of IAC Search & Media, Inc.

Figures 3-22 and 3-23: Courtesy of Google

Figure 3-24: Courtesy of Vivisimo, Inc.

Figure 3-25: Courtesy of © by Jakob Nielsen

Tutorial 4

Figure 4-1: Courtesy of Ask.com, a division of IAC Search and Media, Inc.

Figures 4-2, 4-4, and 4-5: Courtesy of Yahoo! Inc. ® 2007 by Yahoo! Inc. YAHOO! and the YAHOO! logo are trademarks of Yahoo! Inc.

Figure 4-3: Courtesy of Lycosinc.com

Figures 4-6 and 4-8: Courtesy of Google

Figure 4-7: Courtesy of The Internet Public Library

Figure 4-9: Courtesy of AccuWeather.com

Figure 4-10: Courtesy of weather.com and © 2008 Microsoft Corporation. All rights reserved.

Figure 4-11: MapQuest and the MapQuest logo are registered trademarks of MapQuest, Inc. Used with permission.

Figure 4-12: Courtesy of © 2008 Google and © 2008 Microsoft Corporation. All rights reserved.

Figure 4-13: Courtesy of © 2007 Citysearch.com. All rights reserved.

Figure 4-14: Courtesy of Idearc Media Corp

Figure 4-15: Courtesy of StartSpot Mediaworks, Inc.

Figure 4-17: Courtesy of Bartleby.com, Inc.

Figure 4-18: Courtesy of archive.com

Figure 4-20: Copyright © 1998 – 2007 iParadigms, LLC. All rights reserved.

Figure 4-21: Courtesy of © 2005-2007 The Board of Trustees of the Leland Stanford Junior University.

Figure 4-22: Courtesy of ibiblio.org

Figure 4-23: Courtesy of Google

Figure 4-24: Courtesy of © 2008 Adobe Systems Incorporated. All rights reserved.

Tutorial 5
Figure 5-1: Courtesy of © Core FTP. All rights reserved.

Figures 5-2 and 5-6: Courtesy of © 2008 Microsoft Corporation. All rights reserved.

Figure 5-4, 5-5, 5-8 and 5-9: Courtesy of ibiblio.org

Figures 5-10 and 5-11: Copyright 2007 Symantec Corporation. Reprinted with permission.

Figures 5-12 through 5-17: Courtesy of Tim Kosse from the FileZilla Project

Figures 5-18 through 5-20: Courtesy of © 2008 WinZip® International LLC. WinZip is a Registered Trademark of WinZip International LLC.

Figure 5-21: Courtesy of © 2008 Microsoft Corporation. All rights reserved.

Figure 5-22: Courtesy of Box.net, Inc.

Figure 5-23: Courtesy of Zoho/AdventNet, Inc.

Appendix A
Figure A-1: Courtesy of How Stuff Works

Figure A-2: Courtesy of Tucows

Figure A-3: Courtesy of Coldwater Creek

Figure A-4: Courtesy of AAGAMIA/Getty Images

Figure A-7: Courtesy of BNN Technologies

Figure A-8: Image courtesy of Computer History Museum

Figure A-12: Courtesy of MIT Museum; Courtesy of Ted Nelson/Project Xanadu; Courtesy of the Bootstrap Institute

Figure A-13: Reproduced with permission of Yahoo! Inc. ® 2007 by Yahoo! Inc. YAHOO! and the YAHOO! logo are trademarks of Yahoo! Inc.

Objectives

Session 1.1
- Learn about the Internet and the World Wide Web
- Learn how Web browser software displays Web pages
- Learn how Web page addresses are constructed
- Become familiar with Web browsers and the main functions found in this type of software

Session 1.2
- Configure and use the Microsoft Internet Explorer Web browser to navigate the Web
- Save and organize Web addresses using Internet Explorer
- Save Web page text and graphics using Internet Explorer

Session 1.3
- Configure and use the Mozilla Firefox Web browser to navigate the Web
- Save and organize Web addresses using Mozilla Firefox
- Save Web page text and graphics using Mozilla Firefox

Browser Basics

Introduction to the Web and Web Browser Software

Case | Danville Animal Shelter

The Danville Animal Shelter is an organization devoted to helping improve the welfare of animals, particularly unwanted pets, in the local Danville area. Trinity Andrews is the director of the shelter, and she is always looking for ways to improve the services it offers to the community.

The shelter is a charitable organization that is supported mainly by contributions from the local community. Trinity budgets the limited funds that the shelter receives to do the most good for the animals. One of the critical needs of the shelter is to let people in the community know about the pets available for adoption. Trinity has placed some advertising in local newspapers and television stations, but advertising is very expensive, even when the local media outlets provide reduced rates or offer to run stories about the shelter.

The problem with using newspapers and television is that the pets available for adoption change from day to day and, by the time a news story or ad runs, the pet that is featured often has been adopted. Trinity realizes that although newspaper and television advertising and promotion can be a good way for the shelter to get its general message out to the community, these outlets are not the best way to let people know about specific pets that are available for adoption.

You have served as a volunteer at the shelter for several years, and Trinity heard that you were learning to use the Internet. Trinity would like you to help identify ways to use the Internet to let the community know about the shelter and, in particular, about specific pets that are available for adoption. Your college friend, Maggie Beeler, earned her degree in library science. You meet with Maggie at the local public library, where she is working at the reference desk, to discuss how you might use the Web to help the shelter.

Starting Data Files

There are no starting Data Files needed for this tutorial.

Session 1.1

Understanding the Internet and the World Wide Web

Computers can be connected to each other in a configuration called a **network**. If the computers are near each other (usually in the same building), the network is called a **local area network** or a **LAN**. Networked computers that are not located near each other form a **wide area network**, or a **WAN**. When networks are connected to each other, the system is called an **interconnected network** or **internet** (with a lowercase "i"). The **Internet** (with an uppercase "i") is a specific interconnected network that connects computers all over the world using a common set of interconnection standards. Although it began as a large science project sponsored by the U.S. military, the Internet today allows people and businesses all over the world to communicate with each other in a variety of ways.

The part of the Internet known as the **World Wide Web** (or the **Web**) is a subset of the computers on the Internet that use software to make their contents easily accessible to each other. The Web has helped to make information on the Internet easily accessible by people who are not computer scientists. The Internet and the Web give people around the world new ways to communicate with each other, obtain information resources and software, conduct business transactions, and find entertainment. You can read Appendix A to learn more about the history of the Internet and about the technologies that make it work.

The Web is a collection of files that reside on computers, called **Web servers**, that are located all over the world and are connected to each other through the Internet. Most files on computers, including computers that are connected to the Internet, are private; that is, only the computer's users can access those files. The owners of the computer files that make up the Web have made the files publicly available by placing them on the Web servers. Anyone who has a computer connected to the Internet can obtain access to the files.

When you use your Internet connection to become part of the Web, your computer becomes a **Web client** in a worldwide client/server network. A **Web browser** is the software that you run on your computer to make it work as a Web client. The Internet connects many different types of computers running different operating system software. Web browser software lets your computer communicate with all of these different types of computers easily and effectively. Figure 1-1 shows how this client/server structure uses the Internet to provide multiple interconnections among the various kinds of client and server computers.

Client/server structure of the World Wide Web ◀ Figure 1-1

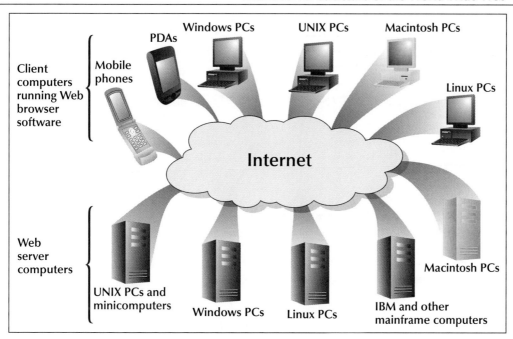

Hypertext, Links, and Hypermedia

The public files on Web servers are ordinary text files, much like the files created and used by word-processing software. To enable Web browser software to read these files, however, the text must be formatted according to a generally accepted standard. The standard used on the Web is **Hypertext Markup Language (HTML)**. HTML uses codes, or **tags**, that tell the Web browser software how to display the text contained in the text file. For example, a Web browser reading the following line of text

```
<B>A Review of the Book <I>Wind Instruments</I></B>
```

recognizes the <B> and </B> tags as instructions to display the entire line of text in bold and the <I> and </I> tags as instructions to display the text enclosed by those tags in italics. Different Web clients that connect to this Web server might display the tagged text differently. For example, one Web browser might display text enclosed by bold tags in a blue color instead of displaying the text in bold. A text file that contains HTML tags is called an **HTML document**.

HTML provides a variety of text formatting tags that can be used to indicate headings, paragraphs, bulleted lists, numbered lists, and other text enhancements in an HTML document. The real power of HTML, however, lies in its anchor tag. The **HTML anchor tag** enables Web designers to link HTML documents to each other. Anchor tags in HTML documents create **hypertext links**, which are instructions that point to other HTML documents or to another section of the same document. Hypertext links also are called **hyperlinks** or **links**. Figure 1-2 shows how these hyperlinks can join multiple HTML documents to create a web of HTML documents across computers on the Internet. The HTML documents shown in the figure can be on the same computer or on different computers. The computers can be in the same room or an ocean away from each other.

Figure 1-2 **Hyperlinks create a web of HTML text across multiple files**

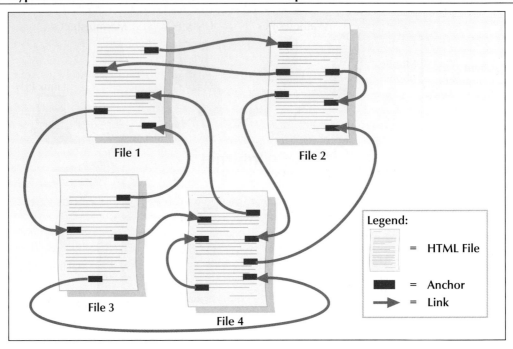

Most Web browsers display hyperlinks in a color that is different from other text in an HTML document and also underline the hyperlinks so they are easy to distinguish. When a Web browser displays an HTML document, it is often referred to as a **Web page**. Maggie shows you a Web page at the World Wide Web Consortium (W3C) Web site. See Figure 1-3. The hyperlinks on this Web page are easy to identify, because the Web browser software that displayed this page shows the hyperlinks as blue, underlined text.

Figure 1-3 **W3C Web page**

Each of the hyperlinks on the Web page shown in Figure 1-3 enables the user to connect to another Web page. In turn, each of those linked Web pages contains hyperlinks to other pages, including one hyperlink that leads back to the original Web page. Hyperlinks can also lead to computer files that contain pictures, graphics, and media objects such as sound and video clips. Hyperlinks that connect to these types of files often are called **hypermedia links**. You are especially interested in learning more about hypermedia links, but Maggie suggests you first need to understand a little more about how people organize Web pages on their Web servers.

The easiest way to move from one Web page to another is to use the hyperlinks that the authors of Web pages have embedded in their HTML documents. Web page authors often use a graphic image as a hyperlink. Sometimes, it is difficult to identify which objects and text are hyperlinks just by looking at a Web page displayed on your computer.

Figure 1-4 shows the pointing index finger icon on a Web page at the World Wide Web Consortium (W3C) site. The mouse pointer was positioned over the Finding Your Way at W3C hyperlink, and the shape of the pointer indicates that if you click the Finding Your Way at W3C text, the Web browser will open the Web page to which that hyperlink points.

Tip

You can determine that a text or graphic object is a hyperlink when the mouse pointer changes into an icon that resembles a hand with a pointing index finger when resting on the text or graphic.

Mouse pointer hovering over a hyperlink ◀ **Figure 1-4**

W3C® WORLD WIDE WEB
consortium

Leading the Web to Its Full Potential...

Activities | Technical Reports | Site Index | New Visitors | About W3C | Join W3C | Contact W3C

The World Wide Web Consortium (W3C) develops interoperable technologies (specifications, guidelines, software, and tools) to lead the Web to its full potential. W3C is a forum for information, commerce, communication, and collective understanding. On this page, you'll find W3C news, links to W3C technologies and ways to get involved. New visitors can find help in *Finding Your Way at W3C*. We encourage organizations to learn more about W3C and about W3C Membership.

Mobile Web   **News**   **Search**

mouse pointer changes to pointing finger when moved over a hyperlink

Web Site Organization

People who create Web pages usually have a collection of related pages stored on one computer that they use as their Web server. A collection of linked Web pages that has a common theme or focus is called a **Web site**. Most Web sites store all of the site's pages in a single location, either on one computer or on one LAN. Some large Web sites, however, are distributed over a number of locations. In fact, it can be difficult to determine where one Web site ends and another begins. One common definition of a Web site is any group of Web pages that relates to one specific topic or organization, regardless of where the HTML documents are located.

The main page that all of the other pages on a particular Web site are organized around and link back to is called the site's **home page**. The term *home page* is used at least three different ways on the Web, and it is sometimes difficult to tell which meaning people intend when they use the term. The first definition of home page indicates the main page for a particular site. This home page is the first page that opens when you visit a particular Web site. The second definition of home page is the first page that opens when you start your Web browser. This type of home page might be an HTML document on your own computer. Some people create such home pages and include hyperlinks to Web sites that they frequently visit. If you are using a computer on your school's or employer's network, its Web browser might be configured to open the main page for the school or firm. The third definition of home page is the Web page that a particular Web browser loads the first time you use it. This page usually is stored at the Web site of the firm or other organization that created the Web browser software. Home pages that meet the second or third definitions are sometimes called **start pages**.

Addresses on the Web

The Internet has no centralized control. Therefore, no central starting point exists for the Web, which is a part of the Internet. However, there is a system for locating a specific computer on the Web.

Domain Name Addressing

Each computer on the Internet has a unique identification number, called an **IP (Internet Protocol) address**. IP addressing is a way of identifying each unique computer on the Web, just like your home address is a way of identifying your home in a city. (You can learn more about IP addressing by reading Appendix A.) Most people do not use the IP address to locate Web sites and individual pages. Instead, the browsers use domain name addressing. A **domain name** is a unique name associated with a specific IP address by a program that runs on an Internet host computer. This program, which coordinates the IP addresses and domain names for all computers attached to it, is called **DNS (domain name system) software**, and the host computer that runs this software is called a **domain name server**. Domain names can include any number of parts separated by periods; however, most domain names currently in use have only three or four parts. For example, the domain name gsb.uchicago.edu is the computer connected to the Internet at the Graduate School of Business (gsb), which is an academic unit of the University of Chicago (uchicago), which is an educational institution (edu). No other computer on the Internet has the same domain name.

Domain names have a hierarchical structure that you can follow from top to bottom if you read the domain names from right to left. The last part of a domain name is called its **top-level domain (TLD)**. For example, DNS software on the Internet host computer that is responsible for the "edu" domain keeps track of the IP addresses for all of the educational institutions in its domain, including "uchicago." Similar DNS software on the "uchicago" Internet host computer would keep track of the academic units' computers in its domain, including the "gsb" computer.

Since 1998, the **Internet Corporation for Assigned Names and Numbers (ICANN)** has had responsibility for managing domain names. In the United States, the six most common TLDs are .com, .edu, .gov, .mil, .net, and .org. Although a seventh TLD, the "us" domain, is approved for general use by any person within the United States, it is most frequently used by state and local government organizations in the United States and by U.S. primary and secondary schools (because the "edu" domain is reserved for post-secondary educational institutions). Internet host computers outside the United States often use two-letter country domain names instead of, or in addition to, the six general TLDs. For example, the domain name uq.edu.au is the domain name for the University of Queensland (uq), which is an educational institution (edu) in Australia (au).

In 2000, ICANN added seven new TLDs. Some of these new TLDs are like the existing TLDs, which are **general TLDs** (or **gTLDs**). A general TLD is maintained by ICANN. Other new TLDs that were introduced in 2000 are **sponsored TLDs** (**sTLDs**), which are maintained by a sponsoring organization other than ICANN.

The four gTLDs introduced in 2000 included .biz (for business organizations), .info (for any person or organization that wanted to provide an informational Web site), .name (for individual persons), and .pro (for licensed professionals, such as accountants, lawyers, and physicians).

The three sTLDs introduced in 2000 that are sponsored by various industry organizations are .aero (for airlines, airports, and the air transport industry), .coop (for cooperative organizations), and .museum (for museums). Each of these domains is maintained by its sponsoring organization, not by ICANN. For example, the .aero domain is maintained by SITA, an air transport industry association.

Although ICANN chose these new domain names after much deliberation and considering more than 100 possible new names, a number of people were highly critical of the selections. In 2005, ICANN again began the process of adding several new TLDs. One of the proposed domains, an .xxx domain for Web sites with adult content, raised considerable controversy. You can learn more about these criticisms and controversies by going to the Online Companion Web page for this tutorial at www.course.com/oc/np/internet7. After logging in, you can click the Tutorial 1 link, and then follow the links in the Additional Information section under the heading "ICANN and Controversy Over Its Rulings." Since 2000, two more gTLDs and several more sTLDs have been added. Figure 1-5 presents a list of the general TLDs, including those added since 2000, and some of the more popular country TLDs.

Common top-level domains (TLDs) ◄ Figure 1-5

Original General TLDs		Country TLDs		General TLDs Added Since 2000	
TLD	Use	TLD	Country	TLD	Use
.com	U.S. Commercial	.au	Australia	.uk	United Kingdom
.edu	U.S. Four-year educational institution	.ca	Canada	.asia	Companies, individuals, and organizations based in Asian-Pacific regions
.gov	U.S. Federal government	.de	Germany	.biz	Businesses
.mil	U.S. Military	.fi	Finland	.info	General use
.net	U.S. General use	.fr	France	.int	International organizations and programs endorsed by a treaty between or among nations
.org	U. S. Not-for-profit organization	.jp	Japan	.name	Individual persons
.us	U.S. General use	.se	Sweden	.pro	Professionals (such as accountants, lawyers, physicians)

Uniform Resource Locators

The IP address and the domain name each identify a particular computer on the Internet, but they do not indicate where a Web page's HTML document resides on that computer. To identify a Web page's exact location, Web browsers rely on Uniform Resource Locators. A **Uniform Resource Locator (URL)** is a four-part addressing scheme that tells the Web browser:

- The transfer protocol to use when transporting the file
- The domain name of the computer on which the file resides
- The pathname of the folder or directory on the computer on which the file resides
- The name of the file

The **transfer protocol** is the set of rules that the computers use to move files from one computer to another on an internet. The most common transfer protocol used on the Internet is the **hypertext transfer protocol (HTTP)**. You can indicate the use of this protocol by typing http:// as the first part of the URL. People do use other protocols to transfer files on the Internet, but most of these protocols were used more frequently before the Web became part of the Internet. Two protocols that you still might see on the Internet are the **file transfer protocol (FTP)**, which is indicated in a URL as ftp://, and the **Telnet protocol**, which is indicated in a URL as telnet://. FTP is just another way to transfer files, and Telnet is a set of rules for establishing a connection between two computers over the Internet that allows a person at one computer to control the other computer.

The domain name was described in the preceding section. The pathname describes the hierarchical directory or folder structure on the computer that stores the file. Most people are familiar with the structure used on Windows and DOS PCs, which uses the backslash character (\) to separate the structure levels. URLs follow the conventions established in the UNIX operating system that use the forward slash character (/) to separate the structure levels. The forward slash character works properly in a URL, even when it is pointing to a file on a Windows or DOS computer.

The filename is the name that the computer uses to identify the Web page's HTML document. On most computers, the filename extension of an HTML document is either .html or .htm. Although many PC operating systems are not case-sensitive, computers that use the UNIX operating system *are* case-sensitive. Therefore, if you are entering a URL that includes mixed-case and you do not know the type of computer on which the file resides, it is safer to retain the mixed-case format of the URL.

Tip

Not all URLs include a filename, so when this is the case, most Web browsers will load the file named index.html, which is the default name for a Web site's home page on most Web servers.

InSight | Filename Extensions for HTML files

Computer engineers have long used the part of a filename that follows the period, called the filename extension, to identify the contents of files. The operating systems of some computers (including Windows PCs) use the filename extension to determine which software program is used with which files. HTML was first created on large computers, and its filename extension was always .html. When Web browsers were developed for PCs, a problem arose. Most operating systems used on PCs at that time limited filename extensions to three characters. Thus, many HTML files were created with the shortened filename extension, .htm, so that they could be used on PCs. Since then, PC operating systems have become able to handle longer filename extensions, but the practice of using both .htm and .html for HTML files has become entrenched, and both are commonly used today.

Figure 1-6 shows an example of a URL annotated to show its four parts.

Structure of a Uniform Resource Locator (URL) ◄ Figure 1-6

The URL shown in Figure 1-6 uses the HTTP protocol and points to a computer that is connected to the Web (www) at the *New York Times* newspaper (nytimes), which is a commercial entity (com). The *New York Times Web* site contains many different kinds of information about the newspaper, including stories that are included in the pages of the printed newspaper each day. The path shown in Figure 1-6 includes two levels. The first level indicates that the information is a story from the pages of the newspaper (pages), and the second level indicates that the page is from the sports section (sports) of the newspaper. The filename (index.html) indicates that this page is the home page in the sports section.

Encountering Error Messages on Web Pages | InSight

You might encounter an error message when you enter a URL in a Web browser. Two common messages that you might see are "server busy" and "DNS entry not found." Either of these messages means that your browser was unable to communicate successfully with the Web server that stores the page you requested. The cause for this inability might be temporary—in which case, you might be able to try the URL later—or the cause might be permanent. The browser has no way of determining the cause of the connection failure, so the browser provides the same types of error messages in either case. Another error message that you might receive appears as a Web page and includes the text "Error 404: File not Found." This error message usually means that the Web page's location has changed permanently or that the Web page no longer exists. You should also keep in mind that if you type a URL incorrectly, you could see either of these error messages, so always double-check your typing before considering other reasons that you were unable to load a particular Web page.

Now that you understand the importance of Internet addressing and URLS, you will notice that you can find URLs in many places; for example, newspapers and magazines often publish URLs of Web sites that might interest their readers. Friends who know about the subject area in which you are interested also are good sources. The best source, however, is the Web itself.

You are eager to begin learning how to use a Web browser. Common elements and similar functionality among most Web browsers make it easy to use any Web browser after you have learned how to use one.

Main Elements of Web Browsers

Now that you know a little more about Web sites, you start to wonder how a particular computer can communicate with other computers over the Internet. Maggie tells you that there are a number of different Web browsers. Web browser software turns your computer into a Web client that can communicate through an Internet service provider (ISP) or a network connection with Web servers all over the world. The two most popular browsers in use today are **Microsoft Internet Explorer**, or simply **Internet Explorer**, and **Mozilla Firefox**, or simply **Firefox**. You will learn more about these and other Web browsers later in this tutorial.

Most Windows programs use a standard graphical user interface (GUI) design that includes a number of common screen elements. Figures 1-7 and 1-8 show the main elements of the Internet Explorer and Firefox program windows, respectively. These two Web browsers share many common Windows elements, such as a title bar at the top of the window, a scroll bar on the right side of the window, and a status bar at the bottom of the window.

Figure 1-7 — **Main elements of the Internet Explorer program window**

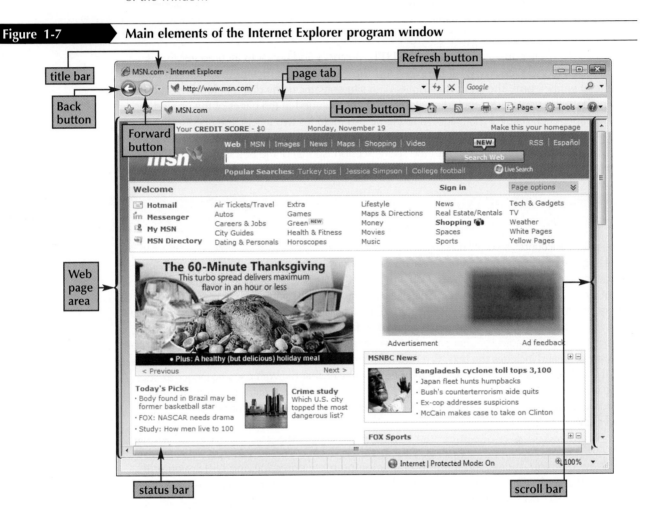

Main elements of the Firefox program window Figure 1-8

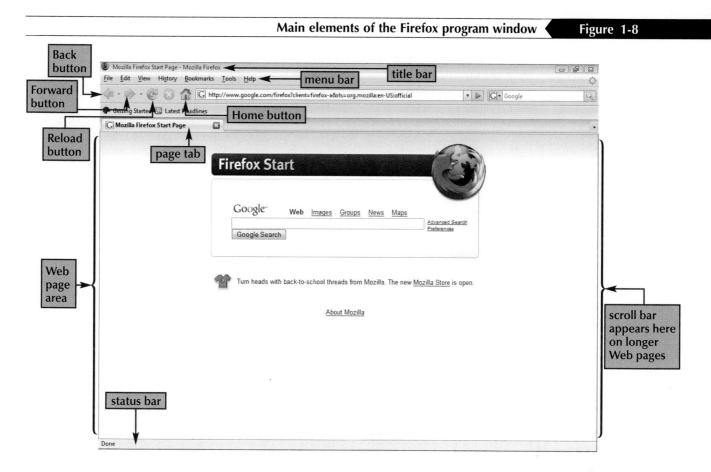

The next section describes the common browser window elements.

Title Bar

A Web browser's **title bar** shows the name of the open Web page and the Web browser's program name. As in all Windows programs, you can double-click the title bar to resize the window quickly. The right side of the title bar contains the **Minimize**, **Restore Down**, and **Close buttons** when the window is maximized to fill the screen. When the window is not maximized, the Restore Down button is replaced by a **Maximize button**; to expand a browser window so it fills the screen, you click the Maximize button.

Scroll Bars

A Web page can be much longer than a Web browser window, so you often need to use the **scroll bar** at the right side of the program window to move the page up or down through the document window. You can use the mouse to click the Up scroll button or the Down scroll button to move the Web page up or down through the window's **Web page area**. You can also use the mouse to click and drag the scroll box up and down in the scroll bar to move the page accordingly.

Tip

Some Web pages can be wider than your browser window. In this case, the browser places another scroll bar at the bottom of the window above the status bar, so you can move the page horizontally through the window.

Status Bar

The **status bar** at the bottom of the browser window includes information about the browser's operations. Each browser uses the status bar to deliver different information, but generally, the status bar indicates the name of the Web page that is loading, the load status (partial or complete), and important messages, such as "Document: Done." Some Web sites send messages as part of their Web pages that are displayed in the status bar as well. You will learn more about the specific functions of the status bar in Internet Explorer and Firefox in Sessions 1.2 and 1.3, respectively.

Menu Bar

The browser's **menu bar** provides a convenient way for you to execute typical File, Edit, View, and Help commands. In addition to these common Windows command sets, the menu bar also provides specialized commands for the browser that enable you to navigate the Web. The menu bar appears just below the title bar in Firefox. The menu bar is hidden by default in Internet Explorer, but some of the common menu options are available from the Page button and the Tools button located on the **Command bar** in Internet Explorer. You will learn more about the options available from these buttons in Session 1.2 as well as how to show the menu bar in Internet Explorer.

Page Tab

Most Web browsers can show multiple Web pages within the Web page area. These Web browsers display a **page tab** for each Web page that shows the title of the Web page. This feature allows you to switch among Web pages that you have opened by clicking the page tabs instead of finding the separate icons on the Windows taskbar that correspond to Web browser windows you have opened. Some users prefer to open multiple Web pages in one browser window and switch among them using the page tabs. This method of using one browser window for all open pages is called **tabbed browsing**.

Home Button

Clicking the **Home button** in Internet Explorer or in Firefox displays the home (or start) page for the browser. Most Web browsers let you specify a page that loads automatically every time you start the program. You might not be able to do this if you are in your school's computer lab because schools often set the start page for all browsers on campus and then lock that setting. Similarly, some companies set a start page for the computers their employees use, so you might not be able to set your own start page if you are using a computer at work. If you are using your own computer, you can choose your own start page. Some people like to use a Web page that someone else has created and made available for others to use. One example of a start page that many people use as their start page is the refdesk.com Web page.

Pages such as the Refdesk.com home page offer links to pages that many Web users frequently visit. The people and organizations that create these pages often sell advertising space on their pages to pay the cost of maintaining their sites. Refdesk.com sells advertising and also accepts donations from users to help defray the cost of operating the site.

Finding Information on the Web Using Search Engines and Web Directories

Web search engines are Web pages that conduct searches of the Web to find the words or expressions that you enter. The result of such a search is a Web page that contains hyperlinks to Web pages that contain matching text or expressions. These pages can give new users an easy way to find information on the Web. Internet Explorer and Firefox each include a toolbar button that opens search engines and Web directories chosen by the companies that wrote the browser software. However, many people prefer to select their own tools for searching the Internet.

Sometimes the number of results from a search conducted using a search engine is overwhelming, and you find that you need to sort through links to pages that only vaguely match your criteria. You can use a **Web directory**, a Web page that contains a list of Web page categories, such as education or recreation, to narrow the results returned for a particular search. The hyperlinks on a Web directory page lead to other pages that contain lists of subcategories leading to other related category lists and Web pages. Instead of relying on a computer to categorize the pages, Web directories employ Web directory editors to categorize Web pages. These editors can weed out the pages that do not fit in a particular category.

Returning to Web Pages Previously Visited

Web addresses can be long and hard to remember. You can store the addresses of specific Web pages in most browsers, and then open the pages by clicking the stored address. You can also return to a page you have visited in the past by using the browser's history feature.

You realize that using the browser to remember important pages will be a terrific asset as you start collecting information for the shelter, so you ask Maggie to explain more about how to return to a Web page.

Using Favorites and Bookmarks

In Internet Explorer, you can save the URL of a site you would like to revisit as a **favorite** in the Favorites folder. In Firefox, you can use a **bookmark** to save the URL of a specific page so you can return to it. You can use Internet Explorer's Favorites feature or a Firefox bookmark to store and organize a list of Web pages that you have visited so you can return to them easily without having to remember the URL or search for the page again. Internet Explorer favorites and Firefox bookmarks work very much like a paper bookmark that you might use in a printed book: They mark the page and help you find the location again quickly.

You can save as many Internet Explorer favorites or Firefox bookmarks as you want. You can mark all of your favorite Web pages, so you can return to pages that you frequently use or pages that are important to your research or tasks.

InSight | **How Web Browsers Store Favorites and Bookmarks**

All Web browsers let you store favorites or bookmarks on your computer, but different browsers store them in different ways. Internet Explorer stores each favorite as a separate file on your computer. Firefox stores all bookmarks in one file on your computer. The Internet Explorer approach of storing each favorite separately offers more flexibility but uses more disk space and can make it hard to find a specific favorite. The Firefox approach of storing all bookmarks in one file uses less disk space and makes the bookmarks easier to find.

Navigating Web Pages Using the History List

As you click hyperlinks to go to new Web pages, the browser stores the location of each page you visit during a single session in a **history list**. You click the **Back button** and the **Forward button** in either Internet Explorer or Firefox to move through the history list.

When you start your browser, both buttons are inactive (dimmed) because no history list for your new session exists yet. After you follow one or more hyperlinks, the Back button becomes active and lets you retrace your path through the hyperlinks you have followed. Once you use the Back button, the Forward button becomes active and lets you move forward through the session's history list.

In most Web browsers, you can right-click either the Back or Forward button to display a portion of the history list. You can reload any page on the list by clicking its name in the list. The Back and Forward buttons duplicate the functions of commands on the browser's menu. You will learn more about the history list for Internet Explorer in Session 1.2 and for Firefox in Session1.3.

Navigating Web Pages Using Page Tabs

If you use the tabbed browsing approach and open Web pages in tabs within one browser window instead of in separate browser windows, you can navigate from page to page by clicking the page tab for the page you want to display. This approach has its limits, however. Depending on the size of the monitor you are viewing, you will only be able to read the titles in the page tabs for a few pages. But if you are doing work that requires frequent back and forth browsing between three or four pages, the page tabs can provide a very handy way to navigate among those pages. You will learn more about how tabbed browsing works in Sessions 1.2 and 1.3.

Reloading a Web Page

When you use your browser to access a Web page, your browser downloads the page to your computer from the Web server on which it is stored. The browser stores a copy of every displayed Web page on your computer's hard drive in a **cache** folder, which increases the speed at which the browser can display pages as you navigate the history list. The cache folder lets the browser reload pages from the cache instead of from the remote Web server. On Windows computers, the cache folder is named Temporary Internet Files.

Clicking the **Refresh button** in Internet Explorer or the **Reload button** in Firefox loads the same Web page that appears in the browser window again. When you click the Refresh or the Reload button, the browser contacts the Web server to see if the Web page has changed since it was stored in the cache folder. If it has changed, the browser gets the new page from the Web server; otherwise, the browser loads the cache folder copy.

Tip

If you want to force the browser to load the most current version of the page from the Web server, hold down the Shift key as you click the Refresh or Reload button.

Stopping a Web Page Transfer

The amount of time it takes for a Web page to arrive from a Web server depends on the size of the page's files (the HTML file, graphics elements, and any active content that is included in the page) and the bandwidth of the Internet connection. Sometimes a Web page takes a long time to load, especially if you are using a low bandwidth connection and the page contains a number of graphics or active content files. When this occurs, you can click the Stop button in Internet Explorer or Firefox to halt the Web page transfer from the server. You can then click the hyperlink again; a second attempt may connect and transfer the page more quickly. You also might want to click the Stop button to abort a transfer when you accidentally click a hyperlink that you do not want to follow.

Cookies

Another issue that Web users should know about is the use of cookies. A **cookie** is a small file that a Web server writes to the disk drive of the client computer (the computer on which the Web browser is running). Cookies can contain information about the user such as login names and passwords. By storing this information on the user's computer, the Web server can perform functions such as automatic login, which makes it easier to quickly return to favorite Web pages. However, the user often is unaware that these files are being written to the computer's disk drive. Most Web browsers allow the user to prohibit the writing of cookies or specify general categories of cookies that will be allowed or not allowed to be written. Internet Explorer, which stores each cookie in a separate file, allows users to delete the individual cookie files if the user can identify the files to delete, which can be difficult. Other browsers, such as Firefox, store all cookies in one file and give users more comprehensive tools for managing the cookies that have been stored on their computers. You will learn more about cookies and managing them in Internet Explorer in Session 1.2 and in Firefox in Session 1.3.

Printing and Saving Web Pages

As you use your browser to view Web pages, you might find some pages that you want to print or store for future use. You can use a Web browser to print a Web page or to save either an entire Web page or just parts of the page, such as selections of text or graphics.

Printing a Web Page

When you execute a print command, the current page (or part of a page, called a **frame**) that appears in the Web page area of the browser is sent to the printer. Most browsers also provide a print preview command that lets you see how the printed page will look. If the page contains light colors or many graphics, you might consider changing the printing options so the page prints without the background or with all black text. You will learn how to change the print settings for Internet Explorer and Firefox in Sessions 1.2 and 1.3, respectively.

Saving a Web Page

Although printing an entire Web page is often useful, there are times when you will want to save all or part of the page to disk. All Web browsers allow you to save copies of most Web pages as files that you can store on your computer's hard disk, a floppy disk, a USB flash drive, or other storage medium. Some Web pages are written to make copying difficult; these pages cannot be saved easily. Internet Explorer and Firefox each perform the save operation somewhat differently, thus you will learn more about saving a Web page and its graphics in Sessions 1.2 and 1.3.

Other Web Browser Choices

After several years of a stable market for Web browsers, many changes occurred in 2004 and 2005. Internet Explorer, which was used by more than 90 percent of all Web users in 2004, saw other browsers begin to make a dent in its dominant position. The media began reporting a number of security issues with Internet Explorer, and users became concerned that the browser was becoming a way for criminals and others with ill intent to attack and take control of their computers. Many organizations and individuals began to doubt whether relying on a single browser was a good idea. Since 2005, many users have installed Firefox. Industry experts estimate that about 25 percent of skilled Web users rely on Firefox as their default browser. Most of the remaining 75 percent still use Internet Explorer and a small percentage of users employ other Web browsers. Beginning Web users tend to use whatever is installed on their computers. Most computer manufacturers still install Internet Explorer, so many people start using that browser and never consider using anything else. In the next section, you will learn about other Web browsers that people are now using instead of or in addition to Internet Explorer and Firefox.

Mozilla Project

Mosaic was one of the first Web browsers developed in the early 1990s. A group of researchers who had helped develop Mosaic left their jobs at the University of Illinois Supercomputing Center to form a new company called Netscape and launched the first commercially successful Web browser, **Netscape Navigator**. Because they wanted to replace Mosaic, they named their development project Mozilla, which was short for "Mosaic Killer." When Navigator was first introduced in 1994, Netscape charged a small license fee for corporate users, but the fee was waived for individuals and academic institutions. During this time, Microsoft began distributing Internet Explorer with its Windows operating system at no additional cost, therefore Netscape was forced to drop its license fee in response and was no longer able to earn a profit on its browser business. AOL bought Netscape's other business assets in 1999, but donated the Netscape browser software to a nonprofit organization that continued developing the browser software and distributing it to users at no cost. The nonprofit group named the browser software development project "Mozilla" in a revival of the browser's original name.

When the Mozilla project started work in 1999, the team focused on a complete rebuild of the internal workings of the browser, called the **browser rendering engine**. In the Mozilla project, the browser rendering engine, which is named the **Gecko engine**, is used in Netscape Navigator, the Mozilla browser, and the Mozilla Firefox browser.

The Mozilla project has been operated on a volunteer basis by programmers working in their spare time since its inception in 1999. In 2003, the Mozilla Foundation was created with an initial contribution of $2 million from Time Warner's AOL division. AOL also contributed equipment, domain names, trademarks, and employees to help with the foundation's initial organization activities. Other corporate supporters of the foundation include Sun Microsystems and Red Hat Software. The foundation will help ensure that the Mozilla project continues into the future.

Today, the development of the Firefox browser (and related projects, such as the Thunderbird email client that you will learn about in the next tutorial) is carried on by the Mozilla Corporation, an entity formed for that purpose. The original Mozilla Foundation continues to develop the Gecko browser engine, new interfaces for Web browsers based on that engine, and a number of related technologies. You can learn more about the Mozilla Foundation's current projects by going to the Online Companion Web page for this tutorial at www.course.com/oc/np/internet7. After logging in, click the Tutorial 1 link, and then follow the links in the Additional Information section under the heading "Current Mozilla Projects."

SeaMonkey Project

Originally, the main focus of the Mozilla Foundation was the continuing development of the **Mozilla Suite**, a combination of Web-related software applications that were created by the Mozilla open source project. This development continues today as the **SeaMonkey Project**, an all-in-one software suite that includes a Web browser that runs on the Gecko engine, an email client, a newsgroup client, an HTML editor, and an instant messaging chat client. The software that Time Warner's AOL division distributes as Netscape Navigator is based on the SeaMonkey software.

The SeaMonkey's Web browser offers tabbed windows (including an option to make your start page a set of multiple tabbed windows), a pop-up ad blocker, an image manager that lets you set the browser so it does not load images until you click the Images button on the toolbar, and a "find as you type" page navigation option. Figure 1-9 shows the SeaMonkey browser displaying the home page for the SeaMonkey Project.

SeaMonkey Web browser Figure 1-9

Opera

Opera started out in 1994 as a research project at Telenor, which is Norway's state telecommunications company. One year later, an independent development company (Opera Software ASA) was formed to continue work on the Opera project. This company continues to develop and sell the Opera Web browser and related software.

Because Opera's program code was written independently and does not use any elements of the Gecko engine or Internet Explorer, Opera is not affected by any security flaws that might be exploited by those attacking any of the Gecko-based browsers or Internet Explorer. Figure 1-10 shows the Opera browser main screen.

Figure 1-10 Opera Web browser

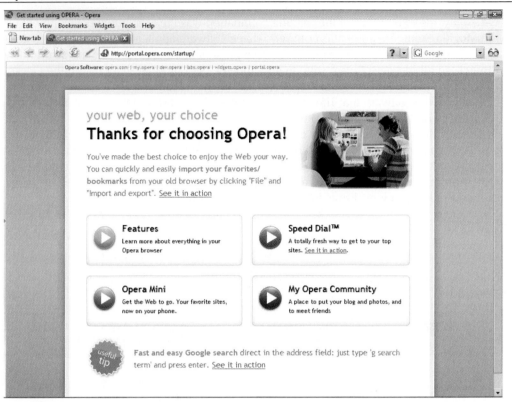

When Opera was first introduced, it was only available as a licensed software product; that is, users had to pay a fee of $39 to use the software. In 2000, Opera began offering a free version of its browser that was supported by advertising. The advertising messages were displayed in the toolbar area of the screen. In 2005, the company decided to make the browser free to all users. Opera still offers a premium support program for an annual fee, but most Opera users today do not enroll in that program. Today, Opera devotes most of its corporate resources to the development of Web browsers for mobile phones and other handheld devices. More than 20 million users worldwide have downloaded a version of Opera.

Opera was the first Web browser to offer tabbed browsing and a search window that the user could configure to run searches in specific search engines automatically. These features have proven to be popular and are now available in most major browsers. Opera also includes a toolbar control that lets users adjust the size of the displayed text in the browser window. Other browsers provide this same function, but the choices are less accessible because they are buried in a menu or submenu.

Browser for Hire: iRider

Internet Explorer, Firefox, SeaMonkey, and Opera are all available at no cost. Several other browsers available today charge a license fee. The most widely used is **iRider**, a browser designed for power users. A power user is a person who is especially knowledgeable about a specific technology and has a high level of skill in using that technology. A power user of Web browsers might regularly have six browsers open at once while shopping for the best deals on airfares, comparing products being auctioned on eBay, or looking up a series of different addresses on Yahoo! Maps.

The current licensing fee for iRider is $29, with a discount available for academic users. The iRider browser allows power users to open and manage multiple Web pages at once. Other browsers do provide this functionality, but they either open the Web pages in separate windows or in separate tabs within a window. Either way, the user only sees a tiny icon and (perhaps) a part of each Web page name. With iRider, the user can view thumbnail images of all open Web pages displayed in a hierarchical map called a Page List.

More important, iRider keeps all open Web pages in memory until the user deletes them, allowing the user to click any thumbnail image in the Page List to open a Web page and review its contents. Most power users find using the Page List to be much easier than using the Back and Forward buttons or a history list because the page thumbnails are displayed as a hierarchy (all Web pages that are linked from a single Web page are shown indented under that page's thumbnail image) instead of being listed in the order in which they were opened (as they would be in a history list). Figure 1-11 shows iRider being used to search for books about Christmas on Amazon.com and Barnes & Noble.com. The user ran searches on each site, opened three product pages on each site, and returned to the Amazon.com start page.

Multiple searches in the iRider Web browser | Figure 1-11

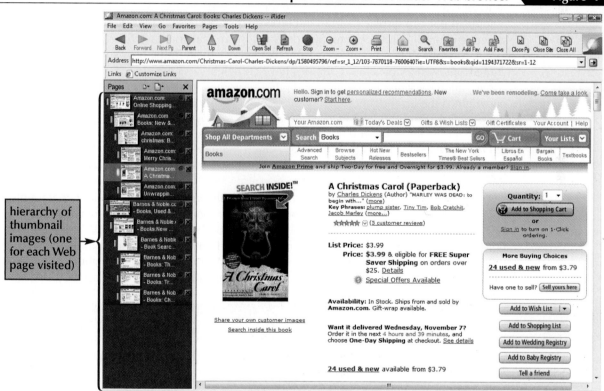

hierarchy of thumbnail images (one for each Web page visited)

Many experienced Web surfers open pages in new windows as a matter of course, but the Web site does not always allow new windows to open, or in some cases, to stay open. In iRider, any window that is opened in the browser remains in the Page List (and thus it is available to be opened again) until the user closes it.

Most airline and travel sites take a few moments to search through all possible flights (or car rentals or hotel rooms) before they return a page of search results. When the search results page appears, a user might decide to try a flight leaving a day earlier or later. Travel sites generally require the user to run the search again, which removes the results of the first search. With iRider, the user can run several searches simultaneously and compare the results, going from page to page as necessary because all of the pages remain available in the Page List. Once again, iRider gives the user more control over which pages remain available and which are closed.

Another useful feature of iRider is that users can select multiple links on a page and iRider will begin to download the pages simultaneously. Each page appears in the Page List when its download is complete so the user can select pages that have downloaded more quickly, rather than waiting for a specific page to download, using the Back button to revisit the search page, clicking and waiting for another page to download, and so on.

The Web provides users with a vast quantity of information and makes it easy for them to view, store, and print the information. However, the ability to access information using a Web browser does not give the user an unfettered right to possess or use that information. These rights are controlled by copyright laws, which exist to protect the owners of the information.

Reproducing Web Pages and Copyright Law

Copyright laws can place significant restrictions on the way that you can use information or images that you copy from another entity's Web site. Because of the way a Web browser works, it copies the HTML code and the graphics and media files to your computer before it can display them in the browser. Just because copies of these files are stored temporarily on your computer does not mean that you have the right to use them in any way other than having your computer display them in the browser window. The United States and most other countries have copyright laws that govern the use of photocopies, audio or video recordings, and other reproductions of authors' original work. A **copyright** is the legal right of the author or other owner of an original work to control the reproduction, distribution, and sale of that work. A copyright comes into existence as soon as the work is placed into a tangible form, such as a printed copy, an electronic file, or a Web page. The copyright exists even if the work does not contain a copyright notice. If you do not know whether material that you find on the Web is copyrighted, the safest course of action is to assume that it is.

U.S. copyright law has a **fair use** provision that allows students to use limited amounts of copyrighted information in term papers and other reports prepared in an academic setting. The source of the material used should always be cited. Commercial use of copyrighted material is much more restricted. You should obtain permission from the copyright holder before using anything you copy from a Web page. The copyright holder can require you to pay a fee for permission to use the material from the Web page.

| InSight | Identifying the Owner of Copyrighted Material |

Although it is important to gain permission to use copyrighted material acquired from the Web, it can be difficult to determine the owner of a source's copyright if no notice appears on the Web page. However, many Web pages provide a hyperlink to the email address of the person responsible for maintaining the page. That person, sometimes called a **Webmaster**, usually can provide information about the copyright status of material on the page. Many Web sites also include the address and telephone number of the company or organization that owns the site.

Now that you understand the basic functions of a browser, you are ready to start using your browser to find information for the Danville Animal Shelter. If you are using Internet Explorer, your instructor will assign Session 1.2; if you are using Firefox, your instructor will assign Session 1.3. The authors recommend, however, that you read both sessions because you might encounter a different browser on a public or employer's computer in the future.

Session 1.1 Quick Check | Review

1. True or False: Web browser software runs on a Web server computer.
2. True or False: You can format text using HTML tags.
3. The Web page that opens when you start your browser is called a(n) _____ or a(n) _____ .
4. The general term for links to graphic images, sound clips, or video clips that appear in a Web page is _____ .
5. A local political candidate is creating a Web site to help in her campaign for office. Describe three things she might want to include in her Web site.
6. What is the difference between IP addressing and domain name addressing?
7. Identify and interpret the meaning of each part of the following URL: http://www.savethetrees.org/main.html.
8. What is the difference between a Web directory and a Web search engine?

Session 1.2

Starting Microsoft Internet Explorer

Microsoft Internet Explorer is Microsoft's Web browser; it is installed with all recent versions of Windows operating system software. In this session, you will use Internet Explorer to begin research work for the Danville Animal Shelter. This introduction assumes that you have Internet Explorer installed on your computer. You should have your computer turned on so the Windows desktop is displayed.

To start Internet Explorer:

▶ 1. Click the **Start** button on the taskbar, point to **All Programs**, and then click **Internet Explorer**. After a moment, Internet Explorer opens.

Trouble? If you cannot find Internet Explorer on the All Programs menu, check to see if an Internet Explorer shortcut icon appears on the desktop, and then double-click it. If you do not see the shortcut icon, ask your instructor or technical support person for help. The program might be installed in a different location on your computer.

▶ 2. If the program does not fill the screen entirely, click the **Maximize** button on the Internet Explorer program's title bar. Your screen should look like Figure 1-12.

Figure 1-12   Internet Explorer main program window

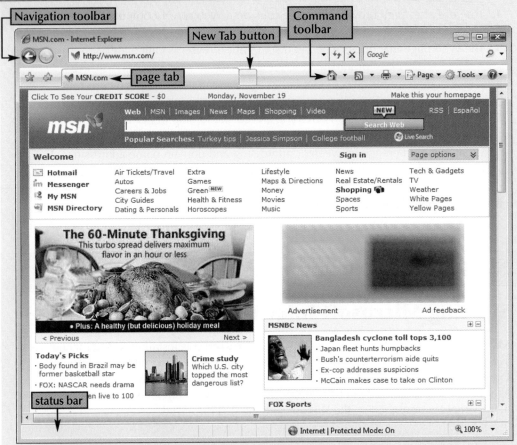

Trouble? Figure 1-12 shows the MSN.com home page, which is the page that Internet Explorer opens the first time it starts. Your computer is likely to be configured to open to a different Web page or no page at all.

Trouble? Figure 1-12 shows the Internet Explorer program window as it appears when it is first installed on a new computer. Many programs add icons and even entire toolbars to the program window, so if you are using a computer that has been used by other people, the program window might include icons and toolbars that are not shown in the figure.

Internet Explorer includes two main toolbars, a Navigation toolbar and a Command toolbar. These toolbars are shown in Figure 1-13. Many of the buttons on these toolbars execute frequently used commands for browsing the Web. You will learn about the functions of the most commonly used toolbar buttons in this session. The toolbars on your Internet Explorer browser might contain icons not shown in Figure 1-13 because the Command toolbar can be customized, which means that icons can be deleted and new icons can be added. Other software programs installed on your computer can place icons on your toolbar so that these programs can be used from within Internet Explorer.

Internet Explorer Navigation toolbar and Command toolbar ◄ Figure 1-13

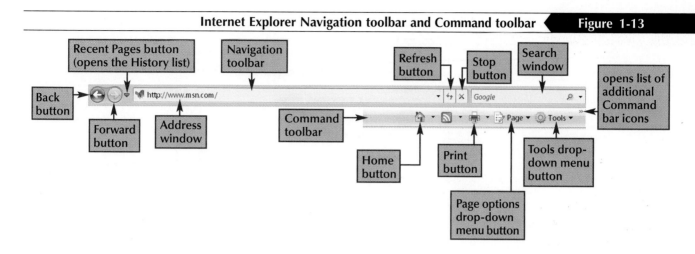

Now that you understand how to start Internet Explorer, you want to learn more about components of the Internet Explorer program window.

Status Bar

The status bar at the bottom of the window includes several panels that give you information about Internet Explorer's operations. The first panel—the **transfer progress report**—presents status messages that show, for example, the URL of a page while it is loading. When a page is completely loaded, this panel displays the text "Done" until you move the mouse over a hyperlink, at which time this panel displays the URL of the hyperlink. While Internet Explorer is loading a Web page from a Web server, a second panel opens and displays a blue **graphical transfer progress indicator** that moves from left to right to indicate how much of a Web page has been loaded. This indicator is especially useful for monitoring progress when the browser is loading large Web pages.

The last (rightmost) element in the status bar is a tool that allows you to adjust the magnification of a Web page. Some Web pages display printed text in a font that is too small for some users to see. Other Web pages have pictures or graphic elements, such as drawings or maps, that users might want to see in a larger or smaller form. This tool lets you increase (or decrease) the magnification level of a Web page.

Just to the left of the screen magnification tool is a panel that displays the **security settings** for the page you are viewing. As part of its security features, Internet Explorer lets you classify Web pages by the security risk you believe they present. You can open the Security tab in the Internet Options dialog box shown in Figure 1-14 by double-clicking the Security Settings panel.

Figure 1-14 **Security tab in the Internet Options dialog box**

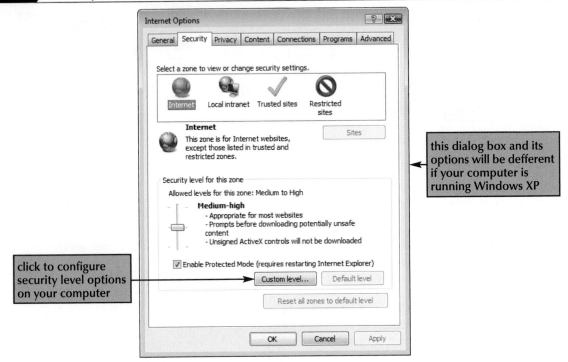

This dialog box lets you set five levels of security-enforcing procedures: High, Medium-High, Medium, Medium-Low, and Low (although not all five options are available for all types of sites; for example, sites in the "Restricted sites" category can only be assigned a level of "High"). In general, the higher the level of security you set for your browser, the slower it will operate. Higher security settings also disable some browser features.

Menu Bar

The menu bar is not displayed by default in recent versions of Internet Explorer. The menu bar gives you access to list menus that contain all of the menu commands available in Internet Explorer. You can display the menu bar by clicking the Tools button arrow and clicking Menu Bar to select it.

Expanding the Web Page Area

Internet Explorer lets you hide its menu bar and toolbars to show more of the Web page area. As stated earlier, the menu bar is hidden by default; however, if you have it displayed, you can click the Tools button arrow and deselect the Menu Bar option to hide the menu bar, or you can select the Full Screen option on the Tools menu. When the window is in **Full Screen**, the toolbars and menu bar are no longer visible. You can display the hidden toolbars by moving the mouse pointer to the top of the screen and holding it there for a few seconds. When you move the mouse pointer away from the toolbars, they will become hidden again. To exit Full Screen mode, move the mouse pointer to the top of the screen until the toolbars appear, click the Tools button arrow, and then click Full Screen to remove the checkmark and deselect this option.

Hiding and Restoring Toolbars in Internet Explorer | Reference Window

- To hide the toolbars, click the Tools button arrow, then click Full Screen to check this option.
- To restore the toolbars, click the Tools button arrow, then click Full Screen to uncheck this option.
- To temporarily restore the toolbars in Full Screen, move the mouse cursor to the top of the screen until the toolbars appear.

To use the Full Screen command:

▶ 1. Click the **Tools button arrow** on the Command toolbar, and then click **Full Screen**. Now, you can see more of the Web page area.

▶ 2. If the toolbars do not immediately roll up out of view, move the mouse pointer away from the top of the screen for a moment.

▶ 3. Move the mouse pointer to the top of the screen. The toolbars scroll back down into view.

▶ 4. Click the **Tools button arrow** on the Command toolbar, and then click **Full Screen** to redisplay the toolbars.

You can add (or delete) buttons that appear on the Command toolbar by clicking the Tools button arrow, pointing to Toolbars, and then clicking Customize to open the Customize Toolbar dialog box.

Entering a URL in the Address Bar

You can use the **Address bar**, which is located on the Navigation toolbar, to enter URLs directly into Internet Explorer. As you learned in Session 1.1, you must enter the URL to identify a Web page's exact location. Although a complete URL includes the name of a file, entering just the IP address or the domain name will usually be enough information to find the home page of the site.

Internet Explorer will try to add standard URL elements to complete partial URLs that you type in the Address bar. For example, if you type cnn.com, Internet Explorer will convert it to http://www.cnn.com and load the home page at that URL.

Entering a URL in the Address Bar | Reference Window

- Click at the end of the current text in the Address bar, and then delete any unnecessary or unwanted text from the displayed URL.
- Type the URL of the location that you want to view.
- Press the Enter key to load the URL's Web page in the browser window.

Trinity has asked you to start your research by examining the home page for the Midland Pet Adoption Agency's Web site. She has given you the URL so that you can find it.

To load the Midland Pet Adoption Agency's Web page:

1. Click three times at the end of the text in the Address bar to position the cursor at that point, and then delete any unnecessary or unwanted text by pressing the **Backspace** key.

   Trouble? Make sure that you delete all of the text in the Address bar so the text you type in Step 2 will be correct.

2. Type **www.midlandpet.com** in the Address bar. This is the URL for the Midland Pet Adoption Agency Web site.

3. Press the **Enter** key. The home page of the Midland Pet Adoption Agency Web site loads, as shown in Figure 1-15.

| Figure 1-15 | Midland Pet Adoption Agency Web page |

Navigating Web Pages Using the Mouse

The easiest way to move from one Web page to another is to use the mouse to click hyperlinks that the authors of Web pages embed in their HTML documents. You can also right-click the mouse on the background of a Web page to open a shortcut menu that includes navigation options.

Navigating Between Web Pages Using Hyperlinks and the Mouse | Reference Window

- Click the hyperlink.
- After the new Web page has loaded, right-click on the Web page's background.
- Click Back on the shortcut menu.

To follow a hyperlink to another Web page and return using the mouse:

▶ **1.** With the Midland Pet Adoption Agency home page open in your browser, move the mouse pointer to position it over the **Training Programs** hyperlink, as shown in Figure 1-16. Note that your pointer changes to the shape of a hand with a pointing index finger, and the status bar displays the URL to which the hyperlink points.

Midland Pet Adoption Agency home page ◀ Figure 1-16

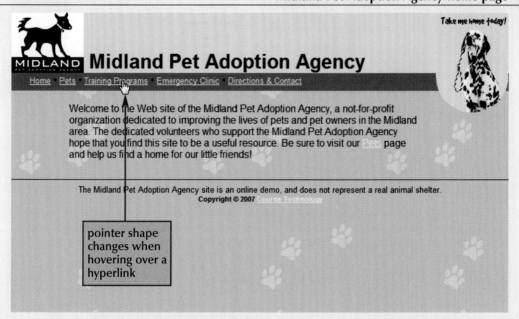

▶ **2.** Click the **Training Programs** hyperlink and move the mouse pointer away from the hyperlink. Watch the left-hand panel in the status bar—when it displays the text "Done," you know that Internet Explorer has loaded the full page. If you do not move the mouse pointer away from the hyperlink, the status bar will continue to display the URL to which the hyperlink points.

▶ **3.** Right-click anywhere in the Web page area that is not a hyperlink to display the shortcut menu, as shown in Figure 1-17.

Figure 1-17 **Using the shortcut menu to go back to the previous page**

Trouble? If you right-click a hyperlink or a graphic Web page element, your short-cut menu will display a list that differs from the one shown in Figure 1-17; there-fore the Back item might not appear in the same position on the menu or not appear at all. If you do not see the shortcut menu shown in Figure 1-17, click any-where outside of the shortcut menu to close it, and then repeat Step 3.

Trouble? Some programs add options to the shortcut menu, so the shortcut menu you see might include items that do not appear on the shortcut menu shown in Figure 1-17.

▶ **4.** Click **Back** on the shortcut menu to return to the Midland Pet Adoption Agency home page.

Returning to Previously Viewed Web Pages

You like the format of the Midland Pet Adoption Agency's home page, so you want to make sure that you can go back to that page later if you need to review its contents. You can write down the URL so you can refer to it later, but an easier way is to store the URL in the Favorites list for future use. You can also use the History list and Back button to return to the pages you have previously visited, and the Home button to return to your browser's start page.

Navigating Web Pages Using the Favorites Center

Internet Explorer's Favorites Center lets you store and organize a list of Web pages that you have visited so you can return to them easily. The Favorites Center button opens the Favorites Center, as shown in Figure 1-18. You can use the Favorites Center to open URLs you have stored as favorites.

Favorites Center in Internet Explorer **Figure 1-18**

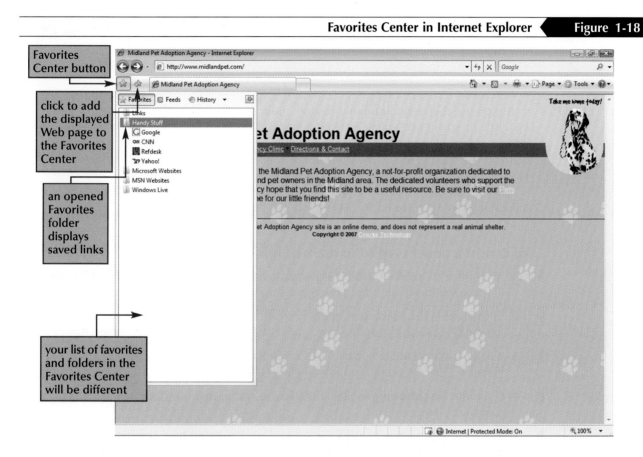

Figure 1-18 shows the hierarchical structure of the Favorites Center. For example, the figure shows four links to Web sites (Google, CNN, Refdesk, and Yahoo!) stored in a folder named "Handy Stuff." You can organize your favorites in whatever way best suits your needs and working style.

Reference Window | **Creating a New Favorites Folder**

- Open the Web page in Internet Explorer.
- Click the Add to Favorites button, then click Add to Favorites.
- Type the title you would like to use for this Favorite in the Name text box (most Web pages will place text that describes the page in the Name text box; you can edit or replace that text).
- Click the New Folder button.
- Type the name of the new folder in the Folder name text box, and then click the Create button.
- Click the Add button.

As you use the Web to find information about pet adoption agencies and other sites of interest, you might find yourself creating many favorites so you can return to sites of interest. When you start accumulating favorites, it is important to keep them organized so that you can quickly locate the site you need. Using folders within the Favorites Center, Internet Explorer helps you keep your favorites organized.

You will save the URL for the Midland Pet Adoption Agency Web page as a favorite in a Pet Adoption Agencies folder, which you will create in the process.

To create a new Favorite in its own folder:

▶ **1.** With the Midland Pet Adoption Agency's home page open, click the **Add to Favorites** button, and then click Add to Favorites. The Add a Favorite dialog box opens.

▶ **2.** If the text in the Name text box is not "Midland Pet Adoption Agency" (without the quotation marks), delete the text, and then type **Midland Pet Adoption Agency**.

▶ **3.** Click the **New Folder** button. The Create a Folder dialog box opens. The new folder will be stored as a subfolder within the Favorites folder.

▶ **4.** Type **Pet Adoption Agencies** in the Folder Name text box, and then click the **Create** button.

▶ **5.** Click the **Add** button to close the Add a Favorite dialog box. The favorite is now saved in Internet Explorer. You can test the favorite by opening it from the Favorites Center.

▶ **6.** Click the **Back** button on the Navigation toolbar to return to the page that had been open in the browser before you opened the Midland Pet Adoption Agency home page, and then click the **Favorites Center** button to open the Favorites Center.

▶ **7.** Click the **Pet Adoption Agencies** folder to open it, as shown in Figure 1-19.

Favorites Center with the new favorite and folder ◀ **Figure 1-19**

8. Click **Midland Pet Adoption Agency**. The Midland Pet Adoption Agency page opens in the browser.

Organizing Favorites

Internet Explorer offers an easy way to organize your folders in a hierarchical structure—even after you have stored them. You can rearrange URLs or even folders within folders in the Favorites Center.

Moving an Existing Favorite into a New Folder | Reference Window

- Click the Favorites Center button.
- Right-click the folder in which you want to add the new folder and click the Create New Folder command to display a new folder in the Favorites Center window.
- Type the name of the new folder, and then press the Enter key.
- Drag the favorite that you want to move into the new folder.

You explain to Maggie that you have created a new folder for Pet Adoption Agencies in the Internet Explorer Favorites Center and stored the Midland Pet Adoption Agency's URL in that folder. Because you might be collecting information about adoption agencies in different states as you conduct your research, Maggie suggests that you organize the information about adoption agencies by state. The Midland Pet Adoption Agency is located in Minnesota, so you decide to put information about the Midland Pet Adoption Agency in a separate folder named MN (which is the two-letter abbreviation for "Minnesota") under the Pet Adoption Agencies folder. As you collect information about other agencies, you will add folders for the states in which they are located, too.

To move an existing favorite into a new folder:

▶ 1. Click the **Favorites Center** button to open the Favorites Center.

▶ 2. Right-click the **Pet Adoption Agencies** folder and click the **Create New Folder** command on the shortcut menu. A new folder appears in the Favorites Center.

▶ 3. Type **MN** to replace the New Folder text, and then press the **Enter** key to rename the folder.

▶ 4. If necessary, click the **Pet Adoption Agencies** folder to open it, and then click and drag the **Midland Pet Adoption Agency** favorite to the new MN folder, and then release the mouse button. Now, the MN folder contains the favorite, as shown in Figure 1-20.

| Figure 1-20 | Moving a favorite to a new folder |

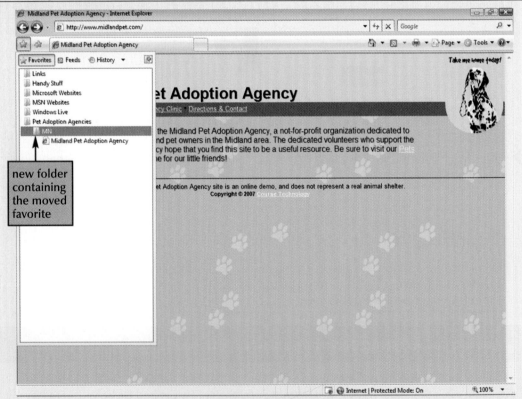

Trouble? If the Midland Pet Adoption Agency favorite is not visible in the Favorites Center, click the MN folder to open that folder and display its contents.

▶ 5. Click the **Favorites Center** button to close the Favorites Center.

Navigating Web Pages Using the History List

The Back and Forward buttons on the Navigation toolbar and the Back and Forward options on the shortcut menu (which you can access by right-clicking a blank area of a Web page) enable you to move to and from previously visited pages. As you move back and forth between pages, Internet Explorer records these visited sites in the history list. To see where you have been during a session, you can open the history list by clicking the Recent Pages button (to the right of the Back and Forward buttons on the Navigation toolbar) or by clicking the Favorites Center button, and then clicking the History button at the top of the Favorites Center window.

To view the history list for this session:

▶ **1.** Click the **Favorites Center** button, and then click the **History** button in the Favorites Center window. The history list appears in a hierarchical structure in a separate window on the left side of the screen. The pages that you have visited are grouped by date of visit, so the last icon in the list will be labeled "Today" and will include Web sites you visited today. The other icons will be labeled with the names of days of the week (Monday, Tuesday, and so on) if Internet Explorer has been used regularly. If not, the icons will be labeled with week names (Last Week, Two Weeks Ago, and so on).

▶ **2.** Click the **Today** icon to open a list of Web sites you visited today. Each page you visited is stored in this list. To return to a particular page, click that page's entry in the list. You can see the full URL of any item in the History list by moving the mouse pointer over the history list item.

▶ **3.** Click the **Favorites Center** button to close the History list.

> **Tip**
>
> If you are using a computer in a computer lab or an Internet café, the History list will include sites visited by anyone who has used the computer, not just you.

Erasing Your History | InSight

In some situations, such as when you are finishing a work session in a school computer lab, you might want to remove the list of Web sites that you visited from the History list of the computer on which you had been working. Erasing your browser history helps protect your personal information and guard your privacy when working on a shared computer. You can do this in Internet Explorer by clicking the Tools button, selecting Internet Options, and clicking the General tab in the Internet Options dialog box. In the Browsing history section, click the Delete button, then click the Delete history button in the Delete Browsing History dialog box. Click Yes to confirm the deletion, and then close the two dialog boxes.

Refreshing a Web Page

The Refresh button on the Navigation toolbar loads a new copy of the Web page that currently appears in the browser window. Internet Explorer stores a copy of every Web page it displays on your computer's hard drive in a **Temporary Internet Files folder** in the Windows folder. Storing this information increases the speed at which Internet Explorer can display pages as you move back and forth through the history list, because the browser can load the pages from a local disk drive instead of reloading the page from the remote Web server. When you click the Refresh button, Internet Explorer contacts the Web server to see if the Web page has changed since it was stored in the Temporary Internet Files folder. If it has changed, Internet Explorer gets the new page from the Web server; otherwise, it loads the copy stored on your computer.

Returning to the Home Page

The Home button on the Command bar displays the home (or start) page for your installation of Internet Explorer. You can set the Home button to display the page you want to use as the default home page.

Reference Window | **Changing the Default Home Page in Internet Explorer**

- Click the Tools button on the Command toolbar, and then click Internet Options.
- Click the General tab in the Internet Options dialog box.
- Select whether you want Internet Explorer to open with the current page, its default page, or a blank page by clicking the corresponding button in the Home page section of the Internet Options dialog box.
- To specify a home page, type the URL of that Web page in the Home page list box. If you want multiple Home pages to open on separate tabs, type the URL for each home page on separate lines in the Home Page list box.
- Click the OK button.

To view the settings for the home page:

▶ 1. Click **Tools** on the Command toolbar, and then click **Internet Options**. The Internet Options dialog box opens, as shown in Figure 1-21. To use the currently loaded Web page as your home page, you would click the Use current button. To use the default home page that was installed with your copy of Internet Explorer, you would click the Use default button. If you don't want a page to open when you start your browser, you would click the Use blank button. If you want to specify a home page other than the current, default, or blank page, you would type the URL for that page in the Home page list box.

Figure 1-21 ▶ **Changing the default home page for Internet Explorer**

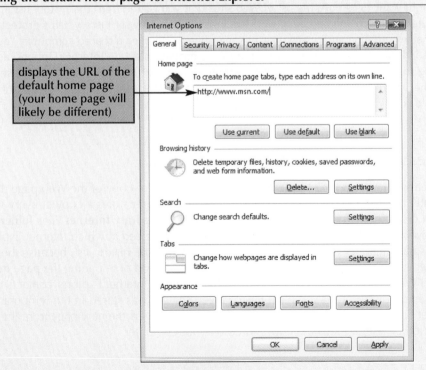

displays the URL of the default home page (your home page will likely be different)

Trouble? If you are working on a computer in a school computer lab or at your employer's place of business, do not change any settings unless you are given permission to do so by your instructor or lab supervisor. Many schools and businesses set the home page defaults on all of their computers and then lock those settings.

▶ **2.** Click the **Cancel** button to close the dialog box without making any changes.

Navigating Web Pages Using Page Tabs

After many years of trailing behind other Web browsers, Internet Explorer added page tabs to its program window. This allows users to navigate from one page to another by opening new Web pages in tabs instead of separate browser windows. This tabbed browsing technique is especially useful when you need to move frequently back and forth between multiple Web pages (up to six). You can click the New Tab button and type a URL in the address window or select a favorite from the Favorites Center, but the most common use of tabbed browsing is to navigate from a page that is already open.

Using Page Tabs to Navigate in Internet Explorer | Reference Window

- Open pages by right-clicking hyperlinks and selecting Open in New Tab on the shortcut menu.
- Click the page tabs to move among open Web pages.

To use page tabs to navigate in Internet Explorer:

▶ **1.** Using the Back and Forward buttons (or the Recent Pages button, or the History list in the Favorites Center), open the Midland Pet Adoption Agency home page in the browser window.

▶ **2.** Right-click the **Pets** hyperlink, and then select **Open in New Tab** on the shortcut menu. Note that the Pets page will not appear until you click the tab (as you will in Step 4).

▶ **3.** Right-click the **Training Programs** hyperlink, and then select **Open in New Tab**. Note that the Training Programs page will not appear until you click the tab (as you will in Step 4).

▶ **4.** Click each visible tab to open its Web page in the browser.

▶ **5.** Close the two tabs you opened by clicking the Close Tab button on the currently displayed tab. The Midland Pet Adoption Agency home page appears again in the browser window.

If you are using tabbed browsing, the page tabs can become rather small as you open more and more tabs. When the page tabs get smaller, the amount of text that is displayed on the tab might not be enough to identify the page. To see the entire Web page title and URL, move the mouse pointer over a page tab and hold it there for a second or two. The information will appear in a box near the mouse pointer. Another way to navigate a large number of open tabs is to use the Quick Tabs button. This button appears to the left of the original tab when a second tab is opened. Clicking the Quick Tabs button opens a page in the browser window that displays small pictures of each Web page that is opened in a tab. Clicking on a picture opens the represented page in the main browser window.

Tip

If you encounter a page that is difficult to print, be sure to look on the Web page for a link to a version of the page that is designed to be printed.

Printing a Web Page

Clicking the Print button arrow on the Command bar opens a menu that gives you choices for printing the current Web page, viewing the page as it will appear when printed (Print Preview), or accessing the Page Setup dialog box, which provides options for adjusting the margins, header, footer, and other attributes of the pages you print (Page Setup).

Reference Window | **Printing the Current Web Page**

- Click the Print button on the Command bar, and then click Print to print the current Web page with the default print settings.

  or
- Click the Print Button arrow on the Command bar, and then click Print to open the Print dialog box.
- In the Print dialog box, select the printer you want to use, and then indicate the pages you want to print and the number of copies you want to make of each page.
- To print a range of pages, click the Pages option button, then type the first page of the range, type a hyphen, and then type the last page of the range.
- Click the Print button.

To print a Web page:

▶ 1. Click the **Print button arrow** on the Command bar, and then click **Print**.

▶ 2. Make sure that the printer selected (highlighted) in the Select Printer list box is the printer you want to use; if not, click the icon of the printer you want to use to change the selection.

▶ 3. Click the **Pages** option button in the Page Range section of the Print dialog box, and then type **1** in the text box to specify that you only want to print the first page. (If the text box already contains a "1" you do not need to change it.)

▶ 4. Make sure that the Number of copies text box displays **1**.

▶ 5. Click the **Print** button to print the Web page and close the Print dialog box.

Changing the Page Setup Settings

Usually, the default settings in the Print dialog box are fine for printing a Web page, but you can use the Page Setup dialog box to change the way a Web page prints. Figure 1-22 shows the Page Setup dialog box and an open Help window that explains the header and footer codes.

Page Setup dialog box and Help window showing header and footer codes ◀ Figure 1-22

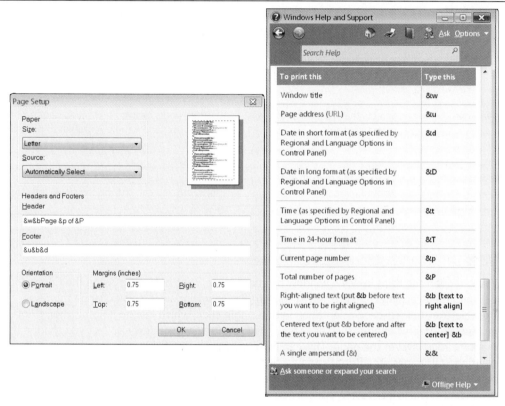

Figure 1-23 describes the options available in the Page Setup dialog box. This dialog box lets you specify the paper orientation, document formatting, margins, and other options.

Figure 1-23 ▷ **Page Setup dialog box options**

Option	Description	Use
Paper Size	Changes the size of the printed page.	Use the Letter size default unless you are printing to different paper stock, such as legal.
Paper Source	Changes the printer's paper source.	Use the default Auto Select unless you want to specify a different tray or manual feed for printing on heavy paper.
Header	Prints information about the Web page at the top of each page.	To obtain details on how to specify exact header printing options, click the Header text box to select it, and then press the F1 key.
Footer	Prints information about the Web page at the bottom of each page.	To obtain details on how to specify exact footer printing options, click the Footer text box to select it, and then press the F1 key.
Orientation	Selects the orientation of the printed output.	Portrait works best for most Web pages, but you can use landscape orientation to print the wide tables of numbers included on some Web pages.
Margins	Changes the margin of the printed page.	Normally, you should leave the default settings, but you can change the right, left, top, or bottom margins as needed.

InSight | **Using Print Preview in Internet Explorer**

You can open the Print Preview window by clicking the Print button arrow on the Command bar, and then clicking Page Preview. The Print Preview window lets you change the page from portrait to landscape orientation with a single click, which can be helpful when printing certain graphic images such as maps. The Print Preview window also lets you change the magnification level of the page. This can help you save a significant amount of paper when printing Web pages. The Print Preview window lets you set the magnification and see the result before you print, so you avoid reducing the magnification to the point that text is unreadable. The Print Preview window also lets you toggle headers and footers on and off with one click.

Checking Web Page Security

Most Web pages are sent from the Web server to the Web browser as plain text and image files. Anyone who intercepts the transmission can read the text and see the images. For most Web pages, which are designed to be viewed by anyone, this is not really a problem. In some cases, however, the Web site and the user would like to have a private interaction. For example, you might not want anyone to know what book titles or what size clothes you are ordering from an online store. You certainly wouldn't want an unauthorized person to intercept your interactions with your bank or stockbroker. To prevent unauthorized persons from reading intercepted transmissions, Web servers can use encryption.

Encryption is a way of scrambling and encoding data transmissions that reduces the risk that a person who intercepts the Web page as it travels across the Internet will be able to decode and read the page's contents. Web sites use encrypted transmission to send and receive information, such as credit card numbers, to ensure privacy. You can determine whether a Web page has been encrypted by examining the page's properties. To open the Properties dialog box for a Web page, right-click the Web page and selectProperties from the shortcut menu. If the Web page is not encrypted, the Connection property in the Properties dialog box will appear as "Not Encrypted." If the Web page is encrypted, the Connection property will display information about the type and level of encryption used to transmit the page from the Web server.

Another protection used by Web sites is to register with a third-party certification authority. A **certification authority** is a company that attests to a Web site's legitimacy. You can see the certificate from the certification authority for a Web site by clicking the Certificates button in the Properties dialog box. Figure 1-24 shows the Properties dialog box and the Certificate for a Web page sent to a user who is placing a product order.

Web page properties and security certificate **Figure 1-24**

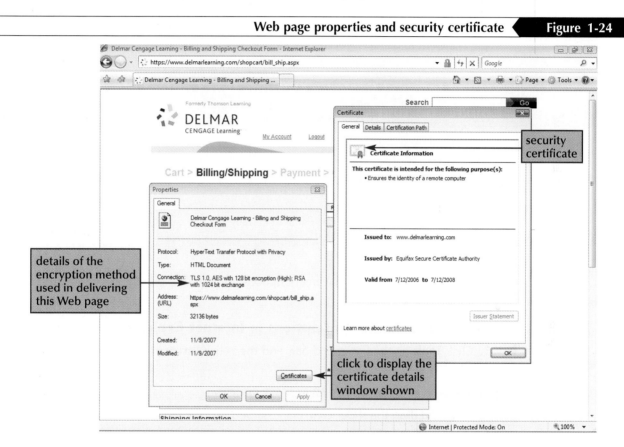

Managing Cookies

Many Web users are concerned about cookies, the small files you learned about in Session 1.1 that some Web servers write to the disk drives of client computers. Unlike most other Web browsers, Internet Explorer stores each cookie in an individual file and does not provide any advanced tools for examining or deleting specific cookies. It does, however, allow you to delete all cookies and set options that control the writing of cookies to your computer's disk drive.

Reference Window | **Deleting All Cookies in Internet Explorer**

- Click the Tools button arrow on the Command bar, and then click Delete Browsing History.
- Click the Delete cookies button in the Delete Browsing History dialog box.
- Click the Close button.

Some cookies provide benefits to users. For example, if you regularly visit a site that requires you to log in, that login information can be stored in a cookie on your computer so you don't have to type your username each time you visit the site. Therefore, you might not want to delete all of the cookies on your computer.

Reference Window | **Setting Internet Explorer Options that Control Placement of Cookies on Your Computer**

- Click the Tools button arrow on the Command bar, and then click Internet Options.
- Click the Privacy tab in the Internet Options dialog box.
- Use the slider control to set the way cookies are handled by Internet Explorer.
- Click the Sites button to specify sites that are allowed (or not allowed) to place cookies on your computer.
- Click the OK button to close the Per Site Privacy Actions dialog box.
- Click the OK button to close the Internet Options dialog box.

You will view the cookie placement options in Internet Explorer.

To view cookie placement options in Internet Explorer:

▶ 1. Click **Tools** on the Command bar, and then click **Internet Options**. The Internet Options dialog box opens.

▶ 2. Click the **Privacy** tab to display these options.

▶ 3. Click and drag the slider control in the Settings section on the Privacy tab to examine the various settings available that control placement of cookies on your computer.

▶ 4. Click the **Cancel** button to close the Internet Options dialog box without saving any of the changes you might have made to the privacy settings.

Getting Help in Internet Explorer

Internet Explorer includes an online Help system. Internet Explorer Help includes information about how to use the browser and how it is different from previous versions of the browser, and provides some tips for exploring the Internet.

*Note:*The Help function in Windows Vista operates differently than the Help function in Windows XP. If you are using Windows XP, the following steps will not work. See your instructor or lab supervisor for assistance.

Opening Internet Explorer Help | Reference Window

- Press the F1 key to open the Windows Help and Support window.
- Click the Browse Help button near the top of the Windows Help and Support window.
- Click a hyperlink to open a specific Help topic.
- Click the Close button.

To open Internet Explorer Help:

▶ 1. Press the **F1** key, the click the Browse Help button. The Windows Help and Support window opens, as shown in Figure 1-25.

Internet Explorer help window ◀ Figure 1-25

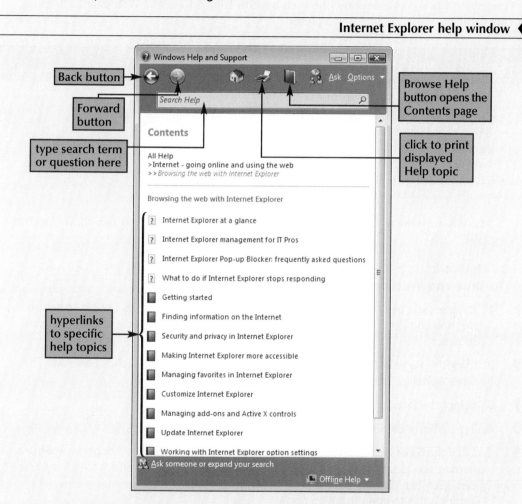

▶ 2. Click the **Browse Help** button to open the Windows Help and Support Contents page. You can explore any of the items in the Help system by clicking the topics displayed as hyperlinks in this window. You can also type terms or questions into the Search Help box to find information in the Help system.

▶ 3. When you are finished exploring the Help system, click the **Close** button.

You want to show Trinity the Midland Pet Adoption Agency Web page, but you are concerned that the Web site might change before she has a chance to visit it on the Web. You can save the Web page as a file on a computer or on a disk. She will then be able to open the Web page on her own computer using her Web browser.

Using Internet Explorer to Save Web Page Content

There will be times when you will want to refer to the information that you have found on a Web page without having to return to the site. In Internet Explorer you can store entire Web pages, selected portions of Web page text, or particular graphics from a Web page to a disk.

Saving a Web Page

You like the Midland Pet Adoption Agency's Web site and want to save a copy of the page to a disk so you can show the Web page to Trinity. To save a Web page, you must have the page open in Internet Explorer.

Reference Window | **Saving a Web Page**

- Open the Web page in Internet Explorer.
- Click the Page button arrow on the Command bar, and then click Save As.
- Select the location for your saved Web page.
- Accept the default filename, or change the filename in the File name text box, but retain the file extension .mht.
- Click the Save button.

You will save the Midland Pet Adoption Agency home page so you can show it to Trinity later.

To save the Web page:

▶ 1. If necessary, use the Back and Forward buttons or the Favorites Center to return to the Midland Pet Adoption Agency home page if it is not already displayed in your browser.

▶ 2. Click the **Page button arrow** on the Command bar, and then click **Save As**. The Save Webpage dialog box opens.

▶ 3. Select the location for your saved Web page.

▶ 4. Type **MidlandHomePageMSIE.mht** in the File name text box.

▶ 5. Click the **Save** button. Now the Web page for the Midland Pet Adoption Agency's home page is saved in the location you specified. When you send it to Trinity, she can open her Web browser and type the file location and name in the browser's Address bar to open the Web page.

Understanding Web Page File Formats | InSight

Internet Explorer by default saves Web pages in a proprietary archive format that can be read by Internet Explorer Web browsers. Not all Web browsers, however, can read this file format. You can change the format in the Save As dialog box by choosing either Webpage, complete (which saves the graphic page elements along with the HTML text), Webpage, HTML only (which saves the Web page's text with the HTML markup codes), or Text File (which saves the Web page's text without the HTML markup codes) in the Save as type list box. Avoiding the Internet Explorer proprietary format will ensure that the page you save can be read by users who are using other Web browsers.

Saving Web Page Text to a File

You can save portions of a Web page's text to a file, so that you can use the text in other programs. You will use WordPad to save text that you will copy from a Web page; however, any word processor or text editor will work.

Copying Text from a Web Page to a WordPad Document | Reference Window

- Open the Web page in Internet Explorer.
- Use the mouse pointer to select the text you want to copy.
- Right-click the selected text to open the shortcut menu, and then click Copy.
- Open WordPad (or another word processor or text editor if WordPad is not available).
- Click Edit on the WordPad menu bar, and then click Paste (or click the Paste button).
- Click the Save button, select the location in which you want to store the file, and then enter a new filename, if necessary.
- Click the Save button.

Trinity will be traveling in Minnesota next week, and she would like to visit the Midland Pet Adoption Agency while she is in the area. She will meet with the director there to learn more about how the agency developed its Web site. You will visit the Midland Pet Adoption Agency's Web site and get the agency's address and telephone number so Trinity can contact the director and schedule a meeting.

To copy text from a Web page and save it as a WordPad document:

1. Return to the Midland Pet Adoption Agency home page if it is not already displayed in your browser.

2. Click the **Directions & Contact** hyperlink to open the Web page that has the address and phone number you want to copy.

3. Click and drag the mouse pointer over the address and telephone number to select it, as shown in Figure 1-26, right-click the selected text, and then click Copy on the shortcut menu to copy the selected text to the Clipboard.

Figure 1-26 Selecting and copying text on a Web page in Internet Explorer

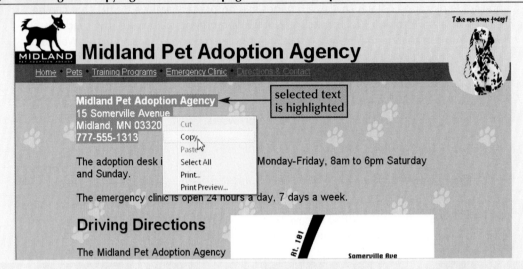

Now, you will start WordPad and then paste the copied text into a new document.

▶ 4. Click the **Start** button on the taskbar, point to **All Programs**, point to **Accessories**, and then click **WordPad** to start the program and open a new document.

▶ 5. Click the **Paste** button on the WordPad toolbar to paste the text into the WordPad document, as shown in Figure 1-27.

Figure 1-27 Pasting text from a Web page into a WordPad document

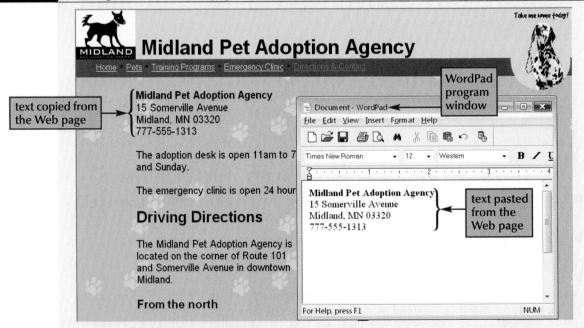

Trouble? If the WordPad toolbar does not appear, click View on the menu bar, click Toolbar, and then repeat Step 5. Your WordPad program window might be a different size from the one shown in Figure 1-27, which does not affect the steps.

▶ 6. Click the **Save** button on the WordPad toolbar to open the Save As dialog box.

▶ 7. Navigate to the location in which you want to save the file.

8. Delete the text in the File name text box, type **MidlandAddressPhoneMSIE.txt**, and then click the **Save** button. Now, the address and phone number of the agency are saved in a text file for future reference.

9. Click the **Close** button on the WordPad title bar to close it.

You can print this information from WordPad and give it to Trinity the next time you see her. As you examine the Web page, you notice a street map that shows the location of the Midland Pet Adoption Agency. You will print this map to give to Trinity as well.

Saving a Web Page Graphic

When a Web page has a graphic or picture that you would like to save or print, you have the option of saving or printing just the image, instead of the entire Web page.

Saving an Image from a Web Page | Reference Window

- Open the Web page in Internet Explorer.
- Right-click the image you want to copy, and then click Save Picture As on the shortcut menu.
- Navigate to the location in which you want to save the image and change the default filename, if necessary.
- Click the Save button.

Now you will save the image of the street map for Trinity.

To save the street map image:

1. Right-click the map image to open its shortcut menu, as shown in Figure 1-28.

Saving the map image ◀ Figure 1-28

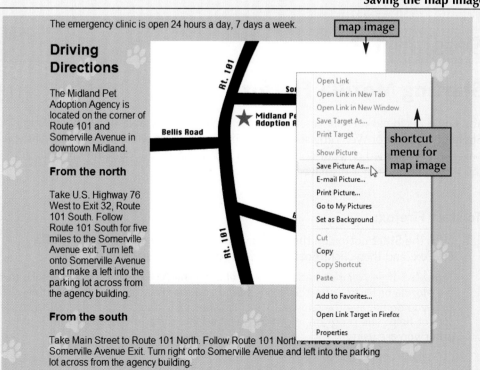

▶ **2.** Click **Save Picture As** on the shortcut menu to open the Save Picture dialog box.

▶ **3.** Navigate to the location in which you want to save the file.

▶ **4.** Delete the text in the File name text box, type **MidlandMapMSIE.gif**, and then click the **Save** button to save the file.

▶ **5.** Close your Web browser.

Now, you have copies of the Midland Pet Adoption Agency home page and map that will show Trinity how to get there during her trip to Minnesota. She will be able to use her Web browser to open the files and print them.

| Review | **Session 1.2 Quick Check** |

1. Describe two ways to increase the Web page area in Internet Explorer.

2. You can use the _____ button in Internet Explorer to visit previously visited sites during your Web session.

3. Clicking the _____ button on the Command bar opens the page that the browser is configured to display when it first starts.

4. List the names of two Favorites folders (in addition to your Pet Adoption Agencies folder) that you might want to add as you continue to gather information for Trinity.

5. To ensure that Internet Explorer loads a Web page from the server rather than from its cache, you can hold down the _____ key as you click the Refresh button.

6. Explain how you can identify encrypted Web pages when viewing them in Internet Explorer.

7. To obtain help in Internet Explorer, press the _____ key.

If your instructor assigned Session 1.3, continue reading. Otherwise complete the Review Assignments and Case Problems at the end of this tutorial.

Session 1.3

Starting Mozilla Firefox

You could decide to do your research on the Web for Trinity and the Danville Animal Shelter with a major Web browser, Mozilla Firefox. This introduction assumes that you have Firefox installed on your computer. You should have your computer turned on so the Windows desktop is displayed.

To start Firefox:

▶ **1.** Click the **Start** button on the taskbar, point to **All Programs**, click **Mozilla Firefox**, and then click **Mozilla Firefox**. After a moment, Firefox opens.

Trouble? If you cannot find Mozilla Firefox on the All Programs menu, check to see if a Mozilla or Firefox shortcut icon appears on the desktop, and then double-click it. If you do not see the shortcut icon, ask your instructor or technical support person for help. The program might be installed in a different location on the computer you are using.

▶ **2.** If the program does not fill the screen entirely, click the **Maximize** button on the Firefox program's title bar. Your screen should look like Figure 1-29.

Firefox main program window | Figure 1-29

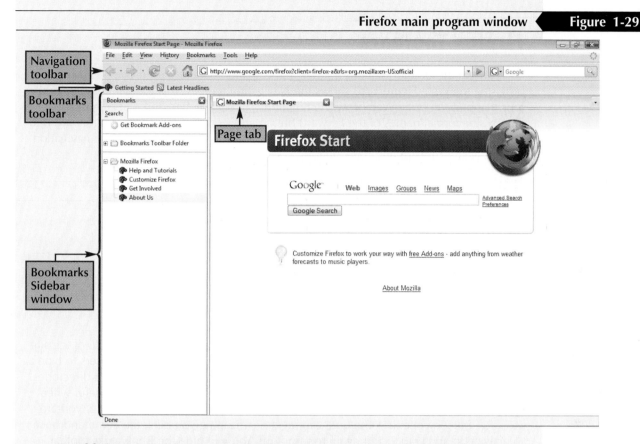

Trouble? Figure 1-29 shows the Firefox Start page, which is the page that Firefox opens the first time the program is started after its initial installation on a computer. Your computer might be configured to open to a different Web page, or no page at all.

Trouble? If you don't see a page tab on your screen, then your browser is set to hide page tabs when only one Web site is open. Click Tools on the menu bar, click Options, click Tabs in the Options dialog box, and then click the Always show the tab bar check box to select it. Click OK to close the dialog box.

Trouble? If the Bookmarks toolbar is not displayed on your screen, click View on the menu bar, point to Toolbars, and then click Bookmarks Toolbar to display the toolbar, as shown in Figure 1-29.

Trouble? If the Bookmarks Sidebar window shown in Figure 1-29 is not visible in your browser window, skip Step 3.

▶ **3.** Click **View** on the menu bar, point to **Sidebar**, and then click the **Bookmarks Sidebar** (or drag the right edge of the Bookmarks Sidebar frame to the left side of the browser window) to close the Bookmarks Sidebar. This will give you more room to view Web pages when using the Firefox browser. You can reopen the Bookmarks Sidebar by selecting View, Sidebar, Bookmarks from the menu bar or by clicking and dragging the left edge of the browser window to the right. The click-and-drag method for restoring the Bookmarks Sidebar works only if you closed it using that method.

Now that you understand how to start Firefox, you want to learn more about the components of the Firefox program window.

Firefox Toolbars

The **Navigation toolbar** includes buttons that execute frequently used commands for browsing the Web. Figure 1-30 shows the Navigation toolbar. This toolbar contains buttons that perform basic Web browsing functions, a Location bar, and a Search bar. In Firefox, the formal names of the Forward button and Back button are the Go forward one page button and Go back one page button, respectively. This text refers to the navigation buttons as the Forward and Back buttons.

| Figure 1-30 | Firefox Navigation toolbar |

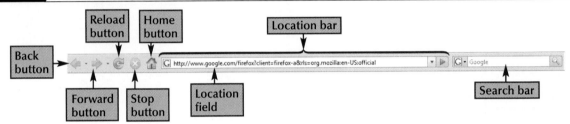

The **Location bar** includes a location field that allows users to type the URL of the site they wish to visit. The Navigation toolbar also has a search bar that allows users to type a search term that Firefox sends to the user's choice of search engines and Web directories.

You can use the View menu to hide or show the Firefox toolbars. This is useful when you want to expand the Web browser window to show more of the Web pages you are viewing. The View menu commands are toggles—meaning you click the command once to activate it, and you click it again to turn it off. You will hide the Bookmarks toolbar.

To hide the Bookmarks toolbar using the View menu:

1. Click **View** on the menu bar, point to **Toolbars**, and then click **Bookmarks Toolbar** to remove its check mark. The Bookmarks toolbar is hidden in the browser window. To redisplay the Bookmarks toolbar, you will repeat the same steps.

   Trouble? If the Bookmarks Toolbar command does not have a check mark next to it, then the Bookmarks toolbar already is hidden.

2. Click **View** on the menu bar, point to **Toolbars**, and then click **Bookmarks Toolbar** to check this command. The toolbar is displayed again.

Firefox will try to add standard URL elements to complete partial URLs that you type in the Address bar. For example, if you type cnn.com, Firefox will convert it to http://www.cnn.com and load the home page at that URL.

Navigating Web Pages Using the Location Bar

You can use the **Location Bar** to enter URLs directly into Firefox. As you learned in Session 1.1, you must enter the URL to identify a Web page's exact location. Although a complete URL includes the name of a file, entering just the IP address or the domain name will usually be sufficient to take you to the home page of the site.

Entering a URL in the Location Bar

- Click at the end of the current text in the location field, and then delete any unnecessary or unwanted text from the displayed URL.
- Type the URL of the site you want to view.
- Press the Enter key to load the URL's Web page in the browser window.

Trinity has asked you to start your research by examining the home page for the Midland Pet Adoption Agency's Web site. She has given you the URL so that you can find it.

To load the Midland Pet Adoption Agency's Web page:

▶ **1.** Click in the Location field and press the **Backspace** key to delete any existing text.

   Trouble? Make sure that you delete all of the text in the Location field so the text you type in Step 2 will be correct.

▶ **2.** Type **www.midlandpet.com** in the Location field. This is the URL of the Midland Pet Adoption Agency Web site.

   Trouble? Depending on how Firefox is configured, the Location field might display a list of suggested URLs as you type. You should ignore these suggestions and continue typing.

▶ **3.** Press the **Enter** key. The home page of the Midland Pet Adoption Agency Web site loads, as shown in Figure 1-31.

Midland Pet Adoption Agency Web page ◀ **Figure 1-31**

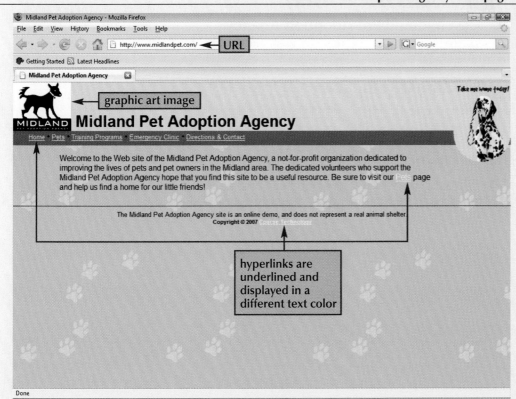

Navigating Web Pages Using the Mouse

The easiest way to move from one Web page to another is to use the mouse to click hyperlinks that the authors of Web pages embed in their HTML documents. You can also right-click the mouse on the background of a Web page to open a shortcut menu that includes navigation options.

Reference Window | **Navigating Between Web Pages Using Hyperlinks and the Mouse**

- Click the hyperlink.
- After the new Web page has loaded, right-click the Web page's background.
- Click Back on the shortcut menu.

To follow a hyperlink to a Web page and return using the mouse:

▶ **1.** Point to the **Training Programs** hyperlink, shown in Figure 1-32, so your pointer changes to an icon of a hand with a pointing index finger.

Figure 1-32   Midland Pet Adoption Agency home page

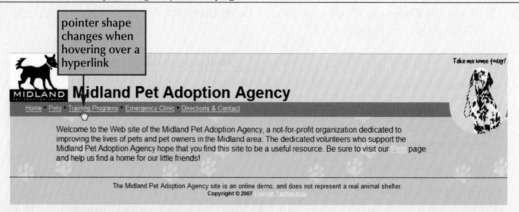

▶ **2.** Click the **Training Programs** link to load the page.

▶ **3.** Right-click anywhere in the Web page area (other than on a graphic or a hyperlink) to open the shortcut menu, as shown in Figure 1-33.

Using the shortcut menu to go back to the previous page ◀ Figure 1-33

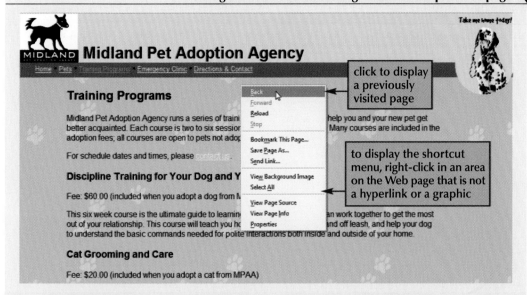

Trouble? If you right-click a hyperlink, your shortcut menu will display a list that differs from the one shown in Figure 1-33; therefore, the Back option might not appear in the same position on the menu. If you don't see the shortcut menu shown in Figure 1-33, click anywhere outside of the shortcut menu to close it, and then repeat Step 3.

▶ 4. Click **Back** on the shortcut menu to go back to the Midland Pet Adoption Agency home page.

Returning to Web Pages Previously Visited

You like the format of the Midland Pet Adoption Agency's home page, so you want to make sure that you can go back to that page later if you need to review its contents. You can write down the URL so you can refer to it later, but an easier way is to store the URL as a bookmark for future use. You can also use the History list and the Back and Forward buttons to return to Web pages you have already visited, and the Home button to return to your browser's start page.

Navigating Web Pages Using Bookmarks

You use the bookmark feature to store and organize a list of Web pages that you have visited so you can return to them easily. Figure 1-34 shows an open Bookmarks Manager window, which contains bookmarks sorted into hierarchical categories.

Figure 1-34 ▶ **Bookmarks sorted into categories**

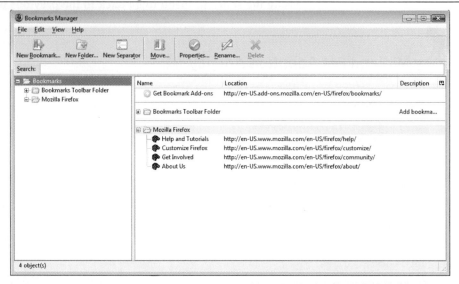

Reference Window | **Creating a New Bookmarks Folder**

- Click Bookmarks on the menu bar, and then click Organize Bookmarks.
- If the Bookmarks entry in the left pane of the Bookmarks Manager window is not high-lighted, click it, and then click the New Folder button.
- Delete the default text in the Name text box, and then type a new folder name.
- Click the OK button.

You will create a bookmark for the Midland Pet Adoption Agency Web page, but first, you need to create a folder in which to store your bookmarks. You will then save your bookmark in that folder. You might not work on the same computer again, so you can save a copy of the bookmark file to a floppy disk, a USB flash drive, or another storage device for future use.

To create a new Bookmarks folder:

▶ **1.** Click **Bookmarks** on the menu bar, and then click **Organize Bookmarks**. The Bookmarks Manager window opens. Maximize the Bookmarks Manager window.

▶ **2.** If the top Bookmarks folder in the left pane of the Bookmarks Manager window is not highlighted, click it, and then click the **New Folder** button. The Properties for "New Folder" dialog box opens with the default text "New Folder" in the Name text box. In the left pane of the Bookmarks Manager window, a new folder is created.

▶ **3.** Delete the default text in the Name text box, type **Pet Adoption Agencies**, and then click the **OK** button. The Pet Adoption Agencies folder appears in the Bookmarks Manager window, as shown in Figure 1-35.

Pet Adoption Agencies folder ◄ **Figure 1-35**

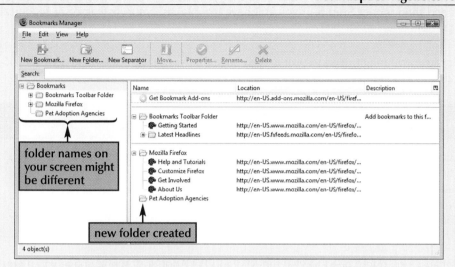

folder names on your screen might be different

new folder created

▶ **4.** Click the **Close** button in the Bookmarks Manager window to close it.

Now that you have created a folder, you can save your bookmark for the Midland Pet Adoption Agency Web page in the new folder.

Saving a Bookmark in a Bookmarks Folder | Reference Window

- Open the page that you want to bookmark in Firefox.
- Click Bookmarks on the menu bar, and then click Bookmark This Page.
- Type a descriptive name in the Name box (or leave the default name for the page as is).
- Select the folder in which you want to save the bookmark.
- Click the OK button.

To save a bookmark for the Midland Pet Adoption Agency Web page in the Bookmarks folder:

▶ **1.** With the Midland Pet Adoption Agency Web page open, click **Bookmarks** on the menu bar, and then click **Bookmark This Page**. The Add Bookmark dialog box opens.

▶ **2.** Type **Midland Pet Adoption Agency** in the Name text box, if it does not already appear.

Trouble? If necessary, delete any existing text that appears in the Name text box before you begin typing the name for the bookmark.

▶ **3.** Click the **Create in** list arrow, scroll down the list to locate the Pet Adoption Agencies folder, click that folder, and then click the **OK** button. The bookmark for Midland Pet Adoption Agency is saved in that folder. You can test your bookmark by using it to visit the site.

▶ **4.** Click the **Back** button on the Navigation toolbar to go to the previous Web page.

▶ **5.** Click **Bookmarks** on the menu bar, point to **Pet Adoption Agencies**, and then click **Midland Pet Adoption Agency**. The Midland Pet Adoption Agency page opens in the browser.

Trouble? If the Midland Pet Adoption Agency page does not open, open the Bookmarks Manager window, make sure that you have the correct URL for the page, and then repeat Step 5. If you still have trouble, ask your instructor or technical support person for help.

Because you might need to visit a Web page that you have bookmarked when you are working at another computer, Firefox lets you save your bookmark file on a disk.

Reference Window | **Saving a Bookmark File to a Disk**

- Click Bookmarks on the menu bar, and then click Organize Bookmarks.
- Click File on the menu bar, and then click Export.
- Select the drive and folder into which you want to save the bookmark file.
- Type a name for the bookmark file.
- Click the Save button.

Because you might need to visit the Midland Pet Adoption Agency page when you are working at another computer, you will save your bookmark file on a disk.

To store the Midland Pet Adoption Agency bookmark file to a disk:

▶ 1. Click **Bookmarks** on the menu bar, and then click **Organize Bookmarks**. The Bookmarks Manager window opens. When you save a bookmark, you save all of the bookmarks, not just the one that you need.

▶ 2. Click **File** on the menu bar in the Bookmarks Manager window, and then click **Export**. The Export bookmark file dialog box opens.

   Trouble? If prompted, insert a disk in the appropriate drive on your computer.

▶ 3. Select the location to which you want to save the bookmarks file in the Save in list box.

   Trouble? If you were prompted to insert a disk in Step 2, then the correct drive and disk should automatically appear in the Save in list box.

   The filename that you give the bookmark file should indicate the Web page you have marked. The file extension must be .htm or .html so the browser into which you load this file will recognize it as an HTML file. Most browsers will recognize either file extension; however, some do not.

▶ 4. Type **MyFirefoxBookmarks.html** in the File name text box. *Note:* You can select the HTML files option in the Save as type list and type the name of the file without typing the file extension; with the HTML files option selected, the program will automatically add the correct file extension.

▶ 5. Click the **Save** button, and then close the Bookmarks Manager window.

When you use another computer, you can open the bookmark file from your disk (or other storage device) by starting Firefox, clicking Bookmarks on the menu bar, and clicking Organize Bookmarks to open the Bookmarks Manager. You can then click File on the Bookmarks Manager menu bar and click Import. Select the device and folder that contains your bookmark file, and then open the bookmark file. Your bookmark file will open in Firefox's Bookmarks Manager window on that computer.

Navigating Web Pages Using the History List

The Back and Forward buttons on the Navigation toolbar and the Back and Forward options on the shortcut menu enable you to move to and from recently visited pages. These buttons duplicate the functions of the commands on the History menu. The options on the History menu enable you to move back and forward through a portion of the history list and allow you to choose a specific Web page from the list. To see where you have been during a session, you also can open the history list for your current session.

To view the history list for this session:

1. Click **History** on the menu bar, and then click **Show in Sidebar** to open the history list in the sidebar window. You will see that the history list is organized into folders that each contain lists of sites that you visited by day (or groups of days). For example, your history list might show folders titled Today, Yesterday, 2 Days Ago, and so on.

2. Click the **plus sign icon** next to the Today folder to open the list of Web sites visited today. (If the icon is a minus sign, you do not need to click it because the list of Web sites is already open.) You can click the file icon next to any entry to return to that specific Web page.

3. Click the **Close** button (the small "x" in a red square near the top-right corner of the sidebar window) on the History sidebar to close it.

Tip
If you are using a computer in a computer lab or an Internet café, the History list will include sites visited by anyone who has used the computer, not just you.

You can change the way that pages are organized in the History list by using the View button in the sidebar window. For example, you can list the pages by Web page title or in the order in which you visited them.

Erasing Your History | InSight

In some situations, such as when you are finishing a work session in a school computer lab, you might want to remove the list of Web sites that you visited from the History list of the computer on which you had been working. Erasing your browser history helps protect your personal information and guard your privacy when working on a shared computer. You can do this in Firefox by clicking Tools on the menu bar, selecting Options, and clicking the Privacy icon at the top of the Options dialog box. In the Private Data section, click the Clear Now button, and then make sure that Browsing History is the only box that is checked. Click the Clear Private Data Now button, and then click the Close button in the Options dialog box.

Reloading a Web Page

The Reload button on the Firefox toolbar loads a new copy of the Web page that currently appears in the browser window. Firefox stores a copy of every Web page it displays on your computer's hard drive in a **Temporary Internet Files folder** in the Windows folder. Storing this information increases the speed at which Firefox can display pages as you move back and forth through the history list, because the browser can load the pages from a local disk drive instead of reloading the page from the remote Web server. When you click the Reload button, Firefox contacts the Web server to see if the Web page has changed since it was stored in the Temporary Internet Files folder. If it has changed, Firefox gets the new page from the Web server; otherwise, it loads the copy stored on your computer.

Returning to the Home Page

The Home button on the Navigation toolbar displays the home (or start) page for your installation of Firefox. You can set the Home button to display the page you want to use as the default home page by using the Options dialog box, which is accessible from the Tools menu.

| Reference Window | **Changing the Default Home Page in Firefox** |

- Click Tools on the menu bar, and then click Options.
- Click the Main icon in the Options dialog box, if it is not already selected.
- In the Startup section of the dialog box, type the URL or filename of the page you want to use as your default home page in the Home Page text box.
- Click the OK button.

To view the settings for the default home page:

▶ 1. Click **Tools** on the menu bar, and then click **Options**. The Options dialog box opens, as shown in Figure 1-36.

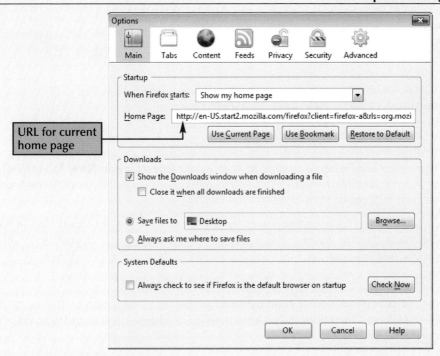

Trouble? If the dialog box does not look like Figure 1-36, make sure that the Main icon near the top of the page is selected.

2. To set the page currently displayed in the browser as your home page, you can click the Use Current Page button in the Startup section of the Options dialog box. To specify a different home page than the one displayed, you would select the text in the Home Page text box and then enter the URL of the Web page you want to use. If you load the Web page that you want as your new home page before beginning these steps, you can click the Use Current Page button to place the page's URL in the Home page text box. You can also choose to use one of your bookmarks as your home page by clicking the Use Bookmark button.

Trouble? If you are using a computer in a school computer lab or at your employer's place of business, do not change any settings unless you are given permission by your instructor or lab supervisor. Many organizations set the home page defaults on all of their computers and lock those settings.

3. Click the **Cancel** button to close the dialog box without making any changes.

Navigating Web Pages Using Page Tabs

Firefox was one of the first Web browsers to follow the lead of Opera and introduce tabbed browsing, which allows users to navigate from one page to another by opening new Web pages in tabs instead of separate browser windows. This tabbed browsing technique is especially useful when you need to move frequently back and forth between five or six Web pages. You can right-click in any existing tab or the area to the right of the page tabs to open a Web page in a new tab, but the most common use of tabbed browsing is to navigate from a page that is already open.

Reference Window | Using Page Tabs to Navigate in Firefox

- Open pages by right-clicking hyperlinks and selecting Open Link in New Tab on the shortcut menu.
- Click the page tabs to move among open Web pages.

To use page tabs to navigate in Firefox:

▶ 1. Using the Back and Forward buttons or the History list, open the Midland Pet Adoption Agency home page in the browser window.

▶ 2. Right-click the **Pets** hyperlink, and then select **Open Link in New Tab** on the shortcut menu. Note that the Pets page will not appear until you click the tab (as you will in Step 4).

▶ 3. Right-click the **Training Programs** hyperlink, and then select **Open Link in New Tab**. Note that the Training Programs page will not appear until you click the tab (as you will in Step 4).

▶ 4. Click each visible tab to open its Web page in the browser.

▶ 5. Close the two tabs you opened by clicking the Close Tab button on the currently displayed tab. The Midland Pet Adoption Agency home page appears again in the browser window.

InSight | Displaying Web Page Information with Tabbed Browsing

If you are using tabbed browsing, the page tabs can become rather small as you open more and more tabs. When the page tabs get smaller, the amount of text that is displayed on the tab might not be enough to identify the page. To see the entire Web page title, move the mouse pointer over a page tab and hold it there for a second or two. The Web page title will appear in a box near the mouse pointer.

Printing a Web Page

The Print command on the File menu lets you print the current Web page. You can use this command to make a printed copy of most Web pages.

Reference Window | Printing the Current Web Page

- Click File on the menu bar, and then click Print.
- In the Print dialog box, select the printer you want to use and indicate the pages you want to print and the number of copies you want to make of each page.
- Click the OK button.

To print a Web page:

1. Click **File** on the menu bar, and then click **Print**. The Print dialog box opens.

2. Make sure that the printer in the Name list box displays the printer you want to use; if not, click the Name list arrow and select the appropriate printer from the list.

3. Click the **Pages** option button in the Print range section of the Print dialog box, type **1** in the from text box, press the **Tab** key, and then, if necessary, type **1** in the to text box to specify that you want to print only the first page.

4. Make sure that the Number of copies text box displays **1**.

5. Click the **OK** button to print the Web page and close the Print dialog box.

   Firefox provides a number of useful print options that allow you to customize the printed format of Web pages. You can use the Page Setup dialog box to create custom formats for printing Web pages in Firefox.

Tip

If you encounter a page that is difficult to print, be sure to look on the Web page for a link to a version of the page that is designed to be printed.

Using Page Setup to Create a Custom Format for Printing a Web Page | Reference Window

- Click File on the menu bar, and then click Page Setup.
- In the Page Setup dialog box, select the orientation, scaling, and print background options you want to use.
- Click the Margins & Header/Footer tab.
- Type the margin settings you want to use.
- Choose elements you want to print in the left, center, and right areas of the page header and footer.
- Click the OK button.

To create a custom format for printing a Web page:

1. Click **File** on the menu bar, and then click **Page Setup** to open the Page Setup dialog box. On the Format & Options tab of this dialog box, you can change settings for page orientation, scale, and background print options. The default settings are good for printing most Web pages, but you can customize any of these settings if you wish.

2. Click the **Margins & Header/Footer** tab in the Page Setup dialog box. See Figure 1-37. In this part of the dialog box you can change the page margins and specify elements of the header and footer that will print with each page. The default settings are good for printing most Web pages, but you can customize any of these settings if you wish.

Tip

The scale settings are especially helpful for saving paper when printing long Web pages.

Figure 1-37 ▶ **Margins & Header/Footer tab in the Page Setup dialog box**

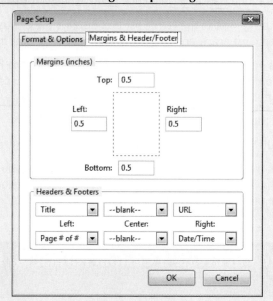

▶ **3.** After you make any changes you wish to the page layout, click the **OK** button to close the dialog box.

You can also set these page print options in the Print Preview window. You can click File on the menu bar, and then click Print Preview to open this window. Some of the page print options are available at the top of the window; all options are available by clicking the Page Setup button, which will open the Page Setup dialog box you worked with in the previous steps. Once you have set the formatting options you want for printing a Web page, you can use the Print button to print the page.

Checking Web Page Security

Most Web pages are sent from the Web server to the Web browser as plain text and image files. Anyone who intercepts the transmission can read the text and see the images. For most Web pages, which are designed to be viewed by anyone, this is not really a problem. In some cases, however, the Web site and the user would like to have a private interaction. For example, you might not want anyone to know what book titles or what size clothes you are ordering from an online store. You certainly wouldn't want an unauthorized person to intercept your interactions with your bank or stockbroker. To prevent unauthorized persons from reading intercepted transmissions, Web servers can use encryption.

Encryption is a way of scrambling and encoding data transmissions that reduces the risk that a person who intercepts the Web page as it travels across the Internet will be able to decode and read the page's contents. Web sites use encrypted transmission to send and receive information, such as credit card numbers, to ensure privacy. You can determine whether a Web page has been encrypted by examining the page's properties.

The **Security indicator button** is a small picture of a padlock that appears at the right edge of the status bar at the bottom of the Firefox browser window when a secure Web page is loaded. The button will appear when the Web page was encrypted during transmission from the Web server. When you double-click this button—or when you click Tools on the menu bar, click Page Info, and then click the Security tab in the Page Info dialog box—you can check some of the security elements of the Web page. If the Web page is not encrypted, the Security tab in the Page Info dialog box will show "Connection Not Encrypted." If the Web page is encrypted, the dialog box will display information about the type and level of encryption used to transmit the page from the Web server.

Another protection used by Web sites is to register with a third-party certification authority. A **certification authority** is a company that attests to a Web site's legitimacy. You can see the certificate from the certification authority for a Web site by clicking the View button on the Security tab of the Page Info dialog box.

Figure 1-38 shows the Security tab of the Page Info dialog box for an encrypted Web page after the user double-clicked the security indicator button. The figure also shows the security certificate for the site in the Certificate Viewer dialog box.

Encryption and security certificate information for a secure Web page in Firefox | Figure 1-38

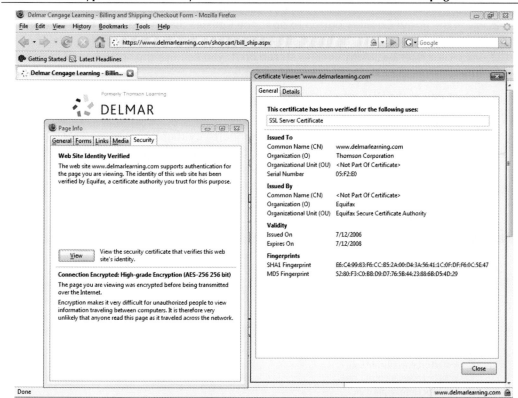

Managing Cookies

Many Web users are concerned about cookies, the small files you learned about in Session 1.1 that some Web servers write to the disk drives of client computers. Firefox stores all cookies in one file, sorted by the name of the Web site that placed each cookie on your computer, and gives users a way to manage the individual cookies.

Reference Window | Managing Cookies in Firefox

- Click Tools on the menu bar, and then click Options to open the Options dialog box.
- Click the Privacy icon to display options for managing privacy issues, and then click the Show Cookies button to open the Cookies dialog box.
- Select a Web site folder, and click the plus sign to the left of the folder. You can then click one of the cookies placed on your computer by that Web site and read the information about that cookie. The cookie information is displayed in the bottom half of the dialog box.
- Select the cookie that you want to delete, and then click the Remove Cookie button.
- Click the OK button.

You will delete a cookie stored on your computer using the Firefox cookie management tool.

To manage cookies in Firefox:

▶ **1.** Click **Tools** on the menu bar, click **Options**, and click the **Privacy** icon in the Options dialog box.

▶ **2.** Click the **Show Cookies** button to open the Cookies dialog box, and then examine the Web site names in the list of sites that appears in the Cookies dialog box. If your computer has many cookies stored on it, you can use the scroll bar to move up and down in the list.

▶ **3.** Select one of the Web site folders displayed in the Cookies dialog box, then click the plus sign to the left of the folder.

▶ **4.** Click one of the cookies placed on your computer by that Web site, and read the cookie information, which is displayed in the bottom half of the dialog box. An example of a Cookies dialog box with several cookies appears in Figure 1-39. Your list of cookies will be different. Information about the selected cookie appears below the list of cookies.

Figure 1-39   Managing cookies in Firefox

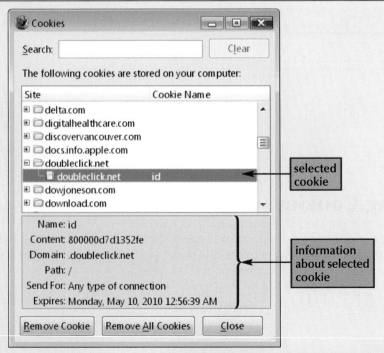

▶ **5.** Find a cookie that you want to delete, click to select it, and then click the **Remove Cookie** button.

Trouble? You might be instructed to delete specific cookies or no cookies at all. Ask your instructor or technical support person for assistance if you are unsure which cookies can be deleted.

▶ **6.** When you are finished exploring and deleting cookies, click the **Close** button to close the Cookies dialog box.

▶ **7.** Click the **Cancel** button in the Options dialog box to end your cookie management activities.

Tip

To delete all the cookies that have been stored on your computer, you can click the Remove All Cookies button.

Advertising Cookies | InSight

You might notice that many of the cookies on your computer are placed there by companies that sell banner advertising on Web pages (AdRevolver or DoubleClick). These companies use cookies to record which ads have appeared on pages you have viewed so that they can present different ads the next time you open a Web page. This can be beneficial because it prevents sites from showing you the same ads over and over again. On the other hand, many people believe that this sort of user tracking is an offensive invasion of privacy.

Getting Help in Firefox

Firefox includes a comprehensive Help facility. You can open the Mozilla Firefox Help window to learn more about the Help options that are available.

Opening Firefox Help | Reference Window

- Click Help on the menu bar, and then click Help Contents.
- In the Mozilla Firefox Help window, click the plus sign next to the general topic for which you want help to open a list of specific topics.
- Click the name of the specific help topic in which you are interested.

You will use Firefox Help to read about browsing the Web.

To use Firefox Help:

▶ **1.** Click **Help** on the menu bar, and then click **Help Contents**. The Mozilla Firefox Help window opens.

▶ **2.** Click the **plus sign icon** next to the Using Mozilla Firefox category to open a list of specific help topics in that category.

▶ **3.** Click **Navigating Web Pages** to view help on that subject. The information for the topic Navigating Web Pages appears in the right panel of the Mozilla Firefox Help window. Examine the page, which should be similar to the one shown in Figure 1-40, scrolling as needed.

Figure 1-40 ▷ **Firefox Help window**

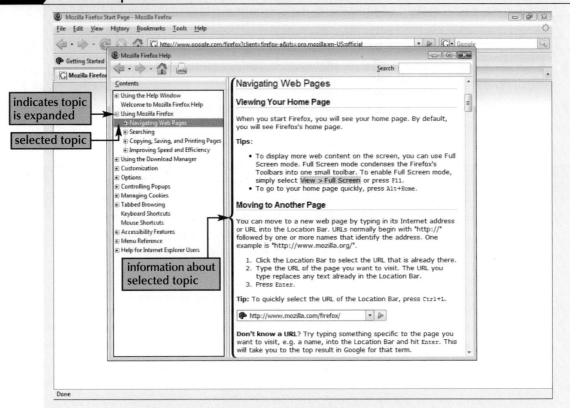

You can click any of the topic titles to obtain help on the specific topics listed.

▶ **4.** Click the **Close** button on the Mozilla Firefox Help window's title bar to close Help.

You want to show Trinity the Midland Pet Adoption Agency Web page, but you are concerned that the Web site might change before she has a chance to visit it on the Web. You can save the Web page as a file on your computer or to a disk. She will then be able to open the Web page on her own computer using her Web browser.

Using Firefox to Save Web Page Content

There will be times when you will want to refer to the information that you have found on a Web page without having to revisit the site. In Firefox, you can store entire Web pages, selected portions of Web page text, or particular graphics from a Web page on your computer or other storage device.

Saving a Web Page

You like the Midland Pet Adoption Agency's Web site and want to save a copy of the page so you can show it to Trinity. That way, she can review the page as it currently appears whenever she wishes. To save a Web page, you must have the page open in Firefox.

Saving a Web Page | Reference Window

- Open the Web page in Firefox.
- Click File on the menu bar, and then click Save Page As.
- Select the location to which you want to save the Web page file.
- Accept the default filename, or change the filename, but retain the file extension .htm or .html.
- Click the Save button.

You will save the Midland Pet Adoption Agency page so you can show it to Trinity later.

To save the Web page:

▶ **1.** Use your bookmark to return to the Midland Pet Adoption Agency page, if necessary.

▶ **2.** Click **File** on the menu bar, and then click **Save Page As**. The Save As dialog box opens.

▶ **3.** Navigate to the location in which you want to save the file, and then type the name **MidlandHomePageMF.htm** in the File name box.

▶ **4.** Select **Web page, HTML only** in the Save as type text box, if necessary.

▶ **5.** Click the **Save** button. Now the HTML document for the Midland Pet Adoption Agency's home page is saved in the location you specified. When you send it to Trinity, she can start her Web browser and then use the Open File command on the File menu to open the Web page.

Trouble? If the Downloads dialog box is open on your screen after you complete this step, click the Close button in the title bar of the Downloads dialog box.

Saving Web Page Graphics | InSight

If a Web page contains graphics, such as photos, drawings, or icons, they are saved in a separate folder with the same name as the HTML document if the Save as type text box is set to Web Page, complete. If you use the Web Page, HTML only setting, the graphic page elements are not saved. To save a graphic, right-click it in the browser window, click Save Image As on the shortcut menu, and then save the graphic to the same location as the Web's HTML document. The graphics file will appear on the HTML document as a hyperlink; therefore, you might have to change the HTML code in the Web page to identify the location of the graphic. Copying the graphics files to the same folder as the HTML document will *usually* work.

Saving Web Page Text to a File

You can save portions of Web page text to a file, so that you can use the file in other programs. You will use WordPad to save text that you will copy from a Web page; however, any word processor or text editor will work.

Reference Window | **Copying Text from a Web Page to a WordPad Document**

- Open the Web page in Firefox.
- Use the mouse pointer to select the text you want to copy.
- Click Edit on the menu bar, and then click Copy.
- Start WordPad (or another word processor or text editor if WordPad is not available).
- Click Edit on the WordPad menu bar, and then click Paste (or click the Paste button).
- Click the Save button, select the folder where you want to store the file, and then enter a new filename, if necessary.
- Click the Save button.

Trinity will be traveling in Minnesota next week, and she would like to visit the Midland Pet Adoption Agency while she is in the area. She will meet with the director there to learn more about how the agency developed its Web site. You will visit Midland Pet Adoption Agency's Web site and get the agency's address and telephone number so Trinity can contact the director and schedule a meeting.

To copy text from a Web page and save the text as a WordPad document:

▶ **1.** Make sure the Midland Pet Adoption Agency home page is open in the browser window.

▶ **2.** Click the **Directions & Contact** hyperlink to open the page with information about Midland's location.

▶ **3.** Find the address and telephone information just under the links to other pages, and then click and drag the mouse pointer over the address and telephone number to select it, as shown in Figure 1-41.

Figure 1-41 ▶ **Selecting and copying text on a Web page in Firefox**

▶ **4.** Click **Edit** on the menu bar, and then click **Copy** to copy the selected text to the Clipboard.

Now, you will start WordPad and then paste the copied text into a new document.

▶ **5.** Click the **Start** button on the taskbar, point to **All Programs**, point to **Accessories**, and then click **WordPad** to start the program and open a new document.

▶ **6.** Click the **Paste** button on the WordPad toolbar to paste the text into the WordPad document, as shown in Figure 1-42. (The bold formatting shown in the figure might not copy when you paste the text into WordPad on your computer.)

Pasting text from a Web page into a WordPad document ◀ **Figure 1-42**

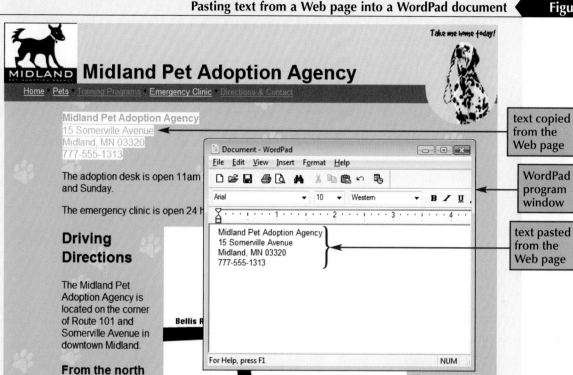

Trouble? If the WordPad toolbar does not appear, click View on the menu bar, click Toolbar, and then repeat Step 6. Your WordPad program window might be a different size from the one shown in Figure 1-42, which does not affect the steps.

▶ **7.** Click the **Save** button on the WordPad toolbar to open the Save As dialog box.

▶ **8.** Click the **Save in** list arrow and select the location in which you would like to save the file.

▶ **9.** Delete the text in the File name text box, type **MidlandAddressPhoneMF.txt**, and then click the **Save** button to save the file. Now, the address and phone number of the agency is saved in a text file for future reference.

▶ **10.** Click the **Close** button on the WordPad title bar to close it.

You can print this information from WordPad and give it to Trinity the next time you see her. As you examine the Web page, you notice a street map that shows the location of the Midland Pet Adoption Agency. Now you will save the map image for Trinity.

Saving a Web Page Graphic

When a Web page has a graphic or picture that you would like to save or print, you have the option of saving or printing just the image, instead of the entire Web page.

Reference Window | **Saving an Image from a Web Page**

- Open the Web page in Firefox.
- Right-click the image you want to copy, and then click Save Image As.
- Select the drive and the folder in which you want to save the image, and change the default filename, if necessary.
- Click the Save button.

To save the street map image:

▶ **1.** Right-click the map image to open its shortcut menu, as shown in Figure 1-43.

Figure 1-43 ▶ Saving the map image

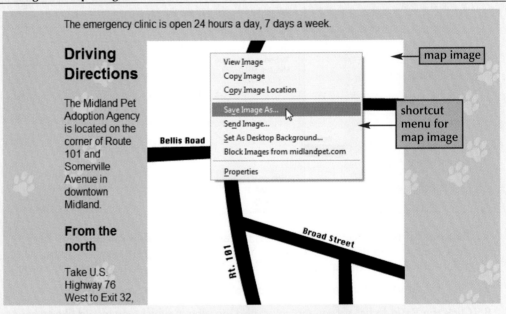

▶ **2.** Click **Save Image As** on the shortcut menu to open the Save Image dialog box.

▶ **3.** Click the **Save in** list arrow, and select the location in which you would like to save the file.

▶ **4.** Delete the text in the File name text box, type **MidlandMapMF.gif**, and then click the **Save** button to save the file.

  Trouble? If the Downloads dialog box is open on your screen after you complete this step, click the Close button in the title bar of the Downloads dialog box.

▶ **5.** Close your Web browser.

Now, you have copies of the Midland Pet Adoption Agency Web home page and a map that will show Trinity how to get there during her trip to Minnesota. She will be able to use her Web browser to open the files and print them.

Session 1.3 Quick Check | Review

1. Describe three ways to load a Web page in the Firefox browser.
2. You can use the _____ in Firefox to visit sites previously visited during your Web session.
3. Why would you hold down the Shift key as you clicked the Reload button?
4. What happens when you click the Home button in the Firefox Web browser?
5. Some Web servers _____ Web page files before returning them to the client to prevent unauthorized access.
6. True or False: You can identify an encrypted Web page when viewing it in Firefox.
7. What is the purpose of the Firefox bookmark feature?

Tutorial Summary | Review

In this tutorial, you learned how Web pages and Web sites make up the World Wide Web. The Web uses a client/server structure in which Web server computers make Web page files available to Web client computers that are running Web browser software. Each server computer on the Internet has an IP address that is mapped to a domain name. The domain name plus the Web page filename make up the Uniform Resource Locator (URL) of that file.

All Web browsers have the same basic elements and can be used to explore the Web in similar ways. Web browsers display Web pages, maintain a history list that can be used to find pages previously visited, and allow users to print and save Web pages and elements of Web pages. You learned about several Web browsers that are currently available at no or low cost.

Internet Explorer and Firefox are the two most widely used Web browsers. You learned how to navigate the Web by opening several different Web pages and to print and save Web page elements using these two browsers.

Key Terms

Common Terms

Back button
browser rendering engine
cache
certification authority
Close button
cookie
copyright
DNS (domain name
    system) software
domain name
domain name server
encryption
fair use
file transfer protocol (FTP)
Firefox
Forward button
frame
general top-level domain
    (gTLD)
Gecko engine
history list
Home button
home page
HTML anchor tag
HTML document
hyperlinks
hypermedia links
hypertext links
Hypertext Markup
    Language (HTML)
hypertext transfer protocol
    (HTTP)
interconnected network

internet
Internet
Internet Corporation for
    Assigned Names and
    Numbers (ICANN)
Internet Explorer
IP (Internet Protocol) address
iRider
local area network (LAN)
links
Maximize button
menu bar
Microsoft Internet Explorer
Minimize button
Mosaic
Mozilla Firefox
Mozilla Suite
Netscape Navigator
network
Opera
page tab
Restore Down button
scroll bar
SeaMonkey project
sponsored top-level domain
    (TLD)
start page
status bar
tabbed browsing
tag
Telnet protocol
Temporary Internet Files
    folder
title bar

toggle
top-level domain (TLD)
transfer protocol
Uniform Resource
    Locator (URL)
Web browser
Web client
Web directory
Web page
Web page area
Web search engine
Web server
Web site
Webmaster
wide area network (WAN)
World Wide Web (Web)

Internet Explorer

Address bar
Command bar
favorite
Full Screen
graphical transfer progress
    indicator
Refresh button
security settings
Temporary Internet Files
    folder
transfer progress report

Firefox

bookmark
Location Bar
Navigation toolbar
Reload button
Security indicator button

Practice	**Review Assignments**

Practice the skills you learned in the tutorial using the same case scenario.

There are no Data Files needed for the Review Assignments.

Trinity is pleased with the information you gathered thus far about the Midland Pet Adoption Agency's Web pages. In fact, she is thinking about having you chair a committee that will supervise the design of a Web site for the Danville Animal Shelter. Because Trinity would like you to be well prepared to direct the committee, she has asked you to compile some information about the Web pages that other animal welfare groups have created. You will examine Web sites for additional background information by completing the following steps.

1. Start your Web browser, go to www.course.com/oc/np/internet7 to open the Online Companion page, click the Tutorial 1 link, and then click the Review Assignments link.

2. Click the hyperlinks listed under the heading Animal Welfare Organizations to explore the Web pages for organizations that have goals and activities similar to those of the Danville Animal Shelter. The list includes a large number of links; however, Web sites change their URLs and even close from time to time. If a link does not lead you to an active site or to a site that you believe is relevant to this assignment, simply choose another link.

3. Choose three interesting home pages, print the first page of each, and then create a bookmark or favorite for each of these sites. Answer the following questions for these three sites:

   a. Which sites include a photograph of the organization's building or any of its physical facilities?

   b. Which sites have photographs of pets available for adoption on the home page?

   c. Which sites provide information about the people who work for the organization (as paid employees or as volunteers)?

   d. Which sites include information about donors who have made contributions to support the organization?

   e. Which sites provide information about their charitable purpose or tax-exempt status?

4. Choose your favorite pet photograph and save it to a file.

5. Do any of the three sites you have chosen provide contact information or directions (with or without a map) to their facilities? If so, which ones? Is this information on the home page, or did you click a hyperlink to find it? Copy the contact information and save it to a text file.

6. Which site made finding specific information (about the organization or about pets available for adoption) the easiest? What did that site do differently from the other sites that made this true?

7. Write a two-page report that summarizes your findings in a form suitable for distribution at your committee's first meeting. Include a recommendation regarding specific elements the Danville Animal Shelter should consider including in its Web site.

8. Close your Web browser.

| Apply | **Case Problem 1** |

Use the skills you learned in the tutorial to find and evaluate Web pages that present business information.

There are no Data Files needed for this Case Problem.

Value City Central   Business Web sites range from very simple informational sites to comprehensive sites that offer information about the firm's products or services, history, current employment openings, and financial information. An increasing number of business sites offer products or services for sale using their Web sites. You just started a position in the marketing department of Value City Central, a large retail chain of television and appliance stores. Your first assignment is to research and report on the types of information that competing businesses offer on their Web sites, which you will do by completing the following steps.

1. Start your Web browser, go to www.course.com/oc/np/internet7 to open the Online Companion page, click the Tutorial 1 link, and then click the Case Problem 1 link.
2. Use the Value City Central hyperlinks to open each business site.

⊕ **EXPLORE**

3. Review the contents of these sites and choose three sites that you believe would be most relevant to your assignment. (*Hint*: Keep in mind that you are looking to identify different types of information, not just different information.)
4. Print the home page for each Web site that you have chosen.
5. Select one site that you feel does the best job in each of the following five categories:
   a. overall presentation of the company's brand or image
   b. description of products offered
   c. ease of use
   d. description of employment opportunities with the company
   e. presentation of financial statements or other financial information about the company
6. Prepare a report that includes one paragraph describing why you believe each of the sites you identified in the preceding step best achieved its goal.
7. Close your Web browser.

| Research | **Case Problem 2** |

Compare four Web browsers, identify features that could be included in future browsers, and recommend a specific browser for a college.

There are no Data Files needed for this Case Problem.

Northwest Community College   Your employer, Northwest Community College, is a school with an enrollment of about 7,000 that prepares students for direct entry into the workforce and for future academic studies at four-year schools. The school has increased its use of computers in all of its office operations. Many of Northwest's computers currently run either Microsoft Internet Explorer or Firefox; however, the administrative vice president (AVP) has decided that the school should support only one browser to save money on user training and computer support personnel costs. The AVP has heard some good things about two other browsers: iRider and Opera. The AVP is wondering whether one of these browsers might be the right product for the school. As the AVP's special assistant, you have been asked to recommend which of these four Web browsers the school should choose to support. You will research the browsers for your report by completing the following steps.

1. Start your Web browser, go to www.course.com/oc/np/internet7 to open the Online Companion page, click the Tutorial 1 link, and then click the Case Problem 2 link.
2. Use the Northwest Community College hyperlinks to learn more about these four Web browsers.

3. Write a two-page memo to the AVP (to submit to your instructor) that outlines the strengths and weaknesses of each product. Recommend one Web browser program and support your decision using the information you collected. Remember that the AVP is concerned about overall cost; not just the cost to license the browser, but the cost of training users and supporting them with technical help. However, the AVP is also concerned about making the school's employees more productive, so if a more expensive browser could increase employee productivity, the AVP would be willing to pay more to install and maintain the software.

EXPLORE

4. Prepare a list of features that you would like to see in a new Web browser software package that would overcome any limitations you see in Firefox, Internet Explorer, iRider, or Opera. (*Hint*: If you do not have access to a computer that runs one or more of these Web browsers, you can develop your list of features by reading what others have written about those browsers.)

5. Close your Web browser.

Research | Case Problem 3

Read Web pages to learn more about cookies and the risks they pose, and compare cookies' risks to their benefits.

There are no Data Files needed for this Case Problem.

Citizens Central Bank   You are a new staff auditor at the Citizens Central Bank. You have had more recent computer training than other audit staff members at Citizens, so Sally DeYoung, the audit manager, asks you to review the bank's policy on Web browser cookie settings. Some of the bank's board members expressed concerns to Sally about the security of the bank's computers. Specifically, they are concerned about the PCs on its networks that are connected to the Internet. One of the board members learned about browser cookies and was afraid that a bank employee might open a Web site that would write a dangerous cookie file that could do damage to the bank's computer network. Not all Web servers write cookies, but those that do can read the cookie file the next time the Web browser on that computer connects to the Web server. The Web server can then retrieve information about the Web browser's last connection to the server. None of the bank's board members knows very much about the detailed technical workings of computers, but all of them became concerned that a virus-laden cookie could significantly damage the bank's computer system. Sally asks you to help her inform the board of directors about cookies and to establish a policy on using them. You will accomplish these tasks by completing the following steps.

1. Start your Web browser, go to www.course.com/oc/np/internet7 to open the Online Companion page, click the Tutorial 1 link, and then click the Case Problem 3 link.

EXPLORE

2. Use the Citizens Fidelity Bank hyperlinks to learn more about cookie files.

3. Choose the three most helpful sites you have visited, and prepare a brief outline of the content on each site.

4. Write a one-page memo in which you list the risks that Citizens Fidelity Bank might face by allowing cookie files to be written to their computers.

5. Write a one-page memo in which you list the benefits that individual users obtain by allowing Web servers to write cookies to the computers that they are using at the bank to access the Web.

6. Close your Web browser.

Create	**Case Problem 4**

Select a model charitable organization Web site and explain why it would be a good example on which to base your organization's site.

There are no Data Files needed for this Case Problem.

Columbus Suburban Area Council The Columbus Suburban Area Council is a charitable organization devoted to maintaining and improving the general welfare of people living in Columbus suburbs. As the director of the council, you are interested in encouraging donations and other support from area citizens and would like to stay informed of grant opportunities that might benefit the council. You are especially interested in developing an informative and attractive presence on the Web and will pursue that goal by completing the following steps.

1. Start your Web browser, go to www.course.com/oc/np/internet7 to open the Online Companion page, click the Tutorial 1 link, and then click the Case Problem 4 link.

⊕ **EXPLORE**

2. Follow the Columbus Suburban Area Council hyperlinks to charitable organizations to find out more about what other organizations are doing with their Web sites.

3. Select three of the Web sites you visited and, for each, prepare a list of the site's contents. Note whether each site included financial information and whether the site disclosed how much the organization spent on administrative or nonprogram-related activities.

⊕ **EXPLORE**

4. Identify which Web site you believe would be a good model for the Columbus Suburban Area Council's new Web site. Prepare a presentation in which you explain to the council why you think your chosen site would be the best example to follow.

5. Close your Web browser.

Create	**Case Problem 5**

Examine the structure of several Web directory pages and use your findings to design a personal start page.

There are no Data Files needed for this Case Problem.

Emma Inkster Your neighbor, Emma Inkster, was an elementary school teacher for many years. She is now retired and has just purchased her first personal computer. Emma is excited about getting on the Web and exploring its resources. She has asked for your help. After you introduce her to what you have learned in this tutorial about Web browsers, she is eager to spend more time gathering information on the Web. Although she is retired, Emma continues to be very active. She is an avid bridge player, enjoys golf, and is one of the neighborhood's best gardeners. Although she is somewhat limited by her schoolteacher's pension, Emma loves to travel to foreign countries and especially likes to learn the languages of her destinations. She would like to have a start page for her computer that would include hyperlinks that would help her easily visit and regularly return to Web pages related to her interests. Her nephew knows HTML and can create the page, but Emma would like you to help her design the layout of her start page. You know that Web directory sites are designed to help people find interesting Web sites, so you begin your search by completing the following steps.

1. Start your Web browser, go to www.course.com/oc/np/internet7 to open the Online Companion page, click the Tutorial 1 link, and then click the Case Problem 5 link.

⊕ **EXPLORE**

2. Use the Emma Inkster hyperlinks to Web directories to learn what kind of organization they use for their hyperlinks. (*Hint*: Links in Web sites can be organized in a linear fashion, in a hierarchy, or in some other logical structure.)

3. You note that many of the Web directories use a similar organizational structure for their hyperlinks and categories; however, you are not sure if this organization structure would be ideal for Emma. You decide to create categories that suit Emma's specific interests. List five general categories around which you would organize Emma's start page. For each category, list three subcategories that would help Emma find and return to Web sites she would find interesting.

4. Write a report of 100 words in which you explain why the start page you designed for Emma would be more useful to her than a publicly available Web directory.

5. Close your Web browser.

Reinforce | **Lab Assignments**

Student Edition Labs

The interactive Student Edition Lab on **Getting the Most Out of the Internet** is designed to help you master some of the key concepts and skills presented in this tutorial, including:

• using a browser to view Web pages
• saving Web pages as favorites
• deleting the files in the Temporary Internet Files folder

This lab is available online and can be accessed from the Tutorial 1 Web page on the Online Companion at www.course.com/oc/np/internet7.

Review | **Quick Check Answers**

Session 1.1

1. False
2. True
3. home page; start page
4. hypermedia links
5. Any three of these: candidate's name and party affiliation; list of qualifications; biography of the candidate; position statements on campaign issues; list of endorsements with hyperlinks to the Web pages of individuals and organizations that support her candidacy; audio or video clips of speeches and interviews; address and telephone number of the campaign office, copies of ads for the candidate that have run on radio or television, a page that allows supporters to make a donation to the campaign fund.
6. A computer's IP address is a unique identifying number; its domain name is a unique name associated with the IP address on the Internet host computer responsible for that computer's domain.

7. "http://" indicates use of the hypertext transfer protocol; "www.savethetrees.org" is the domain name and includes three parts: the ".org" suggests a charitable or not-for-profit organization, "savethetrees" indicates that the organization is probably devoted to forest ecology; and the "www" indicates that it is the address of a site on the World Wide Web. The "main.html" that follows the domain name is the name of the HTML file on the Web server that hosts the Web pages for this site

8. A Web directory contains a hierarchical list of Web page categories; each category contains hyperlinks to individual Web pages. A Web search engine is a Web site that accepts words or phrases you enter and finds Web pages that include those words or expressions.

Session 1.2

1. You can hide its toolbars or click the Full Screen command on the View menu. Two other possible answers (assuming that the window is not maximized already) are to maximize the window or to use the mouse to pull the edges of the browser window out to make the entire browser larger.

2. Recent Pages (A reference to History, the History list, or the History button in the Favorites Center would also be an acceptable answer to this question.)

3. Home

4. Animal Shelters, Humane Societies, Animal Welfare Organizations, Veterinary Offices

5. Shift

6. Right-click a blank area of the Web page and select Properties. Information about any encryption used to send the Web page will appear next to the word "Connection."

7. F1

Session 1.3

1. Any three of these: Type the URL in the location field; click a hyperlink on a Web page; click the Back button; click the Forward button; click the Bookmarks button and select a page; click Go on the menu bar, click History, and then click the entry for the site you want to visit

2. history list (or the Back or Forward buttons)

3. when you wanted to make sure that the browser reloads the page from the Web server instead of from the local cache on your computer

4. Firefox loads the page that is specified as the Home page in the Startup section under the Main tab of the Options dialog box (which you can open from the Tools menu).

5. encrypt

6. True

7. a Firefox feature that enables you to store and organize a list of Web pages that you have visited

Basic Communication on the Internet: Email

Evaluating an Email Program and a Web-Based Email Service

Case | Kikukawa Air

Since 1994, Sharon and Don Kikukawa have operated an air charter service in Maui, Hawaii. At first, Kikukawa Air employed only Sharon, who managed the office, reservations, and the company's financial records, and her husband Don, who flew their twin-engine, six-passenger plane between Maui and Oahu. After many successful years in business, Sharon and Don expanded their business to include scenic tours and charter service to all of the Hawaiian Islands. As a result of their expansion, Kikukawa Air now has six twin-engine planes, two turboprop planes, and a growing staff of more than 30 people.

Because Kikukawa Air has a ticket counter at airports on all of the Hawaiian Islands, many miles now separate the company's employees. Originally, employees used telephone and conference calling to coordinate the business's day-to-day operations, such as schedule and reservation changes, new airport procedures, and maintenance requests. Sharon soon realized that these forms of communication were difficult to coordinate with the growing number of busy ground-service agents and pilots. Most employees already use email to communicate with each other and with outside vendors and clients, but they are not all using the same email program. Sharon believes that Kikukawa Air could benefit from organizing the company's employees so that everyone uses the same email program. This coordination will make it easier to manage the accounts and computers, and will streamline the company's operations.

Sharon has hired you to investigate the different email options available to Kikukawa Air offices and ticket counter facilities. Your job includes evaluating available email systems and overseeing the software's installation. Eventually, you will train the staff members so they can use the new email system efficiently and effectively.

Starting Data Files

Tutorial.02 → Tutorial
Physicals.pdf

Review
KAir.gif

Cases
Recycle.pdf

Session 2.1

What Is Email and How Does It Work?

Electronic mail, or **email**, is a form of communication in which electronic messages are created and transferred between two or more devices connected to a network. Email is one of the most popular forms of business communication, and for many people it is their primary use of the Internet. Email travels to its destination and is deposited in the recipient's electronic mailbox. Although similar to other forms of correspondence, including letters and memos, email has the added advantage of being fast and inexpensive. Instead of traveling through a complicated, expensive, and often slow mail delivery service, such as a postal system, email travels quickly, efficiently, and inexpensively to its destination down the hall or around the world. You can send a message any time you want, without worrying about when the mail is collected and delivered or adding any postage. For many personal and business reasons, people rely on email as an indispensable form of communication.

Email travels across the Internet like other forms of information—that is, in small packets that are reassembled at the destination and delivered to the recipient, whose address you specify in the message. When you send an email message, the message is sent to a **mail server**, which is a hardware and software system that determines from the recipient's address one of several electronic routes on which to send the message. The message is routed from one computer to another and is passed through several mail servers. Each mail server determines the next leg of the message's journey until it finally arrives at the recipient's electronic mailbox.

Sending email uses one of many Internet technologies. Special **protocols**, or rules that determine how the Internet handles message packets flowing on it, are used to interpret and transmit email. **SMTP (Simple Mail Transfer Protocol)** determines which paths an email message takes on the Internet. SMTP handles outgoing messages; another protocol called **POP (Post Office Protocol)** handles incoming messages. POP is a standard, extensively used protocol that is part of the Internet suite of recognized protocols. Other protocols used to deliver mail include IMAP and MIME. **IMAP (Internet Message Access Protocol)** is a protocol for retrieving mail messages from a remote server or messages that are stored on a large local network. The **MIME (Multipurpose Internet Mail Extensions)** protocol specifies how to encode nontext data, such as graphics and sound, so it can travel over the Internet.

When an email message arrives at its destination mail server, the mail server's software handles the details of distributing the message locally, in the same way that a mailroom worker opens a mailbag and places letters and packages into individual mail slots. When the server receives a new message, it is not saved on the recipient's Internet device, but rather, the message is held on the mail server. To check for new email messages, you use a program stored on your Internet device—which might be a personal computer, cellular phone, or other wireless device—to request the mail server to deliver any stored mail to your device. The software that requests mail delivery from the mail server to an Internet device is known as **mail client software**, or an **email program**.

> **Tip**
>
> Most organizations have a single mail server to manage the email sent to and from the domain. For very large organizations, the domain might use multiple mail servers to manage the organization's email.

An **email address** uniquely identifies an individual or organization that is connected to the Internet. To route an email message to an individual, you must identify that person by his or her account name, or **user name**, and also by the name of the mail server that manages email sent to the domain. The two parts of an email address—the user name and the domain name—are separated by an "at" sign (@). Sharon Kikukawa, for example, selected the user name *Sharon* for her email account. Kikukawa Air purchased the domain name KikukawaAir.com to use as both its Internet address (URL) and in the email addresses for its employees. Therefore, Sharon's email address is Sharon@KikukawaAir.com.

A user name usually identifies one person's email account on a mail server. When you are given an email address from an organization, such as your school or an employer, the organization might have standards for assigning user names. Some organizations set standards so user names consist of a person's first initial followed by up to seven characters of the person's last name. Other organizations assign user names that contain a person's first and last names separated by an underscore character (for example, Sharon_Kikukawa). When you are given the opportunity to select your own user name, you might use a nickname or some other name to identify yourself. On a mail server, all user names must be unique.

The domain name is the second part of an email address. The domain name specifies the server to which the mail is to be delivered on the Internet. Domain names contain periods, which are usually pronounced "dot," to divide the domain name. The most specific part of the domain name appears first in the address, followed by the top-level domain name. Sharon's Web site address, KikukawaAir.com (and pronounced "Kikukawa Air dot com"), contains only two names separated by a period. The *com* in the domain name indicates that this company falls into the large, general class of commercial locations. The *KikukawaAir* indicates the unique computer name (domain name) associated with the IP address for KikukawaAir.com.

Most email addresses aren't case-sensitive; in other words, the addresses sharon@kikukawaair.com and Sharon@KikukawaAir.com are the same. It is important for you to type a recipient's address carefully; if you omit or mistype even one character, your message could be undeliverable or sent to the wrong recipient. When a message cannot be delivered, the receiving mail server might send the message back to you and indicate that the addressee is unknown. Sometimes mail that cannot be delivered is deleted on the receiving mail server and no notice is sent to the sender.

Managing More than One Email Address | InSight

Most people have more than one email address to manage their correspondence. It is very common for people to have a primary email address that they use for personal or business correspondence, and a secondary email address that they use for online subscriptions, online purchases, and mailing lists. If you are careful about how you distribute your primary email address, you might reduce the amount of unsolicited mail that you receive. When your secondary email address starts getting a lot of unwanted messages, you can discard it and create a new one. If you keep track of who has your secondary email address, it will be easy to update them if you need to change your secondary email address.

Keep in mind that an email account that you have from your school or employer is subject to the rules of use that the organization has established. Some schools and most employers have policies that dictate the permitted use of their equipment and email accounts. You should not use your employer's email address for personal correspondence unless your employer specifies that your personal use of the email account and your workplace computer is acceptable. In some cases, an employer might terminate employees who abuse the company's resources for personal use.

Common Features of an Email Message

An email message consists of three parts: the message header, the message body, and the signature. The **message header** contains information about the message, and the **message body** contains the actual message content. An optional **signature** might appear at the bottom of an email message and contain standard information about the sender, which the recipient can use to contact the sender in a variety of ways.

Figure 2-1 shows a message that Sharon Kikukawa wrote to Bob Merrell, Kikukawa Air ticket agents, and Don Kikukawa. The message contains an attached file named MaintenanceSchedule.xlsx. Sharon created this file using a spreadsheet program, saved it, and then attached it to the message. Each of the message parts is described in the next sections.

Figure 2-1   **Common features of an email message**

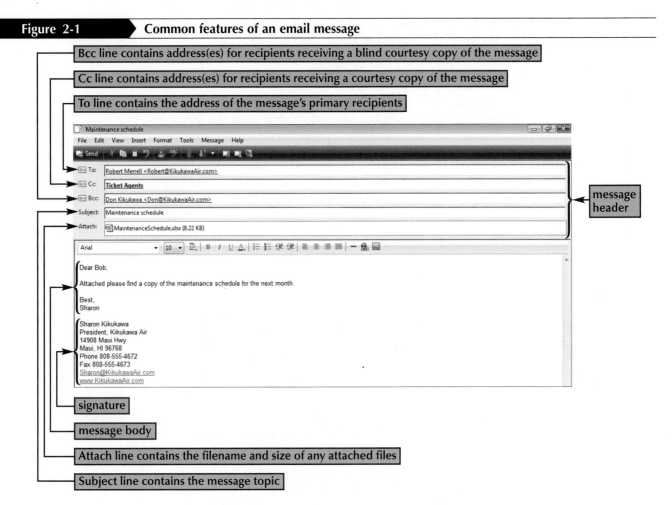

To, Cc, and Bcc

You type the recipient's full email address in the **To line** of a message header. You can send the same message to multiple recipients by typing a comma or semicolon between the recipients' email addresses in the To line. The number of addresses you can type in the To line or in the other parts of the message header that require an address is not limited, but some mail servers will reject messages with too many recipients (usually 50 or more) as a way of controlling unsolicited mail. In Figure 2-1, Sharon used the To line to address her message to one recipient.

You can use the optional **courtesy copy (Cc)** and the **blind courtesy copy (Bcc)** lines to send mail to people who should be aware of the email message, but are not the message's main recipients. When an email message is delivered, every recipient can see the addresses of other recipients, except for those recipients who receive a blind courtesy copy. Because Bcc addresses are excluded from messages sent to addresses in the To and Cc lines, neither the primary recipient (in the To line) nor the Cc recipients can view the list of Bcc recipients. Bcc recipients are unaware of other Bcc recipients, as well. For example, if you send a thank-you message to a salesperson for performing a task especially well, you might consider sending a blind courtesy copy to that person's supervisor. That way, the supervisor knows a customer is happy and that the praise was unsolicited. In Figure 2-1, Sharon sent a blind courtesy copy of her email message to Don Kikukawa so he could monitor the maintenance schedule without Bob or the ticket agents at Kikukawa Air being aware of his involvement.

Sometimes an email address is not one person's address, but rather, a special address called a **group**. In a group, a single email address can represent several or many individual email addresses. In Figure 2-1, the "Ticket Agents" address in the Cc line represents the three email addresses of people who work as ticket agents at Kikukawa Air; there is no "Ticket Agents" user name.

From

The **From line** of an email message includes the sender's name, the sender's email address, or both. Most email programs automatically insert the sender's name and email address in the From line of all outgoing messages. You usually do not see the From line in messages that you are composing, but you can see it in messages that you receive. Figure 2-1 does not show a From line because this is a message that Sharon is composing.

Subject

The content of the **Subject line** is very important. Often the recipient will scan an abbreviated display of incoming messages, looking for the most interesting or important message based on the content in the Subject line. If the Subject line is blank, then the recipient might not read the associated message immediately or at all. Including an appropriate subject in your message helps the reader determine its content and importance. For example, a Subject line such as "Just checking" is less informative and less interesting than "Urgent: new staff meeting time." The email message shown in Figure 2-1, for example, contains the subject "Maintenance schedule" and thus indicates that the message concerns maintenance.

Attachments

Because of the way the messaging system is set up, you can send only text messages using SMTP, the protocol that handles outgoing email. When you need to send a more complex document, such as a Word document or an Excel workbook, you send it along as an attachment. An **attachment** provides a simple and convenient way of transmitting files to one or more people. An attachment is encoded so that it can be carried safely over the Internet, to "tag along" with the message. Frequently, the attached file is the most important part of the email message, and the message body contains only a brief statement, such as "Here's the file that you requested." Sharon's email message (see Figure 2-1) contains an attached file, whose filename and size in kilobytes appear in the Attach line in the message header. (A **kilobyte (KB)** is approximately 1,000 characters.) You can attach more than one file to an email message; if you include multiple recipients in the To, Cc, and Bcc lines of the message header, each recipient will receive the message and the attached file(s). However, keep in mind that an email message with many attachments quickly becomes very large in size, and it might take some recipients with slower Internet connections a long time to download your message. In addition, some Internet service providers (ISPs) place limits on the size of messages that they will accept; in some cases, an email message with file attachments over two megabytes in size might be rejected and returned to the sender.

When you receive an email message with an attached file, you should proceed carefully before opening or viewing it. Email attachments, just like any other computer files,

> **Tip**
>
> If you need to send a large attachment to a recipient, ask for the recipient's preferences in how to send it.

can contain malicious programs called **viruses** that can harm your computer and its files. Some users send attachments containing viruses without realizing that they are doing so; other users send viruses on purpose to infect as many computers as possible. If you receive an email message from a sender that you don't recognize and the message contains an attached file, you should avoid opening that file until you are sure that it doesn't contain a virus. You can install a virus detection software program on your computer to protect it from downloading any files that contain viruses, and some ISPs have built-in virus detection software to accomplish the same goal. The Virus Protection section of the Online Companion page for Tutorial 2 contains links that you can follow to learn more about virus detection software and viruses. (The Online Companion is located at www.course.com/oc/np/internet7. After logging in, click the Tutorial 2 link to access the information and links for this tutorial.)

Email programs differ in how they handle and display attachments. Some email programs identify an attached file with an icon that represents a program associated with the attachment's file type. In addition to an icon, some programs also display an attached file's size and filename. Other email programs display an attached file in a preview window when they recognize the attached file's format, and can start a program on the user's device to open the file. Double-clicking an attached file usually opens the file using a program on the user's device that is associated with the file type of the attachment. For example, if a workbook is attached to an email message, double-clicking the icon for the workbook attachment might start a spreadsheet program and open the workbook. Similarly, a Word document opens in the Word program window when you double-click the icon representing the attached document.

Viewing an attachment by double-clicking it lets you open a read-only copy of the file, but it does not save the file on your device. (A **read-only** file is one that you can view but that you cannot change.) To save an attached file on your computer or other device, you need to perform a series of steps to save the file in a specific location, such as on a hard drive. Some programs refer to the process of saving an email attachment as **detaching** the file. When you detach a file, you must indicate the drive and folder in which to save it. You won't always need to save an email attachment; sometimes you can view it and then delete it. You will learn how to attach and detach files using your email program later in this tutorial.

Message Body and Signature Files

Tip

Most mail servers do not allow you to retract mail after you send it, so you should examine your messages carefully before sending them, and always exercise politeness and courtesy in your messages.

Most often, people use email to write short, quick messages. However, email messages can be many pages in length, although the term "pages" has little meaning in the email world. Few people using email think of a message in terms of page-sized chunks; email is more like an unbroken scroll with no physical page boundaries. An email message is often less formal than a business letter that you might write, but it's still important to follow the rules of formal letter writing when composing an email message. You should begin your messages with a salutation, such as "Dear Sharon," use proper spelling and grammar, and close your correspondence with a signature. After typing the content of your message—even a short message—you should check your spelling and grammar. You can sign a message by typing your name and other information at the end of each message you send, or you can create a signature file.

If you are using email for business communication, a **signature file** usually contains your name, title, and your company's name. Signature files might also contain a mailing address, voice and fax telephone numbers, a Web site address, and a company's logo. If you are using email for personal communication, signatures can be more informal. Informal signatures can include nicknames and graphics or quotations that express a more casual style found in correspondence between friends and acquaintances.

You can set your email program to insert a signature automatically into every message you send so you don't have to repeatedly type its contents. You can modify your signature easily or choose not to include it in selected messages. Most email programs allow you to create multiple signature files so you can choose which one to include when sending a message.

When you create a signature, don't overdo it—it is best to keep a signature to a few lines that identify ways to contact you. Figure 2-2 shows two examples of signatures. The first signature, which Sharon might use in her business correspondence to Kikukawa Air employees, is informal. Sharon uses the second, more formal signature for all other business correspondence to identify her name, title, and contact information to make it easy for people outside of the organization to reach her.

Sample signatures ◀ **Figure 2-2**

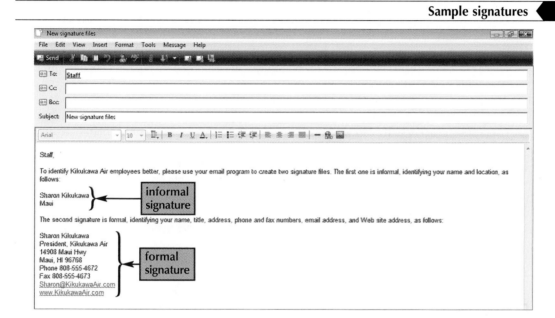

Internet Etiquette (Netiquette)

Netiquette, a term coined from the phrase "Internet etiquette," is the set of commonly accepted rules that represent proper behavior on a network. Just as there are rules of proper conduct on networks that are owned or operated by schools and businesses, the Internet has its own set of acceptable rules. Unlike business networks on which administrators and webmasters set guidelines for acceptable use, and moderators are authorized to restrict usage of that network by users who don't follow those rules, the Internet is self-policing. Email has its own set of rules, which have evolved over time and will continue to evolve as it gains new users.

InSight | **Generally Accepted Rules for Email Messages**

When composing email messages, keep the following generally accepted rules in mind, especially for business correspondence:

- Avoid writing your messages in ALL CAPITAL LETTERS BECAUSE IT LOOKS LIKE YOU ARE SHOUTING.
- Keep your messages simple, short, and focused on their topics.
- Don't forward information about viruses or hoaxes. In many cases, you're forwarding incorrect information. Check with a reputable site for information about viruses or hoaxes.
- Don't use the "Reply All" feature when only the sender needs to know your response.
- Don't assume that everyone you know likes to receive jokes or family pictures. Check with the recipients first.
- When sending messages to a large group, use the Bcc field for the recipients' email addresses to protect them from receiving additional responses from people who use the "Reply All" feature to respond.
- Include a descriptive subject in the Subject line and a signature, so the recipient knows the content of your message and how to get in touch with you.
- Use a spell checker and read your message and correct any spelling or grammatical errors before sending it.
- Don't overuse formatting and graphics, which can make your email message difficult to read. The fonts you select on your device might not be available on the recipient's device and the message might not be displayed as you intended.
- Email is not private—don't divulge private or sensitive information in an email message. It's very easy for the recipient to forward your message to everyone he or she knows, even if it's by accident.
- Use caution when attempting sarcasm or humor in your messages, as the recipient might not appreciate the attempt at humor and might actually misunderstand your intentions. Without the sender's body language and tone of voice, some written statements are subject to misinterpretation.
- Use common courtesy, politeness, and respect in all of your written correspondence.

Because it sometimes takes so little time and effort to compose an email message, you might be tempted to take some shortcuts in your writing, such as omitting the salutation and using acronyms for commonly used phrases, such as the ones shown in Figure 2-3. These shortcuts are fine for informal messages that you might send to your friends and family members but they are not acceptable in business communication. An email message is a business document, just like a memo or letter, and you should treat it with the same formality. Sending a message containing spelling and grammatical errors to a colleague or to an employer at which you are seeking a job is a poor reflection on you and your work. Many employers seeking to fill open positions automatically disregard email messages that do not contain a subject line or information in the message body describing the contents of the attachment and the applicant's intention to apply for the position. In addition, some employers will not seriously consider applications that are sent with email messages that contain typos or demonstrate poor communication skills.

Commonly used email acronyms   Figure 2-3

Acronym	Meaning
atm	At the moment
b/c	Because
btw	By the way
iac	In any case
iae	In any event
imho	In my humble opinion
imo	In my opinion
iow	In other words
jk	Just kidding
thx	Thanks

Email can be an impersonal form of communication, and as a result some writers use emoticons to express emotion. An **emoticon** is a group of keyboard characters that when viewed together represent a human expression. For example, a smiley :-) looks like a smiling face when you turn your head to the left. Other emoticons are a frown :-(a smiley with a wink ;-) and fear or surprise :-o . Some writers use emoticons to show their readers a form of electronic body language. Just like acronyms, emoticons are appropriate in informal correspondence but not in business correspondence.

You can learn more about Netiquette by following the links in the Netiquette section of the Online Companion page for Tutorial 2.

Common Features of Email Programs

Although there are many different ways to send and receive email messages, most email programs have common features for managing mail. Fortunately, once you learn the process for sending, receiving, and managing email with one program, it's easy to use another program to accomplish the same tasks.

Sending Messages

After you finish addressing and composing a message, it might not be sent to the mail server immediately, depending on how the email program or service is configured. A message can be **queued**, or temporarily held with other messages, and then sent when you either exit the program, connect to your ISP or network, or check to see if you have received any new email. Most email programs and services include a "Drafts" folder in which you can store email messages that you are composing but that you aren't ready to send yet. These messages are saved until you finish and send them.

Receiving and Storing Messages

The mail server is always ready to process mail; in theory, the mail server never sleeps. When you receive email, it is held on the mail server until you use your email program to ask the server to retrieve your mail. Most email programs allow you to save delivered mail in any of several standard or custom mailboxes or folders on your Internet device. However, the mail server is a completely different story. Once the mail is delivered to your Internet device, one of two things can happen to it on the server: either the server's copy of your mail is deleted, or it is preserved and marked as delivered or read. Marking mail as delivered or read is the server's way of distinguishing new mail from mail that you have read. For example, when Sharon receives mail on the Kikukawa Air mail server, she might decide to save her accumulated mail on the server—even after she reads it—so she can access her email messages again from another device. On the other hand, Sharon might want to delete old mail to save space on the mail server. Both methods have advantages. Saving old mail on the server lets you access your mail from any device that can connect to your mail server. However, if you automatically delete mail after reading it, you don't have to worry about storing and organizing messages that you don't need, which requires less effort. Some ISPs and email providers impose limits on the amount of material you can store so that you must occasionally delete mail from your mailbox to avoid interruption of service. In some cases, once you exceed your storage space limit, you cannot receive any additional messages until you delete existing messages from the server, or the service deletes your messages without warning to free up space in your mailbox.

Printing a Message

Reading mail on a computer or an Internet device is fine, but there are times when you will need to print some of your messages. Most email programs let you print a message you are composing or that you have received. The Print command usually appears on the File menu, or as a Print button on the toolbar.

Filing a Message

Tip

Filters aren't perfect. When using filters to move mail to specific folders or to the trash, it's a good idea to check your messages occasionally to make sure that your incoming messages are not moved to the wrong folder.

Most email programs let you create folders in which to store related messages in your mailbox. You can create new folders when needed, rename existing folders, or delete folders and their contents when you no longer need them. You can move mail from the incoming folder to any other folder to file it. Some programs let you define and use a **filter** to move incoming mail into a specific folder or to delete it automatically based on the content of the message. Filters are especially useful for moving messages from certain senders into designated folders, and for moving **junk mail** (or **spam**), which is unsolicited mail usually advertising or selling an item or service, to a trash folder. If your email program does not provide filters, you can filter the messages manually by reading them and filing them in the appropriate folders.

Forwarding a Message

You can forward any message that you receive to one or more recipients. When you **forward** a message to another recipient, a copy of the original message is sent to the new recipient you specify without the original sender's knowledge. You might forward a misdirected message to another recipient or to someone who was not included in the original message routing list.

For example, suppose you receive a message intended for someone else, or the message requests information that only a colleague can provide. In either case, you can forward the message you received to the person who can best deal with the request. When you forward a message, your email address and name appear automatically in the From line; most email programs amend the Subject line with the text "Fw," "Fwd," or something similar to indicate that the message has been forwarded. You simply add the recipient's address to the To line and send the message. Depending on your email program and the preferences you set for forwarding messages, a forwarded message might be sent as an attached file or as quoted text. A **quoted message** is a copy of the sender's original message with your inserted comments. A special mark (a > symbol or a solid vertical line) sometimes precedes each line of the quoted message. Figure 2-4 shows a quoted message; notice the > symbol to the left of each line of the original message and the "FW:" text in the Subject line, indicating a forwarded message.

Sample forwarded message ◀ Figure 2-4

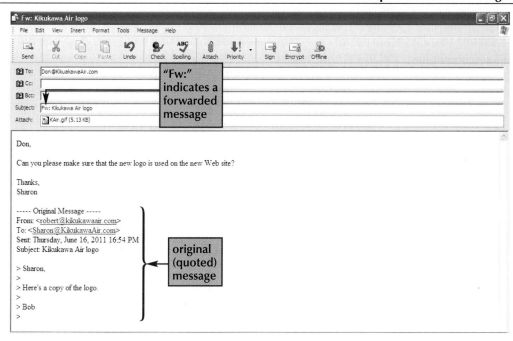

Forwarding Messages Appropriately | InSight

When forwarding a message to a new recipient, and especially when forwarding a message that was forwarded originally to you, keep in mind that a forwarded message includes the email addresses of all the message's previous recipients and senders. Some people might not want to have their addresses sent to other users, who might in turn send them unwanted email messages. If you need to send something you received to a new recipient, and it's not important that the new recipient know who sent you the original message, you should use the Copy and Paste commands in your email program to paste the content of the forwarded message into a new message, thus protecting the privacy of the message's original recipients and making the message easier to read for its new recipients.

Some people routinely send information about Internet viruses and hoaxes or about emotional causes, such as cancer research, to everyone they know in an attempt to "spread the word." Often, these messages contain incorrect information. Before being alarmed by information about viruses or hoaxes, contributing to any charity that you learn about in this way, or forwarding the message to other users, be sure to check one of the many reputable Internet resources for more information. The Virus Protection section of the Online Companion page for Tutorial 2 contains links to sites that contain information about viruses, hoaxes, and fraudulent schemes.

Replying to a Message

Replying to a message is a quick way of sending a response to someone who sent a message to you. Most email programs provide two options for replying to a message that you have received. You can reply to only the original sender using the Reply option, or you can reply to the original sender and all other To and Cc recipients of the original message by using the Reply All option. When you **reply** to a message that you received, the email program creates a new message and automatically addresses it to the original sender (when you choose the Reply option) or to the original sender and all of the original

To and Cc recipients of the message (when you choose the Reply All option). Most email programs will copy the contents of the original message and place it in the message body of the reply. Like forwarded messages, a special mark might appear at the beginning of each line to indicate the text of the original message. When you are responding to more than one question, you might type your responses below the original questions so the recipient can better understand the context of your responses. When you respond to a message that was sent to several people, make sure that you choose the correct option when replying.

Deleting a Message

In most email programs, deleting a message is a two-step process to prevent you from accidentally deleting important messages. First, you temporarily delete a message by placing it in a "trash" folder or by marking it for deletion. Then you permanently delete the trash or marked messages by emptying the trash or indicating to the email program to delete the messages. It is a good idea to delete mail you no longer need because it takes up a lot of space on the drive or server on which your email messages are stored.

Maintaining an Address Book

You use an **address book** to save email addresses and other optional contact information about the people and organizations with which you correspond. The features of an email address book vary by email program. Usually, you can organize information about individuals and groups. Each entry in the address book can contain an individual's full email address (or a group email address that represents several individual addresses), full name, and complete contact information. In addition, most email programs allow you to include notes for each contact. You can assign a unique nickname to each entry so it is easier to address your email messages. A **nickname** might be "Mom" for your mother or "Maintenance Department" to represent all the employees working in a certain part of an organization.

   After saving entries in your address book, you can refer to them at any point while you are composing, replying to, or forwarding a message. You can review your address book and sort the entries in many ways.

Email Programs

Tip

Some domains, such as Yahoo.com, let you send and receive email messages using its Web site. However, you must pay an additional fee to send and receive Yahoo email using an email program.

Different software companies that produce Web browsers might also produce companion email programs that you can use to manage your email. For example, when you install Microsoft Internet Explorer for Windows XP, the Outlook Express email program is also installed. When you install Windows Vista, the Windows Mail email program is installed. Mozilla Firefox users might choose to install the companion Thunderbird email program to manage their email messages. You can use these types of email programs to manage messages that are routed through a domain that sends email messages using the POP protocol. Messages that are routed through a domain in this way are called **POP messages** or **POP3 messages** because of the protocol used to send them. If you have multiple browsers installed on your computer, then you might also have multiple email programs. The choice of which email program to use is up to you.

Before you can use an email program to send and receive your email messages, you must configure it to work with your email accounts. Before you decide which email program to use, you should be familiar with the different ones available. In Session 2.2, you will learn how to configure and use Outlook Express; in Session 2.3, you will learn how to configure and use Windows Mail; and in Session 2.4, you will learn how to configure and use Windows Live Hotmail. Because you might end up using different email programs in the future, it is important to know about two other popular email programs, Mozilla Thunderbird and Opera's M2 email client, which are free email programs available for download.

Mozilla Thunderbird

Mozilla Thunderbird is part of the Mozilla open source project. Although Thunderbird complements the Mozilla Firefox Web browser, Thunderbird is available only as a separate download from the Mozilla Web site. A link to Thunderbird's Web site is provided on the Online Companion page for Tutorial 2.

Starting Thunderbird

When you start Thunderbird for the first time, you might have the option of importing items from other email programs on your computer. If you choose this option, the address book entries and other settings from the email program on your computer that you select will be imported into Thunderbird. You'll also see the Account Wizard, which lets you set up mail and other types of accounts. Figure 2-5 shows the Thunderbird Account Wizard dialog box.

Thunderbird Account Wizard dialog box ◀ Figure 2-5

The first thing you need to set up is your email account so you can send and receive email messages through your ISP. You need to enter your name and email address, your incoming and outgoing mail server information and user name, and the account name you'd like to use to identify your email account. After setting up your email account, you can use Thunderbird to send and receive email messages. Figure 2-6 shows the Thunderbird Inbox window.

Figure 2-6 **Thunderbird Inbox window**

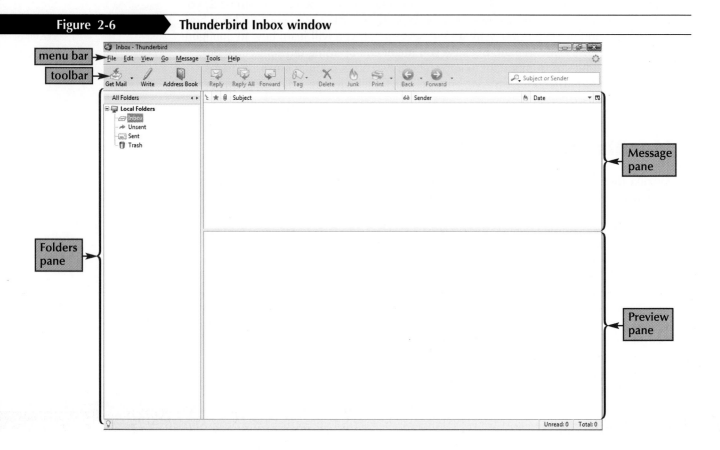

Thunderbird uses a Folders pane, a Message pane, and a Preview pane to organize your email messages.

Sending and Receiving Mail in Thunderbird

To write a message, click the Write button on the toolbar. The Compose window opens, in which you enter the email address of the message's recipient in the To text box. You can send the message to multiple recipients by separating their email addresses with commas. To send Cc or Bcc messages to additional recipients, press the Enter key to move to the next line in the message header, click the To button, select the message recipient type, and then type the recipient's email address. You can also click the Contacts button to open the Contacts pane and view the email addresses you have saved in your Thunderbird address book. You can use the Attach button to attach files, Web pages, or personal cards to your message. Figure 2-7 shows the Compose window after writing a message to Don Kikukawa and attaching a file named Physicals.pdf.

Thunderbird Compose window ◄ Figure 2-7

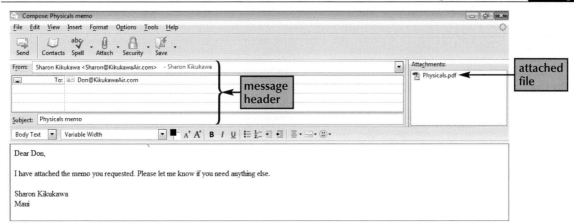

Before sending the message, you can check the document for spelling errors by clicking the Spell button on the toolbar. Clicking the Security button on the toolbar opens a menu that lets you encrypt or digitally sign the message. In addition, you can choose the "View Security Info" option to view certificate and security information about the message you are sending. If you don't want to send the message right away, you can use the options on the Save button menu to save the message as a file, as a draft in the Drafts folder, or as a template. To send the message, click the Send button on the toolbar. By default, messages are sent immediately when you click the Send button, and copies of your sent messages are saved in the Sent folder in the Folders pane.

When you receive a message, the message header appears in the Message pane. Clicking the message opens it in the Preview pane, as shown in Figure 2-8.

Receiving a message in Thunderbird ◄ Figure 2-8

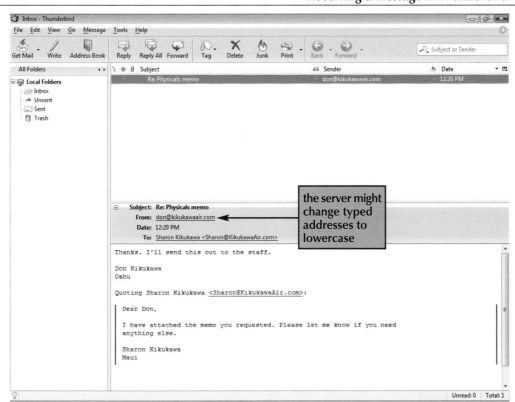

To view an attached file, right-click the filename in the Attachments box, and then click Open on the shortcut menu. An Opening dialog box appears and gives you the choice of opening the file using a program on your computer, or saving the file to disk.

After receiving a message, you can reply to the sender or to all message recipients by clicking the message in the Message pane, and then clicking the Reply or Reply All button on the toolbar. To forward the message to another recipient, click the Forward button on the toolbar. By default, messages are forwarded as attachments. If you prefer to forward inline messages, you can change this setting by clicking Tools on the menu bar in the Compose window, and then clicking Options to open the Options dialog box. Click the Forward messages arrow on the General tab, and then click Inline. To print a message, click the Print button on the toolbar, and then select the printer and other options for printing the message.

Managing Messages in Thunderbird

Just like in other email programs, Thunderbird lets you create folders to manage your messages. To create a new folder in the Folders pane, right-click Local Folders (or your mailbox account name) at the top of the Folders pane to open the shortcut menu, and then click New Folder. In the New Folder dialog box, type the name of the folder, specify where to create it (if necessary), and then click the OK button. To file a message in a folder, drag it from the Message pane to the folder in which you want to save it. To delete a message, select the message in the Message pane, and then click the Delete button on the toolbar. Messages are not permanently deleted until you empty the trash by right-clicking the Trash folder in the Folders pane, and then clicking Empty Trash on the shortcut menu.

Managing Junk Mail in Thunderbird

Tip

If Thunderbird treats a message as junk mail but should not, click the Not Junk button so Thunderbird won't categorize mail from that sender as junk in the future.

A powerful feature of Thunderbird is its adaptive spam and junk mail filters. Based on how you manage your incoming mail, these filters "learn" how to manage your messages for you—with the goal of displaying less junk mail in your Inbox. When you receive junk mail, Thunderbird might automatically mark it as junk mail. You can also click the Junk button on the toolbar, which changes to a Not Junk button after you click it, to designate a message as junk. After clicking the Junk button on the toolbar, Thunderbird changes the message and its sender to junk mail and displays a junk mail icon and notice, as shown in Figure 2-9.

Junk mail identification in Thunderbird ◀ Figure 2-9

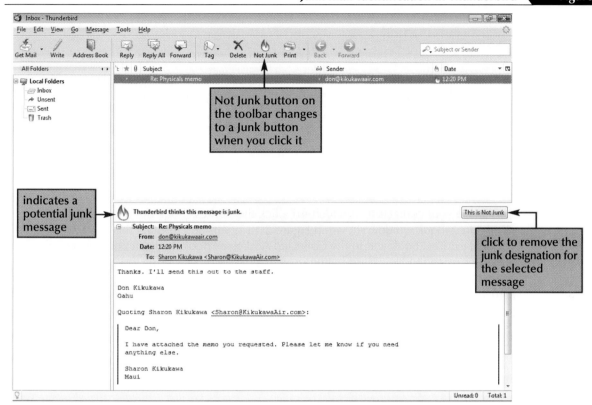

You can set Thunderbird to move messages into a junk folder so it's easy for you to identify and delete unwanted messages later. You can use the "Run Junk Mail Controls on Folder" option located on the Tools menu to set up the junk mail filter so it learns how to identify your incoming mail.

Creating a Saved Search Folder in Thunderbird

To make it easy to find messages based on criteria that you specify, Thunderbird lets you create Saved Search folders. A **Saved Search folder** looks like a regular mail folder, but when you click it, it searches every folder and message for matches using criteria that you specify. To create a Saved Search folder, click File on the menu bar, point to New, and then click Saved Search. The New Saved Search Folder dialog box opens, in which you must specify a Saved Search folder name, location, and the criteria that define the search. For example, you might create a Saved Search folder that finds all messages sent by a specific person, or messages that are older than 60 days. When you run the search, matching messages will appear in the Message pane. Figure 2-10 shows a Saved Search folder named "Don" in the Folders pane. Double-clicking the Don Saved Search folder finds all messages in which Don Kikukawa is the sender.

| Figure 2-10 | Using a Saved Search folder in Thunderbird |

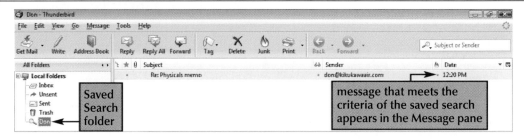

Using the Thunderbird Address Book

To manage your contacts in Thunderbird, click the Address Book button on the toolbar. The Address Book window shown in Figure 2-11 opens and displays the contacts in your Personal Address Book and in the Collected Addresses Book. You can add new email addresses using the New Card button or manage mailing lists using the New List button. To compose a message to someone in your address book, click the person's name, and then click the Write button on the toolbar. Thunderbird lets you store more than just a person's name and email address; if you double-click the contact name in the address book, you can enter a person's phone number, address, and other information, such as a cell phone number.

| Figure 2-11 | Thunderbird Address Book window |

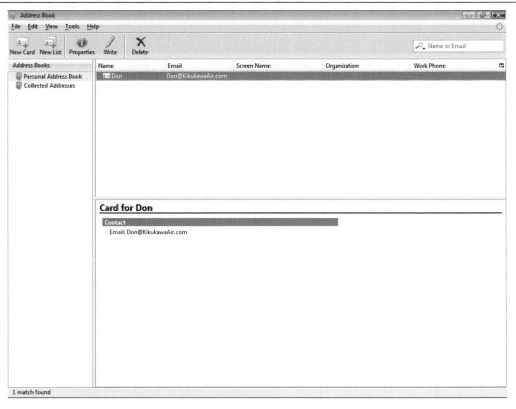

Opera Mail

Another popular email program is the **Opera Mail** built-in email client, which is installed with the Opera Web browser. You can download the Opera browser by following the link on the Online Companion for Tutorial 2.

Starting Opera Mail

When you start the Opera Web browser for the first time, you can use the New account wizard to create an email or other type of account. You can also import information from other email programs.

The first thing you need to set up is your email account so you can send and receive email messages through your ISP. You need to enter your name and email address, your incoming and outgoing mail server information and user name, and the account name you'd like to use to identify your email account. After setting up your email account, you can use Opera to send and receive email messages.

To send and receive messages using the Opera Mail email client, start the Opera browser, and then click the Mail button on the Panels toolbar to open the Mail panel, as shown in Figure 2-12.

Opera Mail panel ◄ **Figure 2-12**

The Mail panel includes buttons to check (receive) and send email, and a Compose button to create new messages. You can close the Mail panel and the Panels bar by pressing the F4 key. You can use whichever method you prefer; most people use the Mail panel to check for new messages quickly without closing the current page being displayed by the browser. To read a message, click the Received folder on the Mail panel to open the Received tab, which displays the message list and a preview pane, a shown in Figure 2-13.

Figure 2-13 Mail received using Opera Mail

Sending and Receiving Email in Opera

To write a message, click the Compose button on the Mail panel. The Compose message tab opens and displays a new message. You can type email addresses in the To, Cc, and Bcc text boxes to add them to your message. To view contacts saved in your address book, click the Contacts button on the Panels toolbar, which opens the Contacts panel to the left of the Compose message tab. Clicking the Add button on the Contacts panel opens a dialog box in which you can enter a person's name, email address, Web site address, and other contact information. To attach a file to your message, click the Attach button on the Compose message toolbar, and then browse to and select the file. After attaching the file, it appears in the Attachment window. Figure 2-14 shows the Compose message tab after writing a message to Don Kikukawa and attaching a file named Physicals.pdf. Notice the promotional message that appears at the bottom of all outgoing messages sent from Opera. This text is actually a signature file that Opera inserts by default into all outgoing messages. If you don't want to include this message in an outgoing email message, you can select the text and delete it from your message before sending it.

Figure 2-14 Composing a message in Opera Mail

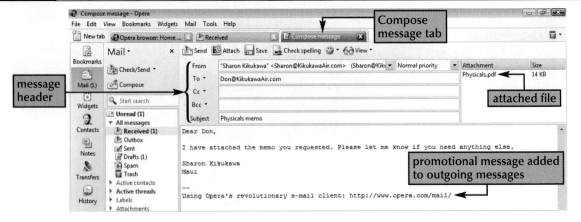

Before sending a message, you can click the Check spelling button on the Compose message toolbar to check the email message for spelling errors. Clicking the View button on the Compose message toolbar lets you show and hide the different parts of the message header, such as the email account name, priority field, and the Cc and Bcc text boxes. To send the message, click the Send button on the Compose message toolbar. A

ScreenTip opens in the lower-left corner of the browser window to indicate that your message is being sent. By default, messages are sent immediately when you click the Send button, and copies of your sent messages are saved in the Sent folder.

To download new messages, click the Check/Send button on the Mail panel. When you receive a new message, a ScreenTip opens in the lower-left corner of the browser window. Figure 2-15 shows that one new message was received.

Receiving a message in Opera | **Figure 2-15**

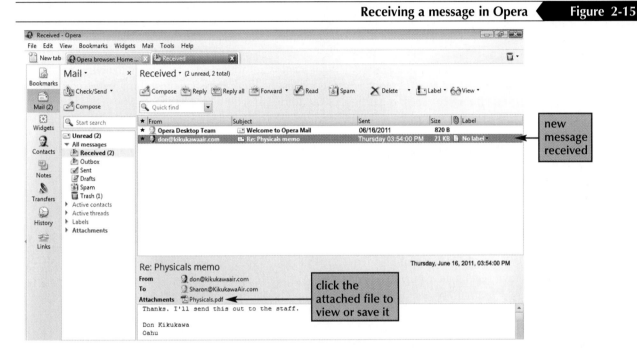

When a message includes an attached file, click the attachment to open a shortcut menu. Click the Open command to open the attachment using a program on your computer, click the "Save to download folder" option to save it to the default download location for Opera files, or click the Save as option to save it in a specific folder or drive on your computer.

After receiving a message, you can reply to the sender or to all recipients by clicking the Reply or Reply all button on the Compose message toolbar. To forward a message to another recipient, click the Forward button on the Compose message toolbar. By default, Opera sends forwarded messages as inline text. To redirect a message to a new recipient, click the Forward button arrow on the Compose message toolbar, and then click Redirect. This option makes it easy to send a message to a new recipient without adding the "Fwd:" prefix to the Subject line. To print a message, click File on the menu bar, and then click Print.

Managing Messages in Opera

After reading a message, you can mark it as read by clicking the Read button on the Compose message toolbar. Clicking the Spam button on the Compose message toolbar flags the sender of the selected message so that future messages sent to you by this sender are automatically saved in the Spam folder. Clicking the Delete button on the Compose message toolbar deletes the message and moves it to the Trash folder. To permanently delete the message, right-click the Trash folder on the Mail panel, and then click Empty trash on the shortcut menu. Clicking the Label button arrow on the Compose message toolbar lets you assign a category to received messages so that you can quickly identify and easily search for important messages, messages that require action, and messages that are funny or valuable. Clicking Labels on the Mail panel lists messages that you have assigned to categories so you can identify and sort them easily. The View button on the Compose message toolbar contains options for displaying relevant information about all of your messages, such as only the message headers or messages received during predefined time periods (such as "last week" or "yesterday").

A unique feature of Opera's email client is how it stores its messages. In other email programs, messages are stored in folders in a mailbox. Opera's messages are stored in a single database so that messages are easy to search for and retrieve. You can sort messages by using the View button on the Compose message toolbar to assign messages to categories as you receive them, or you can create custom filters to sort messages based on their content or sender. Because messages are not saved into folders, viewing messages based on their content or category results in all messages matching your search criteria being selected, regardless of the folder in which they are stored.

Webmail Providers

A **Webmail provider** is an Internet Web site that provides free email addresses and accounts for registered users as well as the capability to use any Web browser with Internet access to send and receive email messages. Some Webmail providers also include options to let you use your free email address with an email program such as Microsoft Outlook Express or Thunderbird. An email address that you get from a Webmail provider is also called **Webmail** because you access the email account through the Webmail provider's Web site. Many people rely on Webmail as their primary email address; others use Webmail to set up a separate, personal address when their employer or other owner of their primary email address restricts the use of personal email. Some popular choices for free Webmail services are Yahoo! Mail, Gmail, and Windows Live Hotmail. You can follow the links in the Email section of the Online Companion page for Tutorial 2 to learn more about these Webmail providers. Figure 2-16 shows a message composed using Windows Live Hotmail.

Message composed using Windows Live Hotmail | Figure 2-16

You might wonder how these companies can provide free email—after all, nothing is free. The answer is advertising. When you use a Webmail provider, you will see advertising, such as the banner shown at the top of the page in Figure 2-16. In addition to showing its account holders advertising messages and providing links to other services, email messages sent from Webmail providers might also contain some sort of advertisement, such as a promotional message or a link to the Webmail provider. Advertising revenues pay for free email, so you must decide whether you are willing to endure some advertising in exchange for using the free email service. Most users of these free services agree that seeing some ads is a small price to pay for the convenience the free email provides.

To get your free email address, use your Web browser to visit the provider's Web site. After locating the link to the site's email service, you will need to provide some basic information about yourself, such as your name, address, and phone number. Then you choose a user name and password. If the email service verifies that your user name is available, it activates your account after you complete a basic registration form and agree to the provider's terms of service. If the user name you selected is in use, the service will ask you to submit a new user name or modify the one you chose. Webmail provides a way for people who do not have an account with an ISP to use email in public libraries, businesses, and other places that provide connections to the Internet. You can access Webmail from anywhere in the world where there is an Internet connection. None of the messages that you send and receive are stored on the device that you use; everything happens on the Webmail provider's servers. The email messages you send and receive are protected by your password and function just like email messages sent from an email program running on your computer.

Google Gmail

When Google launched the test program for its new Webmail service, called **Gmail**, it received a lot of publicity from the media. At the time, other Webmail providers such as Yahoo! and MSN Hotmail had been gradually reducing the free storage space allotted to individual subscribers for email messages from 50 megabytes to two to four megabytes in favor of "premium" services that included additional features and storage capacity for a monthly fee. After Gmail began testing its free Webmail service, which promised more than two gigabytes of storage space for every user, other Webmail providers had to change their offerings quickly to avoid losing their subscribers. Figure 2-17 shows the Gmail Inbox.

Figure 2-17	Gmail Inbox window

One of the initial concerns about Gmail was how Google planned to support it. The service is paid for by adding advertisements to email messages based on searches of those messages. Ads are added to the user's messages based on predefined keywords included in the messages. Although there is no human intervention to produce the advertisements, some users have concerns about the privacy of the email messages they receive because they are scanned and read by computers. Some people do not like the idea of seeing advertisements based on the content of the messages they send and receive because they see it as an invasion of privacy. Gmail has made efforts to make sure that its advertising appears only as targeted text ads. This strategy is different from other email providers that include untargeted advertising in the form of banners and pop-up windows, which some users find to be more invasive. Just like any other free service, it is up to the user to determine the level of advertising they are willing to endure in exchange for the free service provided.

Another issue that concerns many users is how their messages are stored. With substantial storage space, you can save virtually every message you receive—in fact, Google actually encourages you to do so. Because Google performs routine maintenance on its servers, such as backups and archives, your messages might be stored forever in these files. Even if you delete your messages, they still might exist in these files, making your private messages part of a permanent archive. This same scenario applies to most Webmail accounts, regardless of the provider.

Today, anyone can sign up for a Gmail account, which now offers more than 2,900 gigabytes of storage space for free. You can find links to Gmail and to other Webmail providers on the Online Companion page for Tutorial 2.

"You've Got Spam!"

Spam, also known as **unsolicited commercial email (UCE)** or **bulk mail**, includes unwanted solicitations, advertisements, or email chain letters sent to an email address. For most Internet users, spam represents waste in terms of the time it takes to download, manage, and delete. Besides wasting people's time and their computers' disk space, spam can consume large amounts of network capacity. If one person sends a useless email message to hundreds of thousands of people, that unsolicited message consumes Internet resources for a few moments that would otherwise be available to users with legitimate communication needs. Although spam has always been an annoyance, companies are increasingly finding it to be a major problem. In addition to consuming bandwidth on company networks and space on email servers, spam distracts employees who are trying to do their jobs and requires them to spend time deleting unwanted messages. In addition, a considerable number of spam messages include content that is offensive or misleading to its recipients. According to the Messaging Anti-Abuse Working Group (MAAWG), approximately 80% of all email messages sent every day are abusive. In real numbers, this is billions of email messages a day.

Many grassroots and corporate organizations have decided to fight spam aggressively. AOL, for example, has taken an active role in limiting spam through legal channels. Many companies now offer software that organizations can run on their email servers to limit the amount of spam that is delivered to the organization's email addresses. Although individual users can install client-based spam-filtering programs on their computers or set filters that might be available within their email client software, most companies find it more effective and less costly to eliminate spam before it reaches users.

As spam continues to be a serious problem for all email users and providers, an increasing number of approaches have been devised or proposed to combat it. Some of these approaches require new laws, and some require technical changes in the mail handling systems of the Internet. Other approaches can be implemented under existing laws and with current technologies, but only with the cooperation of many organizations and businesses.

One way to limit the amount of spam an organization or individual receives is to reduce the likelihood that a spammer can automatically generate their email addresses. Many organizations create email addresses for their employees by combining elements of each employee's first and last names. For example, small companies often combine the first letter of an employee's first name with the entire last name to generate email addresses for all employees. Any spam sender able to obtain an employee list can generate long lists of potential email addresses using the names on the list. If no employee list is available, the spammer can simply generate logical combinations of first initials and common names. The cost of sending email messages is so low that a spammer can afford to send thousands of messages to randomly generated addresses in the hope that a few of them are valid.

Another way to reduce spam is to control the exposure of your email address in places where spammers look for them. Spammers use software robots to search the Internet for character strings that include the "@" character that appears in every email address. These robots search Web pages, discussion boards, chat rooms, and other online sources that might contain email addresses. If you don't provide your email address to these sources, you reduce the risk of a spammer getting it. A spammer can afford to send thousands of messages to email addresses gathered in this way. Even if only one or two people respond, the spammer can earn a profit because the cost of sending email messages is so low.

Some individuals use multiple email addresses to thwart spam. They use one address for display on a Web site, another to register for access to Web sites, another for shopping accounts, and so on. If a spammer starts using one of these addresses, the individual can stop using it and switch to another. Many Web hosting services include a large number of email addresses—often up to 10,000—as part of their service, so this is a good tactic for people or small businesses with their own Web sites.

The strategies previously described focus on limiting spammer's access to, or use of, an email address. Other approaches use one or more techniques that filter email messages based on their contents. Many U.S. jurisdictions have passed laws that provide penalties for sending spam. In January 2004, the U.S. CAN-SPAM law (the law's name is an acronym for "Controlling the Assault of Non-Solicited Pornography and Marketing") went into effect. Researchers who track the amount of spam noted a drop in the percentage of spam messages in February and March 2004. A MessageLabs study tracked the spam message rate from 62% of all Internet messages sent in January to 59% in February and 53% in March. However, by April, the rate was back up to a new high— 68% of all messages sent. It appears that spammers slowed down their activities immediately after the effective date of CAN-SPAM to see if a broad federal prosecution effort would occur. When the threat did not materialize, the spammers went right back to work.

The CAN-SPAM law is the first U.S. federal government effort to legislate controls on spam, as shown in Figure 2-18. It regulates all email messages sent for the primary purpose of advertising or promoting a commercial product or service, including messages that promote the content displayed at a Web site. The law's main provisions are that unsolicited email messages must identify the sender, contain an accurate message subject and a notice that the message is an advertisement or solicitation, make it possible for the recipient to "opt out" of future mailings within 10 days of receipt of the request, include the sender's physical postal address, and prohibit the sender from selling or transferring an email address with an opt out request to any other entity. Each violation of a provision of the law is subject to a fine of up to $11,000. Additional fines are assessed for those who violate one of these provisions and also harvest email addresses from Web sites, send messages to randomly generated addresses, use automated tools to register for email accounts that are subsequently used to send spam, and relay email messages through a computer or network without the permission of the computer's or network's owner.

CAN-SPAM Act requirements for commercial emailers | Figure 2-18

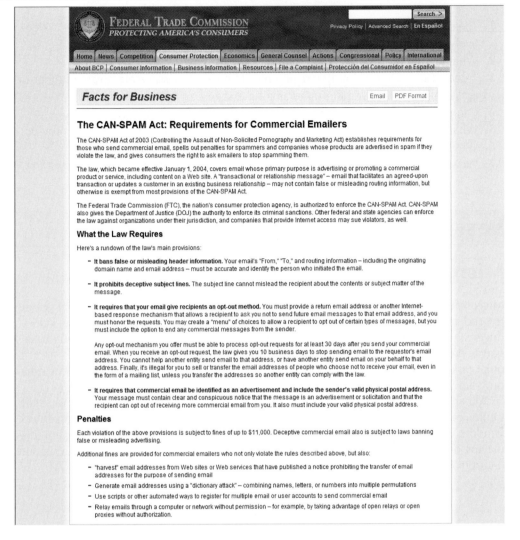

Few industry experts expect CAN-SPAM or similar laws to be effective in preventing spam on the Internet. After all, spammers have been violating existing deceptive advertising laws for years. Many spammers use email servers located in countries that do not have (and that are unlikely to adopt) antispam laws. Enforcement is a problem, too. Spammers can move their operations from one server to another in minutes.

Some critics argue that any legal solution to the spam problem is likely to fail until the prosecution of spammers becomes cost-effective for governments. To become cost-effective, prosecutors must be able to identify spammers easily (to reduce the cost of bringing an action against them) and must have a greater likelihood of winning the cases they file (or must see a greater social benefit to winning). The best way to make spammers easier to find is to make changes in the email transport mechanism in the Internet's infrastructure. To learn more about legislation geared to prevent spam, follow the links in the Email section on the Online Companion page for Tutorial 2.

Now that you understand some basic information about email and email software, you are ready to start using your email program. If you are using Windows XP and Microsoft Outlook Express, your instructor will assign Session 2.2; if you are using Windows Vista and Windows Mail, your instructor will assign Session 2.3; and if you are using Windows Live Hotmail, your instructor will assign Session 2.4.

1. The special rules governing how information is handled on the Internet are collectively called _____ .
2. What are the three parts of an email message?
3. True or False: On receipt, Bcc recipients of an email message are aware of other Bcc recipients who received the same email message.
4. Can you send a Word document over the Internet? If so, how?
5. What are the two parts of an email address and what information do they provide?
6. Why is it important to delete email messages that you no longer need?
7. What is a Saved Search folder and in which program is this feature available?

Session 2.2

Microsoft Outlook Express

Microsoft Outlook Express, or simply **Outlook Express**, is an email program that you use to send and receive email. Outlook Express is installed with Internet Explorer on Windows XP computers. Microsoft Outlook, another email program that you can purchase, is part of the Microsoft Office suite of programs. It lets you send and receive email and do other tasks, such as manage a calendar. (If your computer runs Windows Vista, the email program you will use is Windows Mail, which is covered in Session 2.3.)

You are eager to begin your evaluation of email programs for Kikukawa Air. You start Outlook Express by using the Start menu. Figure 2-19 shows the Outlook Express Inbox window. You can customize Outlook Express in many ways by resizing, hiding, and displaying different windows and their individual elements, so your screen might look different from Figure 2-19.

Outlook Express Inbox window | Figure 2-19

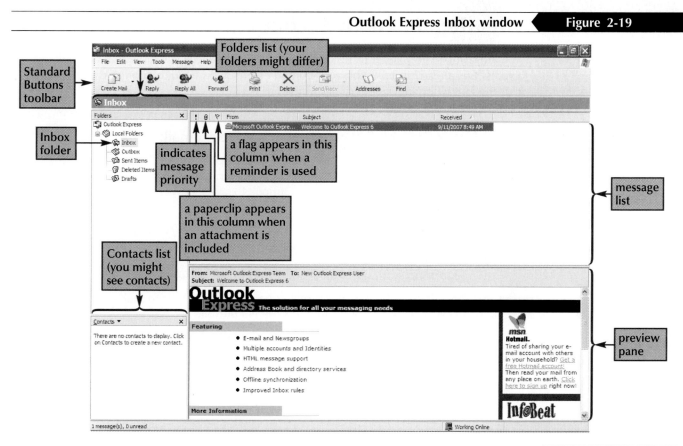

The Inbox window contains four panes: the Folders list, the Contacts list, the message list, and the preview pane. The **Folders list** displays a list of folders for receiving, saving, and deleting mail messages. You might see more folders than those shown in Figure 2-19, but you should see the five default folders. The **Inbox folder** stores messages you have received, the **Outbox folder** stores outgoing messages that have not been sent, the **Sent Items folder** stores copies of messages you have sent, the **Deleted Items folder** stores messages you have deleted, and the **Drafts folder** stores messages that you have written but have not sent. Your copy of Outlook Express might also contain folders you have created, such as a folder in which you store all messages from a certain recipient.

The **Contacts list**, which might be hidden, contains information about the addresses stored in your address book. You can click a contact in the Contacts list to address a new message quickly to an individual or group.

The **message list** contains summary information for each message that you receive. The first three columns on the left might display icons indicating information about the email message. The first column indicates the message's priority: You might see an exclamation point to indicate a message with high priority; a blue arrow icon to indicate a message with low priority; or nothing, which indicates normal priority. The sender indicates a message's priority before sending it; most messages have no specified priority, in which case no icon will appear in the column. The second column displays a paperclip icon when a message includes an attachment. Finally, if you click the third column for a message you have received, a red flag will appear. You can use a flag to remind yourself to follow up on the message later.

The message list also displays the sender's name in the From column, the message's subject in the Subject column, and the date and time the message was received in the Received column. You can sort messages by clicking any column in the message list.

The message that is selected in the message list appears in the preview pane. The **preview pane** appears below the message list and displays the content of the selected message in the message list. You can use the horizontal scroll bar to scroll the message.

Tip

If this is your first time starting Outlook Express, you might receive a message similar to the one shown in Figure 2-19 from Microsoft.

Creating an Email Account

You are ready to get started using Outlook Express. These steps assume that Outlook Express 6 is already installed on your computer. First, you need to configure Outlook Express so it will retrieve your mail from your ISP.

To configure Outlook Express to manage your email:

▶ 1. Click the **Start** button on the Windows taskbar, point to **All Programs**, and then click **Outlook Express** to start the program. Normally, you do not need to be connected to the Internet to configure Outlook Express; however, your system might be configured differently. If necessary, connect to the Internet.

   Trouble? Outlook Express is not installed on computers running the Windows Vista operating system. If you are running Windows Vista, you should complete Session 2.3 on Windows Mail.

   Trouble? If the Internet Connection Wizard starts, click the Cancel button.

   Trouble? If an Outlook Express dialog box opens and asks to make Outlook Express your default mail client, click the No button.

   Trouble? If an Outlook Express dialog box opens and asks to import information from another email program installed on your computer, click the Cancel button.

▶ 2. If necessary, click the **Inbox** folder in the Folders list to select it.

▶ 3. Click **Tools** on the menu bar, click **Accounts**, and then, if necessary, click the **Mail** tab in the Internet Accounts dialog box so you can set up your mail account settings.

   Trouble? If you have already set up your mail account (or if someone has set up an account for you), click the Close button in the Internet Accounts dialog box and skip this set of steps. If you are unsure about any existing account, ask your instructor or technical support person for help.

▶ 4. Click the **Add** button in the Internet Accounts dialog box, and then click **Mail**. The Internet Connection Wizard starts. You use this wizard to identify yourself, your user name, and the settings for your mail server. See Figure 2-20.

| Figure 2-20 | Internet Connection Wizard dialog box |

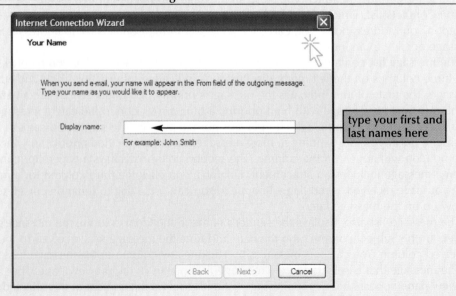

5. Type your first and last names in the Display name text box, and then click the **Next** button to open the next dialog box, in which you specify your email address.

6. Type your full email address (such as student@university.edu) in the Email address text box, and then click the **Next** button. The next dialog box asks you for your incoming and outgoing mail server names.

7. Type the names of your incoming and outgoing mail servers in the text boxes where indicated. Your instructor, technical support person, or ISP will provide this information to you. Usually, an incoming mail server name is POP, POP3, or IMAP followed by a domain name. An outgoing mail server name usually is SMTP or MAIL followed by a domain name. When you are finished, click the **Next** button to continue.

8. In the Account name text box, type your Internet mail user name, as supplied by your instructor, technical support person, or ISP. Make sure that you type your user name and not your domain name (some ISPs might require both).

9. Press the **Tab** key to move the insertion point to the Password text box. To protect your password's identity, Outlook Express displays dots or asterisks in this text box instead of the characters you type. To prevent other users from being able to access your mail account, you will clear the Remember password check box. When you access your mail account, Outlook Express will prompt you for your password. If you are working on a computer to which you have sole access, you might want to set Outlook Express to remember your password, so you don't need to type it every time you access your email.

10. If necessary, click the **Remember password** check box to clear it, and then click the **Next** button.

11. Click the **Finish** button to save the mail account information and close the Internet Connection Wizard. The Internet Accounts dialog box reappears, and your account is listed on the Mail tab. Figure 2-21 shows Sharon Kikukawa's information.

Mail account created for Sharon Kikukawa   **Figure 2-21**

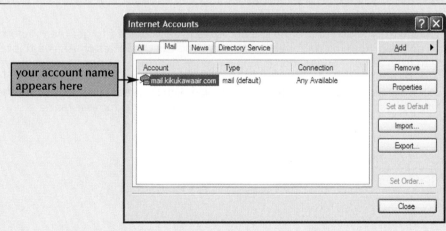

your account name appears here

12. Click the **Close** button in the Internet Accounts dialog box to close it.

Now Outlook Express is configured to send and receive messages, so you are ready to send a message to Don Kikukawa.

Sending a Message Using Outlook Express

You are ready to use Outlook Express to send a message with an attached file to Don. You will send a courtesy copy of the message to your own email address to simulate receiving a message.

Reference Window | **Sending a Message Using Outlook Express**

- Click the Create Mail button on the toolbar to open the New Message window.
- In the To text box, type the recipient's email address. To send the message to more than one recipient, separate additional email addresses with commas or semicolons.
- If necessary, click View on the menu bar, click All Headers to display the Bcc text box, and then type the email address of any Cc or Bcc recipients in the appropriate text boxes. Separate multiple recipients' email addresses with commas or semicolons.
- If necessary, click the Attach button on the toolbar, in the Insert Attachment dialog box browse to and select a file to attach to the message, and then click the Attach button.
- In the message body, type your message.
- Check your message for spelling and grammatical errors.
- Click the Send button on the toolbar.

To send a message with an attachment:

1. Make sure that the **Inbox** folder is selected in the Folders list, and then click the **Create Mail** button on the toolbar to open the New Message window. If necessary, click the **Maximize** button on the New Message window. See Figure 2-22. The New Message window contains its own menu bar, toolbar, message display area, and boxes in which you enter address and subject information. The insertion point is positioned in the To text box when you open a new message.

   Trouble? If you do not see the Bcc text box in the message header, click View on the menu bar, and then click All Headers.

   Trouble? If you don't have the starting Data Files, you need to get them before you can proceed. Your instructor will either give you the Data Files or ask you to obtain them from a specified location (such as a network drive). In either case, make a backup copy of the Data Files before you start so that you will have the original files available in case you need to start over. If you have any questions about the Data Files, see your instructor or technical support person for assistance.

New Message window   Figure 2-22

toolbar with options for working with the message

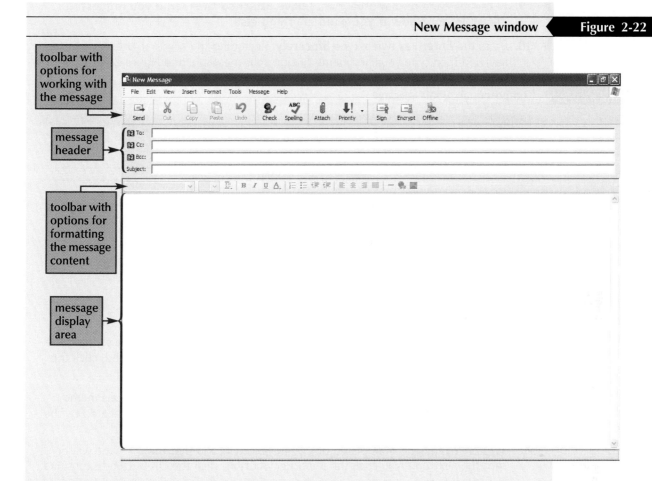

message header

toolbar with options for formatting the message content

message display area

2. In the To text box, type **Don@KikukawaAir.com**, and then press the **Tab** key to move to the Cc text box.

   Trouble? Make sure that you use the address Don@KikukawaAir.com or its lower-case equivalent, don@kikukawaair.com. If you type an email address incorrectly, your message will be returned as undeliverable.

3. Type your full email address in the Cc text box. When you send this message, you and Don will both receive it.

   Trouble? If you make a typing mistake on a previous line, use the arrow keys or click the insertion point in that line so you can correct your mistake. If the arrow keys do not move the insertion point backward or forward in the message header, press Shift + Tab or the Tab key to move backward or forward, respectively.

4. Press the **Tab** key twice to move the insertion point to the Subject text box, and then type **Physicals memo**. Notice that the title bar now displays "Physicals memo" as the window title.

5. Click the **Attach** button on the toolbar. The Insert Attachment dialog box opens.

6. Click the **Look in** list arrow, and then navigate to the location of your Data Files.

7. Double-click the **Tutorial.02** folder, double-click the **Tutorial** folder, and then double-click **Physicals**. The Insert Attachment dialog box closes, and the attached file's icon, filename, and file size appear in the Attach text box.

8. Click in the message display area, type **Dear Don,** (including the comma), and then press the **Enter** key twice to insert a blank line.

Tip

Messages sent to this mail-box are deleted without being opened or read.

▶ 9. In the message display area, type **I have attached the memo you requested. Please let me know if you need anything else.**

▶ 10. Press the **Enter** key twice, type **Sincerely,** (including the comma), press the **Enter** key, and then type your first name to sign your message. See Figure 2-23.

| Figure 2-23 | Composing an email message |

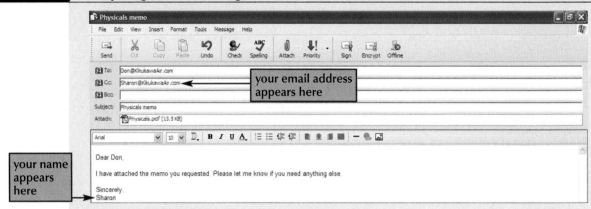

▶ 11. Click the **Spelling** button on the toolbar to check your spelling before sending the message. If necessary, correct any typing errors. When you are finished, click the **OK** button to close the Spelling dialog box.

▶ 12. Click the **Send** button on the toolbar to mail the message. The Physicals memo window closes and the message is stored in the Outbox folder, as indicated by the "(1)" in the Outbox folder.

Trouble? If a Send Mail dialog box opens and tells you that the message will be sent the next time you click the Send/Recv button, click the OK button to continue.

Trouble? If Outlook Express is configured to send messages when you click the Send button, you won't see the "(1)" in the Outbox folder. This difference causes no problems.

Depending on your system configuration, Outlook Express might not send your messages immediately. It might queue (hold) messages until you connect to your ISP or click the Send/Recv button on the toolbar. If you want to examine the setting and change it, click Tools on the menu bar, click Options, and then click the Send tab in the Options dialog box. If the Send messages immediately check box contains a check mark, then Outlook Express sends messages when you click the Send button on the toolbar. Otherwise, Outlook Express holds messages until you click the Send/Recv button.

Receiving and Reading a Message

When you receive new mail, messages that you haven't opened yet are displayed with a closed envelope icon next to them in the message list; messages that you have opened are displayed with an open envelope icon next to them. You check for new mail next.

| Reference Window | **Using Outlook Express to Send and Receive Messages** |

- If necessary, connect to your ISP.
- Click the Send/Recv button on the toolbar.

To check for incoming mail:

▶ 1. Click the **Send/Recv** button on the toolbar, type your password in the Password text box of the Logon dialog box (if necessary), and then click the **OK** button. Depending on your system configuration, you might not need to connect to your ISP and type your password to retrieve your messages. Within a few moments, your mail server transfers all new mail to your Inbox. The Physicals memo message was sent to Don and also to your email address, which you typed in the Cc text box. Notice that the Inbox folder in the Folders list is bold, but other folders are not. A bold folder indicates that it contains unread mail; the number in parentheses next to the Inbox folder indicates the number of unread messages in that folder.

Trouble? If an Outlook Express message box opens and indicates that it could not find your host, click the Hide button to close the message box, click Tools on the menu bar, click Accounts, and then click the Properties button. Verify that your incoming and outgoing server names are correct, and then repeat Step 1. If you still have problems, ask your instructor or technical support person for help.

Trouble? If you do not see any messages in your Inbox, then you either did not receive any new mail or you might be looking in the wrong folder. If necessary, click the Inbox folder in the Folders list. If you still don't have any mail messages, wait a few moments, and then repeat Step 1 until you receive a message.

▶ 2. If necessary, click the **Physicals memo** message in the message list to open the message in the preview pane. See Figure 2-24.

Receiving an email message | Figure 2-24

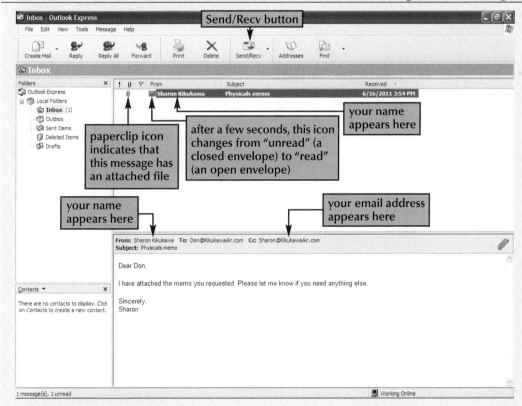

You received a copy of the message that you sent to Don. The paperclip icon indicates the message has an attachment. When you receive a message with one or more attachments, you can open the attachment or save it.

Viewing and Saving an Attached File

You want to make sure that your attached file was sent properly, so you decide to open it. Then you will save the file.

Reference Window | **Viewing and Saving an Attached File in Outlook Express**

- Click the message that contains the attached file in the message list to display its contents in the preview pane.
- Click the paperclip icon in the preview pane to open the shortcut menu, and then click the attached file's name. Close the program window that opens after viewing the file.
- Click the paperclip icon in the preview pane to open the shortcut menu, and then click Save Attachments.
- Click the file to save or click the Select All button to save all attached files, click the Browse button to open the Browse for Folder dialog box, and then change to the drive and folder in which to save the attached file(s).
- Click the OK button.

To view and save the attached file:

▶ **1.** Make sure that the **Physicals memo** message is selected in the message list.

▶ **2.** Click the **paperclip icon** in the upper-right corner of the preview pane to open the shortcut menu. See Figure 2-25.

Figure 2-25 ▶ **Viewing an attached file**

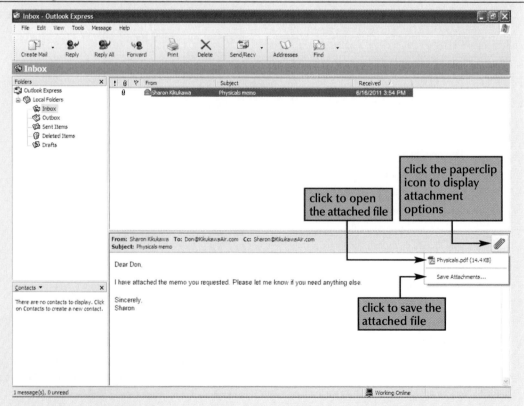

Trouble? If the options on the shortcut menu are dimmed, then Outlook Express is configured to remove all potentially unsafe attachments from messages. Click the paperclip icon to close the menu. If you are working in a public computer lab, ask your instructor or technical support person for help. If you are working on a private computer, click Tools on the menu bar, click Options, click the Security tab in the Options dialog box, and then clear the "Do not allow attachments to be saved or opened that could potentially be a virus." check box. Click the OK button to close the Options dialog box, and then recompose, send, and receive the Test message. It is strongly suggested that you install and configure antivirus software when disabling this option to protect your computer from viruses.

The shortcut menu shows that a file named Physicals.pdf, with a file size of approximately 15 KB, is attached to the message. If this message contained other attachments, they would also appear on the shortcut menu. Clicking Physicals.pdf starts a program on your computer that can open the file. Clicking Save Attachments lets you save the file to the drive and folder that you specify.

▶ 3. Click **Physicals.pdf** on the shortcut menu. Adobe Reader or another program on your computer starts and opens the attached file. If necessary, maximize the program window that opens.

Trouble? If a Mail Attachment dialog box opens warning that the file might contain viruses, click the Open button.

▶ 4. Click the **Close** button on the program window displaying the Physicals document. Now that you have viewed the attachment, you can save it.

▶ 5. Click the **paperclip icon** in the preview pane, and then click **Save Attachments** on the shortcut menu. The Save Attachments dialog box opens. The Physicals.pdf file is already selected for you.

▶ 6. Click the **Browse** button. The Browse for Folder dialog box opens and lists all of the drives on your computer.

▶ 7. Scrolling as necessary, open the drive or folder that contains your Data Files, double-click the **Tutorial.02** folder to open it, click the **Tutorial** folder to select it, and then click the **OK** button. The Save Attachments dialog box appears again. The Save To location indicates that you will save the attached file to the Tutorial.02\Tutorial folder. See Figure 2-26.

Save Attachments dialog box | Figure 2-26

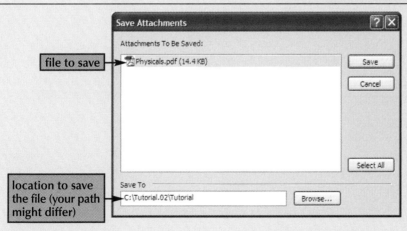

file to save

location to save the file (your path might differ)

▶ 8. Click the **Save** button to save the attached file, and then click the **Yes** button to overwrite the file with the same name.

InSight | **Saving Attachments**

When you receive a message with an attached file, you can view and save the attachment for as long as you store the message. When you delete the message, you delete the file attached to the message. When you detach a file from an email message and save it on a disk or drive, it is just like any other file that you save. Be sure to save any important attachments soon after receiving them, so you do not inadvertently delete the messages containing them.

Replying to and Forwarding Messages

You can forward any message you receive to one or more email addresses. Similarly, you can respond to the sender of a message quickly and efficiently by replying to a message.

Replying to an Email Message

To reply to a message, select the message in the message list, and then click the Reply button on the toolbar to reply only to the sender, or click the Reply All button to reply to the sender and other people who received the original message (those email addresses listed in the To and Cc text boxes). Outlook Express will open a new "Re:" message window and place the original sender's address in the To text box; if you click the Reply All button, then other email addresses that received the original message will appear in the To and Cc text boxes as appropriate. You can leave the Subject text box as is or modify it. Most email programs, including Outlook Express, will copy the original message and place it in the message body. Usually, a special mark to the left of the response indicates a quote from the text of the original message. Figure 2-27 shows a reply to the Physicals memo message.

| Figure 2-27 | **Replying to a message** |

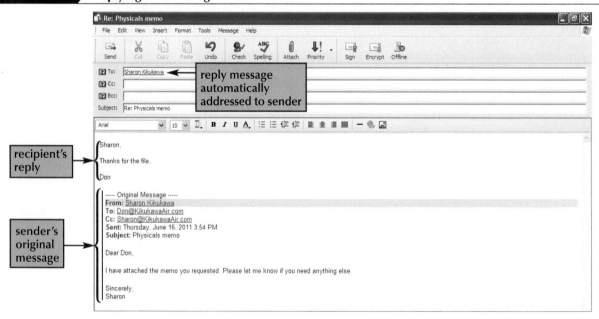

- Click the message in the message list to which you want to reply.
- Click the Reply button on the toolbar to reply only to the sender, or click the Reply All button on the toolbar to reply to the sender and other "To" and "Cc" recipients of the original message.
- Type other recipients' email addresses in the message header as needed.
- Change the text in the Subject text box as necessary.
- Edit the message body as necessary.
- Click the Send button on the toolbar.

Forwarding an Email Message

When you forward a message, you are sending a copy of the message, including any attachments, to one or more recipients who were not included in the original message. (If you do not want to forward the original sender's attached file to the new recipients, select the attachment filename in the Attach text box, and then press the Delete key.) To forward an existing mail message to another user, open the folder containing the message you want to forward, select it in the message list, and then click the Forward button on the toolbar. The "Fw:" window opens, where you can type the address of the recipient in the To text box. If you want to forward the message to several people, type their addresses, separated by commas (or semicolons), in the To text box (or Cc or Bcc text boxes). Outlook Express inserts a copy of the original message in the message display area (as it does when you reply to a message). However, no special mark appears in the left margin to indicate the original message. Figure 2-28 shows a forwarded copy of the Physicals memo message.

Forwarding a message Figure 2-28

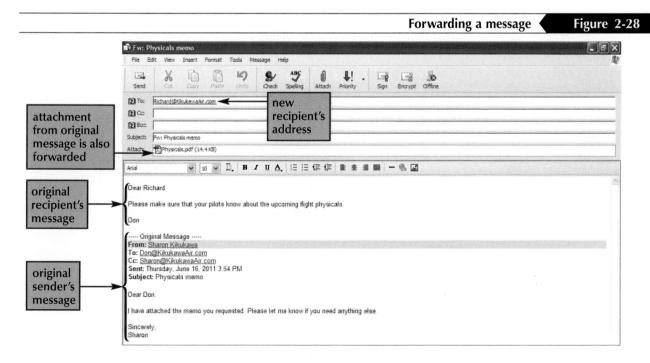

Reference Window | **Forwarding an Email Message Using Outlook Express**

- Click the message in the message list that you want to forward.
- Click the Forward button on the toolbar to open the "Fw:" window, which contains a copy of the original message.
- Click the To text box, and then type one or more email addresses, separated by commas or semicolons.
- Click the blank line above the quoted message, and then type an optional message to add a context for the recipient(s).
- Click the Send button on the toolbar.

Occasionally, you receive important messages, so you want to make sure that you can file and print them as needed.

Filing and Printing an Email Message

You can use the Outlook Express mail folders to file your email messages by topic or category. When you file a message, you move it from the Inbox to another folder. You can also make a *copy* of a message in the Inbox and save it in another folder by right-clicking the message in the message list, clicking Copy to Folder on the shortcut menu, and then selecting the folder in which to store the copy. You file your message in a new folder named "FAA" for safekeeping. Later, you can create other folders to suit your style and working situation.

To create a new folder:

1. Right-click the **Inbox** folder in the Folders list to open the shortcut menu, and then click **New Folder**. The Create Folder dialog box opens. When you create a new folder, first you must select the folder at the level above which to create the new folder. Because the Inbox folder is selected, the new folder that you create is a subfolder of the Inbox folder.

2. Type **FAA** in the Folder name text box. See Figure 2-29.

Figure 2-29 Creating a new folder

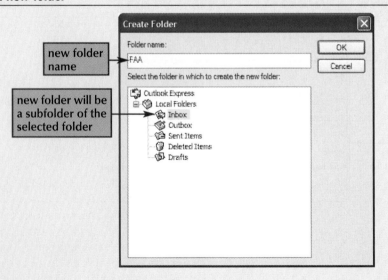

3. Click the **OK** button to create the new folder and close the Create Folder dialog box. The FAA folder appears in the Folders list as a subfolder of the Inbox folder.

After you create the FAA folder, you can transfer messages to it. In addition to copying or transferring mail from the Inbox folder, you can select messages in any other folder and then transfer them to another folder.

To file the Physicals memo message:

1. Click the **Physicals memo** message in the message list to select it.

2. Click and drag the **Physicals memo** message from the message list to the FAA folder in the Folders list. See Figure 2-30.

Filing a message | Figure 2-30

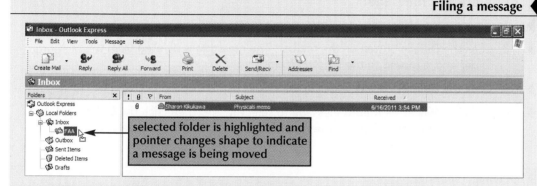

3. When the FAA folder is selected, release the mouse button. The Physicals memo message is now stored in the FAA folder.

4. Click the **FAA** folder in the Folders list to display its contents (the Physicals memo message) in the message list.

You might want to print certain messages for future reference. You print the message next.

To print the email message:

1. Click the **Physicals memo** message in the message list to select it.

2. Click the **Print** button on the toolbar. The Print dialog box opens.

3. If necessary, select your printer in the list of printers.

4. Click the **Print** button. The message is printed.

Deleting an Email Message and Folder

When you don't need a message any longer, select the message in the message list, and then click the Delete button on the toolbar. You can select multiple messages by pressing and holding the Ctrl key, clicking each message in the message list, and then releasing the Ctrl key. When you click the Delete button on the toolbar, each selected message is deleted. You can select folders and delete them using the same process. When you delete a message or a folder, you are really moving it to the Deleted Items folder. To remove items permanently, use the same process to delete the items from the Deleted Items folder.

Reference Window | **Deleting an Email Message or a Folder in Outlook Express**

- Click the message you want to delete in the message list. If you are deleting a folder, click the folder in the Folders list that you want to delete.
- Click the Delete button on the toolbar.
- To delete items permanently, click the Deleted Items folder to open it, select the message(s) or folder(s) that you want to delete permanently, click the Delete button on the toolbar, and then click the Yes button.

  or
- Right-click the Deleted Items folder to open the shortcut menu, click Empty 'Deleted Items' Folder, and then click the Yes button.

To delete the message:

▶ **1.** If necessary, select the **Physicals memo** message in the message list.

▶ **2.** Click the **Delete** button on the toolbar. The message is deleted from the FAA folder and is moved to the Deleted Items folder.

▶ **3.** Click the **Deleted Items** folder in the Folder list to display its contents.

▶ **4.** Click the **Physicals memo** message to select it, and then click the **Delete** button on the toolbar. A dialog box opens and asks you to confirm the deletion. See Figure 2-31.

Figure 2-31 ▶ Deleting a message

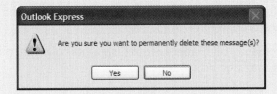

▶ **5.** Click the **Yes** button. The Test message is deleted from the Deleted Items folder.

To delete the FAA folder, you follow the same process.

To delete the FAA folder:

▶ **1.** Click the **FAA** folder in the Folders list to select it. Because this folder doesn't contain any messages, the message list is empty.

▶ **2.** Click the **Delete** button on the toolbar. A dialog box opens and asks you to confirm moving the folder to the Deleted Items folder.

▶ **3.** Click the **Yes** button. The FAA folder moves to the Deleted Items folder. The Deleted Items folder has a plus box to its left, indicating that this folder contains another folder.

▶ **4.** Click the **plus box** to the left of the Deleted Items folder, and then click the **FAA** folder to select it.

▶ **5.** Click the **Delete** button on the toolbar, and then click the **Yes** button in the message box to delete the FAA folder permanently.

▶ **6.** Click the **Inbox** folder in the Folders list to return to the Inbox.

Deleting Messages on a Public Computer | InSight

If you are using a public computer, it is always a good idea to delete all of your messages from the Inbox and then to delete them again from the Deleted Items folder when you finish your session. Otherwise, the next person who uses Outlook Express will be able to access and read your messages.

Maintaining an Address Book

As you use email to communicate with business associates and friends, you might want to save their addresses in an address book to make it easier to enter addresses into the header of your email messages.

Adding a Contact to the Address Book

You can open the Outlook Express address book by clicking the Addresses button on the toolbar. To create a new address, open the address book, click the New button on the toolbar, click New Contact from the list, and then enter information into the Properties dialog box for that contact. On the Name tab, you can enter a contact's name and email address; use the other tabs to enter optional address, business, personal, and other information about that contact. If you enter a short name in the Nickname text box, then you can type the nickname instead of a person's full name when you address a new message.

Adding a Contact to the Outlook Express Address Book | Reference Window

- Click the Addresses button on the toolbar.
- In the Address Book window, click the New button on the toolbar, and then click New Contact.
- On the Name tab of the Properties dialog box, enter the contact's name and email address. Use the other tabs in the Properties dialog box as necessary to enter other information about the contact.
- Click the OK button to add the contact to the address book.
- Click the Close button on the Address Book window title bar.

Now you can add information to your address book. You begin by adding Jenny Mahala's contact information to your address book.

To add a contact to your address book:

► 1. Click the **Addresses** button on the toolbar. The Address Book window opens. If necessary, maximize the Address Book window.

► 2. Click the **New** button on the toolbar, and then click **New Contact**. The Properties dialog box opens with the insertion point positioned in the First text box on the Name tab.

► 3. Type **Jenny** in the First text box. As you type the contact's first name (and eventually the last name), the name of the Properties dialog box changes to indicate that the properties set in this dialog box belong to the specified contact.

▶ **4.** Press the **Tab** key twice to move the insertion point to the Last text box, type **Mahala** in the Last text box, and then press the **Tab** key three times to move the insertion point to the Nickname text box.

▶ **5.** Type **Jen** in the Nickname text box, and then press the **Tab** key to move the insertion point to the E-Mail Addresses text box.

▶ **6.** Type **Jenny@KikukawaAir.com** in the E-Mail Addresses text box, and then click the **Add** button. Jen's contact is complete. See Figure 2-32.

Figure 2-32 ▶ **Adding a contact to the address book**

▶ **7.** Click the **OK** button. The Properties dialog box closes and you return to the Address Book window. Jen's contact now appears in the Address Book window.

▶ **8.** Repeat Steps 2 through 7 to create new contacts for the following Kikukawa Air employees:

First	Last	Nickname	Email Address
Zane	Norcia	Zane	Zane@KikukawaAir.com
Richard	Forrester	Rich	Richard@KikukawaAir.com

▶ **9.** When you are finished entering the contacts, click the **Close** button on the Address Book window title bar to close it. Now the Contacts list shows the entries you just added to your address book.

Now that these email addresses are stored in the address book, when you start typing the first few letters of a nickname or first name, Outlook Express will complete the entry for you. Clicking the Check button on the toolbar in the New Message window changes the names you typed to their matching entries in the address book. If you need to change an address, click to select it and then press the Delete key.

When you receive mail from someone who is not in your address book, double-click the message to open it, right-click the "From" name to open the shortcut menu, and then click Add to Address Book. This process adds the sender's name and email address to your address book, where you can open his or her information as a contact and edit and add information as necessary.

Adding a Group of Contacts to the Address Book

You can use Outlook Express to create a group. Usually you create a group of contacts when you regularly send messages to a group of people.

For example, Sharon frequently sends messages to Zane, Jen, and Rich as a group because they have the same positions at the Kikukawa Air ticket counters. She asks you to create a group of contacts in her address book so she can type one nickname for the group of email addresses, instead of having to type each address separately.

| **Adding a Group of Contacts to the Address Book** | Reference Window |

- Click the Addresses button on the toolbar.
- In the Address Book window, click the New button on the toolbar, and then click New Group.
- In the Properties dialog box, type a nickname for the group in the Group Name text box.
- Click the Select Members button to open the Select Group Members dialog box.
- Click a name in the left list box to add to the group, and then click the Select button. Continue adding names to the group until you have selected all group members.
- Click the OK button twice.

To add a group of contacts to your address book:

1. Click the **Addresses** button on the toolbar, and then, if necessary, maximize the Address Book window.

2. Click the **New** button on the toolbar, and then click **New Group**. The Properties dialog box opens and displays tabs related to group settings.

3. With the insertion point positioned in the Group Name text box, type **Ticket Agents**. This nickname will represent the individual email addresses for employees working in this position.

4. Click the **Select Members** button. The Select Group Members window opens, with existing contacts appearing in a list box on the left side of the window.

5. Click **Jenny Mahala** in the left list box, and then click the **Select** button. A copy of Jenny's contact information is added to the Members list box.

6. Repeat Step 5 to add the contacts for **Richard Forrester** and **Zane Norcia** to the group. Figure 2-33 shows the completed group.

Figure 2-33 ▶ **Creating a group of contacts**

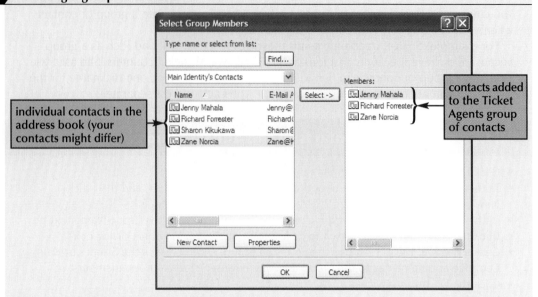

individual contacts in the address book (your contacts might differ)

contacts added to the Ticket Agents group of contacts

▶ **7.** Click the **OK** button to close the Select Group Members dialog box. The Properties dialog box for the Ticket Agents group contains three group members.

▶ **8.** Click the **OK** button to close the Ticket Agents Properties dialog box. The nickname of the new group, Ticket Agents, appears in the address book in the left pane of the window and the members of the group are listed in the right pane.

▶ **9.** Close the Address Book window by clicking the **Close** button on its title bar. The Ticket Agents group appears in the Contacts list.

Now, test the new group of contacts by creating a new message.

To address a message to a group of contacts and close Outlook Express:

▶ **1.** Click the **Create Mail** button on the toolbar. The New Message window opens.

▶ **2.** Type **Ticket Agents** in the To text box. As you type the first two or three letters, Outlook Express might complete your entry for you by selecting the Ticket Agents group.

▶ **3.** Press the **Tab** key.

▶ **4.** Click the **Check** button on the toolbar, right-click **Ticket Agents** in the To text box to open the shortcut menu, and then click **Properties**. The Properties dialog box shows the three group members who will receive messages sent to the Ticket Agents group. Now, when Sharon sends mail to the ticket agents, she can type the group name "Ticket Agents" in any of a message's boxes (To, Cc, or Bcc) instead of typing each address individually.

▶ **5.** Click the **OK** button to close the Ticket Agents Properties dialog box, click the **Close** button on the New Message window title bar, and then click the **No** button to close the message without saving it.

▶ **6.** Click **File** on the menu bar, and then click **Exit**. Outlook Express closes.

When you need to modify a group's members, you can delete one or more members from the group by opening the address book, double-clicking the group name, and then deleting a selected member's name by clicking the Remove button. Similarly, you can add members using the group's Properties dialog box.

In this session, you have learned how to use Outlook Express to create, send, receive, and manage email messages. You have also learned how to create and use an address book to manage email addresses.

Session 2.2 Quick Check | Review

1. The folder that stores messages you have written but have not yet sent is the _____ folder.
2. True or False: You can set Outlook Express so it remembers your Internet account password.
3. What happens when Outlook Express queues a message?
4. When you receive a message with an attachment, what two options are available for the attached file?
5. When you delete a message from the Inbox folder, can you recover it? Why or why not?
6. What information can you store about a person you have added as a contact?

If your instructor assigned Sessions 2.3 or 2.4, continue reading. Otherwise, complete the Review Assignments at the end of this tutorial.

Session 2.3

Microsoft Windows Mail

Microsoft Windows Mail, or simply **Windows Mail**, is an email program that you use to send and receive email. Windows Mail is installed with Internet Explorer on Windows Vista computers. (If your computer runs Windows XP, the email program you will use is Outlook Express, which is covered in Session 2.2.)

You are eager to begin your evaluation of email programs for Kikukawa Air. You start Windows Mail by using the Start button. Figure 2-34 shows the Windows Mail Inbox window. You can customize Windows Mail in many ways by resizing, hiding, and displaying different windows and their individual elements, so your screen might look different from Figure 2-34.

Figure 2-34   **Windows Mail Inbox window**

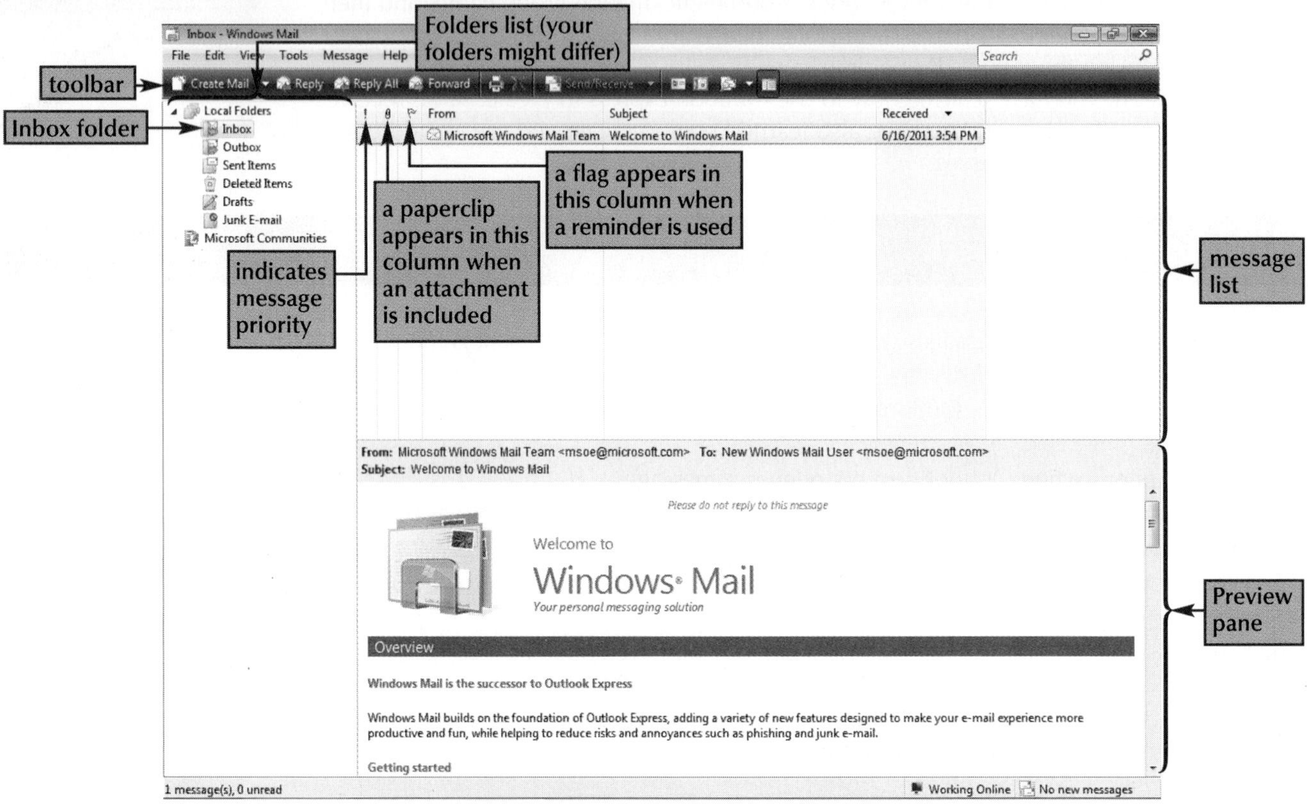

Tip

If this is your first time starting Windows Mail, you might receive a message similar to the one shown in Figure 2-34 from Microsoft.

The Inbox window contains three panes: the Folders list, the message list, and the Preview pane. The **Folders list** displays a list of folders for receiving, saving, and deleting mail messages. You might see more folders than those shown in Figure 2-34, but you should see the six default folders. The **Inbox folder** stores messages you have received, the **Outbox folder** stores outgoing messages that have not been sent, the **Sent Items folder** stores copies of messages you have sent, the **Deleted Items folder** stores messages you have deleted, the **Drafts folder** stores messages that you have written but have not sent, and the **Junk E-mail folder** stores messages that Windows Mail has tagged as junk and unsolicited mail. Your copy of Windows Mail might also contain folders you have created, such as a folder in which you store all messages from a certain recipient.

The **message list** contains summary information for each message that you receive. The first three columns on the left might display icons indicating information about the email message. The first column indicates the message's priority: You might see an exclamation point to indicate a message with high priority; a blue arrow icon to indicate a message with low priority; or nothing, which indicates normal priority. The sender indicates a message's priority before sending it; most messages have no specified priority, in which case no icon will appear in the column. The second column displays a paperclip icon when a message includes an attachment. Finally, if you click the third column for a message you have received, a red flag will appear. You can use a flag to remind yourself to follow up on the message later.

The message list also displays the sender's name in the From column, the message's subject in the Subject column, and the date and time the message was received in the Received column. You can sort messages by clicking any column in the message list.

The message that is selected in the message list appears in the Preview pane. The **Preview pane** appears below the message list and displays the content of the selected message in the message list. You can use the horizontal scroll bar to scroll the message.

Creating an Email Account

You are ready to get started using Windows Mail. These steps assume that Windows Mail is already installed on your computer. First, you need to configure Windows Mail so it will retrieve your mail from your ISP.

To configure Windows Mail to manage your email:

▶ **1.** Click the **Start** button on the Windows taskbar, click **All Programs**, and then click **Windows Mail** to start the program. Normally, you do not need to be connected to the Internet to configure Windows Mail; however, your system might be configured differently. If necessary, connect to the Internet.

Trouble? Windows Mail is not installed on computers running the Windows XP operating system or earlier versions of Windows. If you are not using Windows Vista, you should complete Session 2.2 on Outlook Express.

Trouble? If a Windows Mail dialog box opens and asks to make Windows Mail your default email program, click the No button.

Trouble? If a Windows Mail dialog box opens and asks to import information from another email program installed on your computer, click the Cancel button.

▶ **2.** If necessary, click the **Inbox** folder in the Folders list to select it.

▶ **3.** Click **Tools** on the menu bar, and then click **Accounts**. The Internet Accounts dialog box opens so you can set up your mail account settings.

Trouble? If you have already set up your mail account (or if someone has set up an account for you), click the Close button in the Internet Accounts dialog box and skip this set of steps. If you are unsure about any existing account, ask your instructor or technical support person for help.

▶ **4.** Click the **Add** button in the Internet Accounts dialog box, click **E-mail Account**, and then click the **Next** button. The first step in creating an email account is to enter the name that you want to appear in the From line of your messages. See Figure 2-35.

Dialog box that opens when you create a mail account in Windows Mail ◄ **Figure 2-35**

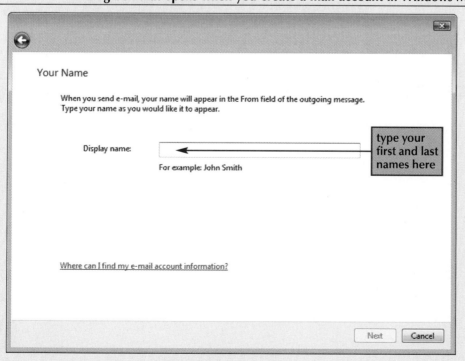

Your Name

When you send e-mail, your name will appear in the From field of the outgoing message.
Type your name as you would like it to appear.

Display name: ⟵   **type your first and last names here**

For example: John Smith

Where can I find my e-mail account information?

Next   Cancel

▶ 5. Type your first and last names in the Display name text box, and then click the **Next** button to open the next dialog box, in which you specify your email address.

▶ 6. Type your full email address (such as student@university.edu) in the Email address text box, and then click the **Next** button. The next dialog box asks you for your incoming and outgoing mail server names.

▶ 7. Type the names of your incoming and outgoing mail servers in the text boxes where indicated. Your instructor, technical support person, or ISP will provide this information to you. Usually, an incoming mail server name is POP, POP3, or IMAP followed by a domain name. An outgoing mail server name usually is SMTP or MAIL followed by a domain name. When you are finished, click the **Next** button to continue.

▶ 8. In the Account name text box, type your email user name, as supplied by your instructor, technical support person, or ISP. Make sure that you type your user name and not your domain name (some ISPs require both a user name and a domain name).

▶ 9. Press the **Tab** key to move the insertion point to the Password text box. To protect your password's identity, Windows Mail displays dots or asterisks in this text box instead of the characters you type. To prevent other users from being able to access your mail account, you will clear the Remember password check box. When you access your mail account, Windows Mail will prompt you for your password. If you are working on a computer to which you have sole access, you might want to set Windows Mail to remember your password, so you don't need to type it every time you access your email.

▶ 10. If necessary, click the **Remember password** check box to clear it, and then click the **Next** button.

▶ 11. Click the **Finish** button to save the mail account information and close the dialog box. The Internet Accounts dialog box reappears, and your new mail account is listed. Figure 2-36 shows Sharon Kikukawa's information.

Figure 2-36 ▶ **Mail account created for Sharon Kikukawa**

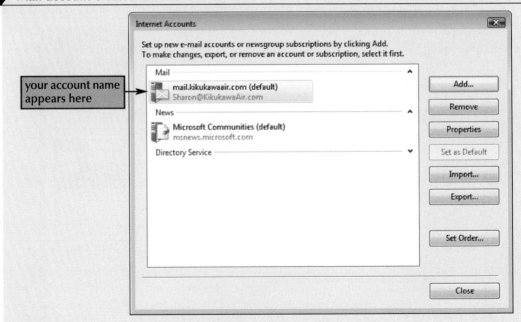

Trouble? If a Windows Security dialog box opens, click the Cancel button to close it.

Trouble? If a Windows Mail dialog box opens, click the Close button on the title bar to close it.

▶ **12.** Click the **Close** button in the Internet Accounts dialog box to close it.

Now Windows Mail is configured to send and receive messages, so you are ready to send a message to Don Kikukawa.

Sending a Message Using Windows Mail

You are ready to use Windows Mail to send a message with an attached file to Don Kikukawa. You will also send a courtesy copy of the message to your own email address to simulate receiving a message.

Sending a Message Using Windows Mail	Reference Window

- Click the Create Mail button on the toolbar to open the New Message window.
- In the To text box, type the recipient's email address. To send the message to more than one recipient, separate additional email addresses with commas or semicolons.
- If necessary, click View on the menu bar, click All Headers to display the Bcc text box, and then type the email address of any Cc or Bcc recipients in the appropriate boxes. Separate multiple recipients' email addresses with commas or semicolons.
- If necessary, click the Attach File To Message button on the toolbar, in the Open dialog box browse to and select a file to attach to the message, and then click the Open button.
- In the message body, type your message.
- Check your message for spelling and grammatical errors.
- Click the Send button on the toolbar.

To send a message with an attachment:

▶ **1.** Make sure that the **Inbox** folder is selected in the Folders list, and then click the **Create Mail** button on the toolbar to open the New Message window. If necessary, click the **Maximize** button on the New Message window. See Figure 2-37. The New Message window contains a menu bar and toolbar for working with the message options. It also contains the message display area, a toolbar for formatting the message content, and boxes in which you enter address and subject information. The insertion point is positioned in the To text box when you open a new message.

Trouble? If you do not see the Bcc text box in the message header, click View on the menu bar, and then click All Headers.

Trouble? If you don't have the starting Data Files, you need to get them before you can proceed. Your instructor will either give you the Data Files or ask you to obtain them from a specified location (such as a network drive). In either case, make a backup copy of the Data Files before you start so that you will have the original files available in case you need to start over. If you have any questions about the Data Files, see your instructor or technical support person for assistance.

Figure 2-37   New Message window

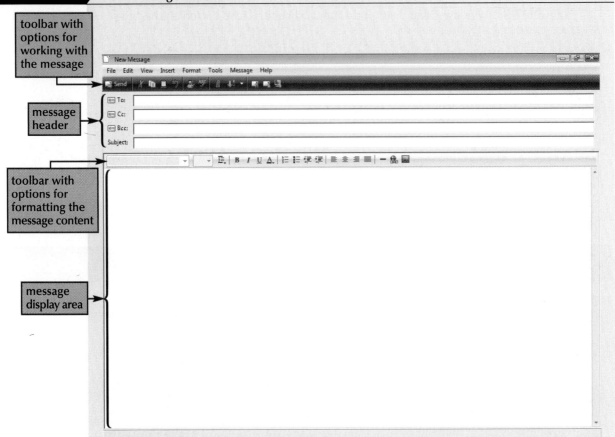

toolbar with options for working with the message

message header

toolbar with options for formatting the message content

message display area

Tip

Messages sent to this mail-box are deleted without being opened or read.

▶ **2.** In the To text box, type **Don@KikukawaAir.com**, and then press the **Tab** key to move to the Cc text box.

    Trouble? Make sure that you use the address Don@KikukawaAir.com or its lower-case equivalent, don@kikukawaair.com. If you type an email address incorrectly, your message will be returned as undeliverable.

▶ **3.** Type your full email address in the Cc text box. When you send this message, you and Don will both receive it.

    Trouble? If you make a typing mistake on a previous line, use the arrow keys or click the insertion point in the line so you can correct your mistake. If the arrow keys do not move the insertion point backward or forward in the message header, press Shift + Tab or the Tab key to move backward or forward, respectively.

▶ **4.** Press the **Tab** key twice to move the insertion point to the Subject text box, and then type **Physicals memo**. Notice that the title bar now displays "Physicals memo" as the window title.

▶ **5.** Click the **Attach File To Message** button on the toolbar. The Open dialog box appears.

▶ **6.** Browse to the location that contains your Data Files.

▶ **7.** Double-click the **Tutorial.02** folder, double-click the **Tutorial** folder, and then double-click **Physicals.pdf**. The Open dialog box closes, and the attached file's icon, filename, and file size appear in the Attach text box.

▶ **8.** Click in the message display area, type **Dear Don,** (including the comma), and then press the **Enter** key twice to insert a blank line.

▶ **9.** In the message display area, type **I have attached the memo you requested. Please let me know if you need anything else.**

▶ **10.** Press the **Enter** key twice, type **Sincerely,** (including the comma), press the **Enter** key, and then type your first name to sign your message. See Figure 2-38.

Composing an email message   Figure 2-38

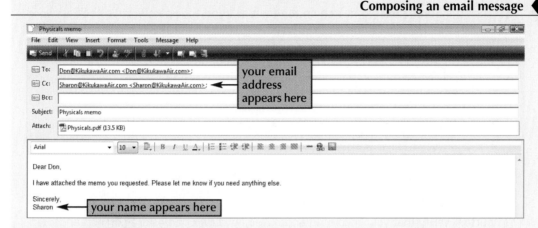

▶ **11.** Click the **Spelling** button on the toolbar to check your spelling before sending the message. If necessary, correct any typing errors. When you are finished, click the **OK** button to close the Spelling dialog box.

▶ **12.** Click the **Send** button on the toolbar to mail the message. The Physicals memo window closes and the message is sent.

    Trouble? If a Send Mail dialog box opens and tells you that the message will be sent the next time you click the Send/Receive button, click the OK button to continue.

    Trouble? If Windows Mail is configured to queue messages, the message will be stored in the Outbox folder, as indicated by a "(1)" in the Outbox folder. This difference causes no problems.

Depending on your system configuration, Windows Mail might not send your messages immediately. It might queue (hold) messages until you connect to your ISP or click the Send/Receive button on the toolbar. If you want to examine the setting and change it, click Tools on the menu bar, click Options, and then click the Send tab in the Options dialog box. If the Send messages immediately check box contains a check mark, then Windows Mail sends messages when you click the Send button on the toolbar. Otherwise, Windows Mail holds messages until you click the Send/Receive button.

Receiving and Reading a Message

When you receive new mail, messages that you haven't opened yet are displayed with a closed envelope icon next to them in the message list; messages that you have opened are displayed with an open envelope icon next to them. You check for new mail next.

Reference Window | **Using Windows Mail to Send and Receive Messages**

- If necessary, connect to your ISP.
- Click the Send/Receive button on the toolbar.

To check for incoming mail:

▶ 1. Click the **Send/Receive** button on the toolbar, type your password in the Password text box of the Logon dialog box (if necessary), and then click the **OK** button. Depending on your system configuration, you might not need to connect to your ISP and type your password to retrieve your messages. Within a few moments, your mail server transfers all new mail to your Inbox. The Physicals memo message was sent to Don and also to your email address, which you typed in the Cc text box. Notice that the Inbox folder in the Folders list is bold, but other folders are not. A bold folder indicates that it contains unread mail; the number in parentheses next to the Inbox folder indicates the number of unread messages in that folder.

   Trouble? If a Windows Mail message box opens and indicates that it could not find your host, click the Hide button to close the message box, click Tools on the menu bar, click Accounts, click your email account, and then click the Properties button. Verify that your incoming and outgoing server names are correct, and then repeat Step 1. If you still have problems, ask your instructor or technical support person for help.

   Trouble? If you do not see any messages in your Inbox, then you either did not receive any new mail or you might be looking in the wrong folder. If necessary, click the Inbox folder in the Folders list. If you still don't have any mail messages, wait a few moments, and then repeat Step 1 until you receive a message.

▶ 2. If necessary, click the **Physicals memo** message in the message list to open the message in the Preview pane. See Figure 2-39.

| Figure 2-39 | **Receiving an email message** |

Tip

The Search text box on the menu bar searches for text in messages you have sent and received. It is not a way to search the Help system. To access Help, click Help on the menu bar, and then click View Help.

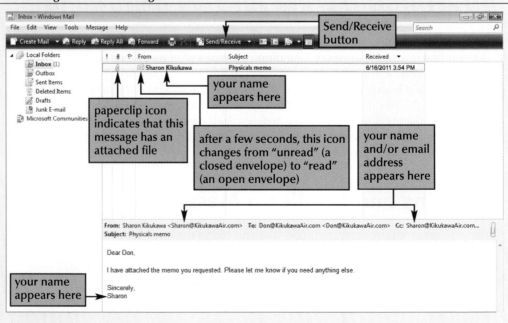

You received your copy of the message that you sent to Don. The paperclip icon indicates the message has an attachment. When you receive a message with one or more attachments, you can open the attachment or save it.

Viewing and Saving an Attached File

You want to make sure that your attached file was sent properly, so you decide to open it. Then you will save the file.

Viewing and Saving an Attached File in Windows Mail | Reference Window

- If necessary, click the message that contains the attached file in the message list to display its contents in the Preview pane.
- To view a file, click the paperclip icon in the Preview pane to open the shortcut menu, and then click the attached file's name. Click the Open button to open the file, or choose a program from the list to select a program to open the file. Close the program window that opens after viewing the file.
- To save a file, click the paperclip icon in the Preview pane to open the shortcut menu, and then click Save Attachments.
- Click the file to save or click the Select All button to save all attached files, click the Browse button, and then change to the drive and folder in which to save the attached file(s). Click the OK button.
- Click the Save button.

To view and save the attached file:

▶ **1.** Make sure that the **Physicals memo** message is selected in the message list.

▶ **2.** Click the **paperclip icon** in the upper-right corner of the Preview pane to open the shortcut menu. See Figure 2-40.

Viewing an attached file ◀ Figure 2-40

Trouble? If the options on the shortcut menu are dimmed, then Windows Mail is configured to remove all potentially unsafe attachments from messages. Click the paperclip icon to close the menu. If you are working in a public computer lab, ask your instructor or technical support person for help. If you are working on a private computer, click Tools on the menu bar, click Options, click the Security tab, and then clear the "Do not allow attachments to be saved or opened that could potentially be a virus" check box. Click the OK button to close the Options dialog box, and then recompose, send, and receive the Physicals memo message. It is strongly suggested that you install and configure antivirus software when disabling this option to protect your computer from viruses.

The shortcut menu shows that a file named Physicals.pdf, with a file size of approximately 15 KB, is attached to the message. If this message contained other attachments, they would also appear on the shortcut menu. Clicking Physicals.pdf starts a program on your computer that can open the file. Clicking Save Attachments lets you save the file to the drive and folder that you specify.

▶ **3.** Click **Physicals.pdf** on the shortcut menu, and then, if necessary, click the **Open** button. Adobe Reader or another program on your computer starts and opens the attached file. If necessary, maximize the program window that opens.

▶ **4.** Click the **Close** button on the program window displaying the Physicals memo document. Now that you have viewed the attachment, you can save it.

▶ **5.** Click the **paperclip icon** in the Preview pane, and then click **Save Attachments** on the shortcut menu. The Save Attachments dialog box opens. The Physicals.pdf file is already selected for you.

▶ **6.** Click the **Browse** button. The Browse For Folder dialog box opens and lists all of the drives on your computer.

▶ **7.** Scrolling as necessary, open the drive or folder that contains your Data Files, click the **Tutorial.02** folder to open it, click the **Tutorial** folder to select it, and then click the **OK** button. The Save Attachments dialog box appears again. The Save To location indicates that you will save the attached file to the Tutorial.02\Tutorial folder. See Figure 2-41.

Figure 2-41 ▶ **Save Attachments dialog box**

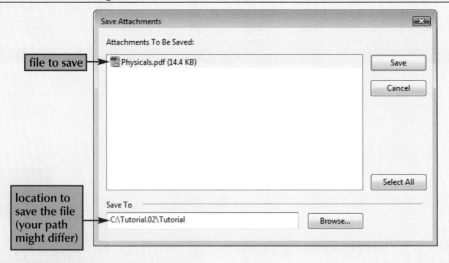

file to save

location to save the file (your path might differ)

▶ **8.** Click the **Save** button to save the attached file, and then click the **Yes** button to overwrite the file with the same name.

When you receive a message with an attached file, you can view and save the attachment for as long as you store the message. When you delete the message, you delete the file attached to the message. When you detach a file from an email message and save it on a disk or drive, it is just like any other file that you save. Be sure to save any important attachments soon after receiving them, so you do not inadvertently delete the messages containing them.

Replying to and Forwarding Messages

You can forward any message you receive to one or more email addresses. Similarly, you can respond to the sender of a message quickly and efficiently by replying to a message.

Replying to an Email Message

To reply to a message, select the message in the message list, and then click the Reply button on the toolbar to reply only to the sender, or click the Reply All button to reply to the sender and other people who received the original message (those email addresses listed in the To and Cc text boxes). Windows Mail will open a new "Re:" message window and place the original sender's address in the To text box; if you clicked the Reply All button, then other email addresses that received the original message will appear in the To and Cc text boxes as appropriate. You can leave the Subject text box as is or modify it. Most email programs, including Windows Mail, will copy the original message and place it in the message body. Usually, a special mark to the left of the response indicates a quote from the text of the original message. Figure 2-42 shows a reply to the Physicals memo message.

Replying to a message | **Figure 2-42**

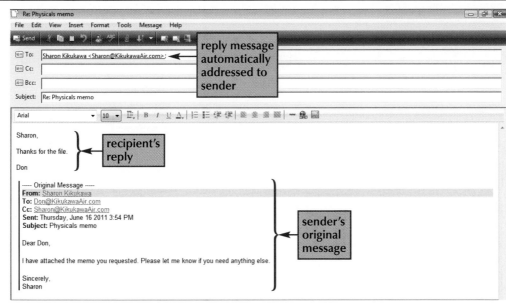

Replying to a Message Using Windows Mail

- Click the message in the message list to which you want to reply.
- Click the Reply button on the toolbar to reply only to the sender, or click the Reply All button on the toolbar to reply to the sender and other "To" and "Cc" recipients of the original message.
- Type other recipients' email addresses in the message header as needed.
- Change the text in the Subject text box as necessary.
- Edit the message body as necessary.
- Click the Send button on the toolbar.

Forwarding an Email Message

When you forward a message, you are sending a copy of your message, including any attachments, to one or more recipients who may not have been included in the original message. (If you do not want to forward the original sender's attached file to the new recipients, select the attachment filename in the Attach text box, and then press the Delete key.) To forward an existing mail message to another user, open the folder containing the message you want to forward, select it in the message list, and then click the Forward button on the toolbar. The "Fw:" window opens, where you can type the address of the recipient in the To text box. If you want to forward the message to several people, type their addresses, separated by commas (or semicolons), in the To text box (or Cc or Bcc text boxes). Windows Mail inserts a copy of the original message in the message display area (as it does when you reply to a message). However, no special mark appears in the left margin to indicate the original message. Figure 2-43 shows a forwarded copy of the Physicals memo message.

Figure 2-43 **Forwarding a message**

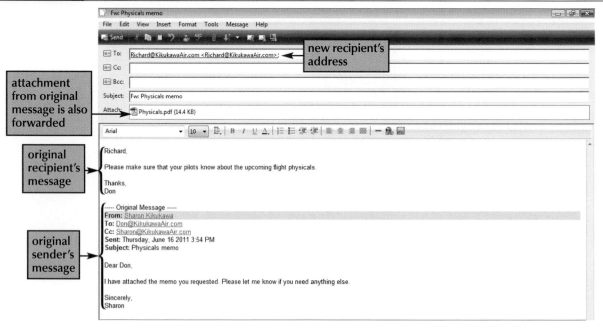

Forwarding an Email Message Using Windows Mail | Reference Window

- Click the message in the message list that you want to forward.
- Click the Forward button on the toolbar to open the "Fw:" window, which contains a copy of the original message.
- Click the To text box, and then type one or more email addresses, separated by commas or semicolons.
- Click the blank line above the quoted message, and then type an optional message to add a context for the recipient(s).
- Click the Send button on the toolbar.

Occasionally, you receive important messages, so you want to make sure that you can file and print them as needed.

Filing and Printing an Email Message

You can use the Windows Mail folders to file your email messages by topic or category. When you file a message, you move it from the Inbox to another folder. You can also make a *copy* of a message in the Inbox and save it in another folder by right-clicking the message in the message list, clicking Copy to Folder on the shortcut menu, and then selecting the folder in which to store the copy. You will file your message in a new folder named "FAA" for safekeeping. Later, you can create other folders to suit your style and working situation.

To create a new folder:

▶ **1.** Right-click the **Inbox** folder in the Folders list to open the shortcut menu, and then click **New Folder**. The Create Folder dialog box opens. When you create a new folder, first you must select the folder at the level above which to create the new folder. Because the Inbox folder is selected, the new folder that you create is a subfolder of the Inbox folder.

▶ **2.** Type **FAA** in the Folder name text box. See Figure 2-44.

Creating a new folder ◀ **Figure 2-44**

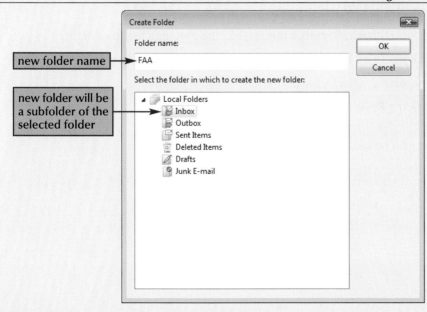

new folder name ➤

new folder will be a subfolder of the selected folder

▶ **3.** Click the **OK** button to create the new folder and close the Create Folder dialog box. The FAA folder appears in the Folders list as a subfolder of the Inbox folder.

After you create the FAA folder, you can transfer messages to it. Besides copying or transferring mail from the Inbox folder, you can select messages in any other folder and then transfer them to another folder.

To file the Physicals memo message:

▶ **1.** Click the **Physicals memo** message in the message list to select it.

▶ **2.** Drag the **Physicals memo** message from the message list to the FAA folder in the Folders list. See Figure 2-45.

| Figure 2-45 | Filing a message |

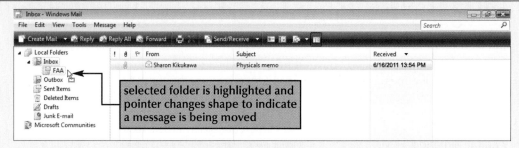

▶ **3.** When the FAA folder is selected, release the mouse button. The Physicals memo message is now stored in the FAA folder.

▶ **4.** Click the **FAA** folder in the Folders list to display its contents. The Physicals memo message appears in the FAA folder, and its contents (the Physicals memo message) appear in the message list.

You might want to print certain messages for future reference. You can print a message at any time—when you receive it, before you send it, or after you file it. You print the message next.

To print the email message:

▶ **1.** Click the **Physicals memo** message in the message list to select it.

▶ **2.** Click the **Print** button on the toolbar. The Print dialog box opens.

▶ **3.** If necessary, select your printer in the list of printers.

▶ **4.** Click the **Print** button. The message is printed.

When you no longer need a message, you can delete it.

Deleting an Email Message and Folder

When you don't need a message any longer, select the message in the message list, and then click the Delete button on the toolbar. You can select multiple messages by pressing and holding the Ctrl key, clicking each message in the message list, and then releasing the Ctrl key. When you click the Delete button on the toolbar, each selected message is deleted. You can select folders and delete them using the same process. When you delete a message or a folder, you are really moving it to the Deleted Items folder. To remove items permanently, use the same process to delete the items from the Deleted Items folder.

Deleting Messages on a Public Computer | InSight

If you are using a public computer in a university computer lab, it is always a good idea to delete all of your messages from the Inbox and then to delete them again from the Deleted Items folder when you finish your session. Otherwise, the next person who uses Windows Mail will be able to access and read your messages.

Deleting an Email Message or a Folder in Windows Mail | Reference Window

- Click the message you want to delete in the message list. If you are deleting a folder, click the folder in the Folders list that you want to delete.
- Click the Delete button on the toolbar. If you are deleting a folder, click the Yes button.
- To delete items permanently, click the Deleted Items folder to open it, select the message(s) or folder(s) that you want to delete permanently, click the Delete button on the toolbar, and then click the Yes button.
  or
- Right-click the Deleted Items folder to open the shortcut menu, click Empty 'Deleted Items' Folder, and then click the Yes button.

To delete the message:

▶ 1. If necessary, select the **Physicals memo** message in the message list.

▶ 2. Click the **Delete** button on the toolbar. The message is deleted from the FAA folder and is moved to the Deleted Items folder.

▶ 3. Click the **Deleted Items** folder in the Folder list to display its contents.

▶ 4. Click the **Physicals memo** message to select it, and then click the **Delete** button on the toolbar. A dialog box opens and asks you to confirm the deletion. See Figure 2-46.

Deleting a message | Figure 2-46

▶ **5.** Click the **Yes** button. The Physicals memo message is deleted from the Deleted Items folder.

To delete the FAA folder, you follow the same process.

To delete the FAA folder:

▶ **1.** Click the **FAA** folder in the Folders list to select it. Because this folder doesn't contain any messages, the message list is empty.

▶ **2.** Click the **Delete** button on the toolbar. A dialog box opens and asks you to confirm moving the folder to the Deleted Items folder.

▶ **3.** Click the **Yes** button. The FAA folder moves to the Deleted Items folder. The Deleted Items folder has an arrow to its left, indicating that this folder contains another folder.

▶ **4.** Click the **arrow** to the left of the Deleted Items folder, and then click the **FAA** folder to select it.

▶ **5.** Click the **Delete** button on the toolbar, and then click the **Yes** button in the message box to delete the FAA folder permanently.

▶ **6.** Click the **Inbox** folder in the Folders list to return to the Inbox.

Maintaining Your Windows Contacts

As you use email to communicate with business associates and friends, you can save their addresses in an address book to make it easier to enter addresses into the header of your email messages. In Windows Mail, the address book is called **Windows Contacts**.

Adding a Contact to Windows Contacts

You can open the Windows Contacts window by clicking the Contacts button on the toolbar. To create a new address, click the Contacts button on the toolbar to open the Windows Contacts window, and then click the New Contact button on the toolbar. The Properties dialog box opens, in which you can enter information about the new contact. On the Name and E-mail tab, you can enter a contact's name and email address; you can use the other tabs to enter optional address, business, personal, and other information about that contact. If you enter a short name in the Nickname text box, you can type the nickname instead of a person's full name when you address a new message.

| Reference Window | **Adding a Contact to Windows Contacts** |

- Click the Contacts button on the toolbar.
- In the Windows Contacts window, click the New Contact button on the toolbar.
- On the Name and E-mail tab of the Properties dialog box, enter the contact's name and email address. Use the other tabs in the Properties dialog box as necessary to enter other information about the contact.
- Click the OK button to add the contact to the address book.
- Click the Close button to close the Windows Contacts window.

Now you can add information to your address book. You begin by adding Jenny Mahala's contact information to Windows Contacts.

To add a contact to Windows Contacts:

1. Click the **Contacts** button on the toolbar. A window opens and displays your computer's drives and folders in the pane on the left and any existing contacts in the pane on the right. If necessary, maximize the window.

2. On the toolbar, click the **New Contact** button. The Properties dialog box opens with the insertion point positioned in the First text box on the Name and E-mail tab.

   Trouble? If you do not see the New Contact button on the toolbar, right-click a blank area in the pane on the right to open the shortcut menu, click Properties to open the Contacts Properties dialog box, and then click the Customize tab. Click the Use this folder as a template button arrow, click Contacts in the list, and then click the OK button to close the Contacts Properties dialog box. If you still do not see the New Contact button on the toolbar, ask your instructor or technical support person for help.

3. Type **Jenny** in the First text box. As you type the contact's first name (and eventually the last name), the name of the Properties dialog box changes to indicate that the properties set in this dialog box belong to the specified contact.

4. Press the **Tab** key twice to move the insertion point to the Last text box, type **Mahala** in the Last text box, and then press the **Tab** key three times to move the insertion point to the Nickname text box.

5. Type **Jen** in the Nickname text box, and then press the **Tab** key to move the insertion point to the E-mail text box.

6. Type **Jenny@KikukawaAir.com** in the E-mail text box, and then click the **Add** button. Jenny's contact is complete. See Figure 2-47.

Adding a contact to Windows Contacts | Figure 2-47

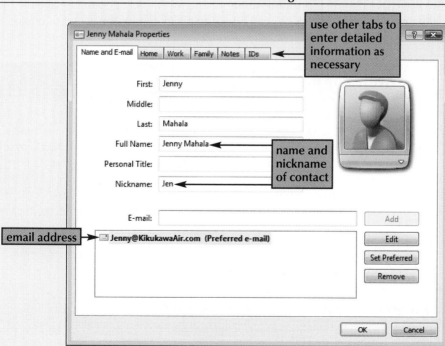

7. Click the **OK** button. The Properties dialog box closes and you return to the Contacts window. Jenny's contact now appears in the pane on the right.

> **8.** Repeat Steps 2 through 7 to create two new contacts for the following Kikukawa Air employees:
>
> | First | Last | Nickname | Email Address |
> |---|---|---|---|
> | Zane | Norcia | Zane | Zane@KikukawaAir.com |
> | Richard | Forrester | Rich | Richard@KikukawaAir.com |
>
> **9.** When you are finished entering the contacts, click the **Close** button on the Contacts window title bar to close it.

Now that these email addresses are stored in Windows Contacts, when you create a new message and start typing the first few letters of a nickname or first name in a text box in the message header, Windows Mail will complete the entry for you. Clicking the Check Names button on the toolbar in the New Message window changes the names you typed to their matching entries in Windows Contacts. If you need to change an address, click to select it and then press the Delete key.

When you receive mail from someone who is not in Windows Contacts, double-click the message to open it, right-click the "From" name to open the shortcut menu, and then click Add to Contacts. This process adds the sender's name and email address to Windows Contacts, where you can open his or her information as a contact and edit and add information as necessary.

Adding a Group of Contacts to Windows Contacts

You can use Windows Mail to create a group of email addresses. Usually, you create a group of contacts when you regularly send messages to a group of people.

For example, Sharon frequently sends messages to Zane, Jen, and Rich as a group because they have the same positions at the Kikukawa Air ticket counters. She asks you to create a group of contacts so she can type one nickname for the group of email addresses, instead of having to type each address separately.

Reference Window	**Adding a Group of Contacts to Windows Contacts**

- Click the Contacts button on the toolbar.
- In the Windows Contacts window, click the New Contact Group button on the toolbar.
- In the Properties dialog box, type a nickname for the group in the Group Name text box.
- Click the Add to Contact Group button to open the Add Members to Contact Group window.
- Click a name in the pane on the right, and then click the Add button. To select more than one name at a time, click the first name, press and hold down the Ctrl button, click the other names, and then click the Add button.
- Click the OK button.

To add a group of contacts to Windows Contacts:

> **1.** Click the **Contacts** button on the toolbar, and then, if necessary, maximize the Windows Contacts window.

> **2.** Click the **New Contact Group** button on the toolbar. The Properties dialog box opens and displays tabs related to group settings.

3. With the insertion point positioned in the Group Name text box, type **Ticket Agents**. This nickname will represent the individual email addresses for employees working in this position.

4. Click the **Add to Contact Group** button. The Add Members to Contact Group window opens. The pane on the right displays the existing contacts in Windows Contacts.

5. Click **Jenny Mahala.contact** in the pane on the right to select her as the first contact in the group.

6. Press and hold down the **Ctrl** key, click the contacts for **Richard Forrester** and **Zane Norcia** to the group, and then release the **Ctrl** key.

7. Click the **Add** button. Figure 2-48 shows the completed group. The Properties dialog box for the Ticket Agents group contains three group members.

Creating a group of contacts | Figure 2-48

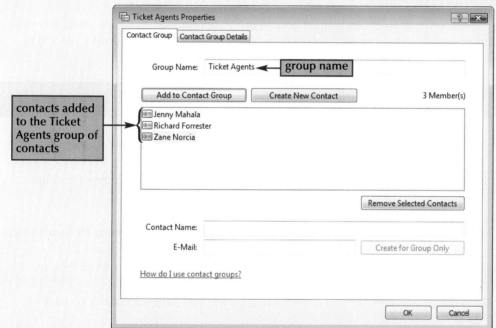

8. Click the **OK** button to close the Ticket Agents Properties dialog box. The nickname of the new group, Ticket Agents.group, appears in the pane on the right in the Windows Contacts window.

9. Click the **Close** button on the Windows Contacts window to close it.

Now, test the new group of contacts by creating a new message.

To address a message to a group of contacts and close Windows Mail:

1. Click the **Create Mail** button on the toolbar. The New Message window opens.

2. Type **Ticket Agents** in the To text box. As you type the first two or three letters, Windows Mail might complete your entry for you by selecting the Ticket Agents group.

3. Press the **Tab** key. The Ticket Agents nickname changes to bold and underlined, indicating that Windows Mail recognizes it as a contact group.

▶ **4.** Right-click **Ticket Agents** in the To text box to open the shortcut menu, and then click **Properties**. The Ticket Agents Properties dialog box shows the three group members who will receive messages sent to the Ticket Agents group. Now, when Sharon sends mail to the ticket agents, she can type the group name "Ticket Agents" in any of a message's boxes (To, Cc, or Bcc) instead of typing each address individually.

▶ **5.** Click the **OK** button to close the Ticket Agents Properties dialog box, click the **Close** button on the New Message window title bar, and then click the **No** button to close the message without saving it.

▶ **6.** Click **File** on the menu bar, and then click **Exit**. Windows Mail closes.

When you need to modify a group's members, you can delete one or more members from the group by opening Windows Contacts, double-clicking the group name in the pane on the right, and then deleting a selected member's name by clicking the Remove Selected Contacts button. Similarly, you can add members using the Add to Contact Group button.

In this session, you have learned how to use Windows Mail to create, send, receive, and manage email messages. You have also learned how to use Windows Contacts to manage email addresses.

| Review | | **Session 2.3 Quick Check** |

1. The folder that stores messages you have written but have not yet sent is the _____ folder.
2. True or False: You can set Windows Mail so it remembers your Internet account password.
3. What happens when Windows Mail queues a message?
4. When you receive a message with an attachment, what two options are available for the attached file?
5. When you delete a message from the Inbox folder, can you recover it? Why or why not?
6. What information can you store about a person you have added as a contact?

If your instructor assigned Session 2.4, continue reading. Otherwise, complete the Review Assignments at the end of this tutorial.

Session 2.4

Windows Live Hotmail

Windows Live Hotmail is a Webmail provider from Microsoft that you use to send and receive email. To use Windows Live Hotmail, you must use a Web browser to connect to the Windows Live Hotmail Web site, where you create and sign in to an account to retrieve and send email messages.

Most people who use Windows Live Hotmail and other Webmail providers have Internet access from their employer, school, public library, or friend. The Windows Live Hotmail service is free, but you must have a way to access it using a Web browser and an existing Internet connection, which someone else might supply for you. Many public and school libraries provide free Internet access from which you can access your Windows Live Hotmail account. No matter where you are in the world, if you can connect to the Internet, you can access your Windows Live Hotmail account. This portability makes Webmail a valuable resource for people who travel or do not have a computer or other device on which to send and receive email.

You are eager to begin your evaluation of email services for Kikukawa Air. To begin using Windows Live Hotmail, you need to use your Web browser to connect to the Windows Live Hotmail Web site. Then you can create a user account and send and receive messages.

Creating a Windows Live ID and Hotmail Account

The steps in this session assume that you have a Web browser and can connect to the Internet. Before you can use Windows Live Hotmail, you need to establish a Windows Live ID. If you have an existing Hotmail email address or a Passport, you can use these user names as your Windows Live ID.

To begin setting up a Windows Live ID:

▶ **1.** Start your Web browser, open the Online Companion page at **www.course.com/oc/np/internet7** and log in to your account, click the **Tutorial 2** link, click the **Session 2.4** link, and then click the **Windows Live Hotmail** link. The sign-in page for Windows Live Hotmail opens in your browser. See Figure 2-49.

Windows Live Hotmail sign-in page ◢ **Figure 2-49**

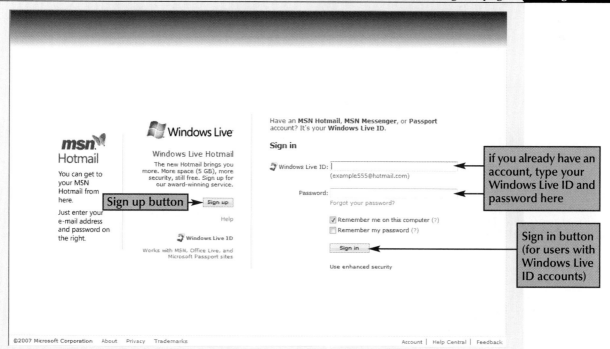

Trouble? The Windows Live Hotmail sign-in page and other Windows Live Hotmail pages might change over time. Check the Online Companion page for Tutorial 2 for notes about any differences you might encounter.

> **Trouble?** You must have an Internet connection to set up a Windows Live ID. If you cannot connect to the Internet, ask your instructor or technical support person for help.
>
> **Trouble?** If you already have a Windows Live ID, MSN Hotmail account, or Passport account, use the Sign in section to enter your Windows Live ID and password, click the Sign in button, and then skip this set of steps.

2. Click the **Sign up** button. (If you do not see a Sign up button, Windows Live Hotmail may have redesigned the Web site. Examine the page carefully until you find the button or tab that lets you create a Windows Live ID or Hotmail account.)

The Windows Live options page shown in Figure 2-50 opens (this page will change over time). Currently, Windows Live offers two types of accounts: Windows Live Hotmail and Windows Live services (including Hotmail). You will create a free Windows Live Hotmail account.

Figure 2-50	Windows Live options page

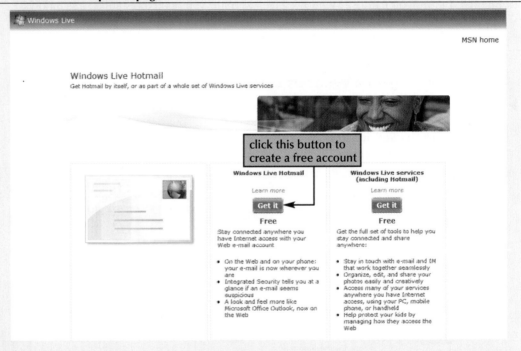

3. Click the **Get it** button for Windows Live Hotmail (or the button that lets you create a free Windows Live Hotmail account). The Sign up for Windows Live page shown in Figure 2-51 opens.

Trouble? If Windows Live Hotmail discontinues its free email service, use the links in the Email Services section of the Online Companion page for Tutorial 2 to create an email account with another provider.

Trouble? The Windows Live sign up page might change over time. If your page looks different, follow the on-screen instructions to create a Windows Live Hotmail account.

The first step in creating a free email account is to create a **Windows Live ID** (Windows Live Hotmail also calls this a sign-in name, an email address, or a Passport), which will be your Windows Live Hotmail email address. A Windows Live ID can contain letters, numbers, or underscore characters (_), but it cannot contain any spaces. After creating a Windows Live ID, you must create a password containing letters and/or numbers, but no spaces. You type your password twice to ensure that you entered it correctly. Finally, to help remember your password in the event that you forget it, you enter a question and its secret answer so Windows Live Hotmail can verify your identity in the future, as necessary.

To finish setting up a Windows Live ID:

▶ **1.** Click in the **Windows Live ID** text box, and then type a user name. You can use any name you like, but it must be unique. You can try your first and last name, separated by an underscore character, followed optionally by your birth date or year of birth, such as sharon_kikukawa0922. Windows Live Hotmail addresses can contain only letters, numbers, periods, hyphens, and underscores.

Trouble? If you need help creating a user name, click the "Get help with this" link on the page to get help.

▶ **2.** Click the **Check availability** button to see if the Windows Live ID you selected is available. A message appears that tells you whether the Windows Live ID you selected is available. If it is not, try a different Windows Live ID until you find one.

Trouble? Do not continue to Step 3 until you find an available Windows Live ID.

▶ **3.** Scroll down the page and type a password with at least six characters in the Type password text box. The most effective passwords are ones that are not easily guessed and that contain letters and numbers. As you type your password, dots or asterisks appear in the Password text box to protect your password from being seen by other users. In addition, the Password strength indicator analyzes the password you typed to identify its strength. A weak password is one that contains only letters, such as "pencil." A stronger password includes letters and numbers, such as "pencil87." The strongest password is one that does not form a word and that includes mixed-case letters, numbers, and special characters, such as "p2nc1L%."

▶ **4.** Press the **Tab** key to move to the Retype password text box, and then type your password again. Make sure to type the same password you typed in Step 3.

▶ **5.** Press the **Tab** key to move to the Alternate e-mail text box. If you have an existing email address, enter it in the Alternate e-mail text box. This is the email address that Windows Live Hotmail will send your password to in case you forget it. If you don't have another email address, don't enter anything in this text box.

▶ **6.** Click the **Question** arrow, and then select a category that you know the answer for.

▶ **7.** Click in the **Secret answer** text box, and then type the answer to your question. Your answer must contain at least five characters.

Now that you have created a Windows Live ID and a password, you need to enter your account information.

To enter your account information:

▶ **1.** Click in the **First name** text box, type your first name, press the **Tab** key to move to the Last name text box, and then type your last name. Your first and last names will appear in all Windows Live Hotmail email messages that you send.

▶ **2.** Click the appropriate **option** button in the Gender section to indicate your gender.

▶ **3.** Click in the **Birth year** text box, and then type the four-digit year of your birth.

▶ **4.** If necessary, click the **Country/Region** arrow, and then click the country or region in which you live.

5. If necessary, click the **State** or **Province** arrow, and then choose the state or province that you live in.

6. If necessary, click in the **ZIP code** or **Province** text box, and then type your zip code or postal code. Windows Live Hotmail will use this information to provide you with additional services, such as local weather forecasts, that you might request in the future.

The last part of creating a Windows Live Hotmail email address is to prove to Windows Live Hotmail that you are a person and not an automated program, and also to read and accept the agreements that govern the use of a Windows Live Hotmail account.

To finish creating a Windows Live Hotmail account:

1. Scroll down the page so that you see characters in a picture. See Figure 2-52.

Required character entry to prevent abuse | Figure 2-52

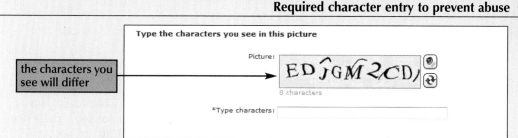

2. Click in the **Type characters** text box, and then type the characters you see in the picture. Make sure to type the characters shown in the picture on your screen. (Do not type the characters you see in Figure 2-52.) This process ensures that a person is creating a Windows Live Hotmail account, instead of an automated program. This registration check protects Windows Live Hotmail users from service delays and from receiving junk email messages.

3. Read the agreements, which appear as hyperlinks in the "Review and accept the agreements" section. After reading these agreements, click the **I accept** button. Your registration is complete when the page shown in Figure 2-53 (or a similar page) opens.

Tip

If you can't read the characters in the picture, click the Refresh button to the right of the box to get a new collection of characters.

Figure 2-53   Choosing the user interface

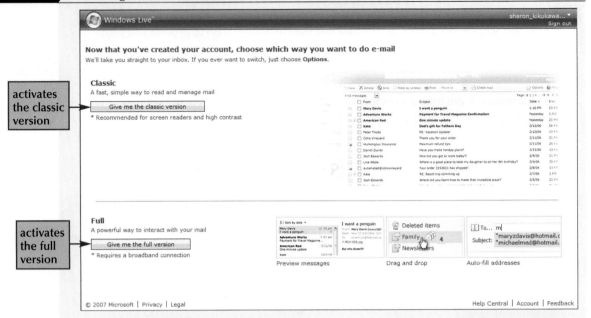

activates the classic version

activates the full version

Trouble? Windows Live Hotmail might redesign its Web site, in which case your screen might not match the one shown in Figure 2-53. If you do not see a page like the one shown in Figure 2-53, or if your page indicates that you did not successfully create a Windows Live Hotmail account, follow the on-screen instructions to correct any identified problems. If you are asked to sign in to your account again, complete the steps to create your account to continue.

Now that you have created a Windows Live ID and an email address, you need to choose which version of Windows Live Hotmail you would like to use. The classic version is recommended for screen readers (which assist visually impaired users) and provides a high contrast. The full version requires a broadband connection and provides additional features not found in the classic version; the steps and figures in this book will show the full version of Windows Live Hotmail. After selecting a version, you can change it later by clicking the Options button on the Inbox page. After choosing a version, Windows Live Hotmail will open your Inbox.

To choose the full version of Windows Live Hotmail, open your Inbox, and sign out of your account:

▶ **1.** Click the **Give me the full version** button. Windows Live Hotmail opens your Inbox. See Figure 2-54.

Windows Live Hotmail Inbox (full version)　　Figure 2-54

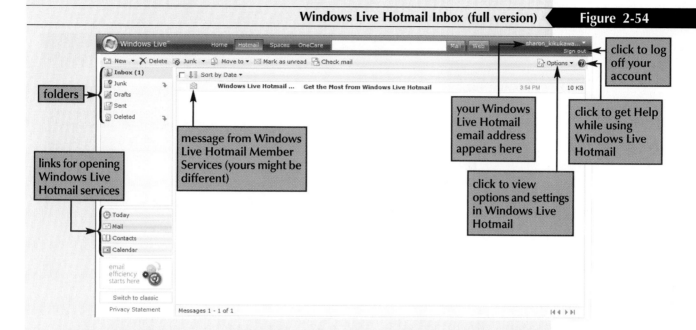

Trouble? The figures in this book show the full version of Windows Live Hotmail. If you choose the classic version of Windows Live Hotmail, you will encounter differences in the steps and figures shown in this book. If you have problems following the steps, ask your instructor or technical support person for help.

So that you can practice signing into your Windows Live Hotmail account, you'll sign out. Signing out closes your account and logs you out of the system. You should always sign out of your account when you have finished working so that other users cannot access your email or send messages using your email address.

2. In the upper-right corner of the window, click the **Sign out** link. The MSN home page (or another page) appears in your browser.

3. Return to the Online Companion page for Tutorial 2, and then click the **Windows Live Hotmail** link. The Windows Live sign-in page opens. See Figure 2-55.

Figure 2-55	Windows Live Hotmail sign-in page

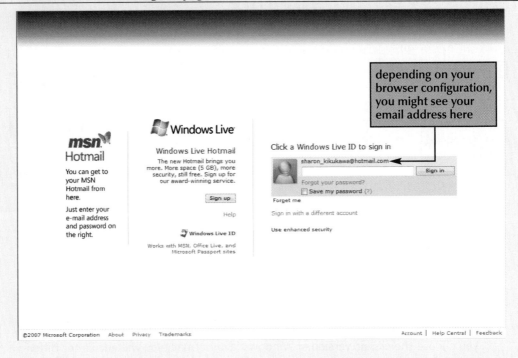

Securing Your Email Account on Private and Public Computers | InSight

Depending on your browser configuration, you might see your email address on the sign-in page for Windows Live Hotmail. If you see your email address, clicking it will open a text box into which you can enter your password and then click the Sign in button to log into your account. If you will be using your Windows Live Hotmail account on your own computer, you might choose to enter your password and then click the Save my password check box to put a check mark in it so you don't have to enter it in the future. This option is the least secure; anyone with access to your computer can log into your account, because your Windows Live ID and password appear automatically in the sign-in page when your browser loads the page.

You might also see someone else's Windows Live ID account information on the page; in this case, you can click the "Sign in with a different account" link to enter your Windows Live ID and password so you can log into your account.

If you forget your password, you can enter your Windows Live Hotmail email address and then click the "Forgot your password?" link. The system will ask you the question you specified when you created your account so you can provide your secret answer. If you also provided a second email address, the system will send your password information or instructions for resetting your password to that email address. If you did not provide a second email address when you signed up for your account, the system will help you reset your password.

Finally, you can use the "Forget me" link to tell your browser not to display your Windows Live ID when it loads this page. This option is the most secure for users who access their email from public computers, because your Windows Live ID and password information are never displayed until you log on to the system. If you choose this option, you can specify how you want the computer to remember you. Clicking the "Remember me on this computer" check box to add a check mark to it remembers your email address; clicking the "Remember my password" check box to add a check mark to it remembers your password. If you clear both check boxes, the computer won't "remember" your email address or your password.

The privacy you expect on the computer you are using to access your Windows Live Hotmail account should help you decide which login method to choose. Always choose the method that provides the most security, so you won't risk having your account accessed by unauthorized users.

Next, you'll log into your Windows Live Hotmail account and open your Inbox.

To log into your Windows Live Hotmail account:

▶ 1. If necessary, click your Windows Live ID or enter it as instructed, type your password, and then click the **Sign in** button. The "Today" page opens and displays current stories from MSN.com.

   Trouble? If you receive a message that your email address or password is not found, clear the Email address and Password text boxes, and then re-enter your information. If you are still having problems, you may have entered your password incorrectly. Click the Forgot your password? link and follow the on-screen directions to retrieve your password, and then try logging into your Windows Live Hotmail account again. If you are still having problems, ask your instructor or technical support person for help.

▶ 2. Click the **Inbox** folder in the Folders pane on the left side of your screen to open your Inbox. You might see one new message from Windows Live Hotmail, welcoming you to the service. (You might see other messages, as well.)

   Trouble? If you don't see a message in the Inbox, skip Step 3.

▶ 3. Click the sender's name to open the message. See Figure 2-56.

Figure 2-56	Message from Windows Live Hotmail

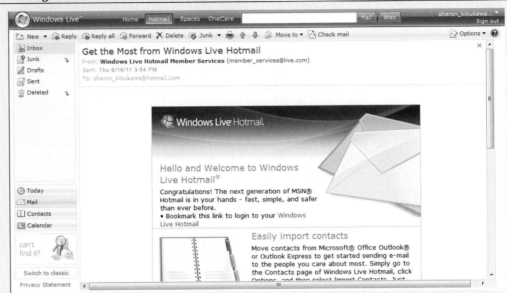

Trouble? Your message might look different from the one shown in Figure 2-56. This difference causes no problems.

Trouble? Depending on your computer's security features, you might see advertisements when you view your email messages. Windows Live Hotmail is a free service; the money that advertisers pay to display their ads makes the Windows Live Hotmail service possible.

Figure 2-56 displays the default mail folders for your account. The **Inbox folder** stores messages you have received, the **Junk folder** stores messages that Windows Live Hotmail thinks are unsolicited, the **Drafts folder** stores messages that you have written but have not sent, the **Sent folder** stores copies of messages that you have sent, and the **Deleted folder** stores messages you have deleted. Figure 2-56 also displays the Today, Mail, Contacts, and Calendar links on the left side of the screen. The **Today page** opens when you log in to your Windows Live Hotmail account. It includes the latest information about the day's current events, your mailbox, and appointments that you have scheduled using your calendar. You can also use the hyperlinks near the bottom of the page to open other pages in the MSN site with information about shopping, finances, and other topics.

The **Mail page** displays a list of messages that you have received and provides options for working with email messages. "Windows Live Hotmail Member Services" might send a message to you with the subject "Get the Most from Windows Live Hotmail" or a similarly worded subject when you first access your Windows Live Hotmail account. As mentioned earlier, the **Folders pane** on the left side of the window shows you how many messages are stored in each of the specified folders. Clicking a folder name in the Folders pane opens that folder and displays its contents.

The **Contacts page** contains options for managing information about your contacts. The **Calendar page** contains options for organizing your scheduled appointments and daily calendar. You can click the Options and Help buttons near the upper-right corner of the page to access pages containing program options and help for Windows Live Hotmail users, respectively.

Now that you have created a Windows Live Hotmail account, you are ready to send a message to Don.

Sending a Message Using Windows Live Hotmail

You are ready to use Windows Live Hotmail to send a message with an attached file to Don. You will also send a courtesy copy of the message to your own email address to simulate receiving a message.

Sending a Message Using Windows Live Hotmail | Reference Window

- Click the Inbox folder, and then click the New button.
- In the To text box, type the recipient's email address. To send the message to more than one recipient, separate additional email addresses with commas or semicolons.
- If you need to address the message to Cc and Bcc recipients, click the Show Cc & Bcc link on the right side of the message header, and then type the email address of any Cc or Bcc recipients in the appropriate text boxes. Separate multiple recipients' email addresses with commas or semicolons.
- If necessary, click the Attach button, click File, browse to and select the file to attach, and then click the Open button.
- Click in the message body, and type your message.
- Check your message for spelling and grammatical errors.
- Click the Send button.

To send a message with an attachment:

1. Click the **New** button. The New Message page opens. See Figure 2-57.

New message created | Figure 2-57

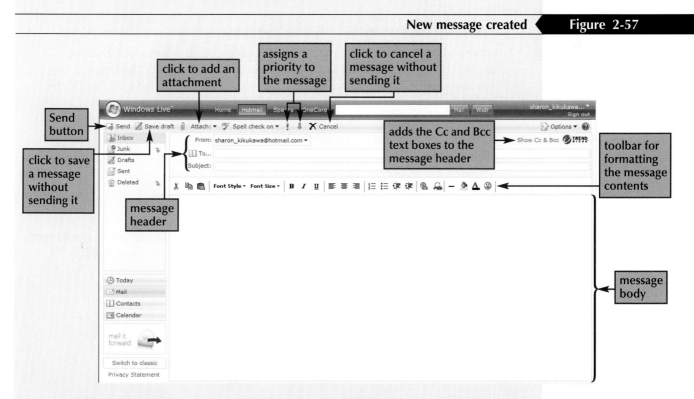

Trouble? Depending on the speed of your Internet connection, it might take a few seconds to load new pages. Check your browser's status bar to make sure that pages have fully loaded before using them.

Trouble? Your screen might look slightly different, depending on your computer's operating system, the browser you are using to access your email, and future changes to the Windows Live Hotmail site. These differences should not affect how Windows Live Hotmail functions.

Trouble? If you don't have the starting Data Files, you need to get them before you can proceed. Your instructor will either give you the Data Files or ask you to obtain them from a specified location (such as a network drive). In either case, make a backup copy of the Data Files before you start so that you will have the original files available in case you need to start over. If you have any questions about the Data Files, see your instructor or technical support person for assistance.

2. In the To text box, type **Don@KikukawaAir.com**.

   Trouble? Make sure that you use the address Don@KikukawaAir.com or its lower-case equivalent, don@kikukawaair.com. If you type an email address incorrectly, your message will be returned as undeliverable.

3. In the right corner of the message header, click the **Show Cc & Bcc** link to add the Cc and Bcc text boxes to the message header.

4. Click in the **Cc** text box, and then type your full email address. When you send this message, you and Don will both receive it.

   Trouble? If you make a typing mistake on a previous line, use the arrow keys or click the insertion point to return to a previous line so you can correct your mistake. If the arrow keys do not move the insertion point backward or forward in the message header, press Shift + Tab or the Tab key to move backward or forward, respectively.

5. Click in the **Subject** text box, and then type **Physicals memo**.

6. Click the **Attach** button, and then click **File**. The Choose file dialog box opens.

   Trouble? If you are using Firefox, click the Browse button that appears below the Subject text box to open the File Upload dialog box, and then continue with Step 7.

7. Browse to the location of your Data Files, double-click the **Tutorial.02** folder, double-click the **Tutorial** folder, click **Physicals**, and then click the **Open** button. The message header now shows the attached file's name and size in the Attachments text box. If you are using Firefox, click the Attach button below the Subject text box to finish attaching the file to the message, and then continue with Step 8. If you omit this step, the file will not be sent with the message.

8. Click in the message display area, type **Dear Don,** (including the comma), and then press the **Enter** key twice to insert a blank line.

9. In the message display area, type **I have attached the memo you requested. Please let me know if you need anything else.**

10. Press the **Enter** key twice, type **Sincerely,** (including the comma), press the **Enter** key, and then type your first name to sign your message. See Figure 2-58.

Completed message ◂ **Figure 2-58**

The default setting for the spell check feature in Windows Live Hotmail is "on," as indicated by the "Spell check on" button. If the spell check is turned on, misspelled words and words not in the dictionary (such as proper names) will appear with a red, wavy underline. When you right-click one of these words, you have the choice of selecting a word from a menu, ignoring the word, or adding it to the dictionary. If you don't see the correct word in the menu, you can correct the misspelled word directly. If you see the "Spell check off" button, Windows Live Hotmail will not flag words it doesn't recognize. In either case, it is still important to read your message and make any necessary corrections before sending it.

▶ **11.** Review your message for typing or grammatical errors, and if necessary, correct any errors.

▶ **12.** Click the **Send** button to mail the message. A message confirmation page opens and shows that your message has been sent. See Figure 2-59.

Figure 2-59   Message confirmation page

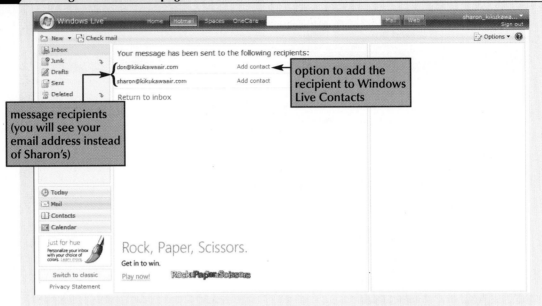

If the email addresses in your message are not already saved in your Windows Live Hotmail contacts, Windows Live Hotmail provides an option for you to add new contacts to your account by selecting the "Add contact" link. If the contact already exists, you'll see an "Already a contact" note. You will add contacts to your account later, so no action is necessary now.

Receiving and Reading a Message

When you receive new mail, messages that you have not opened are displayed with closed envelope icons, and messages that you have opened are displayed with open envelope icons. You check for new mail next.

To check for incoming mail:

1. Click the **Inbox**. The Physicals memo message appears in the Inbox. To read the message, you click it.

2. Click the **Physicals memo** message. The message opens and displays the message header and content. See Figure 2-60.

Message received ◀ Figure 2-60

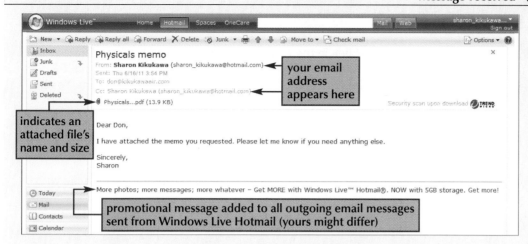

You received your copy of the Physicals memo message that you sent to Don. The file-name in the Attachment section indicates that you received an attached file with the message. When you receive a message with one or more attachments, you can open the attachment or save it.

Viewing and Saving an Attached File

You want to make sure that your attached file was sent properly, so you decide to open it. You then save the file.

| Viewing and Saving an Attached File in Windows Live Hotmail | Reference Window |

- In the Inbox, click the message that contains the attachment.
- To open the file using a program on your computer, click the attached file's name in the message header, and then click the Open button in the File Download dialog box.
- To save the file, click the attached file's name in the message header, click the Save button in the File Download dialog box, browse to the drive and folder in which to save the attached file, click the Save button, and then click the Close button.

To view and save the attached file:

▶ 1. Click the **Physicals.pdf** link in the message header. The File Download dialog box opens.

   Trouble? If you are using Firefox, the dialog box that opens is named Opening Physicals.pdf. Click the Open with option button in the Opening Physicals.pdf dialog box, click the OK button, and then continue with Step 3.

▶ 2. Click the **Open** button. Adobe Reader or another program on your computer starts and opens the attached file. If necessary, maximize the program window that opens.

▶ **3.** Click the **Close** button on the program window's title bar. Now that you have viewed the attachment, you can save it.

Trouble? If a Downloads dialog box is open, click the Close button on its title bar to close it.

▶ **4.** Click the **Physicals.pdf** link in the Attachment section, click the **Save** button, browse to the drive or folder containing your Data Files, open the **Tutorial.02** folder, open the **Tutorial** folder, click the **Save** button, and then click the **Yes** button to overwrite the existing file with the same name.

Trouble? If you are using Firefox, the Opening Physicals.pdf dialog box opens. Click the Save to Disk option button, and then click the OK button. The file is saved on the desktop unless you specified a different folder in which to download files. Move the downloaded Physicals.pdf file from the desktop into the Tutorial.02\Tutorial folder, click the Yes button to overwrite the existing file with the same name, and then skip Step 5.

Trouble? If a Downloads dialog box is open, click the Close button on its title bar to close it.

▶ **5.** If you are using Internet Explorer, click the **Close** button. You return to the message.

| InSight | | **Saving Attachments** |

When you receive a message with an attached file, you can view and save the attachment for as long as you store the message. When you delete the message, you delete the file attached to the message. When you detach a file from an email message and save it on a disk or drive, it is just like any other file that you save. Be sure to save any important attachments soon after receiving them, so you do not inadvertently delete the messages containing them.

Replying to and Forwarding Messages

You can forward any message you receive to one or more email addresses. Similarly, you can respond to the sender of a message quickly and efficiently by replying to a message. Replying to and forwarding messages are common tasks for email users.

Replying to an Email Message

To reply to a message, click the Reply button to reply only to the sender, or click the Reply all button to reply to the sender and other people who received the original message (those email addresses listed in the To and Cc text boxes). Windows Live Hotmail will open a reply message and place the original sender's address in the To text box; other email addresses that received the original message will appear in the To and Cc text boxes as appropriate. You can leave the Subject text box as is or modify it. Most programs, including Windows Live Hotmail, will copy the original message and place it in the response window. The > symbol might appear to the left of the response, or the response might be indented to indicate the text of the original message. Figure 2-61 shows a reply to the Physicals memo message.

Replying to a message | **Figure 2-61**

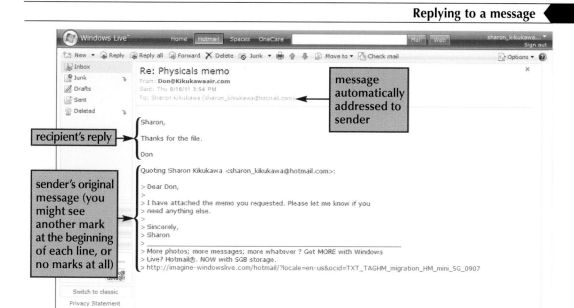

Replying to a Message Using Windows Live Hotmail | Reference Window

- Open the message to which you want to reply.
- Click the Reply button to reply only to the sender, or click the Reply all button to reply to the sender and other "To" and "Cc" recipients of the original message.
- Type other recipients' email addresses in the message header as needed.
- Change the text in the Subject text box if necessary.
- Edit the message body as necessary.
- Click the Send button.

Forwarding an Email Message

When you forward a message, you are sending a copy of your message, including any attachments, to one or more recipients who were not included in the original message. (If you do not want to forward the original sender's attached file to the new recipients, click the Remove link next to the attachment.) To forward an existing mail message to another user, open the message you want to forward, and then click the Forward button. The Forward page opens, where you can type the address of the recipient in the To text box. If you want to forward the message to several people, type their addresses, separated by commas, in the To text box (or Cc or Bcc text boxes). Windows Live Hotmail indents the original message in the message display area and adds a line above it. Figure 2-62 shows a forwarded copy of the Physicals memo message.

Figure 2-62 **Forwarding a message**

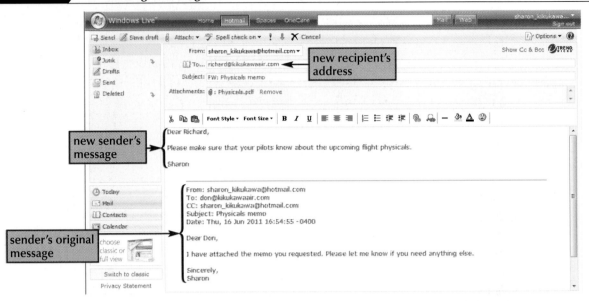

new recipient's address

new sender's message

sender's original message

Forwarding an Email Message Using Windows Live Hotmail

- Open the message that you want to forward.
- Click the Forward button.
- Click the To text box, and then type one or more email addresses, separated by commas. Add Cc and Bcc email addresses as necessary.
- Click the blank line above the quoted message, and then type an optional message to add a context for the recipient(s).
- Click the Send button.

Occasionally, you receive important messages, so you want to make sure that you can file and print them as needed.

Filing and Printing an Email Message

You can use the Windows Live Hotmail folders to file your email messages by category. When you file a message, you move it to another folder. You file your message in a new folder named "FAA" for safekeeping. Later, you can create other folders to suit your style and working situation.

To create the new folder:

1. Click the **Inbox**, click the **New button arrow** to open the menu, and then click **Folder**. A new folder is added with the default name "New folder" selected. See Figure 2-63.

Creating a new folder | Figure 2-63

point to an envelope to display a check box

new folder created

2. With the default folder name selected, type **FAA**, and then press the **Enter** key. The FAA folder appears in the list of folders.

After you create the FAA folder, you can transfer messages to it. Besides transferring mail from the Inbox folder, you can select messages in any other folder and then transfer them to another folder.

To file the Physicals memo message:

1. Point to the envelope icon to the left of the **Physicals memo** message to display a check box, and then click the **check box** to add a check mark to it.

2. Click the **Move to** button, and then click **FAA**. The message is transferred to the FAA folder.

3. Click the **FAA** folder in the Folders pane. The Physicals memo message appears in the FAA folder.

You might want to print certain messages for future reference. You can print a message at any time—when you receive it, before you send it, or after you file it. You print the message next.

To print the email message:

1. Click the **Physicals memo** message to open it.

2. Click the **Print** button. A new window opens and displays a "printer-friendly" version of the message, and the Print dialog box opens.

3. If necessary, select your printer in the list, and then click the **Print** button (or the **OK** button). The message is printed.

4. Close the window with the printer-friendly version of the message, and then click the **Inbox**.

When you no longer need a message, you can delete it.

Deleting an Email Message and Folder

When you don't need a message any longer, you can delete it by opening the message and clicking the Delete button. You can delete a folder by selecting it and then clicking the Delete button. When you delete a message or folder, you are simply moving it to the Deleted folder. The default setting for Windows Live Hotmail accounts is for the system to periodically delete all messages in the Deleted folder. However, if you want to remove items permanently and right away, you can delete them from the Deleted folder.

Reference Window | **Deleting an Email Message Using Windows Live Hotmail**

- Open the folder that contains the message you want to delete, point to the envelope icon to display a check box, click the check box to add a check mark to it, and then click the Delete button.
- To delete items permanently, right-click the Deleted folder to open the shortcut menu, click Empty folder, and then click the Yes button.

To delete the message:

▶ **1.** Click the **FAA** folder in the Folders section.

▶ **2.** Point to the envelope icon for the Physicals memo message, and then click the **check box** that appears to add a check mark to it. This action selects the message.

▶ **3.** Click the **Delete** button. The message is deleted from the FAA folder and is moved to the Deleted folder.

▶ **4.** Click the **Deleted** folder in the Folders pane. The Physicals memo message appears in the folder.

▶ **5.** Point to the envelope icon for the Physicals memo message so it changes to a check box, click the **check box** to add a check mark to it, and then click the **Delete** button. The Physicals memo message is deleted from the Deleted folder.

To delete the FAA folder, you follow a similar process.

Reference Window | **Deleting a Windows Live Hotmail Folder**

- Right-click the folder you want to delete to open the shortcut menu.
- Click Delete folder on the shortcut menu.
- Click the Yes button.

To delete the FAA folder:

▶ **1.** Click the **FAA** folder in the Folders section. The FAA folder is empty.

▶ **2.** Right-click the **FAA** folder to open the shortcut menu, and then click **Delete folder**. A dialog box opens and warns that deleting the folder also deletes any messages stored in the folder.

▶ **3.** Click the **OK** button. The FAA folder is deleted.

Maintaining Windows Live Contacts

As you use email to communicate with business associates and friends, you might want to save their addresses in an address book to make it easier to enter addresses into the header of your email messages. In Windows Live Hotmail, the address book is called **Windows Live Contacts**.

Adding a Contact to Windows Live Contacts

You can open the Windows Live Contacts by clicking the Contacts link. To create a new contact, click the New button, and then use the text boxes to enter a contact's information.

Adding a Contact to Windows Live Contacts | Reference Window

- Click the Contacts link.
- Click the New button.
- Enter the contact's information in the appropriate text boxes on the Edit contact details page.
- Click the Save button.

Now you can add information to your address book. You begin by adding Jenny Mahala's contact information to Windows Live Contacts.

To add a contact to Windows Live Contacts:

▶ 1. Click the **Contacts** link.

▶ 2. Click the **New** button. The Edit contact details page opens and displays text boxes for entering a contact's first name, last name, nickname, personal email address, Windows Live ID, and mobile phone number. Clicking the Show all fields link opens a more detailed page that you can use to enter other information about a contact, such as business contact information and a birth date.

▶ 3. Click in the **First name** text box, and then type **Jenny**.

▶ 4. Press the **Tab** key, type **Mahala** in the Last name text box, and then press the **Tab** key to move to the Nickname text box.

▶ 5. Type **Jen**, and then press the **Tab** key to move to the Personal e-mail text box.

▶ 6. Type **Jenny@KikukawaAir.com**. Jen's contact is complete. See Figure 2-64.

> **Tip**
>
> Clicking the New button opens a new contact. Clicking the New button arrow lets you create a new message, folder, contact, or group.

Adding a contact to Windows Live Contacts ◀ **Figure 2-64**

▶ **7.** Click the **Save** button. Jen's information appears as a contact.

▶ **8.** Repeat Steps 2 through 7 to create new contacts for the following Kikukawa Air employees:

First	Last	Nickname	Email Address
Zane	Norcia	Zane	Zane@KikukawaAir.com
Richard	Forrester	Rich	Richard@KikukawaAir.com

Now that these email addresses are stored in Windows Live Contacts, you can click the Choose a contact button that appears to the left of a To, Cc, or Bcc text box in a new message, and then click a name in the Contacts list to enter that person's email address in the message header.

When you send mail to someone who is not in Windows Live Contacts, the message confirmation page includes an "Add contact" link that you can click to add the contact to Windows Live Contacts.

Adding a Group to Windows Live Contacts

You can use Windows Live Contacts to create a group. Usually, you create a group when you regularly send messages to a specific group of people.

For example, Sharon frequently sends messages to Zane, Jen, and Rich as a group, because they have the same positions at the Kikukawa Air ticket counters. She asks you to create a group in Windows Live Contacts so she can type one nickname for the group of email addresses, instead of having to type each address separately.

Reference Window | **Adding a Group to Windows Live Contacts**

- Click the Contacts link.
- Click the New button arrow, and then click Group.
- Type a group name for the group, and then press the Enter key.
- Click the first member of the group in the Contacts list, click the Add to group button, and then click the group name to add the contact to the group. Continue adding contacts to the group until you have entered all contacts to the group.

To add a group to Windows Live Contacts:

▶ **1.** Click the **Contacts** link, click the **New button arrow**, and then click **Group**. A new group is created using the default name "New group."

▶ **2.** Type **Ticket Agents** as the group name, and then press the **Enter** key. The group has zero in parentheses to its right to show that the group has no contacts.

▶ **3.** In the Contacts list, click **Jen** to select this contact, click the **Add to group** button, and then click **Ticket Agents**. Jen is added to the group. Notice that the number in parentheses to the right of the group name changes to 1, indicating that the group has one contact.

▶ **4.** In the Contacts list, click **Rich**, click the **Add to group** button, and then click **Ticket Agents**. Rich is the second contact in the group.

▶ **5.** Repeat Step 4 to add **Zane** to the Ticket Agents group.

▶ **6.** Click the **Ticket Agents** group. The group contains three contacts. See Figure 2-65.

Group added to Windows Live Contacts — Figure 2-65

Now, test the new group by creating a new message.

To address a message to a group:

1. Click the **Mail** link, and then click the **Inbox** folder.

2. Click the **New** button.

3. Click the **Choose a contact** button to the left of the To text box, and then click **"Ticket Agents"** in the list. The Ticket Agents nickname is added to the To text box. The menu stays open until you close it, so you can add additional recipients to the message if necessary.

4. Click the **Close** button on the Contacts list.

5. Click the **Show Cc & Bcc** link to add the Cc and Bcc text boxes to the message header.

6. Click the **Choose a contact** button to the left of the Cc text box, click your email address in the list, and then close the Contacts list. Your email address is added to the Cc text box. See Figure 2-66.

Using Windows Live Contacts to address a message — Figure 2-66

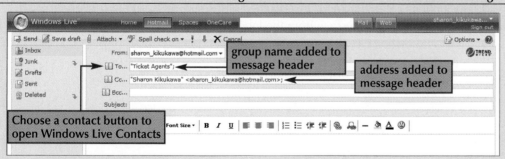

7. Click the **Cancel** button to cancel the message, click the **OK** button in the message box asking you to confirm discarding the message (if necessary), and then click the **Inbox** folder.

When you need to modify a group's members, you can do so by clicking the Contacts link, clicking the group's nickname, and then using the Edit, Delete, Remove from group, and Add to group buttons to change details about the group, delete the group (but not the individual contacts), remove individual contacts from the group, or to add new contacts to the group, respectively.

You are finished evaluating Windows Live Hotmail, so you need to log off your Windows Live Hotmail account and close your browser. It is important that you log off before closing the browser to ensure the security of your email and to prevent unauthorized access. Your Windows Live Hotmail account is active if you use it. If you do not sign into your Windows Live Hotmail account within 10 days after creating it, or for 120 days at any point after that, your account will become inactive. If you do not sign in to your Windows Live Hotmail account for more than 210 days, it is permanently deleted.

To log off Windows Live Hotmail and close your browser:

▶ **1.** Click the **Sign out** link near the upper-right corner of the page. The MSN.com home page (or another Web page) opens.

▶ **2.** Click the **Close** button on your browser's title bar to close the browser.

In this session, you learned how to use Windows Live Hotmail to create, send, receive, and manage email messages. You also learned how to create and use Windows Live Contacts to manage information about contacts.

Review | **Session 2.4 Quick Check**

1. To set up a Windows Live Hotmail account, what information must you provide?
2. True or False: If you are using a computer in a public library to access your Windows Live Hotmail account, you should log off your account when you are finished viewing your messages to protect your privacy.
3. Does Windows Live Hotmail queue a message or send it right away?
4. When you receive a message with an attachment in Windows Live Hotmail, what two options are available for the attached file?
5. When you delete a message from the Inbox, can you recover it? Why or why not?
6. What information can you store about a person using Windows Live Contacts?

Tutorial Summary | Review

In this tutorial, you learned how to use email as a form of communication and how to send and receive email messages. You also learned how to print, file, save, delete, respond to, and forward email messages. You created an address book into which you stored the name, email address, and other important details about a person or a group of people. Now that you have learned these important skills, you can use the email program of your choice to send and receive your own email messages. As you use your email program, expand your skills by using its Help system to explore the many other features that it includes.

Key Terms

Common Terms
address book
attachment
blind courtesy copy (Bcc)
bulk mail
courtesy copy (Cc)
detaching
electronic mail
email
email address
email program
emoticon
filter
forward
From line
Gmail
group
IMAP (Internet Message
    Access Protocol)
junk mail
kilobyte (KB)
mail client software
mail server
message body
message header
MIME (Multipurpose
    Internet Mail
    Extensions)
Mozilla Thunderbird
netiquette
nickname

Opera Mail
POP (Post Office Protocol)
POP message
POP3 message
protocol
queued
quoted message
read-only
reply
Saved Search folder
signature file
SMTP (Simple Mail
    Transfer Protocol)
spam
Subject line
To line
unsolicited commercial
    email (UCE)
user name
virus
Webmail
Webmail provider

Outlook Express
Contacts list
Deleted Items folder
Drafts folder
Folders list
Inbox folder
message list
Microsoft Outlook Express

Outbox folder
Outlook Express
preview pane
Sent Items folder

Windows Mail
Deleted Items folder
Drafts folder
Folders list
Inbox folder
message list
Microsoft Windows Mail
Outbox folder
Preview pane
Sent Items folder
Windows Contacts
Windows Mail

Windows Live Hotmail
Calendar page
Contacts page
Deleted folder
Drafts folder
Inbox folder
Junk folder
Mail page
Sent folder
Today page
Windows Live Contacts
Windows Live Hotmail
Windows Live ID

| Practice | Review Assignments |

Practice the skills you learned in the tutorial using the same case scenario.

Data File needed for the Review Assignments: KAir.gif

Now that you have learned about different types of email programs, Sharon asks you to submit a recommendation about which program to use for Kikukawa Air. Sharon also wants to see how graphics are sent over the Internet, so she asks you to send her the Kikukawa Air logo to simulate how it will appear when sent by Kikukawa Air employees. To evaluate email alternatives for Sharon, complete the following steps.

1. Start your email program or log on to your Webmail provider.
2. Add your instructor's full name and email address and Sharon Kikukawa's full name and email address (Sharon@KikukawaAir.com) to the address book. Create an appropriate nicknames that will be easy for you to remember.
3. Add a group contact to the address book using the full names and email addresses of three of your classmates. Create appropriate nicknames for each person.
4. Create a new message. Use nicknames to send the message to Sharon and to your instructor. Send a courtesy copy of the message to yourself, and use the group contact you created to send a blind courtesy copy of the message to your classmates. Use the subject **Email Recommendation** for the message.
5. In the message body, type three or more sentences describing your overall impressions about the different email programs or services that you have learned about in this tutorial. Recommend the program that Kikukawa Air should use based on the program's features, ease of use, and other important considerations that you determine.
6. In the message body, press the Enter key twice, and then type your full name and email address on separate lines.
7. Attach the file named **KAir.gif**, from the Tutorial.02\Review folder included with your Data Files, to the message.
8. Check your spelling before you send the message and correct any mistakes. Proofread your message and verify that you have created it correctly, and then send the message.
9. Wait about one minute, check for new mail (enter your password, if necessary), and then open the message you sent to Sharon and your instructor. Print the message.
10. Forward the message and the attached file to only your instructor. In the message body, describe the appearance of the file you attached to the message and explain your findings in terms of attaching a graphic to an email message. Send the message.
11. Permanently delete the messages you received and *sent* from your email program. (*Hint:* Delete messages from the folder where you receive messages and also from the folder that stores a copy of all sent messages. Make sure to delete messages from the folder that stores your deleted messages, as well.)
12. Exit your email program or log off your Webmail provider.

Apply | Case Problem 1

Apply the skills you learned to save an email message to a file.

There are no Data Files needed for this Case Problem.

Worldwide Golf Resorts   Worldwide Golf Resorts is a corporation based in Kansas City, Missouri that owns and operates golf resorts in 22 countries worldwide. These resorts are popular destinations for people on vacation, and two of them host annual professional golf tournaments. You work for the regional vice president, Michael Pedersen, and handle all of his business correspondence. The Information Technology department just installed Michael's new computer, and now you need to send a test message to make sure that Michael's email account is working correctly. You will create and send the message by completing the following steps.

1. Start your email program or log on to your Webmail provider.
2. Add to your address book the full name, nickname, and email address of your instructor and two classmates.
3. Create a group contact for the two classmates you added to the address book in Step 2 using the nickname **managers**.
4. Create a new message addressed to your instructor. On the Cc line, enter the group nickname you added to the address book in Step 3. On the Bcc line, enter your email address. Use the subject **Worldwide Golf Resorts test message**.
5. In the message display area, type a short note telling the recipients that you are sending a message for Michael and ask them to respond to you when they receive your message. Sign your message with your first and last names.
6. Send the message, wait a minute, and then retrieve your messages from the server. Print the message you sent to your instructor.

✪ **EXPLORE**
7. If you are using Outlook Express or Windows Mail, save the message in the Tutorial.02\Cases folder included with your Data Files, using the message's subject as the filename. Choose the option to save the file in HTML format.
8. Create a mail folder or mailbox named **Golf**, and then file the message you received in the Golf folder.

✪ **EXPLORE**
9. Permanently delete the messages you received and *sent* from your email program and the Golf folder. (*Hint:* Delete the folder and message, delete the message you sent from the folder that stores sent messages, and then empty the folder that stores deleted items.)
10. Exit your email program or log off your Webmail provider.

Challenge | Case Problem 2

Use the Help system for your email program to learn how to create a signature for your outgoing email messages.

There are no Data Files needed for this Case Problem.

Grand American Appraisal Company You are the office manager for Grand American Appraisal Company, a national real-estate appraisal company with its corporate headquarters in Los Angeles. Grand American handles appraisal requests from all over the United States and maintains a large list of approved real-estate appraisers located throughout the country. When an appraisal request is phoned into any regional office, an office staff member phones or faxes the national office to start the appraisal process. The appraisal order desk in Los Angeles receives the request and is responsible for locating an appraiser in the community in which the property to be appraised is located. After the Los Angeles office identifies and contacts an appraiser by phone, the appraiser has two days to perform the appraisal and either phone or fax the regional office with a preliminary estimate of the property's value. The process of phoning the regional office and then phoning or faxing the national office is both cumbersome and expensive.

Your supervisor asks you to use your email program to set up an account for yourself so you can use email for the appraisal requests instead of the current fax system. You will create a signature file to attach to your messages that identifies your name, city, email address, and appraiser license number by completing the following steps.

1. Start your email program or log on to your Webmail provider.
2. Obtain the email address of a classmate, who will assume the role of the Los Angeles order desk. Add your classmate's full name, nickname, and email address to the address book.
3. Add your instructor's full name, nickname, and email address to the address book.
4. Use your classmate's nickname to address a new message to him or her. Type your email address and your instructor's nickname in the Cc line, and then type **Request for appraisal** in the Subject line.
5. Type a short message that requests the assignment of an appraiser. Include your street address and the request date in the message.

⊕ EXPLORE
6. Use the Help system to learn how to create a signature file with your first and last names on the first line, your city and state on the second line, your email address on the third line, and **License number** plus any six-digit number on the fourth line. (*Hint:* If you are using Outlook Express or Windows Mail, search Help using the Index tab for **signatures, personal** and then follow the directions. If you are using Windows Live Hotmail, click the Options button, click More options in the list, and then click the Personal e-mail signature link to create a signature.)

⊕ EXPLORE
7. Include your signature in the new message. (*Hint:* In Outlook Express or Windows Mail, click Insert on the menu bar, and then click Signature. Windows Live Hotmail will attach your signature file automatically.)

8. Send the message, wait a minute, and then retrieve your messages from the server. Print the message you sent to your classmate.

⊕ EXPLORE
9. Permanently delete the messages you received and *sent* from your email program. (*Hint:* Delete the message from the folder where you receive messages and also from the folder that stores a copy of all sent messages. Make sure to delete messages from the folder that stores your deleted messages, as well.)

⊕ EXPLORE
10. If you are using Outlook Express or Windows Mail, delete your signature. (*Hint:* Select your signature on the Signatures tab in the Options dialog box, and then click the Remove button.)

11. Exit your email program or log off your Webmail provider.

Challenge | Case Problem 3

Use the Help system for your email program to learn how to create a signature for your outgoing email messages.

Data File needed for this Case Problem: Recycle.pdf

Recycling Awareness Campaign   You are an assistant in the Mayor's office in Cleveland, Ohio. The mayor has asked you to help with the recycling awareness campaign. Your job is to use email to increase awareness of the recycling centers throughout the city and to encourage Cleveland's citizens and businesses to participate in the program. You will send an email message to members of the city's chamber of commerce with an invitation to help increase awareness of the program by forwarding your message and its attached file to their employees and colleagues by completing the following steps.

1. Start your email program or log on to your Webmail provider.
2. Add the full names, email addresses, and nicknames of five classmates to your address book to act as chamber of commerce members. After creating individual entries in the address book for your classmates, add them to a group contact named **Chamber** in your address book. Then add the full name, email address, and nickname of your instructor to your address book.
3. Create a new message and address it to the Chamber group. Add your instructor's nickname to the Cc line and your email address to the Bcc line. Use the subject **Recycling campaign for businesses**.

⊕ **EXPLORE**   4. Write a two- or three-line message urging the chamber members to promote the city's new business recycling campaign by forwarding your message and the attached file to local businesses. Make sure to thank them for their efforts on behalf of the Mayor's office.

5. Attach the file named **Recycle.pdf**, located in the Tutorial.02\Cases folder included with your Data Files, to the message.

⊕ **EXPLORE**   6. Use the Help system in your email program to learn how to create and use a signature file. Your signature should include your full name on the first line, the title **Assistant to the Mayor** on the second line, and your email address on the third line. (*Hint:* If you are using Outlook Express or Windows Mail, search Help using the Index tab for **signatures, personal** and then follow the directions. If you are using Windows Live Hotmail, click the Options button, click More options in the list, and then click the Personal e-mail signature link to create a signature.)

⊕ **EXPLORE**   7. Include your signature file in the new message. (*Hint:* In Outlook Express or Windows Mail, click Insert on the menu bar, and then click Signature. Windows Live Hotmail will attach your signature file automatically.)

8. Proofread and spell check your message, and then send your message. After a few moments, retrieve your email message from the server and print it.
9. Forward the message to one of the classmates in your address book. Add a short message to the forwarded message that asks the recipient to forward the message to appropriate business leaders per your program objectives.

⊕ **EXPLORE**   10. Save a *copy* of your message in a new subfolder of the Inbox named **Recycling**, and then delete the message from the Inbox.

⊕ **EXPLORE**   11. Permanently delete the messages you received and *sent* from your email program and the Recycling folder. (*Hint:* Delete the folder and message, delete the message you sent from the folder that stores sent messages, and then empty the folder that stores deleted items.)

12. If you are using Outlook Express or Windows Mail, delete your signature file. (*Hint:* Select your signature on the Signatures tab in the Options dialog box, and then click the Remove button.)
13. Exit your email program or log off your Webmail provider.

Apply | Case Problem 4

Apply the skills you learned in this tutorial to create a group contact for a group of students.

There are no Data Files needed for this Case Problem.

Student Study Group   In two weeks, you have a final exam, and you want to organize a study group with your classmates. Everyone in your class has an email account provided by your school. You want to contact some classmates to find out when they might be available to get together in the next week to study for the exam. To create a study group, you will complete the following steps.

1. Start your email program or log on to your Webmail provider.
2. Obtain the email addresses of at least four classmates, and then enter them in the To line of a new message. In the Cc line, enter your email address, and then in the Bcc line, enter your instructor's email address. Do *not* add these names to your address book.
3. Use the subject **Study group** for the message. In the message body, tell your classmates about the study group by providing possible meeting times and locations. Ask recipients to respond to you through email by a specified date if they are interested. Sign the message with your full name and email address.
4. Proofread and spell check your message, and then send your message. After a few moments, retrieve your email message from the server and open it.
5. Add each address in the To and Cc lines to your address book.
6. Create a new group contact named **study group** using the addresses you added to your address book in Step 5. Then forward a copy of your message to the study group.
7. Send your message. After a few moments, retrieve your email message from the server and print it.

⊕ **EXPLORE**
8. Permanently delete the messages you received and *sent* from your email program. (*Hint:* Delete the messages from the Inbox, delete the message you sent from the folder that stores sent messages, and then empty the folder that stores deleted items.)
9. Exit your email program or log off your Webmail provider.

Create | Case Problem 5

Expand the skills you learned in this tutorial to create a document that you can send to a group of recipients as an email attachment.

There are no Data Files needed for this Case Problem.

Murphy's Market Research Services   You work part-time for Murphy's Market Research Services, a company that surveys students about various topics of interest to college students. A local music store, CD Rocks, wants you to send a short survey via email to students at your university to learn more about student-buying habits for music CDs. You need to find out the names of three of their favorite music CDs, where they prefer to shop for music CDs, and how much time they spend each day listening to music. You will create the survey using any word-processing program, such as Microsoft Word, WordPad, or WordPerfect, and then you will attach the survey to your email message. You need to receive the survey results within three weeks, so you will ask the respondents to return the survey via email within that time period. You will create and send the survey by completing the following steps.

1. Using any word-processing program, create a new document named **Survey** and save it with the program's default filename extension in the Tutorial.02\Cases folder included with your Data Files.

2. Create the survey by typing the following questions (separate each question with two blank lines) in the new document:

   a. What are the titles of your three favorite music CDs?

   b. Where is the best place (online or retail) to shop for music CDs?

   c. Approximately how much time per day do you spend listening to music?

3. At the bottom of the document, type a sentence that thanks respondents for their time, and then on a new line, type your first and last names. Save the document, and then close your word-processing program.

4. Start your email program or log on to your Webmail provider.

5. Obtain the email addresses of three classmates, and then enter them in the To line of a new message. In the Cc line, enter your email address, and then in the Bcc line, enter your instructor's email address. Do *not* add these names to your address book.

6. Use the subject **Music survey** for the message. In the message body, ask recipients to open the attached file and to complete the survey by typing their responses into the document. Make sure that recipients understand that you need them to return the survey within three weeks. As an incentive for completing the survey, ask recipients to return the survey via email but to print their completed survey and bring it to their local CD Rocks outlet for a $2 discount on any purchase. Sign the message with your full name, the company name (Murphy's Market Research Services), and your email address.

7. Attach the survey to your email message, and then send the message. After a few moments, retrieve your email message from the server.

⊕ **EXPLORE**　8. Open the attached file, and then complete the survey. Before saving the file, use your word-processing program's Print command to print the document.

⊕ **EXPLORE**　9. In your word-processing program, click File on the menu bar, and then click Save As. Browse to the Tutorial.02\Cases folder included with your Data Files and then save the file as **Completed Survey**, using the program's default filename extension. Close your word-processing program.

10. Forward the message to your instructor, attach the **Completed Survey** file to the message, make sure that the original message text appears in the message body, type a short introduction (such as "Here is my completed survey."), sign your message with your full name and email address, and then send the message.

⊕ **EXPLORE**　11. Permanently delete the messages you received and *sent* from your email program. (*Hint:* Delete the messages from the Inbox, delete the message you sent from the folder that stores sent messages, and then empty the folder that stores deleted items.)

12. Exit your email program or log off your Webmail provider.

Student Edition Labs

The interactive Student Edition Lab **Email** is designed to help you master some of the key concepts and skills presented in this tutorial, including:

- sending and receiving email messages
- replying to email messages
- storing and deleting email messages

This lab is available online and can be accessed from the Tutorial 2 Web page on the Online Companion at www.course.com/oc/np/internet7.

Session 2.1

1. protocols
2. message header, message body, signature
3. False
4. Yes; you can attach the Word document file to an email message.
5. The user name identifies a specific individual, and the domain name identifies the computer on which that individual's account is stored.
6. By deleting unnecessary messages, you clear space on the drive or server on which your email messages are stored.
7. A folder that contains a saved search; clicking the folder runs the search and finds all messages that match the search criteria. This feature is available in Thunderbird.

Session 2.2

1. Drafts
2. True
3. Outlook Express holds messages that are queued until you connect to your ISP and click the Send/Recv button on the toolbar.
4. You can view the attached file if your computer has a program that can open it, or you can save the attached file on your computer.
5. Yes, you can recover the message because it is stored in the Deleted Items folder.
6. name, email address, nickname, address, business information, personal information, and so on

Session 2.3

1. Drafts
2. True
3. Windows Mail holds messages that are queued until you connect to your ISP and click the Send/Receive button on the toolbar.
4. You can view the attached file if your computer has a program that can open it, or you can save the attached file on your computer.
5. Yes, you can recover the message because it is stored in the Deleted Items folder.
6. name, email address, nickname, address, business information, personal information, and so on

Session 2.4

1. Your name, preferred language, country, state, zip code, time zone, gender, and birth date; you must also submit a unique sign-in name, a password, and a secret question and answer.
2. True
3. Windows Live Hotmail sends messages right away because all work is completed with a live Internet connection.
4. You can view the attached file if your computer has a program that can open it, or you can save the attached file on your computer.
5. Yes, you can recover the message because it is stored in the Trash Can folder.
6. name, email address, nickname, address, business information, personal information, and so on

Reality Check

In Tutorials 1 and 2, you learned that every computer on the Internet has a unique IP address, and that this IP address is more commonly called a domain name. When you use a Web browser to load a Web page or an email program to send and receive email messages, you use the domain name as a way of identifying the Web site or email address that you need.

In Tutorial 1, you learned that the not-for-profit organization that coordinates and ensures unique domain names and IP addresses on the Internet is ICANN. ICANN is also responsible for accrediting domain name registrars. A **registrar** is a for-profit organization that collects information about new or renewed domains and submits information about it to a database of all Internet domain names, called the **registry**. The registry contains the necessary information to associate a specific domain name with an IP address, and to connect this information to a specific computer. The registry also contains information that delivers email messages sent to a domain to the correct computer.

Some registrars simply register a domain for a yearly fee; other registrars register the domain and offer additional services, such as Web site hosting and creation or email forwarding. Because registrars often provide different services, the amount that you pay to register a domain differs. Some registrars will provide a free yearly domain name when you use the registrar to host a Web site. When you purchase a domain name, you might choose to purchase it for one year. Some registrars offer discounted annual fees when you purchase a domain for longer than one year. However, ICANN does not permit registrars to sell domain names for longer than a period of 10 years at a time.

When you use a registrar to register a domain, you must provide your contact information. This information is stored in the registry; some registrars offer additional services so that your information is held private in the registry for an additional fee. The domain is registered for you for the duration of the registration term. At the end of the registration term, the domain will expire. Before a domain expires, most registrars will contact the domain name owner using the information that was collected during registration. When the domain expires, you have the choice of renewing it or relinquishing it. Some registrars provide additional services to prevent the loss of a domain name when it expires. If you fail to renew a domain name, the Web site you host at that domain and all email accounts associated with it might be deleted from the Internet. In some cases, another person or organization might purchase the domain and associate it with its Web site, causing you to lose access to your site and all email sent to it.

ICANN maintains a list of accredited registrars on its Web site. When you purchase a domain through an accredited registrar, you are protected by certain legal rights about how your domain name will be registered and protected. ICANN has accredited over 800 registrars that can register a domain name. Some registrars are not accredited directly by ICANN because they are resellers of domain names from accredited registrars. ICANN suggests working with accredited registrars for maximum consumer protection.

In this exercise, you'll use the Internet to learn more about how to register a domain name that you can use for a Web site and email accounts. You will send an email to your instructor summarizing your findings.

1. Start your Web browser, open the Online Companion page at **www.course.com/oc/np/internet7** and log in to your account, click the Tutorial 2 link, and then click the Reality Check link.

2. Click the ICANN FAQs link and wait while your browser opens the Web page. Read the information on the page to learn more about what it means to register a domain and how to register a domain. In an email message addressed to your instructor, describe how to register a domain.

3. Return to the Online Companion page for Tutorial 2, and then click the Network Solutions Registry Whois link to open the Web page. Read the information provided on this page to learn about the Whois service. In your email message to your instructor, describe the Whois service.

4. Click in the Search WHOIS domain name registration records for this term text box on the page, enter the domain name **course.com**, make sure the Domain Name option button is selected, and then click the Search WHOIS button. In your email message to your instructor, note the name of the registrant for this domain and when the domain record expires.

5. Near the top of the page, click the E-Mail link to open a page that contains information about email hosting services. In your email message to your instructor, describe the features that are provided with email hosting services.

6. Use your browser's Back button to return to the WHOIS page, and then enter your full name, followed by a period and the top-level domain **com** in the Search WHOIS domain name registration records for this term text box. Make sure that the Domain Name option button is selected, and then click the Search WHOIS button. Is the domain name available? If not, who owns it and when does it expire? Add this information to your email message to your instructor.

7. Add your full email address to the Cc line of your message and an appropriate subject, and then send the message.

8. Close your Web browser.

Objectives

Session 3.1
- Determine whether a research question is specific or exploratory
- Learn how to formulate an effective Web search strategy to answer research questions
- Learn how to use Web search engines, Web directories, and Web metasearch engines effectively

Session 3.2
- Use Boolean logic and filtering techniques to improve your Web searches
- Use advanced search options in Web search engines
- Assess the validity and quality of Web research resources
- Learn about the future of Web search tools

Searching the Web

Using Search Engines and Directories Effectively

Case | International Executive Reports

International Executive Reports (IER) is a company that publishes a variety of weekly newsletters, monthly reports, and annual reviews of major trends in economic conditions and management developments. IER's clients are top-level managers and other people who serve on the governing boards of large companies and not-for-profit organizations. IER publications are mailed or emailed to subscribers. The subscription rates range from $300 to $900 per year.

The IER writing staff provides content for all of its publications. In some cases, content that is developed for one publication is edited and used in other publications. Anne Hill, the managing director for content at IER, has recruited an excellent staff of editors, writers, and researchers who work together to create a wide variety of content. Anne has hired you to fill an intern position on the research staff. Your job will involve conducting online research and fact-checking for two of the staff writers, Dave Burton and Ranjit Singh. Dave is an international business specialist and Ranjit is an economist who writes about current economic trends.

You are just learning to use the Web yourself, but Anne is counting on you to become skilled in conducting Web searches. She can help you with questions you might have as you find your way around the Web.

Starting Data Files

There are no starting Data Files needed for this tutorial.

Session 3.1

Types of Search Questions

Dave and Ranjit will need different kinds of help because of their different writing goals. Dave will need quick answers to specific questions. For example, he might need to know the population of Bolivia or the languages spoken in Thailand. Ranjit will be looking for help finding new perspectives and a wide range of information on broad topics. For example, he might need you to find Web sites that contain collections of research papers that discuss the causes of the Great Depression.

Dave uses the Internet to obtain information about every country in the world and do background research on most major businesses and industries. To support Dave, you need to be able to "get the facts."

Ranjit writes longer, more thought-provoking pieces about broad economic and business issues and will count on you to provide him with new ideas that he can explore in his columns. The Web is a good place to find unusual and interesting views on the economy and general business practices. Ranjit needs you to use the Web as a source of interesting concepts and new angles on old ideas, rather than as a place to find fast answers to specific questions.

You can use the Web to obtain answers to both of these question types—specific and exploratory—but each requires a different search strategy. A **specific question** is a question that you can phrase easily and one for which you will recognize the answer when you find it. In other words, you will know when to end your search. The search process for a specific question is one of narrowing the field down to the answer you seek. In contrast, an **exploratory question** is an open-ended question that can be harder to phrase; it also is difficult to determine when you find a good answer. The search process for an exploratory question requires you to fan out in a number of directions to find relevant information.

Specific questions require you to start with broad categories of information and gradually narrow the search until you find the answer to your question. Figure 3-1 shows this process of sequential, increasingly focused questions.

| Figure 3-1 | Specific research question search process |

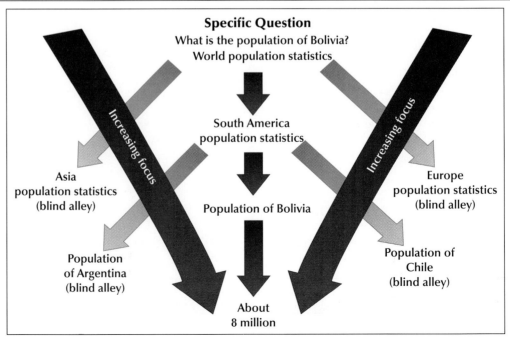

As you narrow your search, you might find that you are heading in the wrong direction or down a blind alley. In that case, you need to move back up the funnel shown in Figure 3-1 and try another path.

An exploratory search starts with general questions that lead to other, less general questions. The answers to the questions at each level should lead you to more information about the topic in which you are interested. This information then leads you to more questions. Figure 3-2 shows how this questioning process leads to a broadening scope as you gather information pertinent to the exploratory question.

Exploratory research question search process ◀ **Figure 3-2**

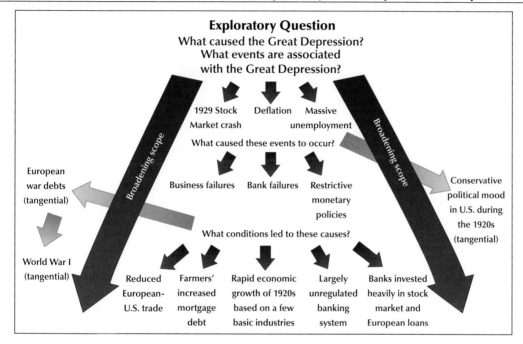

As your exploratory search expands, you might find yourself collecting tangential information. Tangential information is data that is somewhat related to your topic but does not help answer your exploratory question.

Determining Useful Information	InSight

The boundary between useful and tangential information can be difficult to identify for exploratory search questions. Sometimes, what appears to be tangential information can turn out to be useful information that leads you to expand your exploratory search in a fruitful direction. Do not be too quick to classify information as tangential. Remember, an exploratory search involves examining a wide range (that is, exploring) of information.

Web Search Strategy

Now that you understand the different types of questions that you will need to answer, you should learn something about searching the Web. You know the Web is a collection of interconnected HTML documents, and you know how to use Web browser software to navigate the hyperlinks that connect these documents. The search tools available on the Web are an integral part of these linked HTML documents, or Web pages.

Before you begin any Web search, you must decide whether your question is specific or exploratory. Then you can begin the actual Web search process, which includes four steps. The first step is to carefully formulate and state your question. Next, you select the appropriate tool or tools to use in your search. After obtaining your results from a Web search tool, you need to evaluate these results to determine whether they answer your question. If they do not, you continue the search by refining or redefining your question and then selecting a different search tool to see if you get a different result. The first three steps are the same for both specific and exploratory questions, but the determination of when your search process is completed is different for the two types of questions. Figure 3-3 illustrates the search process.

Figure 3-3 ⟩ **Web search process**

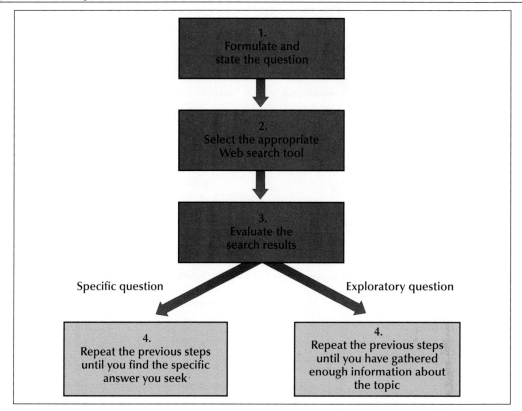

| Repeating the Search Process | | InSight |

You can repeat the search process as many times as necessary until you obtain the specific answer you seek or a satisfactory range of information regarding your exploratory topic. Sometimes, you might find that the nature of your original question is different than you had originally thought. You also might find that you need to reformulate, or more clearly state, your question. As you restate your question, think of synonyms for each word. Unfortunately, many words in the English language have multiple meanings. For example, the word *mogul* can mean an influential businessperson, an Indian person of Mongolian or Persian descent, or a small bump in a ski run. If you use a word in your search that is common and has many meanings, you can be buried in irrelevant information or be led down many blind alleys. Identifying unique phrases that relate to your topic or question is a helpful way to avoid some of these problems. For example, if you are searching for sites that discuss ways to ski safely over a mogul, you could include the word "skiing" or "slope" in your search expression to reduce the chances of obtaining results that link to Web pages about Indians or business magnates.

An important part of any search is evaluating the search results you obtain. You will learn how to assess the validity and reliability of Web pages you find during your searches in the next tutorial.

Using Search Engines

To implement any Web search strategy, you will use one or more Web search tools. **Web search tools** include four broad categories of sites: search engines, directories, metasearch engines, and other Web resources such as Web bibliographies. The Additional Information section of the Online Companion page for Tutorial 3 includes links to many of these Web search tools. (The Online Companion page is located at www.course.com/oc/np/internet7.)

In this section, you will learn the basics of using each type of search tool. Remember that searching the Web is a challenging task using any of these tools. No one knows exactly how many pages exist on the Web, but the number is now in the billions. Each of these pages might have thousands of words, images, or links to downloadable files. Thus, the content of the Web is far greater than any library. Unlike the content of a library, however, the content of the Web is not indexed in any standardized way. Fortunately, the tools you have to search the Web are powerful.

Understanding Search Engines

A Web **search engine** is a Web site (or part of a Web site) that finds other Web pages that match a word or phrase you enter. This word or phrase is called a **search expression** or a **query**. A search expression or query might also include instructions that tell the search engine how to search; you will learn how to formulate search expressions that include additional search instructions later in this tutorial. The basic search page for AltaVista, an early but still popular search engine site, is shown in Figure 3-4.

Figure 3-4   AltaVista basic search page

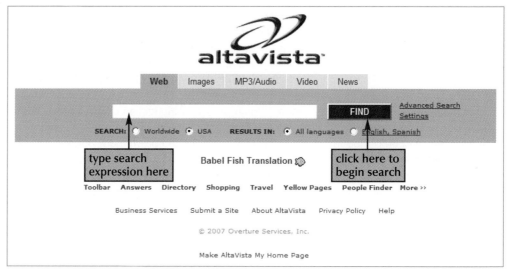

Reproduced with permission of Yahoo! Inc. ® 2007 by Yahoo! Inc. YAHOO! and the YAHOO! logo are trademarks of Yahoo! Inc.

A basic search page includes a text box for entering a search expression and a command button to begin the search. The basic search page for Google, one of the most popular search engines, appears in Figure 3-5.

Figure 3-5   Google basic search page

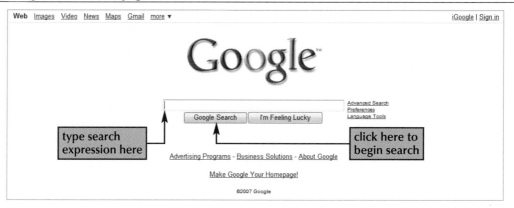

A search engine does not search the Web to find a match; it searches only its *own* database of information about Web pages that it has collected, indexed, and stored. A search engine's database includes the URL of the Web page (recall from Tutorial 1 that a Web page's URL, or uniform resource locator, is its address). If you enter the same search expression into different search engines, you will often get different results because each search engine has collected a different set of information in its database, and each search engine uses different procedures to search its database. Later in this session, you will learn more about variations in how search engines work.

Most search engines report the number of hits they find. A **hit** is a Web page that is indexed in the search engine's database and that contains text that matches a specific search expression. All search engines provide a series of **results pages**, which are Web pages that list hyperlinks to the Web pages containing text that matches your search expression. An example of a search results page (for a search on the word "car") from the Google search engine appears in Figure 3-6.

Google search results for the search term "car" — Figure 3-6

Each search engine uses a Web robot to build its database. A **Web robot**, also called a **bot** or a **spider**, is a program that automatically searches the Web to find new Web sites and update information about old Web sites that already are in the database. One of a Web robot's more important tasks is to delete information in the database when a Web site no longer exists. The main advantage of using an automated searching tool is that it can examine far more Web sites than an army of people ever could. However, the Web changes every day, and even the best search engine sites cannot keep their databases completely updated. When you click hyperlinks on a search engine results page, you will find that some of the Web pages no longer exist. A hyperlink to a Web page that no longer exists or has been moved to another URL is called a **dead link**.

People who create Web pages want their sites to be found by people who are interested in the content of those pages. Most search engines allow Web page creators to submit the URLs of their pages to the databases of search engines. This gives search engines another way to add Web pages to their databases. Most companies that operate search engines screen Web page submissions to prevent a Web page creator from submitting a large number of duplicate or similar Web pages. When the search engine receives a submission, it sends its Web robot out to visit the submitted URL and collect data about the site.

The organizations that operate search engines often sell advertising space on the search engine Web page and on the results pages. An increasing number of search engine operators also sell paid placement rights on results pages. A **paid placement** is the right to have a link to your Web site appear on the search results page when a user enters a specific search term. For example, Toyota might want to purchase the right to have its site listed on the search results page whenever a user enters the search term "car." When you enter a search expression that includes the word "car," the search engine creates a results page that will have a link to Toyota's Web site at or near the top of the results page. Most, but not all, search engines label these paid placement links as "sponsored," and they are usually called **sponsored links**. If the advertising appears in a box on the page (usually at the top, but sometimes along the side or at the bottom of the page), it is usually called a **banner ad**.

Search engines use the revenue from sponsored links and banner ads to generate profit after covering the costs of maintaining the computer hardware and software required to search the Web and to create and search the database. The only price a user pays for access to these excellent search tools is that you will see banner ads on many of the pages, and you might have to scroll through a few sponsored links at the top of results pages; otherwise, your usage is free.

Figure 3-6 shows the sponsored links to advertisers that have paid for the placement on this page.

Your first research assignment is to find the amount of average rainfall in Belize for Dave. This search question is a specific question, not an exploratory question, because you are looking for a fact and you will know when you have found that fact. You can use the four steps from Figure 3-3 as follows:

1. Formulate and state the question. You have identified key search terms in the question that you can use in your search expression: *Belize*, *rainfall*, and *annual*. You use these terms because they all should appear on any Web page that includes the answer to the question. None of these terms are articles, prepositions, or other common words, and none have multiple meanings. The term *Belize* should be especially useful in narrowing the search to relevant Web pages.

2. Because the question is very specific, you decide that a basic search engine would be a good tool to use.

3. When you obtain the results, review and evaluate them and then decide whether they provide an acceptable answer to your question.

4. If the results do not answer the question to your satisfaction, you need to redefine or reformulate the question so it is more specific, and then conduct a second search using a different tool, question, or search expression until you find the fact you seek.

To find the average annual rainfall in Belize:

1. Start your Web browser, go to **www.course.com/oc/np/internet7** to open the Online Companion page, log in to your account, click the **Tutorial 3** link, and then click the **Session 3.1** link.

2. Select any one of the search engines in the Basic Search Engines section, click the link to that search engine, and then wait while the browser opens that search engine's Web page.

3. Type **Belize annual rainfall** in the search text box.

4. Click the appropriate button to start the search. The search results appear on a new page. This page should indicate that there are hundreds, perhaps even thousands, of Web pages that might contain the answer to your question.

5. Scroll down the results page and examine your search results. Click some of the links until you find a page or several pages that provide annual rainfall information for Belize. If you do not find any useful links on the first page of search results, click the link to view more search results pages (usually located at the bottom of the first results page). Click the **Back** button on your Web browser to return to the results page after going to each hyperlink. You should find that Belize has several climate zones and that the annual rainfall ranges from 50 to 180 inches, or 130 to 470 centimeters.

You probably expected that you would find one rainfall amount that would be representative of the entire country, but that is not the case. Web searches often disclose information that helps you adjust the assumptions you made when you formulated the original research question.

You discuss the results of your search with Dave and explain that you obtained several different rainfall amounts for different regions within Belize. Dave finds your results interesting and will use them to expand the story he is working on. Since you are fact-checking for a story that IER will publish, Dave asks you to search again using a different search engine just to confirm what you found.

Using More Than One Search Engine

To get a confirmation of your results, you decide to search for the same information in another search engine.

To conduct the same search to confirm your results:

1. Return to the Online Companion page for Session 3.1, and then click a link to another of the search engines in the Basic Search Engines section.

2. Type **Belize annual rainfall** in the search text box.

3. Click the appropriate button to start the search. You will most likely see a completely different set of links on your search results page.

4. Scroll down the results page and examine your search results, and then click some of the links until you find a page that provides the average annual rainfall for Belize. Return to the results page after going to each hyperlink. Once again, you should find that Belize has several climate zones and that the annual rainfall ranges from 50 to 180 inches, or 130 to 470 centimeters.

Your second search returned a different set of links because each search engine includes different Web pages in its database and because different search engines use different rules to evaluate search expressions. Some search engines will return hits for pages that include *any* of the words in the search expression. Other search engines return hits only for pages that include *all* of the words in the search expression.

The best way to determine how a specific search engine interprets search expressions is to read the Help pages on the search engine Web site. As you become an experienced Web searcher, you will find that you primarily rely on two or three particular search engines. Read the Help pages on those Web sites regularly because search engines do change the way they interpret search expressions from time to time. Figure 3-7 shows the Help page for the AltaVista site's basic search function.

Figure 3-7   AltaVista Help page for basic searches

Home › AltaVista Help › **Search**

Different Types of Searches

Web	Video
Image	News
Audio	Webmaster Search

AltaVista Features

AltaVista Toolbar	Settings
Advanced Web Search	Family Filter
AltaVista Shortcuts	Report offensive pages (Yahoo!)
Special search terms	

Basic Web search tips

AltaVista invites you to search its digital content collection containing billions of Web pages, data resources and multimedia files by simply typing a query and clicking the Search button.

> information about how basic search expressions are interpreted

- When you type multiple words in the search box, AltaVista looks for Web pages that contain all of the words.
- Be as specific as you can. (Example: **Baltimore Ravens** instead of just **Ravens**)
- Enter words that you think will appear on the Web page you want. AltaVista indexes all of the words on each Web page.
- To search for an exact phrase, put it in quotes (Example: **"to be or not to be"**).
- Uppercase and lowercase are treated the same. To maintain a certain capitalization, put the word in quotes.
- Words with punctuation between them are treated as if they are surrounded in quotes. All punctuation marks are treated equally.
  (Example: **Ford.mustang/convertible** gives the same results as **"ford mustang convertible"**.)
- If you get results in other languages, either Translate the Web pages or select your preferred language in the search box menu.
- If you include an accent in a query word, AltaVista only matches words with that particular accent. If you do not include an accent, AltaVista will match words both with and without accents. This means you can search for French, German or Spanish words, even if you have an English-only keyboard.

To help focus your search further, use Advanced Web Search or Special search terms.

> links to Help pages with more information about search terms and expressions

Types of Web results

Doing different types of searches

AltaVista's search tabs, located on top of the search box, allow you to instantly search in different areas: Web, Images, Audio, Video, Directory or News.

To try a different type of search, just click a tab. AltaVista takes the words that are currently in the search box and automatically perform the search for you. (Sorry, this doesn't work on all browsers.)

Features in your Web search results page

Translate: This link lets you easily translate a Web page into any of nine languages. When you translate a page, AltaVista automatically translates all of the pages you link to from that page.

More pages from [this site]: When a site contains multiple pages that closely match your query, clicking on this link lets you see all of them. If a second page is very close in relevance to the first page, AltaVista automatically shows the second page indented below the first one.

PDF files: AltaVista searches various types of files in response to your queries. When a relevant PDF file is found you will see a note saying "File Format: PDF" and a link to easily download the free Adobe Acrobat Reader software, which is required to view a PDF file.

Business Services   Submit a Site   About AltaVista   Privacy Policy   Help

© 2007 Overture Services, Inc.

Reproduced with permission of Yahoo! Inc. ® 2007 by Yahoo! Inc. YAHOO! and the YAHOO! logo are trademarks of Yahoo! Inc.

If you found the same information after running both searches, you can confirm the information you found in your first search. If not, you should run additional searches to determine the reason your answers are not consistent, or report to Dave that you have obtained inconsistent results for your search.

You might have noticed that many of the links on the results pages led to Web sites that have no information about Belize rainfall at all. This is why most researchers routinely use several search engines; answers that are difficult to find using one search engine are often easy to find with another.

Understanding Search Engine Databases

Search engine databases store different collections of information about the pages that exist on the Web at any given time. Many search engine robots do not search all of the Web pages at a particular site. Further, each search engine database uses a different approach to index the information it has collected from the Web. Some search engine robots collect information only from a Web page's title, description, keywords, or HTML tags; others read only a certain number of words from each Web page. Figure 3-8 shows the first few lines of HTML from a Web page that contains information about electronic commerce.

Meta tags in a Web page   Figure 3-8

```
<HEAD>

<TITLE>
Current Developments in Electronic Commerce
</TITLE>

<META NAME ="description" CONTENT="Current
news and reports about electronic commerce
developments.">

<META NAME ="keywords" CONTENT ="electronic
commerce, electronic data interchange,
value added reseller, EDI, VAR, secure
socket layer, business on the internet">

</HEAD>
```

The description and keywords tags are examples of HTML meta tags. A **meta tag** is HTML code that a Web page creator places in the page header for the specific purpose of informing Web robots about the content of the page. Meta tags do not cause any text to appear on the page when a Web browser loads it; rather, they exist solely for the use of search engine robots.

The information contained in meta tags can become an important part of a search engine's database. For example, the "keywords" meta tag shown in Figure 3-8 includes the phrase "electronic data interchange." These keywords could be a very important phrase in a search engine's database because the three individual words *electronic, data,* and *interchange* are common terms that often are used in search expressions that have nothing to do with electronic commerce. The word *data* is so common that many search engines are programmed to ignore it. A search engine that includes the full phrase "electronic data interchange" in its database will greatly increase the chances that a user interested in that topic will find this particular page.

Some search engines store the entire content of every Web page they index; other search engines store only parts of Web pages. Search engines that store a Web page's full content are called **full text indexing** engines. If you use a search engine that is not full text indexing, and the terms you use in your search expression are not in the part of the Web page that the search engine stores in its database, the search engine will not return a hit for that page. Many search engines, even those that claim to be full text indexed search engines, omit common words such as *and, the, it,* and *by* from their databases. These common words are called **stop words**. For example, if you enter a search expression of "Law and Order" (without the quotes) while looking for pages related to the television show of that name, a search engine that omits stop words will return a large number of irrelevant links because it will search on the two words "law" and "order."

Most, but not all, search engines will include stop words if you include them as part of a phrase enclosed in quotes. You can find out how a particular search engine handles stop words by examining the search engine Web site's Help pages; many search engines include information about their search engines, robots, and databases on their Help or About pages.

Search Engine Features

One advance in search engine technology is page ranking. **Page ranking** is a way of grading Web pages by the number of other Web pages that link to them. The URLs of Web pages with high rankings are presented first on the search results page. A page that has more Web pages linking into it (these connections are called **inbound links**) is given a higher ranking than a page that has fewer pages linking into it. In complex page ranking schemes, the value of each link varies with the linking page's rank.

For example, a Web page with many inbound links might have a lower ranking than another Web page that has fewer inbound links if the second page's inbound links are from Web pages that, in turn, have a large number of inbound links themselves. As you can imagine, calculating page ranks can be complex, but the rankings can effectively identify pages that are likely to meet the needs of users. Google has been a leader in the use of page ranking and in the development of highly sophisticated page ranking algorithms.

Most search engines use **stemming** to search for variants of keywords automatically. For example, if you search using the keywords *Canada travel guide*, most search engines will return hits that include the keywords "Canadian" and "Canada," as well as pages containing the plural form of the word "guide." Unfortunately, you cannot dictate which variant of your keywords the search engine will use.

Another feature that some search engines have attempted to include in their pages is natural language querying. A **natural language query interface** allows users to enter a question exactly as they would ask a person that question. For example, using a natural language query, you might phrase the Belize rainfall search as "How much rain does Belize get each year?" You could ask the same question in various ways. The search engine analyzes the question using knowledge it has been given about the grammatical structure of questions and then uses that knowledge to convert the natural language question into a search query. This procedure of converting a natural language question into a search expression is sometimes called **parsing**.

One of the first search engines to offer a natural language query interface was Ask.com. After several years, however, Ask.com decided that most users' search questions were not long enough for parsing to work well. Ask.com decided to use alternatives to the natural language query to obtain better search results such as making suggestions on how to improve search expressions that users enter. You decide to see how Ask.com handles the Belize rainfall question.

To examine the Ask.com search suggestion approach:

▶ 1. Return to the Online Companion page for Session 3.1, and then click the **Ask.com** link to open the Ask.com search engine page.

▶ 2. Type **annual rainfall Belize** in the text box, as shown in Figure 3-9.

   Trouble? Depending on how the options are set for this Web site on the computer you are using, you might see a balloon appear below the text box as you type. This balloon will contain Ask.com suggestions for completing your query. Ignore these suggestions and continue typing the text shown in Step 2.

Typing a search expression into the Ask.com search engine ◄ Figure 3-9

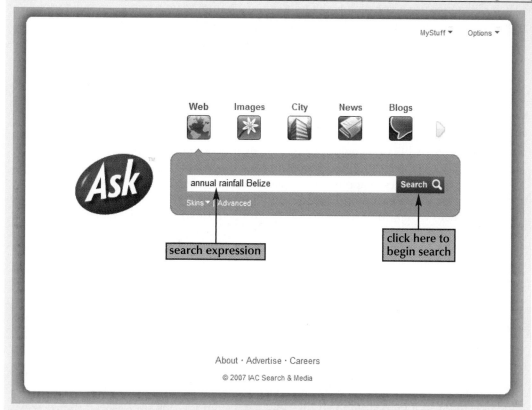

3. Click the **Search** button to run the search. The search results appear on a new page.

4. Scroll down the results page and examine your search results, and then click some of the links to determine whether Ask.com's interface has provided a good list of search suggestions (see the left side of the search results page). You can click any of these search suggestions to see if a reformulated search query offers better results than your original query. Return to the results page after going to each hyperlink.

Search engines provide a powerful tool for executing keyword searches of the Web. However, most search engine URL databases are built by computers running programs that perform the search automatically, so they can miss important classification details that a human searcher would notice instantly. For example, if a search engine's robot found a Web page with the title "Test Data: Do Not Use," it would probably not recognize the text as a warning and would include content from the page in the search engine database. If a person were to read such a warning in a Web page title, that person would know not to include the page's contents. However, with billions of Web pages on the Web, it is impossible to have people screen every Web page.

Using Directories and Hybrid Search Engine Directories

Web directories use a completely different approach from search engines to build useful indexes of information on the Web. A **Web directory** is a listing of hyperlinks to Web pages that is organized into hierarchical categories. The difference between a search engine and a Web directory is that the Web pages included in a Web directory are selected and organized into categories before visitors use the directory. In a search engine, the database is searched in response to a visitor's query, and results pages are created in response to each specific search. Most Web directories have human editors who decide which Web pages will be included in the directory and how they will be organized; however, some Web directories use computers to perform these tasks. Web directory editors, who are knowledgeable experts in one or more subject areas and skilled in various classification techniques, review candidate Web pages for inclusion in the directory. When these experts decide that a Web page is worth listing in the directory, they determine the appropriate category in which to store the hyperlink to that page. The main weakness of a directory is that users must know which category is likely to yield the information they desire. If users begin searching in the wrong category, they might follow many hyperlinks before they realize that the information they seek is not in that category. Some directories overcome this limitation by including hyperlinks in category levels that link to lower levels in other categories.

Tip

Most Web directories allow a Web page to be indexed in several different categories.

InSight | Paying to Submit URLs

Many Web directories, including Yahoo!, allow businesses that have Web sites to pay a fee and submit their URLs to the directory editors so they can consider including the Web site in their directory. In most cases, the fee does not guarantee that the site will be included in the directory, but it does ensure that the editors will know that the site exists. A new site on the Web that does not use a paid directory submission can wait months before a directory editor notices it and considers including it.

One of the oldest and most respected directories on the Web is Yahoo!. David Filo and Jerry Yang, two Stanford doctoral students who wanted a way to keep track of interesting sites they found on the Internet, started Yahoo! in 1994. Since then, Yahoo! has grown to become one of the most widely used resources on the Web. Yahoo! currently lists hundreds of thousands of Web pages in its categories—a sizable collection, but only a small portion of the billions of pages on the Web. Although Yahoo! does use some automated programs for checking and classifying its entries, it relies on human experts to do most of the selection and classification work. The Yahoo! Web directory home page appears in Figure 3-10.

Yahoo! Web directory home page | Figure 3-10

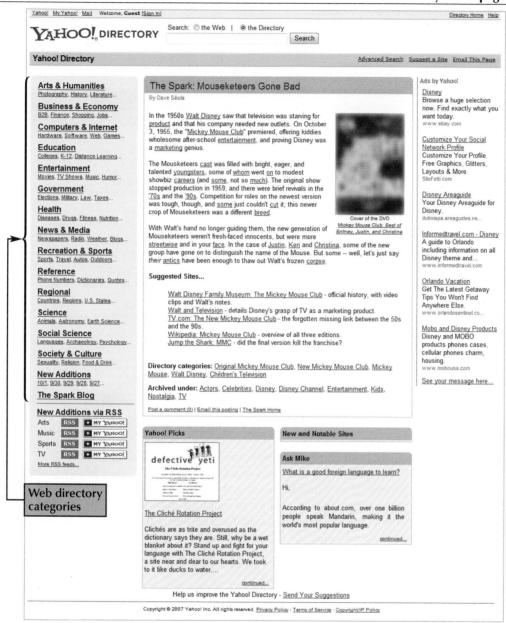

The search tool that appears near the top of the page is a search engine within the Yahoo! directory. You can enter search terms into this tool, and Yahoo! will search its listings to find a match. This combination of search engine and directory is sometimes called a **hybrid search engine directory**; however, most directories today include a search engine function, so many people simply call these sites Web directories. No matter what it is called, the combination of search engine and directory provides a powerful and effective tool for searching the Web. Using a hybrid search engine directory can help you identify which category in the directory is likely to contain the information you need. After you enter a category, the search engine is useful for narrowing a search even further; you can enter a search expression and limit the search to that category.

The Yahoo! Web directory includes 16 main categories, each with several subcategories. These are not the only subcategories; they are just a sample of those that are the largest or most used. You can click a main category hyperlink to see all of the subcategories under that category.

The Open Directory Project is different from most other Web directories because the editors volunteer their time to create the directory's entries. The home page for the Open Directory Project is shown in Figure 3-11.

Figure 3-11   **Open Directory Project home page**

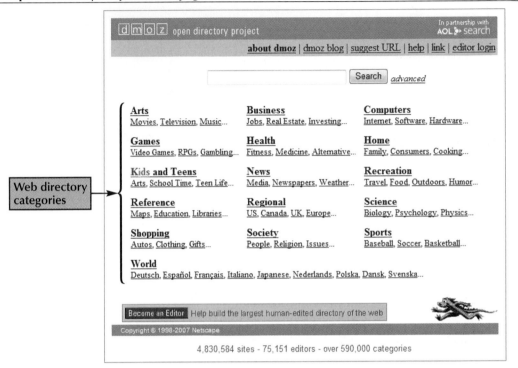

Your next assignment from Dave is to find some background information on The Conference Board, an organization that does research on business issues and publishes statistics about economic growth and business activity. Dave would like to know about the history of the organization and what kinds of reports it publishes. Following the guidelines for searching on the Web that you learned earlier in this tutorial, you decide that Dave's question is about a specific fact and you:

1. Identify key search terms—*Conference Board*, *business*, and *organization*—that you will use in your search.
2. Use a Web directory to find the answer, so you can search in the business directory instead of searching the entire Web.
3. Examine the results and decide whether a second search using different search terms or a different category is necessary.
4. Plan to repeat the first three steps until you determine whether The Conference Board provides any information about itself on the Web.

To find The Conference Board on the Web:

▶ **1.** Return to the Online Companion page for Session 3.1, choose one of the sites in the Web Directories section and click the link for the site you chose.

▶ **2.** Examine the categories on the directory's home page and click a link that is likely to contain information about The Conference Board. A link that contains the word "Business" or "Economics" would be a good choice.

3. Examine the page that loads in your browser. Search for links to subcategories that include words such as "organizations," "industry groups," "statistics," or "indicators." You might need to search several levels down in the directory to find information about The Conference Board. Some Web directories include a search function that lets you search within a category once you have found a likely candidate. If the Web directory you chose to use includes this feature, be sure to try it.

4. If you do not find the information you seek in one category, try another. You can also try a different Web directory if you are unable to find the information in the first Web directory you chose to use. Figures 3-12 and 3-13 show the results pages for searches in two Web directories, Yahoo! and Gigablast, respectively. Your results will probably be somewhat different, even if you use the same Web directory sites.

Yahoo! Web directory search results page ◄ **Figure 3-12**

link to The Conference Board Web site

Figure 3-13 ▶ **Gigablast Web directory search results page**

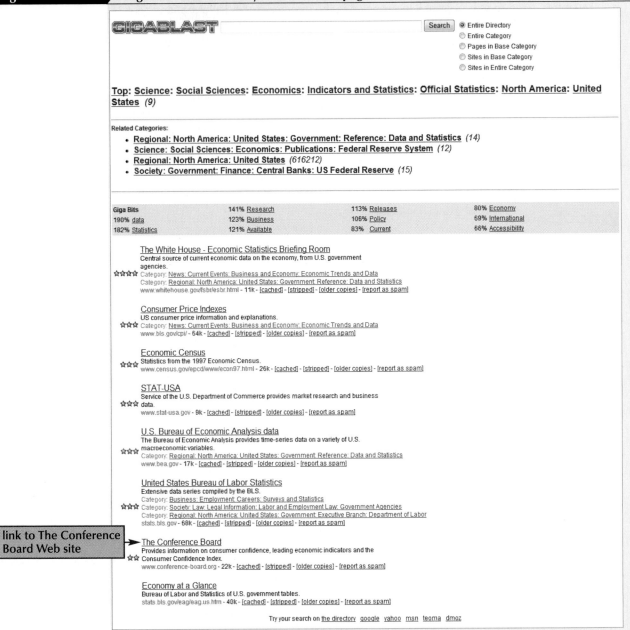

You should be able to find information about The Conference Board at one or more of the sites listed. After you have reviewed the sites, you can develop an outline of the background information that Dave asked you to find. Now that you have seen how to use a search engine and a hybrid search engine directory, you are ready to use an even more powerful combination of Web research tools: the metasearch engine.

Using Metasearch Engines

A **metasearch engine** is a tool that combines the power of multiple search engines. Some metasearch tools also include directories. The idea behind metasearch tools is simple. Each search engine on the Web has different strengths and weaknesses because each search engine:

- Uses a different Web robot to gather information about Web pages.
- Stores a different amount of Web page text in its database.
- Selects different Web pages to index.
- Has different storage resources.
- Interprets search expressions somewhat differently.

You have already seen how these differences cause various search engines to return vastly different results for the same search expression. To perform a complete search for a particular question, you might need to use several individual search engines. Using a metasearch engine lets you search several engines at the same time, so you need not conduct the same search many times. Metasearch engines do not have their own databases of Web information; instead, a metasearch engine transmits your search expression to several search engines. These search engines run the search expression against their databases of Web page information and return results to the metasearch engine. The metasearch engine then reports consolidated results from all of the search engines it queried.

A few years ago, some Web search experts believed that metasearch engines would become unnecessary as the larger search engines expanded their coverage of the Web. But the Web continues to grow so rapidly that it outpaces the abilities of any single search engine to keep up with it. Metasearch engines still make it easier to do a complete search of the Web.

Mamma.com was one of the first metasearch engines on the Web. Mamma.com forwards search queries to a number of major search engines and Web directories, including About.com, Google, MSN, Open Directory, Wisenut, and others. The specific search engines and directories that Mamma.com uses change from time to time because newer and better search tools become available and older tools disappear. Each entry on the search results page is labeled with the search engine or Web directory that found it. When more than one source provides the same result, that entry is labeled with all of the sources. Figure 3-14 shows the Mamma.com metasearch engine home page.

Mamma metasearch engine home page | Figure 3-14

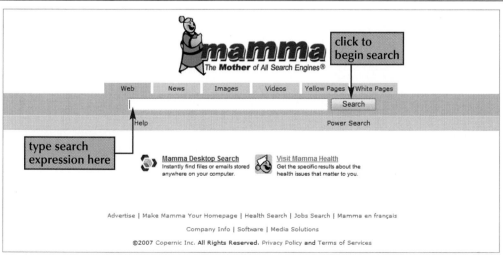

You want to learn how to use metasearch engines so that you can access information faster. You decide to test a metasearch engine using Dave's Belize rainfall question.

| Reference Window | **Using a Metasearch Engine** |

- Formulate your search question.
- Open the metasearch engine home page in your Web browser.
- Enter the search expression into the metasearch engine.
- Evaluate the results and decide whether to revise the question or your choice of search tools.

To use a metasearch engine:

▶ **1.** Return to the Online Companion page for Session 3.1, choose one of the sites in the Metasearch Engines section and click the link for the site you chose.

▶ **2.** Type **Belize annual rainfall** in the search text box.

▶ **3.** Execute the search by clicking the appropriate button.

▶ **4.** Examine and evaluate your search results. If you did not find the information you were seeking, repeat your search using a different metasearch engine.

As you scroll through the search results pages, you can see that there is a wide variation in the number and usefulness of the results provided by each search engine and directory. You might notice a number of duplicate hits; however, most of the Web pages returned by one search tool are not returned by any other.

Figure 3-15 shows the results page from one of the more interesting metasearch engines, KartOO. KartOO presents results in a graphic format. Each image is a link and the images are clustered around words that appear in the results pages. When you move the pointer over a word, the links appear as lines between the word and the images. In the figure, the pointer is over the word "temperature," which adds that word to the end of the search expression and the clustering of links based on that term are shown as orange lines. The list of links on the left side of the page also changes to reflect the addition of the term.

KartOO metasearch graphic results | **Figure 3-15**

word added to end of search expression when pointer is over the word "temperature"

lines connect results pages that contain term being pointed to

pointer

Using Other Web Resources

In addition to search engines, Web directories, and metasearch engines, the Web includes **Web bibliographies**, another category of resource for searching the Internet. Web bibliographies can be very useful when you want to obtain a broad overview or a basic understanding of a complex subject area.

As their name suggests, Web bibliographies are similar to print bibliographies, but instead of listing books or journal articles, they contain lists of hyperlinks to Web pages. Just as some bibliographies are annotated, many of these resources include summaries or reviews of Web pages. Web bibliographies are also called **resource lists**, **subject guides**, **clearinghouses**, and **virtual libraries**. Sometimes they are called Web directories, which can be somewhat confusing. Web bibliographies are usually more focused on specific subjects than Web directories, and Web bibliographies usually do not include a tool for searching within their categories.

Using a search engine to locate broad information on a complex subject is likely to turn up a narrow list of references that are too detailed and that assume a great deal of prior knowledge. For example, using a search engine or directory to find information about quantum physics will probably give you many results that link to technical papers and Web pages devoted to current research issues in quantum physics. However, your search probably will yield very few Web pages that provide an introduction to the topic. In contrast, a Web bibliography page can offer hyperlinks to information regarding a particular subject that is presented at various levels. Many of these resources include annotations and reviews of the sites they list. This information can help you identify Web pages that fit your level of knowledge or interest.

Some Web bibliographies, such as the Librarian's Index to the Internet, are general references. Most are more focused, such as Martindale's The Reference Desk, which emphasizes science-related links. Some Web bibliographies, such as the Scout Report and the Argus Clearinghouse, are no longer actively updated, but they are maintained on the Web as useful information resources.

Tip

Remember, you can often find useful subject guides by entering the search term along with the words "subject guide" into a regular search engine.

Many Web bibliographies are created by librarians at university and public libraries. You can find Web bibliographies on specific subjects by entering a search term along with the words "subject guide" into a search engine. The results of an example search on the words "Native American subject guide" conducted in the Google search engine appear in Figure 3-16.

Figure 3-16   **Results of a search on "Native American subject guide"**

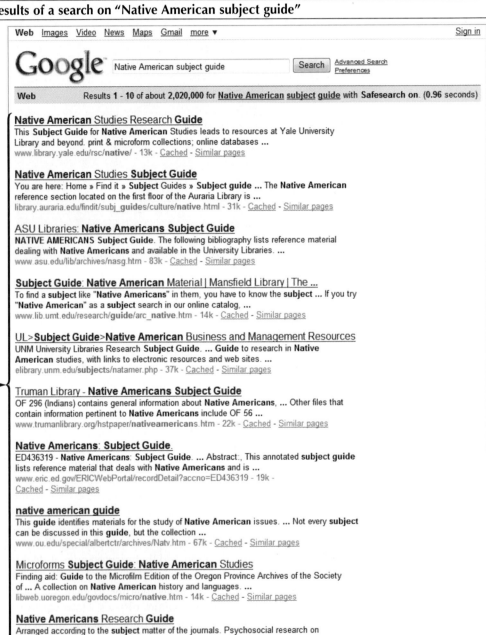

search results include several links to Web bibliographies about Native Americans

Another way to find Web bibliographies is to use a Web directory site. Many Web directories include links to subject-specific Web bibliographies within the category listings for those subjects. For example, the Yahoo! Web directory includes a link titled "Web Directories" within its Social Science category. This link leads to a list of Web bibliographies on the subject of social science. It also has similar links in many of the social science subcategories, such as Economics. Other Web directories include similar links.

Ranjit is planning a series of pieces on the business and economic effects of current trends in biotechnology, including information about the potential effects of genetic engineering research. You need to find some Web sites that Ranjit can use to learn more about biotechnology trends in general and genetic engineering research in particular. You determine that an exploratory search will locate the required information, and you decide to use a Web bibliography site for your research. Biotechnology is a branch of the biological sciences, so you will use three category terms: *biotechnology, genetic engineering*, and *biology* as your search categories. Many Web bibliographies contain hyperlinks to other useful sites. You can collect information from these pages by printing copies of the Web pages, sending the URLs by email, or saving the Web pages and attaching them to an email message. You can also copy and paste relevant text from the Web pages into an email or a document.

Tip

If you regularly do research in a specific field, it can be helpful to ask other researchers who work in the field if they know of useful Web bibliographies that specialize in relevant subjects.

To use a Web bibliography to conduct an exploratory search:

▶ **1.** Return to the Online Companion page for Session 3.1, choose one of the sites in the Web Bibliographies and click its link.

▶ **2.** Examine the page for links that might lead to information about biotechnology, genetic engineering, or biology. Follow those links to gather information relative to your search. Make a note of any article titles that you think would be interesting to Ranjit.

▶ **3.** Examine your search results and determine whether you have gathered sufficient useful information to provide to Ranjit. If you have not, repeat the search using a different Web bibliography.

▶ **4.** Close your browser.

You have completed your search for Web sites containing information about genetic engineering and biotechnology. Because your answer to Ranjit's question involves so many pages at different sites, your best approach would be to send an email message with a list of relevant URLs.

Session 3.1 Quick Check | Review

1. What are the key characteristics of an exploratory search question?
2. True or False: Many Web search engine operators use advertising revenue to cover their expenses and to earn a profit.
3. The part of a search engine site that is a program that automatically searches the Web to find new Web sites is called a(n) _____ .
4. A search engine that uses page ranking will list a Web page near the top of search results pages if the page has many _____ .
5. True or False: Most search engines index all Web page contents in their databases.
6. List one advantage and one disadvantage of using a Web directory instead of a Web search engine to locate information.

7. How does a hybrid search engine directory overcome the disadvantages of using either a search engine or a directory alone?
8. How does a metasearch engine process the search expression you enter into it?
9. What are the key features offered by Web bibliographies?

Session 3.2

Complex Searches with Boolean Logic and Filtering Techniques

The most important factor in obtaining good results from a search engine, a metasearch engine, or a search tool within a hybrid search engine directory is careful selection of the search terms you use. When the object of your search is straightforward, you can usually choose one or two words that will work well. More complex search questions require more complex queries, which you can use along with Boolean logic, search expression operators, wildcard operators, or filtering techniques, to broaden or narrow your search expression. In the next four sections, you will learn how to research various topics for Dave and Ranjit using these advanced techniques.

The Boolean operators and filtering techniques you will learn to use in this session can also be helpful when you are doing searches in library databases. These databases, which can be very expensive to purchase, provide much information that cannot be found on the Internet and are often available at school libraries, company libraries, or your local public libraries. Each database has its own implementation of Boolean operators and filtering tools, but the principles you learn here will help you in formulating your searches of these library databases.

Boolean Operators

When you enter a single word into a Web search tool, it searches for matches to that word. When you enter a search expression that includes more than one word, the search tool makes assumptions about the words that you enter. You learned in Session 3.1 that some search engines assume that you want to match *any* of the keywords in your search expression, whereas other search engines assume that you want to match *all* of the keywords. These differing assumptions can result in dramatic differences in the number and quality of hits returned. Some search engines are designed to offer both options because users might want to match all of the keywords on one search and any of the keywords on a different search. One way of implementing these options is to use Boolean operators in the search expression.

George Boole was a nineteenth-century British mathematician who developed **Boolean algebra**, the branch of mathematics and logic that bears his name. In Boolean algebra, all values are reduced to one of two values. In most practical applications of Boole's work, these two values are *true* and *false*. Although Boole did his work a hundred years before computers became commonplace, his algebra is still useful to computer engineers and programmers. At the very lowest level of analysis, all computing is a manipulation of two values—a single computer circuit's on and off states. Unlike the algebra you might have learned in your math classes, Boolean algebra does not use numbers or mathematical operators. Instead, Boolean algebra uses words and logical relationships.

Some parts of Boolean algebra are useful in search expressions. **Boolean operators**, also called **logical operators**, are a key part of Boolean algebra. Boolean operators specify the logical relationship between the elements they join, just as the plus sign arithmetic operator specifies the mathematical relationship between the two elements it joins. Three basic Boolean operators—AND, OR, and NOT—are recognized by most search engines. You can use these operators in many search engines by simply including them with search terms. For example, the search expression "exports AND France" returns hits for pages that contain both words, the expression "exports OR France" returns hits for pages that contain either word, and "exports NOT France" returns hits for pages that contain the word *export* but not the word *France*. Some search engines use "AND NOT" to indicate the Boolean NOT operator.

Some search engines recognize variants of the Boolean operators, such as "must include" and "must exclude" operators. For example, a search engine that uses the plus sign to indicate "must include" and the minus sign to indicate "must exclude" would respond to the expression "exports + France - Japan" with hits that included anything about exports and France, but only if those pages did not include anything about Japan.

Figure 3-17 shows several ways to use Boolean operators in more complex search expressions that contain the words *exports*, *France*, and *Japan*. The figure shows the matches that a search engine will return if it interprets the Boolean operators correctly. Figure 3-17 also describes information-gathering tasks in which you might use these expressions.

Using Boolean operators in search expressions ◄ Figure 3-17

Search Expression	Search Returns Pages That Include	Use to Find Information About
exports AND France AND Japan	All of the three search terms.	Exports from France to Japan or from Japan to France.
exports OR France OR Japan	Any of the three search terms.	Exports from anywhere, including France and Japan, and all kinds of information about France and Japan.
exports NOT France NOT Japan	Exports, but not if the page also includes the terms France or Japan.	Exports to and from any countries other than France or Japan.
exports AND France NOT Japan	Exports and France, but not Japan.	Exports from France to anywhere but Japan or to France from anywhere but Japan.

Other Search Expression Operators

When you join three or more search terms with Boolean operators, it is easy to become confused by the expression's complexity. To reduce the confusion, you can use precedence operators, a tool you probably learned in basic algebra, along with the Boolean operators. A **precedence operator**, also called an **inclusion operator** or a **grouping operator**, clarifies the grouping within a complex expression and is usually indicated by the parentheses symbols. Figure 3-18 shows several ways to use precedence operators with Boolean operators in search expressions.

Figure 3-18 **Using Boolean and precedence operators in search expressions**

Search Expression	Search Returns Pages That Include	Use to Find Information About
Exports AND (France OR Japan)	Exports and either France or Japan.	Exports from or to either France or Japan.
Exports OR (France AND Japan)	Exports or both France and Japan.	Exports from anywhere, including France and Japan, and all kinds of other information about both France and Japan.
Exports AND (France NOT Japan)	Exports and France, but not if the page also includes Japan.	Exports to and from France, except those to or from Japan.

Some search engines use double quotation marks to indicate precedence grouping; however, most search engines use double quotation marks to indicate search terms that must be matched exactly as they appear within the double quotation marks. Using an exact match search phrase can be particularly useful because most search engines ignore stop words by default. You can force most search engines to include a stop word (that they would, by default, ignore) in a search expression by enclosing it in double quotation marks (or by including it in an exact search phrase that is enclosed in double quotation marks).

Another useful search expression tool is the location operator. A **location operator**, or **proximity operator**, lets you search for terms that appear close to each other in the text of a Web page. The most common location operator offered in Web search engines is the NEAR operator. If you are interested in French exports, you might want to find only Web pages in which the terms *exports* and *France* are close to each other. Unfortunately, each search engine that implements this operator uses its own definition of "NEAR." One search engine might define NEAR to mean "within 10 words," whereas another search engine might define NEAR to mean "within 20 words." To use the NEAR operator effectively, you must read the search engine's Help file carefully.

Wildcard Characters

A few search engines support some use of a wildcard character in their search expressions. A **wildcard character** allows you to omit part of a search term. The search engines that include this function most commonly use the asterisk (*) as the wildcard character. For example, the search expression "export*" would return pages containing the terms *exports, exporter, exporters,* and *exporting* in many search engines. Some search engines let you use a wildcard character in the middle of a search term. For example, the expression "wom*n" would return pages containing both *woman* and *women*.

Search Filters

Many search engines allow you to restrict your search by using search filters. A **search filter** eliminates Web pages from search results. The filter criteria can include such Web page attributes as language, date, domain, host, or page component (URL, hyperlink, image tag, or title tag). For example, many search engines provide a way to search for the term *exports* in Web page titles and ignore pages in which the term appears in other parts of the page.

Performing Complex Searches

Most search engines implement many of the operators and filtering techniques you have learned about in this session. The way in which various search engines apply these techniques can differ; some search engines provide separate advanced search pages for these techniques, while others allow you to use advanced techniques such as Boolean operators on their simple search pages.

This section describes how to conduct complex searches in several specific search engines. The steps are correct as this book is printed, but the Web is a changing medium. When you perform these steps, the screens you see might look different and you might need to modify the steps. If you encounter difficulties, ask your instructor for assistance or read the Help pages on the search engine site. If major changes occur, the Online Companion Web site will be updated to indicate how to make the searches work.

Using AltaVista Advanced Search

Ranjit is writing about the role that trade agreements play in limiting the flow of agricultural commodities between countries. His current project concerns the German economy. Your job is to find some Web page references that might provide useful background information. Ranjit is especially interested in learning more about the German perspective on trade issues.

You recognize this as an exploratory question and decide to use the advanced query capabilities of the AltaVista search engine to conduct a complex search for Web pages. AltaVista offers very good support for Boolean and precedence operators.

To create a useful search expression, you must identify search terms that might lead you to appropriate Web pages. Some terms you might use for the search are *Germany*, *trade*, *treaty*, and *agriculture*. You want to locate a reasonable number of hyperlinks to Web pages, but you do not want to search through thousands of URLs, so you decide to combine the search terms using Boolean logic to increase the chances that the search engine will return only useful sites.

Conducting a Complex Search Using AltaVista | Reference Window

- Open the AltaVista search engine in your Web browser.
- Select the Advanced Search option.
- Formulate the Boolean search.
- Enter the search terms in the query builder in accordance with the Boolean logic rules.
- Click the Find button.
- Evaluate the results and, if necessary, revise your search expression.

To perform a complex search using AltaVista:

▶ 1. Start your Web browser, go to **www.course.com/oc/np/internet7** to open the Online Companion page, log in to your account, click the **Tutorial 3** link, click the **Session 3.2** link, and then click the **AltaVista** link.

▶ 2. Click the **Advanced Search** link on the AltaVista page.

▶ 3. To obtain results that include, in Boolean terms (Germany AND trade), along with (treaty OR agriculture), type **Germany trade** in the **all of these words** text box (AltaVista applies the Boolean AND operator to terms in this text box), and then type **treaty agriculture** in the **any of these words** text box (AltaVista applies the Boolean OR operator to terms in this text box).

▶ 4. Click the **Find** button to start the search. The results appear in Figure 3-19.

Figure 3-19	Complex search in AltaVista

Reproduced with permission of Yahoo! Inc. ® 2007 by Yahoo! Inc. YAHOO! and the YAHOO! logo are trademarks of Yahoo! Inc.

Filtered Search in Ask.com

Some search engines provide specific filtering options in addition to or instead of Boolean operators. The Ask.com search engine offers several such options on its Advanced Search page, including filters for date and geographic region.

Dave is writing about the upcoming corn harvest in Brazil. He wants you to check on developments that have occurred during the past six months in that country. You decide to use the Ask.com search engine to run a filtered search query.

Conducting a Filtered Search Using Ask.com | Reference Window

- Open the Ask.com search engine page in your Web browser.
- Click the Advanced link.
- Formulate and enter a suitable search expression.
- Set any filters you want to use for the search.
- Click the Advanced Search button.
- Evaluate the results and, if necessary, revise your search expression.

To perform a filtered search using Ask.com:

▶ **1.** Return to the Online Companion page for Session 3.2, and then click the **Ask.com** link.

▶ **2.** Click the **Advanced** link to open the Ask.com Advanced Search page.

▶ **3.** Type **corn harvest** in the Find results with all of the words text box.

▶ **4.** Click the **Country** list arrow, and then click **Brazil** to set the Country filter.

▶ **5.** Click the **Page modified** list arrow, and then click **Last 6 months** to set the date filter. Figure 3-20 shows the Ask.com Advanced Search page with the search expression entered and the filters set.

Using search filters in Ask.com ◀ **Figure 3-20**

> **6.** Click the **Advanced Search** button to start the search. Figure 3-21 shows the search results page, where you can see the search expression, the filter settings, and a list of hyperlinks to related Web pages. The results also include suggestions for search terms you can use to narrow your search if you wish.

Figure 3-21 ▶ **Ask.com filtered search results page**

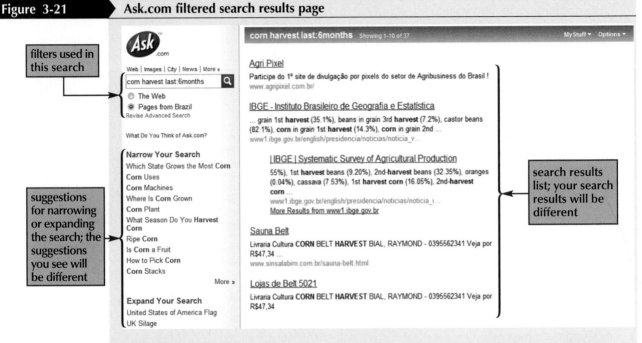

> **7.** Examine your search results and determine whether you have gathered sufficient useful information to complete the search. Since the search returned some links that contain information relevant to Dave's query, you can conclude the search by forwarding the URLs to Dave.

Filtered Search in Google

Dave is writing an item about Finland and would like to interview a professor he once met who taught graduate business students there. He does not remember the professor's name or the name of the university at which the professor teaches, but he does remember that the professor taught business subjects at a university in Finland. Dave is confident that he would recognize the university's name if he saw it again. He asks if you can search the Web to find the names of some Finnish universities.

You decide to use the Google search engine for this task. To create a useful search expression, you must identify search terms that might lead you to appropriate Web pages. You decide to include *Finland* as a search term. Also, Dave told you that graduate schools of business in Europe are often called Schools of Economics, so you decide to include the exact phrase *School of Economics* in your search. You know that the country code for Finland is *.fi*, so you decide to limit the search to Web pages in this top-level domain. Because Dave reads only English, you also decide to limit the search to pages that are in English.

| **Conducting a Filtered Search Using Google Advanced Search** | Reference Window |

- Open the Google search engine page in your Web browser.
- Click the Advanced Search link.
- Formulate and enter suitable search expression elements.
- Formulate and set appropriate search filters.
- Click the Google Search button.
- Evaluate the results and, if necessary, revise your search expression.

To perform a filtered search using Google Advanced Search:

1. Return to the Online Companion page for Session 3.2, and then click the **Google** link.

2. Click the **Advanced Search** link to open the Google Advanced Search page.

3. Click in the **Find results with all of the words** text box at the top of the page, and then type **Finland**.

4. Click in the **Find results with the exact phrase** text box, and then type **School of Economics**.

5. Click the arrow on the **Language** drop-down selection box, and then click **English**.

6. Click in the **Domain** text box, and then type **.fi**. Figure 3-22 shows the Google Advanced Search page with the search expressions entered and the filters set.

Tip

You might need to try different combinations of filters to get a set of search results that works.

Google Advanced Search page ◄ **Figure 3-22**

7. Click the **Google Search** button to start the search. The top portion of the search results page appears in Figure 3-23 and includes a number of links to Finnish universities.

Figure 3-23   **Google Advanced Search results page**

filters and exact search expressions used in this search

search results list; your search results will be different

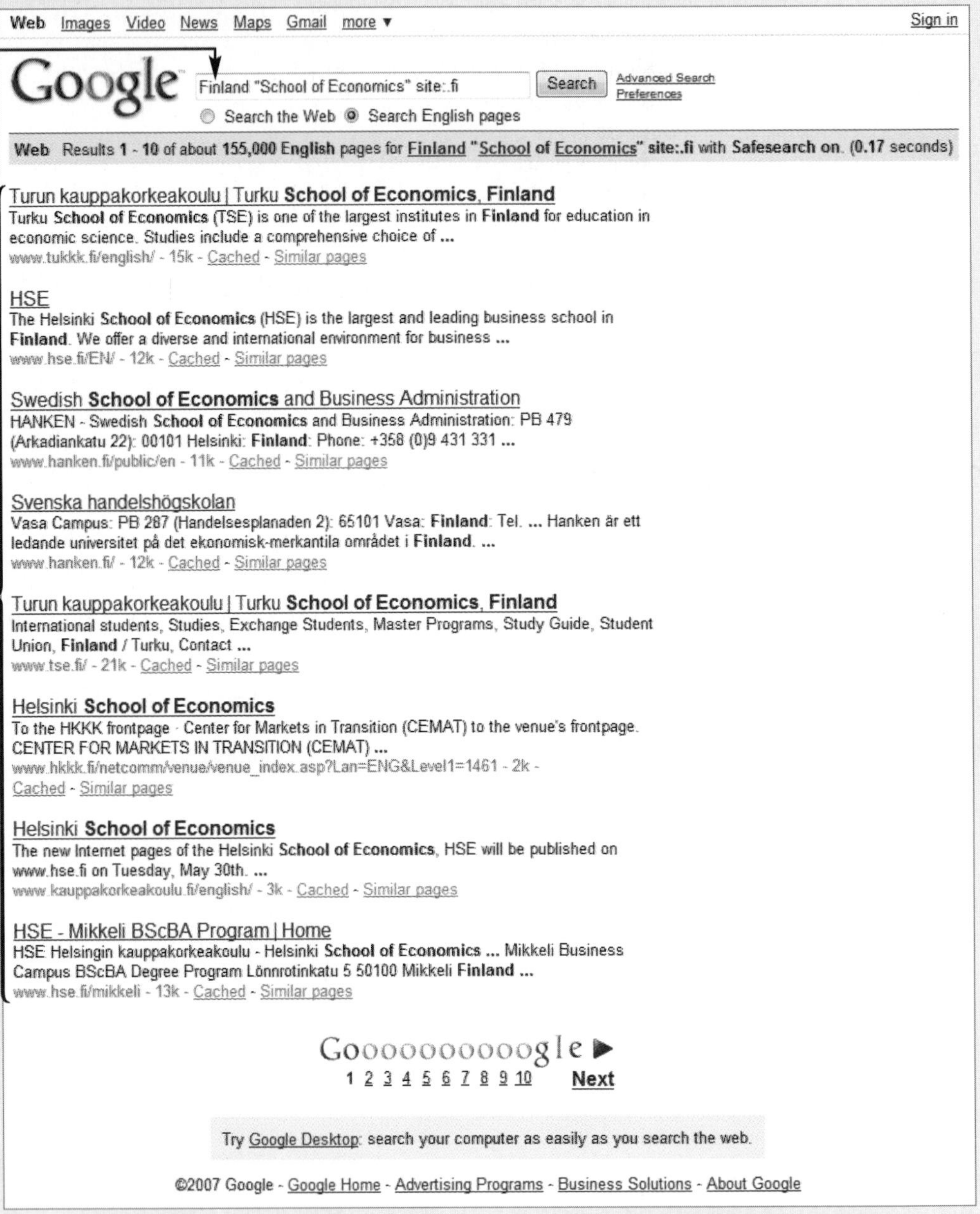

8. Examine your search results and determine which of the hyperlinks in the search results lead to Finnish universities. You can send a list of these links to Dave in an email message. Remember that you might need to examine several pages of search results to find exactly what you need.

Search Engines with Clustering Features

One problem with using search engines is that they often generate thousands (or even millions) of hits. Scrolling through hundreds of results pages looking for useful links is not very efficient. Clusty is a search engine that uses an advanced technology to group its results into clusters. The clustering of results provides a filtering effect; however, the filtering is done automatically by the search engine after it runs the search. You would like to try this search engine to see if its clustering feature provides results that are easier to review.

Ranjit is writing about fast-food franchises in various developing countries. He needs your help gathering information on this industry's experience in Indonesia. You decide to run this search using the Clusty search engine. To create a useful search expression, you must identify search terms that might lead you to appropriate Web pages. Some terms you might use include *Indonesia*, *fast food*, and *franchise*. You are not interested in Web pages that have the individual terms *fast* and *food*, so you will use double quotation marks to specify the phrase "fast food." The Clusty search engine uses its clustering feature as a substitute for Boolean logic, so you will enter a simple expression and let Clusty filter your results into searchable categories.

Obtaining Clustered Search Results Using Clusty		Reference Window

- Open the Clusty search engine page in your browser.
- Formulate and enter a suitable search expression.
- Click the Search button.
- Evaluate the results and, if necessary, revise your search expression.

To obtain clustered search results using Clusty:

▶ 1. Return to the Online Companion page for Session 3.2, and then click the **Clusty** link.

▶ 2. Click in the Search text box, and then type **Indonesia "fast food" franchise**. Make sure that you type the quotation marks so that you find the phrase "fast food" instead of the individual terms *fast* and *food*.

▶ 3. Click the **Search** button to start the search. Figure 3-24 shows the search results page, which includes a number of promising hyperlinks.

Figure 3-24 ▷ **Clusty search results page**

search expression

search results collected into clusters of related hyperlinks

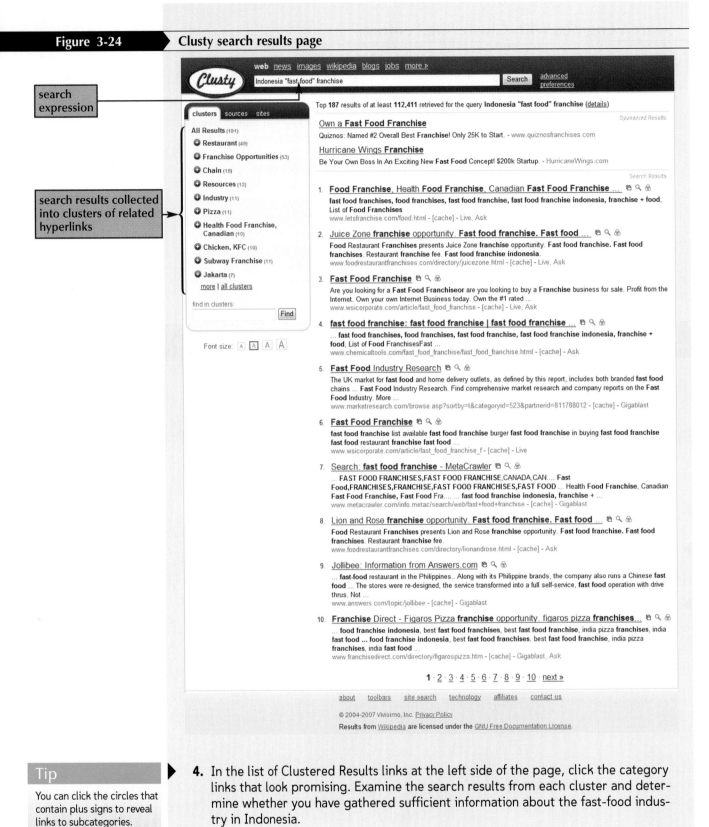

▶ **4.** In the list of Clustered Results links at the left side of the page, click the category links that look promising. Examine the search results from each cluster and determine whether you have gathered sufficient information about the fast-food industry in Indonesia.

A unique feature of Clusty is that it collects search results into clusters and runs the clustering algorithms as the search results are returned. That is, instead of classifying Web pages into categories in its database, it creates the categories dynamically after it processes the search expression. Clusty defines its clusters using artificial intelligence. The clustering is done in real time for each search and depends on the search expression and the clustering algorithm, which is continually revised. Your search provides a number of useful links for Ranjit.

Future of Web Search Tools

Many different companies and organizations are working on ways to make searching the Web easier and more successful for the increasing numbers of people who use the Web. One weakness of most current search engines and Web directories is that they only search static Web pages. A **static Web page** is an HTML file that exists on a Web server computer. The robots used by search engines to build their databases can find and examine these files.

An increasing number of Web sites do not store information as HTML files. Instead, they store information in a database, and when a user submits a query in the search function of the site, the site's Web server searches the database and generates a Web page on the fly that includes information from the database. These generated Web pages are called **dynamic Web pages**. For example, if you visit Amazon.com and search for books about birds, the Amazon.com Web server queries a database that contains information about books and generates a dynamic Web page that includes that information. This Web page is not stored permanently on the Web server and cannot be found or examined by search engine robots. Much of the information stored in these databases can only be accessed by users who have a login and password to the Web site that generates dynamic pages from the database.

Several researchers have explored the difficulties that search engine robots face when trying to include information contained in the databases that some Web sites use to generate their dynamic pages. Some researchers call this information the **deep Web**; other researchers use the terms **hidden Web** and **invisible Web**.

You also learned earlier in this tutorial that KartOO uses graphic display technology to present its search results.

Using People to Enhance Web Directories

One company, About.com, hires people with expertise in specific subject areas to create and manage its Web directory entries in those areas. Although both Yahoo! and MSN Search use subject matter experts this way, About.com takes the idea one step further and identifies its experts. Each About.com expert, called a Guide, hosts a page with hyperlinks to related Web pages, moderates discussion areas, and provides an online newsletter. This creates a community of interested persons from around the world that can participate in maintaining the Web directory.

The Open Directory Project uses the services of more than 40,000 volunteer editors who maintain listings in their individual areas of interest. The Open Directory Project offers the information in its Web directory to other Web directories and search engines at no charge. Many of the major Web directory, search engine, and metasearch engine sites regularly download and store the Open Directory Project's information in their databases. For example, AlltheWeb, AltaVista, DogPile, and Google all include Open Directory Project information in their databases.

Evaluating Web Research Resources

One of the most important issues in conducting research on the Web is assessing the validity and quality of the information provided on the Internet. Because the Web has made publishing so easy and inexpensive, virtually anybody can create a Web page on almost any subject. Research published in scientific or literary journals is subjected to peer review. Similarly, books and research monographs are often reviewed by peers or edited by experts in the appropriate subject area. However, information on the Web is seldom subjected to the review and editing processes that have become a standard practice in print publishing.

When you search the Web for entertainment or general information, you are not likely to experience significant harm as a result of gathering inaccurate or unreliable information. When you are searching the Web for an answer to a serious research question, however, the risks of obtaining and relying on inaccurate or unreliable information can be significant.

You can reduce your risks by carefully evaluating the quality of any Web resource on which you plan to rely for information related to an important judgment or decision. To develop an opinion about the quality of the resource, you can evaluate three major components of any Web page: the Web page's authorship, content, and appearance.

Author Identity and Objectivity

The first thing you should try to do when evaluating a Web research resource is to determine who authored the page. If you cannot easily find authorship information on a Web site, you should question the validity of the information included on the site. A Web site that does not identify its author has very little credibility as a research resource. Any Web page that presents empirical research results, logical arguments, theories, or other information that purports to be the result of a research process should identify the author *and* present the author's background information and credentials. The information on the site should be sufficient to establish the author's professional qualifications. You should also check secondary sources for corroborating information. For example, if the author of a Web page indicates that he or she is a member of a university faculty, you can find the university's Web site and see if the author is listed as a faculty member. The Web site should also provide author contact information, such as a street, email address, or telephone number, so that you can contact the author or consult information directories to verify the addresses or telephone numbers.

You also should consider whether the qualifications presented by the author pertain to the material that appears on the Web site. For example, the author of a Web site concerned with gene-splicing technology might list a Ph.D. degree as a credential. If the author's Ph.D. is in history or sociology, it would not support the credibility of the gene-splicing technology Web site. If you cannot determine the specific areas of the author's educational background, you can look for other examples of the author's work on the Web. By searching for the author's name and terms related to the subject area, you should be able to find other sites that include the author's work. The fact that a Web site author has written extensively on a subject can add some evidence—though not necessarily conclusive—that the author has expertise in the field.

In addition to identifying the author's identity and qualifications, author information should include details about the author's affiliations—either as an employee, owner, or consultant—with organizations that might have an interest in the research results or other information included in the Web site. Information about the author's affiliations will help you determine the level of independence and objectivity that the author can bring to bear on the research questions or topics. For example, research results supporting the contention that cigarette smoke is not harmful presented in a site authored by a researcher with excellent scientific credentials might be less compelling if you learn that the researcher is the chief scientist at a major tobacco company. By reading the page content carefully, you might be able to identify potential bias in the results presented.

Determining Web Site Ownership | InSight

In some cases, it can be difficult to determine who owns a specific Web server or provides the space for the Web page. You can make a rough assessment, however, by examining the domain identifier in the URL. If the site claims affiliation with an educational or research institution, the domain should be .edu for educational institution. A not-for-profit organization would most likely have the .org domain, and a government unit or agency would have the .gov domain. These are not hard-and-fast rules, however. For example, some perfectly legitimate not-for-profit organizations have URLs with a .com domain.

Content

The relevance of a site's content to your search for information can be more difficult to judge than the author's identity and objectivity; after all, you were searching for Web sites so you could learn more about your search topic, which implies that you probably are not an expert in that content area. However, you can look for some things in the Web site's presentation to help determine the quality of information. If the Web page has a clearly stated publication date, you can determine the timeliness of the content. You can read the content critically and evaluate whether the included topics are relevant to the research question at hand. You might be able to determine whether important topics or considerations were omitted. You also might be able to assess the depth of treatment the author gives to the subject.

Form and Appearance

A Web site that is a legitimate source of accurate information presents the information in a professional form that helps convey its validity. The Web does contain pages full of mis-information and outright lies that are nicely laid out, include professionally produced graphics, and have grammatically correct and properly spelled text. However, many pages that contain low-quality or incorrect information are poorly designed and not well edited. For example, a Web page devoted to an analysis of Shakespeare's plays that contains spelling errors indicates a low-quality resource. Loud colors, graphics that serve no purpose, and flashing text are all Web page design elements that often suggest a low-quality resource.

Evaluating the Quality of a Web Site

Now that you understand the principles of assessing Web page quality, Anne asks you to evaluate a Web page. Anne has been doing research on how companies can appeal to children on the Web by promoting products while not taking advantage of the children who visit their sites. Anne would like you to evaluate the quality of a URL titled "Kids' Corner."

Reference Window | **Evaluating a Web Research Resource**

- Open the Web page in your Web browser.
- Identify the author, if possible. If you can identify the author, evaluate his or her credentials and objectivity.
- Examine the content of the Web site.
- Evaluate the site's form and appearance.
- Draw a conclusion about the site's overall quality.

To evaluate the quality of the Kids' Corner Web page:

► **1.** Return to the Online Companion page for Session 3.2.

► **2.** Click the **Kids' Corner** link. The browser loads the Web page that appears in Figure 3-25. Examine the content of the Web page, read the text, examine the titles and headings, and consider the page's appearance.

Kids' Corner Web page   **Figure 3-25**

Jakob Nielsen's Alertbox, April 14, 2002:

Kids' Corner: Website Usability for Children

Summary:
Our usability study of kids found that they are as easily stumped by confusing websites as adults. Unlike adults, however, kids tend to view ads as content, and click accordingly. They also like colorful designs, but demand simple text and navigation.

Millions of children already use the Internet, and millions more are coming online each year. Many websites specifically target children with educational or entertainment content, and even mainstream websites are adding "kids' corner" sections for children -- either as a public service or to build brand loyalty from an early age.

Despite this growth in users and services, very little is known about how children actually use websites or how to design sites that will be easy for them to use. Most website designs for kids are based on **pure folklore about how kids supposedly behave** -- or, at best, by insights gleaned when designers observe their own children, who are hardly representative of average kids, typical Internet skills, or common knowledge about the Web.

Testing Children's Web Use

To find out how kids really use the Web, we conducted usability studies with 55 children who varied in age from 6 to 12 (first through fifth graders). We tested 39 kids in the United States and 16 in Israel, to broaden the international applicability of our recommendations.

We observed the children interacting with 24 sites designed for children, and three mainstream sites designed for adults (Amazon, Yahoo!, and Weather.com). For the targeted sites, we tested some sites specifically devoted to children, such as Alfy, MaMaMedia, and Sesame Street, and several kid-oriented subsites produced by mainstream companies, such as ABC News for Kids and Belmont Bank's Kids' Corner.

Even though participants in our study were very young, they often had the **greatest success using websites intended for adults**. Sites such as Amazon and Yahoo! are committed to utter simplicity and compliance with Web design conventions, and have become so easy to use that they support little kids very well. In contrast, many of the children's sites had complex and convoluted interaction designs that stumped our test users. As one first-grade boy said, *"The Internet is a lot of times BORING because you can't find anything when you go on to it."*

Usability Problems Hurt Kids

The idea that children are **masters of technology** and can defeat any computer-related difficulty is a myth. Our study found that children are **incapable of overcoming many usability problems**. Also, poor usability, combined with kids' lack of patience in the face of complexity, resulted in many simply leaving websites. A fourth-grader said, *"When I don't know what to do on a Web page, I just go look for something else."*

Also, children don't like slow downloads any more than adults do. As one first-grade girl said, *"Make it go faster! Maybe if I click it, it will go faster..."*

Young children often have **hand-me-down computers**, whether at home (where they often inherit older machines when their parents upgrade) or at school (where budget constraints mandate keeping machines in service for many years). Kids also typically have slow connections and outdated software. Given these limitations, websites must **avoid technical problems** or crashes related to access by low-end equipment. Faced with an error message, kids in our study told us that they see them a lot, and that the best thing to do is to ignore them or close the window and find something else to do.

Several types of **classic Web usability problems** caused difficulties for the kids in our study:

- **Unclear navigational confirmation** of the user's location confused users both within sites and when leaving them.
- **Inconsistent navigation** options, where the same destination was referred to in different ways, caused users to visit the same feature repeatedly, because they didn't know they had already been there.
- **Non-standard interaction techniques** caused predictable problems, such as making it impossible for users to select their preferred game using a "games machine."
- **Lack of perceived clickability** affordances, such as overly flat graphics, caused users to miss features because they overlooked the links.
- **Fancy wording** in interfaces confused users and prevented them from understanding the available choices.

Age-Appropriate Content

Extensive text was problematic for young children, who are just beginning to read. We observed severe usability problems when kids were inadvertently thrown into sections that were written above their current reading level.

Also, kids are **keenly aware of their age** and differentiate sharply between material that is appropriate for them and material for older or younger kids, however close in age they might be. At one website, a six-year-old said, *"This website is for babies, maybe four or five years old. You can tell because of the cartoons and trains."*

You can see that the author of the page is Jakob Nielsen and that the page has a clear, simple design. You note that the grammar and spelling are correct and the content is neither inflammatory nor overly argumentative, although it does reflect a strong specific viewpoint on the issue. The date on which the page was published is clearly stated at the top of the page. You note that this page appears to be a part of a Web publication called "Alertbox" by looking at the page's URL and by noting the link at the top of the page.

3. Click the **Alertbox** link near the top of the Web page to learn more about the Web publication.

You see that the full title of the publication is *Alertbox: Current Issues in Web Usability* and that it is written by Dr. Jakob Nielsen, a principal of the Nielsen Norman Group. You can also see that the site offers a free email newsletter and that it has a clearly stated privacy policy that governs use of any email addresses submitted. Although some sites state policies that they do not follow, the existence of a clearly stated policy is a good indicator of a high quality site.

4. Click the links to the **Jakob Nielsen** biography page and to the **Nielsen Norman Group** information page. These links appear under the publication title near the top of the page. Review the information on these pages and use it along with the information you gained in the previous steps to evaluate the quality of the Kids' Corner page.

5. Close your Web browser.

The information you examined should lead you to conclude that the Kid's Corner page is of high quality. Dr. Nielsen and his organization are both well respected in the field of Web site usability research. If you would like to do an additional exploration regarding this topic, you could use your favorite search engine to conduct searches on combinations of terms such as "Nielsen" and "Web usability." The determination of Web site quality is not an exact science, but with practice, you can develop your skills in this area.

Wikipedia

Wikipedia is a Web site that hosts a community-edited set of online encyclopedias in more than a dozen different languages. The concept behind Wikipedia is similar to that behind the Open Directory Project you learned about earlier in this tutorial. Instead of hiring experts to review and edit entries, which is what all print encyclopedias do, Wikipedia relies on contributions from anyone for its entries. Those entries then can be edited by anyone who reads them and thinks they should be changed in some way. The idea is that with enough people reading, editing, and re-editing the entries, the information on the site will evolve to a higher degree of accuracy.

The result of Wikipedia's open nature to date is that it contains a great deal of useful information and much of that information is valid. However, Wikipedia's content is only as good as its contributors, and consequently, some of the information on the site is inaccurate, incomplete, or biased.

One of the most important tools you have for assessing the quality of information on the Web is the author's identity. On Wikipedia, contributors may post and edit articles anonymously, in which case the author is identified only by the IP address of his or her connection to the Internet. Even when the author or editor of an article chooses to be identified, it is through a Wikipedia account name and the biographical information included on the user page is entered by the account holder. That is, the information can be as limited or incorrect as the account holder chooses.

Conducting Research Online | InSight

Although Wikipedia can be an interesting place to visit, it can be a risky place to do serious research. Very few teachers or employers would accept a research project that referenced Wikipedia as a primary source. In fact, it is always a good idea to check with your instructor before using online resources in your research.

Your research efforts have provided Dave and Ranjit with a great deal of valid information. Anne is impressed with your work.

Session 3.2 Quick Check | Review

1. The three basic Boolean operators are _____ , _____ , and _____ .

2. Write a search expression using Boolean and precedence operators that returns Web pages containing information about wild mustang horses in Wyoming but not information about the Ford Mustang automobile.

3. True or False: The NEAR location operator always returns phrases that contain all keywords within 10 words of each other in a search expression.

4. True or False: In most search engines, the wildcard character is a * symbol.

5. Name three kinds of filters you can include in a Google search run from its Advanced Search page.

6. In an advanced or Boolean search expression, parentheses are an example of a(n) _____ operator.

7. Name one distinguishing feature of the Clusty search engine.

8. List three features to consider when evaluating the quality of a Web site.

In this tutorial, you learned how to formulate specific and exploratory research questions and how to use a structured Web search process to find information on the Web. You learned how to develop search expressions, which you used in three types of Web search tools: search engines, Web directories, and metasearch engines. You learned what Boolean operators, precedence operators, and location operators are and how they work in several major search engines. You also learned how to use wildcards in search expressions and how to use several types of filtering techniques to narrow your search results. You learned how to use information about Web page author identity and objectivity along with the content, form, and appearance of the Web pages themselves to evaluate their validity and reliability.

Key Terms

banner ad
Boolean algebra
Boolean operator
bot
clearinghouse
dead link
deep Web
dynamic Web page
exploratory question
full text indexing
grouping operator
hidden Web
hit
hybrid search engine
   directory
inbound links

inclusion operator
invisible Web
location operator
logical operator
meta tag
metasearch engine
natural language query
   interface
page ranking
paid placement
parsing
precedence operator
proximity operator
query
resource list
results page

search engine
search expression
search filter
specific question
spider
sponsored links
static Web page
stemming
stop words
subject guide
virtual library
Web bibliography
Web directory
Web robot
Web search tools
Wikipedia
wildcard character

Practice	Review Assignments

Practice the skills you learned in the tutorial using the same case scenario.

There are no Data Files needed for the Review Assignments.

Anne, Dave and Ranjit are keeping you busy at IER. You have noticed that Dave and Ranjit frequently need information about the economy and economic forecasts. Your internship will be over soon, so you would like to leave them with links to some resources that they might find useful after you leave. To create the links, complete the following steps:

1. Start your Web browser, go to www.course.com/oc/np/internet7 to open the Online Companion page, log in to your account, click the Tutorial 3 link, and then click the Review Assignments link. The Review Assignments section of the Tutorial 3 page contains links organized under three headings: Search Engines, Web Directories, and Metasearch Engines.

2. Choose at least one search tool from each category and conduct searches using combinations of the search terms "economy," "economics," "forecasts," "conditions," and "outlook."

3. Expand or narrow your search using each tool until you find five Web sites that you believe are comprehensive guides or directories that Anne, Dave, and Ranjit should include in their bookmarks or favorites lists to help them locate information about international business stories.

4. For each Web site, record the URL and write a paragraph that explains why you believe the site would be useful to an international business news writer. Identify each site as a guide, directory, or other resource.

5. For each Web site, conduct an evaluation of the quality of the site. Write a paragraph for each site rating the site's quality as low, medium, or high, and explain the reasons for your rating.

6. When you are finished, close your Web browser.

Apply	Case Problem 1

Apply the skills you learned in this tutorial to choose a search tool and use it to find geographic information.

There are no Data Files needed for this Case Problem.   *Tutorial 4 Case 1*

Midland University Earth Sciences Institute   You are an intern at the Midland University Earth Sciences Institute. The Institute conducts research on the primary effects of earthquakes on land stability, soil composition, and water redirection. The Institute also examines secondary effects such as changes in plant and animal life in the earthquake zone. When an earthquake strikes, the Institute sends a team of geologists, soil chemists, biologists, botanists, and civil engineers to the quake's site to examine the damage to structures, land formations, lakes, and rivers. An earthquake can occur without warning nearly anywhere in the world, so the Institute needs quick access to information about local conditions in various parts of the world, including the temperature, rainfall, money exchange rates, demographics, and local customs. It is early July when you receive a call that an earthquake has just occurred in northern Chile. To obtain information about local mid-winter conditions there so that you can help the Institute prepare its team, complete the following steps.

1. Start your Web browser, go to www.course.com/oc/np/internet7 to open the Online Companion page, log in to your account, click the Tutorial 3 link, and then click the Case Problem 1 link. The Case Problem 1 section contains links to lists of search engines, directories, and metasearch engines.

⊕ **EXPLORE**

2. Choose one of the search tools you learned about in this tutorial to conduct searches for information on local conditions in northern Chile. For the weather conditions information, be sure to obtain information about conditions during the month of July. (*Hint:* You might need to conduct preliminary searches to identify terms that you can use to limit your searches to northern Chile.)

3. Prepare a short report that includes the daily temperature range, average rainfall, current exchange rate for U.S. dollars to Chilean pesos, and any information you can obtain about the characteristics of the local population.

4. When you are finished, close your Web browser.

| Apply | | **Case Problem 2** |

Apply the skills you learned in this tutorial to find information about companies that sell a specific product.

There are no Data Files needed for this Case Problem.

Lightning Electrical Generators, Inc. You work as a marketing manager for Lightning Electrical Generators, Inc., a firm that has built generators for more than 50 years. The generator business is not as profitable as it once was. John Delaney, the firm's president, has asked you to investigate new markets for the company. One market that John would like to consider is the uninterruptible power supply (UPS) business. A UPS unit supplies continuing power to a single computer or to an entire computer system if the regular source of power fails. Most UPS units provide power only long enough to allow an orderly shutdown of the computer. John wants you to study the market for UPS units in the United States. He also wants to know which firms currently make and sell UPS products. Finally, he would like some idea of the power ratings and prices of individual units. To provide John the information he needs, complete the following steps.

1. Start your Web browser, go to www.course.com/oc/np/internet7 to open the Online Companion page, log in to your account, click the Tutorial 3 link, and then click the Case Problem 2 link. The Case Problem 2 section contains links to lists of search engines, directories, and metasearch engines.

⊕ **EXPLORE**

2. Use one of the search tools to conduct searches for information about specific UPS products for John. You should design your searches to find the manufacturers' names and information about the products that they offer. (*Hint*: Try searching on the full term, "uninterruptible power supply," in addition to the acronym, "UPS.")

3. Prepare a short report that includes the information you have gathered for at least five UPS products, including the manufacturer's name, model number, product features, and suggested price.

4. When you are finished, close your Web browser.

| Apply | | **Case Problem 3** |

Apply the skills you learned in this tutorial to find and evaluate the quality of specific Web Page content.

There are no Data Files needed for this Case Problem.

Eastern College English Department You are a research assistant in the Eastern College English Department. The department head, Professor Garnell, has a particular interest in Shakespeare. She has spent years researching the question of whether William Shakespeare actually wrote the plays and poems attributed to him. Some scholars, including Professor Garnell, believe that most of Shakespeare's works were written by Christopher Marlowe. Professor Garnell would like to include links on the department Web page to other researchers who agree with her, but she wants only high-quality sites represented. To gather the URLs that Professor Garnell wants, complete the following steps.

1. Start your Web browser, go to www.course.com/oc/np/internet7 to open the Online Companion page, log in to your account, click the Tutorial 3 link, and then click the Case Problem 3 link. The Case Problem 3 section contains links to lists of search engines, directories, and metasearch engines.

2. Use one of the search tools to find Web sites that contain information about the Shakespeare-Marlowe controversy.

⊕ **EXPLORE**

3. Use the procedures outlined in this tutorial to evaluate the quality of the sites you found in the previous step. (*Hint*: Most useful sites will have some connection to a university or research library.)

4. Choose at least five Web sites that Professor Garnell might want to include on her Web page. For each Web site, record the URL and write at least one paragraph in which you describe the evidence you have gathered about the site's quality. You should include at least one site that is low quality in your collection.

5. When you are finished, close your Web browser.

| Research | **Case Problem 4** |

Research the Web to find specific information, then evaluate the information.

There are no Data Files needed for this Case Problem.

Glenwood Employment Agency   You work as a staff assistant at the Glenwood Employment Agency. Eric Steinberg, the agency's owner, wants you to locate Web resources for finding open positions in your geographic area. Eric would like this information to gauge whether his own efforts are keeping pace with the competition. He wants to monitor a few good pages but does not want to conduct exhaustive searches of the Web every week. To help Eric find current employment information, complete the following steps.

1. Start your Web browser, go to www.course.com/oc/np/internet7 to open the Online Companion page, log in to your account, click the Tutorial 3 link, and then click the Case Problem 4 link. The Case Problem 4 section contains links to lists of search engines, directories, and metasearch engines.

⊕ **EXPLORE**

2. Use one of the search tools to find Web sites containing information about job openings in your geographic area. (*Hint*: You can use search expressions that include Boolean and precedence operators to limit your searches.)

3. Prepare a list of at least five URLs of pages that you believe would be good candidates for Eric's monitoring program.

4. For each URL that you find, write a paragraph that explains why you selected it and then identify any particular strengths or weaknesses of the Web site based on Eric's intended use.

5. When you are finished, close your Web browser.

| Create | **Case Problem 5** |

Create a report that evaluates the effectiveness of a search tool you chose to find specific information.

There are no Data Files needed for this Case Problem.

Lynda's Fine Foods   For many years, Lynda Rice has operated a small store that sells specialty foods, such as pickles and mustard, and related gift items. Lynda is thinking about selling her products on the Web because they are small, inexpensive to ship relative to their product prices, and easy to ship. She believes that people who buy her products might appreciate the convenience of ordering over the Web. Lynda would like to find some specialty food store sites on the Web to learn about possible competitors and to obtain some ideas that she might use when she creates her own Web site. To research selling specialty food items on the Web, complete the following steps.

1. Start your Web browser, go to www.course.com/np/internet7 to open the Online Companion page, log in to your account, click the Tutorial 3 link, and then click the Case Problem 5 link. The Case Problem 5 section contains links to lists of search engines, directories, and metasearch engines.

2. Use one of the search tools to find Web sites that offer gift items such as pickles or mustard. You can use search expressions that include Boolean and precedence operators to limit your searches.

3. Repeat your search using one of the Web directory tools.

4. Compare the results you obtained using a search engine and using a Web directory. Explain in a memorandum of about 100 words which search tool was more effective for this type of search. Your instructor might ask you to prepare a presentation to your class in which you summarize your conclusions.

5. When you are finished, close your Web browser.

Review | Quick Check Answers

Session 3.1

1. open-ended, hard to phrase, difficult to determine when you have found a good answer

2. True

3. Web robot, bot, or spider

4. inbound links from other Web pages

5. False. Most search engines exclude stop words such as *and* or *the*.

6. Advantage: Experts have selected, examined, and classified the entries in a Web directory. Disadvantage: You must know which category to search to find information.

7. The power of the search engine operates on the expert-selected and classified entries in the directory.

8. It forwards the expression to a number of other search engines, and then presents and organizes the search results it receives from them.

9. They offer lists of hyperlinks to other Web pages, frequently including summaries or reviews of the Web sites, organized by subject.

Session 3.2

1. AND, OR, NOT

2. One possibility is: (mustang OR horse) AND Wyoming NOT (Ford OR automobile OR auto OR car)

3. False. The number of words will be different in different search engines.

4. True

5. Any three of these: language, file format, date, where the search terms appear on the Web page, domain, and Safe Search

6. precedence, inclusion, or grouping

7. It organizes search results into clusters of related hyperlinks; it performs this clustering dynamically after it has processed the search expression and gathered the results from its database.

8. identity and objectivity of author(s), content, form, and appearance

Information Resources on the Web

Finding, Evaluating, and Using Online Information Resources

Case | Cosby Promotions

You have just started a new position as the executive assistant to Marti Cosby, the president of Cosby Promotions—a growing booking agency that handles promotion and concert contract negotiations for musicians and bands. Cosby Promotions works with a wide variety of music acts. Current clients include bands that play pop, Latin, heavy metal, techno, industrial, and urban styles of music. The agency does not currently handle many country music acts, but Marti wants to expand its country music business over the next few years. The music business is dynamic because of the fluctuating popularity of musical artists; promotion and booking strategies that work best for a particular client one month might not work well the next month. Promotional tie-ins and spon-sorships are also important revenue sources for music acts, and the needs of specific sponsors change with shifts in customer preferences.

Your primary job is to use your basic understanding of Web searching techniques to help Cosby Promotions' staff stay current on entertainment news and trends that might affect the agency's clients. Your other duties include updating agency execu-tives and clients about local conditions at travel destinations and working with the agency's Web site design team to develop an effective Web presence.

In addition to working with Marti and the executive team, you will work closely with Susan Zhu, the agency's research director. Susan has worked at Cosby Pro-motions for six years in a variety of research jobs. The research department con-ducts background investigations when dealing with the agency's clients. For example, whenever Marti starts working on a booking for a concert hall or other venue that is new for the agency, she asks Susan to provide background on the venue. Susan is looking forward to having you work with her as part of the Cosby Promotions research team.

Starting Data Files

There are no starting Data Files needed for this tutorial.

Session 4.1

Current Information on the Web

In earlier tutorials, you learned how to use search engines, directories, and other resources to find information on the Web. Many of your assignments for Cosby Promotions will involve finding recent news and information about clients, potential sponsors, performance venues, and changes in the music industry. In this session, you will learn how to use search engines and directories to find recent news stories and other current information. Remember to use the techniques you learned in Tutorial 3 to assess the reliability of the information you gather in this tutorial.

To help you find current news and information, many search engines and directories include sections devoted to news items. For example, the Excite directory's home page includes a collection of hyperlinks to general news stories, sports scores, stock market reports, and weather, as shown in Figure 4-1.

Figure 4-1	Excite home page

Tip

If you are willing to register with Excite, you can follow the Personalize links (near the top of the Web page) to specify the kind of information that appears on this page when you log on.

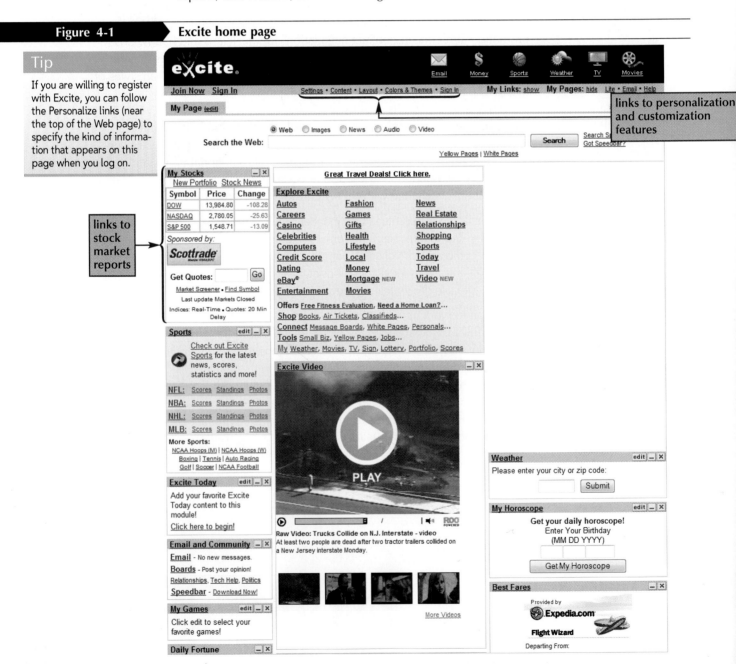

links to personalization and customization features

links to stock market reports

Yahoo! offers similar information on its home page, including an "In the News" tab that includes general news stories. The page also includes tabs titled "World," "Local," and "Finance" that include corresponding types of news stories. The Yahoo! home page also offers links to current entertainment, sports, and weather information, as shown in Figure 4-2.

Yahoo! home page   **Figure 4-2**

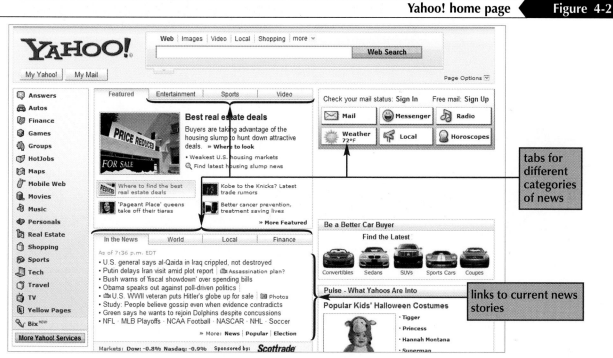

Reproduced with permission of Yahoo! Inc. ® 2007 by Yahoo! Inc. YAHOO! and the YAHOO! logo are trademarks of Yahoo! Inc.

Search engines can also be useful tools for finding news stories. Many search engines allow you to choose a date range when you enter a search expression. HotBot is a Web site that lets you run date-filtered searches on Ask.com. HotBot's Advanced Search page, shown in Figure 4-3, provides two ways to perform date-related searches. You can choose one of HotBot's preset time range options, such as "in the last week" or "in the last 3 months," to limit your search to sites that were last modified within your selected time period. Alternatively, you can limit searches to dates before or after a specific date. In the section of the HotBot Advanced Search page that appears in Figure 4-3 you can see the two date filter options.

Figure 4-3 | **Date filters on the HotBot Advanced Search page**

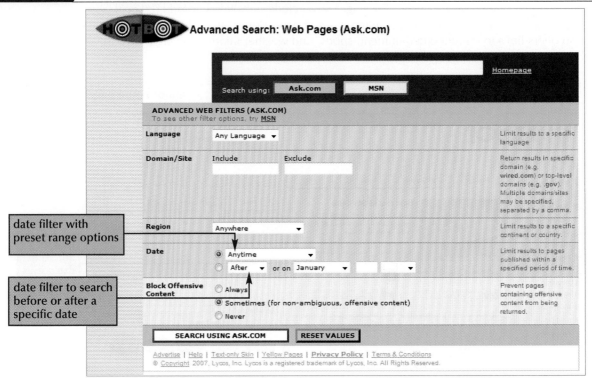

date filter with preset range options

date filter to search before or after a specific date

HotBot does not, however, provide a way to search for sites modified within a specified date range. For example, you could not limit a HotBot search to sites modified between April 24, 2006, and November 11, 2006. As you learned in Tutorial 3, a good Internet researcher will always know how to use more than one search tool. To search for sites modified between specific dates, you could use the AltaVista search engine, which allows you to set an exact "between" date range on its Advanced Search page. Figure 4-4 shows the AltaVista Advanced Web Search page with an exact date range set.

Date filters on the AltaVista Advanced Web Search page | Figure 4-4

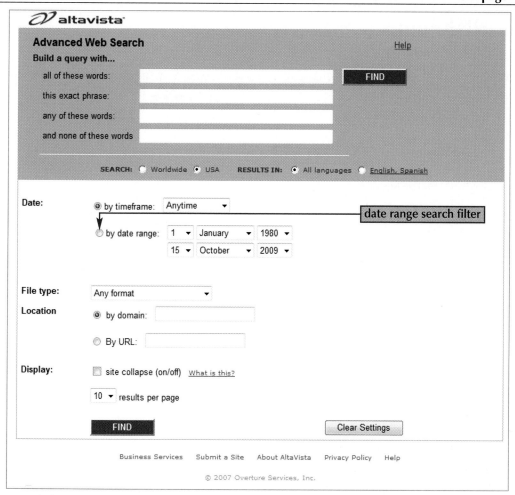

Reproduced with permission of Yahoo! Inc. ® 2007 by Yahoo! Inc. YAHOO! and the YAHOO! logo are trademarks of Yahoo! Inc.

The AlltheWeb search engine uses a slightly different approach. It allows you to set separate "after" and "before" date filters. By setting both of these filters, you can construct an exact "between" date filter. Figure 4-5 shows these filters on the AlltheWeb Advanced Search page with an exact date range set.

Figure 4-5   Date filters on the AlltheWeb Advanced Search page

Reproduced with permission of Yahoo! Inc. ® 2007 by Yahoo! Inc. YAHOO! and the YAHOO! logo are trademarks of Yahoo! Inc.

Your first assignment for Cosby Promotions requires research on recent news about Honda. The company wants to increase its appeal to younger drivers and is looking to sponsor a band that will appeal to that market. Marti knows that other agencies will be pitching bands to Honda for this sponsorship, so she wants as much background information on Honda as possible before she meets with them next week. She would like you to search the Web and collect the URLs of sites that mention Honda; she is especially interested in learning more about the kinds of promotional activities the company is already doing. Marti needs the most recent information available, so you will search for sites that have been modified within the last few months.

Finding Web Sites that Have Been Modified Recently | Reference Window

- Go to the Web site for a search engine or directory that allows date-range restrictions.
- Formulate your search expression.
- Set the date-range restriction in the search tool.
- Run the search.
- Evaluate the search results. If you do not find useful results, select an alternative search tool, and then run the search again.

Consider the search tools available. Your search term—*Honda*—is a brand name, so it is likely that Web directories will collect many useful sites that include the term in their databases. Another option is to use a search engine for this query. Search engines might include more recent listings because the editorial review process of many Web directories takes time to complete.

To find specific Web pages based on last modified dates:

▶ **1.** Start your Web browser, go to **www.course.com/oc/np/internet7** to open the Online Companion page, log on to your account, click the **Tutorial 4** link, and then click the **Session 4.1** link.

▶ **2.** Choose one of the search tools in the Search Engines and Web Directories with Date Filters section, and then click the link to the tool you have chosen to open its advanced search page.

▶ **3.** Formulate a search expression that will locate promotions for Honda. For most of the search tools, typing the expression **Honda promotion** in the search text box should work.

▶ **4.** Select a date filter to limit your search to the most recent few months (depending on the search tool you chose, you will use either a preset filter for the last three or four months or an exact date filter), and then click the appropriate tool's **Search** (or similar) button to start the search.

▶ **5.** Examine your search results to determine whether you have found any valuable information. If not, return to the Online Companion page for Tutorial 4, select a different search engine or Web directory from the list, and then repeat Steps 2 through 4 using that search tool.

Tip

Remember, if you do not find what you are looking for with one search tool, you can try your search again using different tools until you are satisfied with your results.

Figure 4-6 shows a part of the results page generated by the Google search engine for this query. The page includes several results that might be useful to Marti. Your results, even if you use Google, will be different.

Figure 4-6 ▷ **Google date-filtered search results**

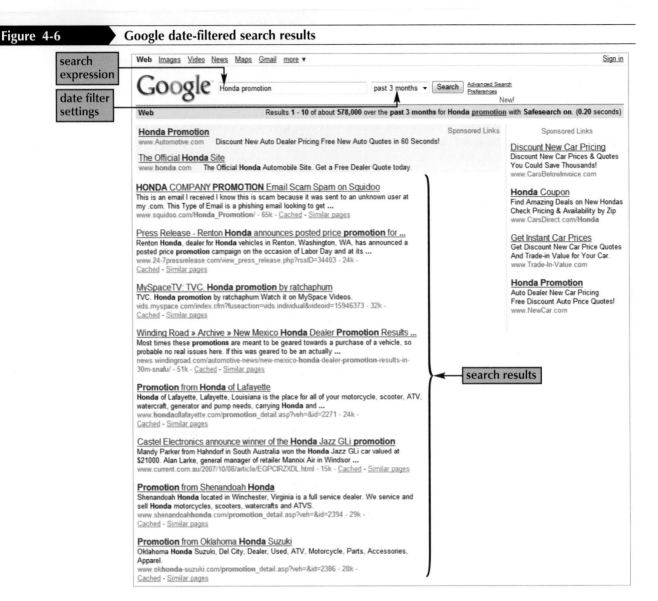

You can email the URLs to Marti or you can tell her how to obtain the same search results. For now, you decide to copy and paste the URLs that look promising and send them to her in an email message.

Getting the News

Marti is pleased with many of the recently modified Web pages you found. Now, she asks you to find current news stories about Honda that might not appear in a search of recently modified Web pages.

Finding current news stories on the Web can be easy if you know where to look. Most search engines and Web directories include links to broadcast networks, wire services, and newspapers. A **wire service** (also called a press agency or news service) is an organization that gathers and distributes news to newspapers, magazines, broadcasters, and other organizations that pay a fee to the wire service. Although there are hundreds of wire services in the world, most news comes from the four largest wire services: United Press International (UPI) and the Associated Press (AP) in the United States, Reuters in Great Britain, and Agence France-Presse in France. In addition to selling stories to news-outlets around the world, these major wire services all display current news stories on their Web sites.

Web News Directories and News Search Engines

All of the major U.S. broadcast networks, including ABC, CBS, CNN, Fox, MSNBC, NBC, and NPR have Web sites that carry news features. Broadcasters in other countries, such as the BBC, also provide news reports on their Web pages. Major newspapers, such as *The New York Times*, the *Washington Post*, and the *Los Angeles Times*, have Web sites that include current news and many other features from their print editions. Many of these broadcast news, wire service, and newspaper Web sites include search features that allow you to search the site for specific news stories.

The Internet Public Library's Online Newspapers site includes hyperlinks to hundreds of international and domestic newspapers. Sites like the Internet Public Library, which offer categorized links to news outlets or to specific stories on the Web pages of news outlets, are called **Web news directories**. You can explore a number of Web news directories by opening the Online Companion page, clicking the Tutorial 4 link, and then following the links in the "Web News Directories" section. Figure 4-7 shows the Newspapers page of the Internet Public Library Web site, which is hosted by the University of Michigan.

Figure 4-7 ▶ Internet Public Library links to newspaper Web sites

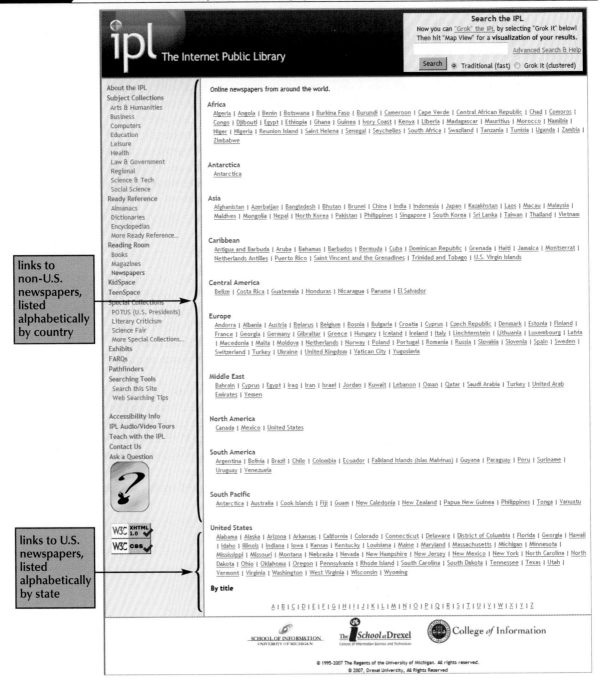

links to non-U.S. newspapers, listed alphabetically by country

links to U.S. newspapers, listed alphabetically by state

The search feature of the Internet Public Library Newspapers page searches only the title and the main entry for each newspaper and does not search the newspaper sites' contents. Therefore, you could use it to identify all of the newspapers in New Jersey or all of the newspapers that had the word Tribune in their titles, but you could not use it to find news stories that include the word Honda. You need to select a newspaper, go to the newspaper site, and conduct your search there. To search a hundred newspapers, you would need to do your search a hundred times. This drawback is shared by most Web news directory sites.

Fortunately, a number of Web sites let you search the content of current news stories in multiple publications and wire services. These sites are often called **news search engines**. In the early days of the Web, a number of these sites were independently operated and offered links to specific stories on the Web sites of newspapers and other media outlets. One of these early sites, NewsHub, is still in operation, but most Web search engines today are operated by the major search engines you learned about in earlier tutorials. The databases for the news search engine components of these sites are separate from their main Web search databases, but the search mechanism is usually similar to that used on the sites' main search pages.

Yahoo! News includes stories from the major wire services along with news it purchases from newspapers and magazines. Google News includes stories from similar news sources. Some news search engines provide ways to search **Web logs** (also called **Weblogs** or **blogs**), which are Web sites that contain commentary on current events written by individuals. You will learn more about blogs in Session 4.2.

You decide to use a news search engine to find recent news stories about Honda.

> **Tip**
>
> To obtain both breadth and currency of coverage, experienced searchers often run the same query using more than one search tool.

Searching Current News Stories | Reference Window

- Select a news search engine site.
- Open the site in your Web browser.
- Enter your search expression into the search text box.
- Set any date filters you want to use to limit your search.
- Run the search and evaluate your results.

To find recent news stories on the Web that mention Honda:

▶ **1.** Return to the Online Companion page for Session 4.1, choose one of the tools in the News Search Engines section to use in your search, and then click the link to the tool you have chosen to open its search page.

▶ **2.** Type the search term **Honda** in your chosen site's search text box, and then click the site's **Search** (or similar) button to start the search.

▶ **3.** Select a date filter to limit your results to the most recent few weeks.

▶ **4.** Examine your search results to determine whether you have found any information that might be useful to Marti. If not, repeat Steps 1 through 3 using a different search tool.

Figure 4-8 shows a part of the results page generated by the Google news search engine for this query. Your results, even if you use Google News, will be different.

Figure 4-8   **Google News search results page**

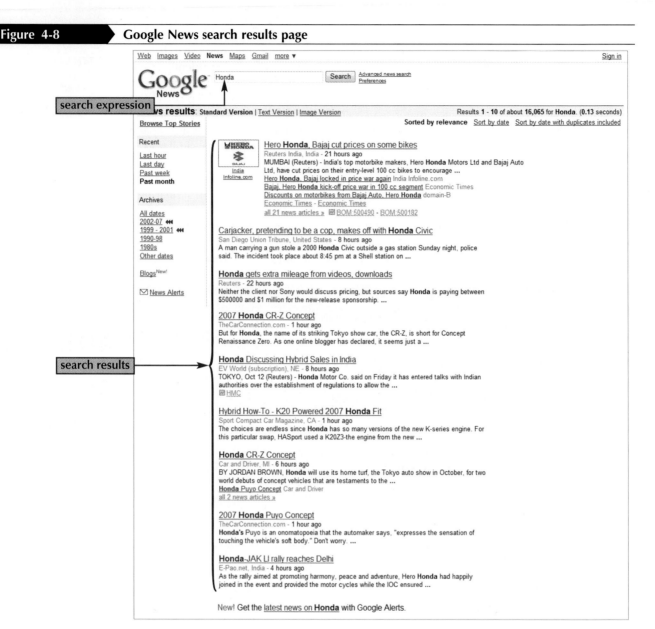

You have compiled a list of useful URLs about Honda's current promotional and sponsorship activities for Marti. You have also gained experience in searching for current topics by examining Web pages that have been modified recently and by using tools that search the Web specifically for news reports.

Weather Reports

Marti will travel to Nashville later in the week to meet with some new country music artists that she hopes to sign as clients for the agency. Marti is interested in the weather forecast for the area. A number of Web sites offer weather information and forecasts. The two most popular—The Weather Channel and AccuWeather—provide weather forecast information to many other Web sites, such as Excite, *USA Today*, and Yahoo!. The Accu-Weather home page appears in Figure 4-9.

AccuWeather home page | Figure 4-9

enter zip code or name of city here to obtain local weather forecast

InSight | Using Local Weather Forecasts

Local television stations offer weather information on their Web sites. Some of these sites purchase weather information from major weather Web sites such as AccuWeather or the Weather Channel, but many of them employ their own meteorologists and have their own weather prediction equipment. You might find that these local weather forecasts are more accurate and detailed than those provided by the major weather Web sites for your area. To find these sites, enter a search expression that includes your local television station's call letters into a search engine and follow the links in the search results.

You decide to check two weather sources for Marti because you know that meteorology is not an exact science.

Reference Window | Finding a Weather Forecast

- Open a weather information Web site in a Web browser.
- Locate the weather report for the city or area in which you are interested.
- Repeat the steps to find other weather forecasts in different weather information Web sites.

To find weather forecasts for the Nashville area:

▶ **1.** Return to the Online Companion page for Session 4.1.

▶ **2.** Choose one of the tools in the Weather Information Web Sites section to use in your search, and then click the link to the site you have chosen to open its home page. Most of these sites allow you to search on either the name of the city or its zip code.

▶ **3.** Type the city name and state, **Nashville**, **TN**, or the zip code for downtown Nashville, **37201**, in your chosen site's search text box, and then click the site's **Go** (or similar) button to find the local Nashville forecast. Note the forecast for the time that corresponds with Marti's visit.

▶ **4.** Repeat Steps 1 through 3 using a different weather information site.

Tip

Usually, weather-forecasting sites will report slightly different (and sometimes completely different) forecasts for the same time period in the same area.

Figure 4-10 shows a part of the Nashville local forecast page on The Weather Channel site. It includes a report on current conditions, a forecast, and a Doppler radar image. It also includes a link to a 10-day local forecast. The page you see, even if you use The Weather Channel site, will be different.

The Weather Channel local forecast page for Nashville   Figure 4-10

type city name or zip code here to obtain another weather forecast

current weather

current forecast

link to 10-day local forecast

Doppler radar image

Obtaining Maps and Destination Information

Marti would like to include a stop at Ryman Auditorium, the original home of the Grand Ole Opry, which is at 116 Fifth Avenue North. You offer to find a map of Nashville on the Web that shows the location of Ryman Auditorium. A number of Web sites provide maps and driving directions. Although the information provided by these sites is not perfect (new roads and detours caused by current construction work are not included), many people find them to be helpful travel aids. One of the most popular of these sites is MapQuest. A portion of the MapQuest home page appears in Figure 4-11.

Figure 4-11	MapQuest home page

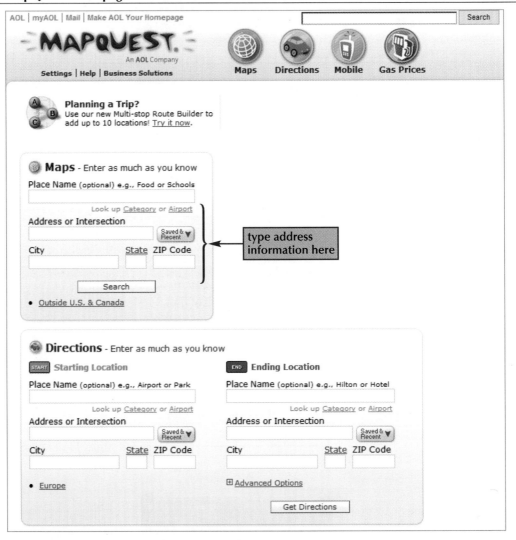

Finding a Local Area Map on the Web | Reference Window

- Open a Web site that offers maps in your Web browser.
- Enter the location of the map you need to find.
- Zoom the map scale in or out to suit your requirements.
- Print or download the finished map.

To obtain a map of the Nashville area near Ryman Auditorium:

▶ **1.** Return to the Online Companion page for Session 4.1, choose one of the tools in the Web Sites with Maps and Directions section to use in your search, and then click the link to the site you have chosen to open its home page.

▶ **2.** Type the address, **116 Fifth Avenue North**, the city name, **Nashville**, and the state abbreviation, **TN**, in the appropriate text boxes of your chosen site's Web page. Then click the site's **Get Map** (or similar) button to open a page that includes a map of the area near Ryman Auditorium.

▶ **3.** When the page that includes the map loads, use the controls on the page to zoom in or out until you have a map image that you think will meet Marti's needs.

Downloading Maps | InSight

Some sites allow you to email the map image or download it to your computer or a handheld device such as a personal digital assistant (PDA) or a mobile phone. These sites usually include links to terms and conditions that govern your use of any maps you download, print, or email. Be sure to review those terms and conditions for your chosen site.

Figure 4-12 shows the results of this search using two Web sites, Google Maps and MSN Maps & Directions. The map you obtain, even if you use one of these sites, might look different. Each site offers a slightly different view of the area, with different features displayed. Each of these features might be more or less important in a given situation. For example, if Marti is planning to drive to Ryman Auditorium, she might find the MSN site's freeway exit numbers helpful. Because these differences exist, many people regularly use two or three different Web sites when they are planning a trip.

Figure 4-12 Ryman Auditorium area map in Google Maps and MSN Maps & Directions

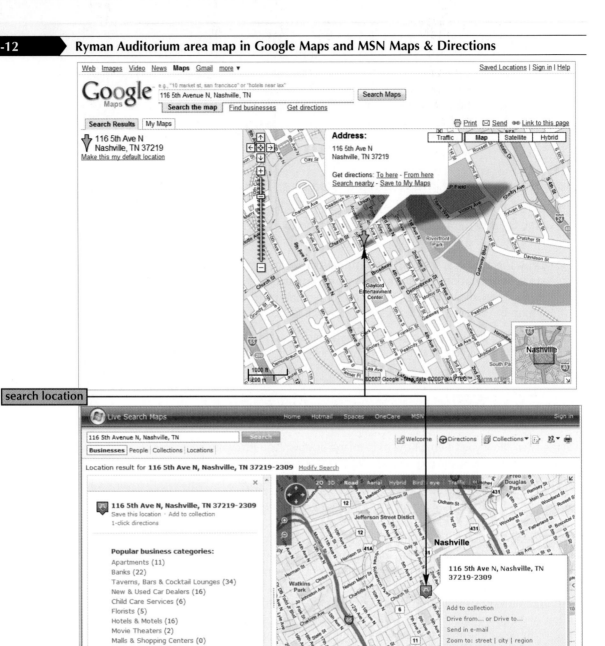

You have located a map that will meet Marti's needs. To further help Marti on her Nashville trip, you want to find some information about restaurants and other points of interest in Nashville. The Web offers a number of sites with information about cities that are popular travel destinations.

Obtaining Travel Destination Information | Reference Window

- Go to a city guide Web site in your Web browser.
- Search the site for your destination city, region, or country.
- Explore the hyperlinks provided by the site for your destination.

To obtain information about Nashville restaurants and entertainment:

▶ **1.** Return to the Online Companion page for Session 4.1, choose one of the tools in the City Guides section to use in your search, and then click the link to the site you have chosen to open its home page.

▶ **2.** Find your chosen site's page for Nashville, TN. The procedure you use will depend on which site you chose; however, most sites require you to type **Nashville** in a search text box or click a **Nashville** link. If you are unable to find an entry for Nashville on your chosen site, select a different site for your search.

▶ **3.** Examine the results page to find information about restaurants and entertainment in Nashville.

You can find a variety of useful information using city guide sites. In addition to information about entertainment and restaurants, you can often obtain useful information about specific attractions. For example, Figure 4-13 shows detailed information about the Ryman Auditorium that you might find by using the Citysearch site.

Figure 4-13 Citysearch Ryman Auditorium page

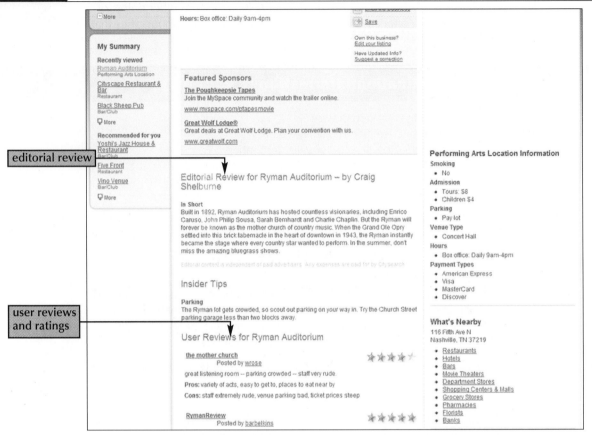

Finding Businesses and People on the Web

Some Web sites include listings of businesses and people, much like the print directories that you have probably used to find telephone numbers. These sites often include search engines that specialize in finding information about people and businesses on the Web.

Finding Businesses

Over the next few years, Marti is planning to develop reciprocal relationships with local booking agencies in Nashville. She would like to make some initial contacts during this trip and asks you to search the Web to find a list of booking agencies in Nashville. Web sites that store information about businesses only are often called **yellow pages directories**. You can use a yellow pages directory to find booking agencies located in Nashville.

Finding Business Listings on the Web | Reference Window

- Navigate to a yellow pages directory site in your Web browser.
- Enter information about the nature and geographic location of the business that you want to find.
- Run the search.
- Examine and evaluate the results to determine whether you should revise your search or try another search engine.

To find Nashville booking agencies on the Web:

▶ **1.** Return to the Online Companion page for Session 4.1, choose one of the tools in the Yellow Pages Directories section to use in your search, and then click the link to the site you have chosen to open its home page.

▶ **2.** The exact procedure you will use for your search will depend on which directory you chose. Most sites require you to enter a search term for the category of the business you want to find. For this search, you should try terms such as *agent*, *artist*, *recording artist*, or *booking agent*. Enter the location information in the appropriate field, and then click the **Search** (or similar) button. If your first search is unsuccessful, try another search with a different search term. If none of the search terms yields satisfactory results, return to the Online Companion page for Session 4.1 and try using a different yellow pages directory site.

▶ **3.** Examine your results pages to find information about booking agencies in Nashville.

This search can be challenging because there is no single category description that is universally used by companies that book performing musicians. Figure 4-14 shows the results page for a search using the term "agent" on the SuperPages.com yellow pages directory site. The search returned several categories, one of which was the category "Talent Agencies & Casting Services." This category includes a number of listings for booking agencies in Nashville. Your search will yield different categories, depending on which directory you use. In fact, your search will probably yield a different list of booking agencies, even if you use the SuperPages.com directory and click the "Talent Agencies & Casting Services" category.

Figure 4-14 SuperPages.com search results page

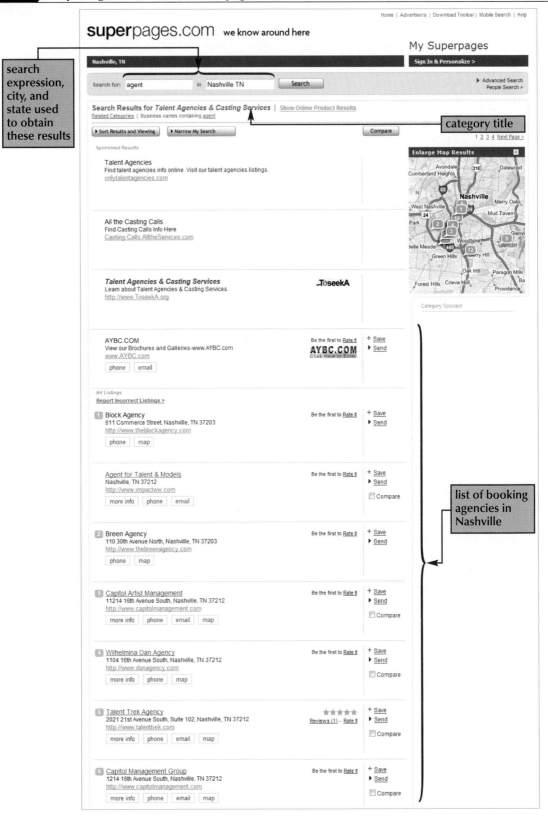

You are satisfied that you have found enough information about Nashville weather, attractions, and booking agencies.

In addition to using the Web to find businesses, you can use it to find individuals.

Finding People

Many Web sites let you search for individuals' names, addresses, and telephone numbers. These sites, often called **white pages directories**, collect information from published telephone directories and other publicly available information and index it by last name.

Some Web sites make unpublished and unlisted telephone numbers available for public use. Other sites group individual listings by categories such as religious or political affiliation. Many people expressed concerns about privacy violations when this type of information became easily accessible on the Web. In response to these privacy concerns, most white pages sites offer people a way to remove their listings. For example, Switchboard will accept a list removal request made on its Web page or sent by email. You might want to determine whether white pages directories have a correct listing for you and whether you want your listing to appear in a white pages site.

Searching for Your White Pages Listing | Reference Window

- Open a white pages directory Web site in your Web browser.
- Enter your name and part of your address.
- Run the search, and then examine the search results.
- Consider repeating the search with various combinations of partial address information or variants of the correct spelling of your name.

To search for your listing on a white pages directory:

▶ **1.** Return to the Online Companion page for Session 4.1, choose one of the tools in the White Pages Directories section to use in your search, and then click the link to the site you have chosen to open its home page.

▶ **2.** The exact procedure you will use for your search will depend on which directory you chose; however, most sites require you to enter your first name, your last name, and a part of your address such as the city and state.

   Trouble? If your telephone number is listed under another person's name, such as a parent or roommate, use that person's name to find your listing.

   Trouble? If you do not find your listing, try searching for a friend's listing or your parents' listing. You can also try your search in a different white pages directory.

▶ **3.** Examine your listing and, if you wish, follow the site's instructions for modifying or deleting your listing.

▶ **4.** Close your Web browser and, if necessary, log off your Internet connection.

You have accomplished many tasks and helped Marti quite a bit. Next, you will learn about multimedia resources on the Web and the copyright issues that arise when you use them.

1. Reuters is an example of a(n) _____ .
2. When would you use a search engine with a date filter rather than a news directory or news search engine?
3. Explain why you might want to consult two or three Web resources for weather information.
4. List two advantages of using a Web map and directions site instead of a paper map or atlas.
5. Describe three types of information that you might obtain from a city guide Web page.
6. True or False: City guide Web sites are usually created by an agency of the city government.
7. A Web site that helps people find businesses by name or category is often called a(n)_____ .
8. A Web site that helps people find the telephone numbers or email addresses of other individuals is often called a(n) _____ .

Session 4.2

Online Library, Text, and Multimedia Resources

Because the Web has made publishing so easy and inexpensive, virtually anybody can create a Web page on almost any subject. These pages contain many useful items of information and form a collective online library of sorts. The resources of this vast online library include text, graphics, and multimedia files. **Multimedia** is a general term for files that contain sound, music, or video recordings. In this session you will learn how to find these resources, use them in compliance with copyright laws, and properly cite their sources.

Library Resources

Despite the proliferation of online resources, the Web has made existing libraries more accessible to more people. Traditional libraries and online collections of works that have serious research value now recognize each other as complementary rather than competing information sources, and library users have started to see many new and interesting research resources. One online collection that is both comprehensive and valuable is the LibrarySpot Web site, which is a collection of hyperlinks organized in the same general way that a physical library might arrange its collections.

To explore the LibrarySpot Web site:

▶ 1. Start your Web browser, go to **www.course.com/oc/np/internet7** to open the Online Companion page, log on to your account, click the **Tutorial 4** link, and then click the **Session 4.2** link. Click the **LibrarySpot** hyperlink, and then wait while your Web browser loads the Web page shown in Figure 4-15.

LibrarySpot home page   Figure 4-15

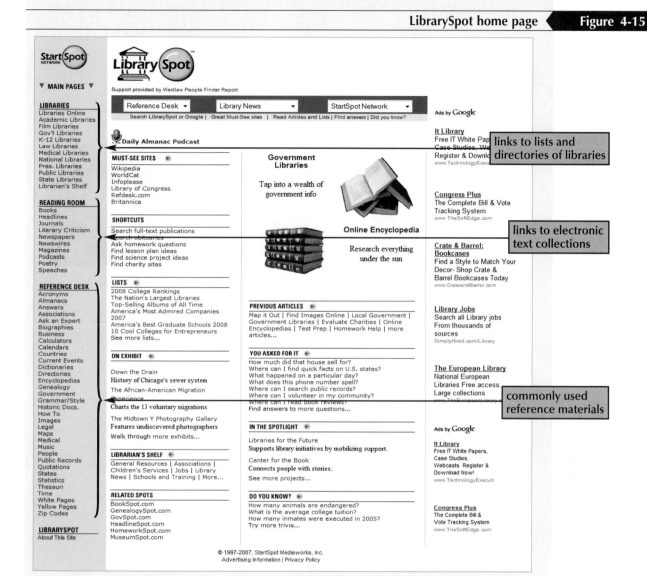

As you can see in Figure 4-15, the LibrarySpot site includes many of the same things you would expect to find in a public or school library. It lets you access reference materials, electronic texts, and other library Web sites from one central Web page. Unlike a public or school library, this library is open 24 hours a day and seven days a week.

Marti had asked you to find the name of the river that runs through Nashville.

▶ **2.** Using the links listed under the heading "Reference Desk" on the LibrarySpot home page, search for information about Nashville to find the river's name. A good place to start would be the **Encyclopedias** link. Note the river's name so that you can include it in your report to Marti about Nashville.

Another useful resource is the U.S. Library of Congress Web site, which includes links to a huge array of research resources, ranging from the Thomas Legislative Information site to the Library of Congress archives. The home page of the Library of Congress Web site is shown in Figure 4-16.

Figure 4-16   U.S. Library of Congress home page

The Thomas Legislative Information Web site provides you with search access to the full text of bills that are before Congress, the *Congressional Record*, and Congressional Committee Reports. The American Memory link leads you to archived photographs, sound and video recordings, maps, and collections of everything from 17th century dance instruction manuals to baseball cards. The Exhibitions link leads you to information about current and past displays sponsored by the Library of Congress.

The Online Companion page for Tutorial 4 contains many other hyperlinks to useful library and library-related Web sites in the Additional Information section under the Library Information Sites heading. Consider exploring the library resources on the Web the next time you need to complete a research assignment for school or your job.

Text and Other Archives on the Web

The Web contains a number of text resources, including dictionaries, thesauri, encyclopedias, glossaries, and other reference works. Many people find reference works easier to use when they have a computerized search interface. For example, when you open a dictionary to find the definition of a specific word, the structure of the bound book actually interferes with your ability to find the answer you seek. A computer interface allows you to enter a search term—in this case, the word to be defined—and saves you the trouble of scanning several pages of text to find the correct entry.

Of course, publishers sell dictionaries and encyclopedias on CDs, but the Web provides many alternatives, ranging in quality from very low to very high. Some of the best resources offered on the Web require you to pay a subscription fee. The free reference works on the Web are also worth investigating; many are good enough to provide useful answers to a wide range of questions. In addition to dictionaries and encyclopedias, the Web includes grammar checkers, rhyming dictionaries, and language-translation pages. The Online Companion page for this tutorial includes a collection of links to a number of these reference resources in the Additional Information section under the heading Reference Resources.

The Web also includes sites that offer full-text copies of works that are no longer protected by copyright. Two well-known full-text sites are the Project Gutenberg and Bartleby.com Web sites. These volunteer efforts have collected the contributions of many people throughout the world who have spent enormous amounts of time entering or converting printed text into electronic form. The Project Gutenberg site is supported by donations. The Bartleby.com site, which is named for the main character in Herman Melville's famous short story "Bartleby the Scrivener," was converted into a privately held corporate site in 1999. Since then, it has used advertising to generate revenue to support its operations. The Bartleby.com home page appears in Figure 4-17.

Figure 4-17   Bartleby.com home page

The Web itself has become the subject of archivists' attention. The Internet Archive's Wayback Machine provides researchers a series of snapshots of Web pages as they were at various points in the history of the Web. The Internet Archive site also stores text, moving image, audio, and other files that have been contributed to the site. The wide array of information at the Internet Archive site makes it a valuable resource for a variety of research projects. The Internet Archive home page is shown in Figure 4-18.

Internet Archive home page ◀ **Figure 4-18**

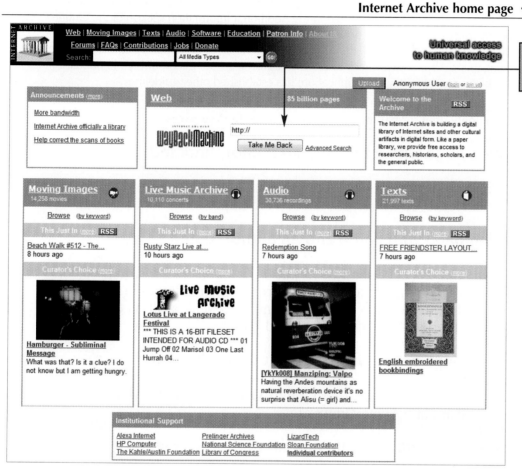

The Online Companion page for Tutorial 4 includes links to Web sites that offer electronic texts and archives in the Additional Information section under the heading Electronic Texts and Archives.

Citing Web Resources

As you search the Web for research resources, you should collect information about the sites you visit so you can include a proper reference to your sources in any research report you write based on your work. You should record the URL and name of any Web site that you use, either in a word-processor document, as a Firefox bookmark, or as an Internet Explorer favorite.

Citation formats are well-defined for print publications, but formats for electronic resources are still emerging. For academic research, the two most widely followed standards for print citations are those of the American Psychological Association (APA) and the Modern Language Association (MLA). The APA and MLA formats for Web page citations are similar and both include: name of the author or Web page creator (if known);

title of the Web site in italics (if the page is untitled, provide a description of the page but do not italicize the description); name of the site's sponsoring organization (if any); date the page was retrieved; and the URL. Some authorities recommend that you enclose the URL in chevron symbols (< >). If you do not enclose the URL in chevron (or other) symbols, do not add a period at the end of the URL. This prevents readers from thinking that the period is a part of the URL.

Figure 4-19 shows examples of Web page citations that conform to the APA and MLA citation styles. Links to these two Web sites, and to additional sites that contain citation style and formatting resources, are listed in the Additional Information section of the Online Companion page for this tutorial under the heading Citation Style and Formatting for Web References. Be sure to check the APA and MLA Web sites for updates to these styles before using them. Also, always check to see if your instructor (for classroom work) or editor (for work you are submitting for publication) has established other guidelines.

| Figure 4-19 | Commonly used formatting style for references to Web pages |

Web page with a title and an author, undated

Hinman, L.M. *Ethics Updates*. (n.d.). University of San Diego. Retrieved March 12, 2009, from http://ethics.sandiego.edu

Web page with a title and an author, dated

Loveland, T. (2004, Fall). *Journal of Technology Education* 16(1). Technology education standards implementation in Florida. Retrieved April 19, 2009, from http://scholar.lib.vt.edu/ ejournals/JTE/v16n1/loveland.html

Web page with a title but no author, undated

The Linux Home Page. (n.d.). Linux Online, Inc. Retrieved May 15, 2009, from http://www.linux.org/

Web page with no title and no author, undated

United States Postal Service home page. (n.d.). Retrieved June 18, 2009, from http://www.usps.com

The APA and MLA formats for citations to books, journal articles, and other research resources that were published in print form but are also accessible on the Web are more complex than the formats for Web pages. You should consult the APA and MLA Web sites for the latest rules.

InSight | Formatting URL Linebreaks

One of the problems that both the APA and MLA face when setting standards is the difficulty of typesetting long URLs in print documents. No clear standards specifying where or how to break long URLs at the end of a print line have emerged. Most authorities currently agree that the URL should be broken at a slash that appears in the URL and that a hyphen should not be added at the end of the line that occurs in the middle of the URL.

Any method of citing Web pages faces one serious and yet unsolved problem—moving and disappearing URLs. The Web is a dynamic medium that changes constantly. The citation systems that academics and librarians use for published books and journals work well because the printed page has a physical existence. A Web page exists only in an HTML document on a Web server computer. If the file's name or location changes, or if the Web server is disconnected from the Internet, the page is no longer accessible. Perhaps future innovations in Internet addressing technologies will solve this problem. Until then, at least one alternative is being used. Publishers of scholarly academic journals have begun assigning a unique alphanumeric identifier to journal articles and similar documents. This identifier, called a **digital object identifier (DOI)**, is issued by CrossRef.org, which is an independent registration agency. The DOI provides a uniform way to identify content and provide a persistent link to its location as long as the content continues to be located somewhere on the Internet.

Copyright Issues

Marti would like to create a Web page for each musical artist that the agency represents. Many of the agency's artists have their own Web sites, but Marti would like to have a page for each artist on the Cosby Promotions Web site and provide a standard set of information (including a link to the artist's own Web site, if one exists). She would like you to undertake a long-term assignment for her by paying close attention to the multimedia elements of the Web pages you view as you undertake searches for the agency's staff members. She asks you to note any particularly effective uses of Web page design elements and to forward any relevant URLs to her. So that you will understand how these elements work and be better able to gather this information, Marti has asked Susan to give you a tour of multimedia elements in Web pages. The first issue Susan wants to discuss with you is how copyright law governs the use of the text and multimedia elements you obtain online.

Many Web page elements and other items you can find online are a form of **intellectual property**, a general term that includes all products of the human mind, including original ideas. These products can be tangible or intangible. Intellectual property rights include the protections afforded to individuals and companies by governments through governments' granting of copyrights and patents, and through registration of trademarks and service marks.

As you learned in Tutorial 1, a copyright is, quite literally, the right of a person to make copies of his or her work. Copyright laws enforce the idea of copyright by exclusion; that is, the laws prohibit anyone other than the copyright holder from making copies of the work. Copyrights are granted by a government to the author or creator of a literary or artistic work, in other words, to those who create a tangible expression of an idea. The right is for the specific length of time provided in the copyright law and gives the author or creator the sole and exclusive right to print, publish, or sell the work. Creations that can be copyrighted include virtually all forms of artistic or intellectual expression, including books, music, artworks, recordings (audio and video), architectural drawings, choreographic works, product packaging, and computer software. In the United States, works created after 1977 are protected for the life of the author plus 70 years. Works copyrighted by corporations or not-for-profit organizations are protected for 95 years from the date of publication or 120 years from the date of creation, whichever is earlier.

In the past, many countries (including the United States) required the creator of a work to register the work to obtain copyright protection. U.S. law still allows registration, but registration is no longer required. A work that does not include the words "copyright" or "copyrighted," or the copyright symbol (©), and that was created after 1977, is copyrighted automatically by virtue of the copyright law unless the creator makes a specific statement on the work that it is not copyrighted.

Once the term of the copyright has expired, the work is in the **public domain**, which means that anyone is free to copy the files without requesting permission from the source. Older literary works, such as Dickens' *A Tale of Two Cities*, are in the public domain and may be copied and reprinted freely. An author or creator can intentionally place work into the public domain at any time. For example, some Web sites provide graphics files that you can use free of charge. Even though you can freely use public domain information, you should check the site carefully for requirements about whether and how you should acknowledge the source of the material when it is used.

A copyright can protect a particular expression of a creative work in addition to the work itself. For example, a Mozart symphony is in the public domain because it was written hundreds of years ago and is no longer protected by Austrian copyright law. But Mozart's creative work was writing the notes of the symphony down on paper in a particular form. If the Cleveland Symphony makes an audio recording of that public domain Mozart symphony, its performance can be copyrighted by the Cleveland Symphony and protected under current copyright laws.

Copyrights and Ideas

The *idea* contained in a product is not copyrightable. The particular form of expression of an idea creates a work that can be copyrighted. For example, you cannot copyright the idea to write a song about love, you can copyright only the song you end up writing. If an idea cannot be separated from its expression in a work, that work cannot be copyrighted. For example, mathematical calculations cannot be copyrighted.

A collection of facts can be copyrighted, but only if the collection is arranged, coordinated, or selected in a way that causes the resulting work to rise to the level of an original work. For example, the Yahoo! Web Directory is a collection of links to URLs. These facts existed before Yahoo! selected and arranged them into the form of its directory. However, most intellectual property lawyers would argue that the selection and arrangement of the links into categories probably makes the directory copyrightable.

Copyright Protection and Internet Technologies

When you use your Web browser to read text on a Web page, view a graphic image, listen to a sound, or watch a video clip, your Web browser downloads the multimedia element from the Web server and stores it in a temporary file on your computer's hard drive. This technological process creates a new, intermediate level of ownership that did not exist before the emergence of the Web. For example, when you go to an art gallery and view a picture, you do not take possession of the picture in any way. When you visit an online art gallery, however, your Web browser—software running on your computer—temporarily owns a copy of the file containing the image. As you have learned in earlier tutorials, it is easy to make a permanent copy of Web page images—even though your copy might violate the image owner's rights.

The potential for users to violate copyright laws when viewing Web pages is much greater than when using other types of media. Web site managers who incorporate multimedia elements frequently violate copyright law when including graphics, video, and audio clips on their pages—sometimes without realizing they have done anything wrong.

Some Web site owners attempt to avoid liability under copyright laws by including on their sites hyperlinks to copyright-violating multimedia elements located on *other* Web pages. Their intent is to claim that they did not have any copyright violations on their sites because the multimedia element was located on the site to which they linked. This strategy has not yet been tested sufficiently in the courts to determine whether it is an effective shield against liability.

Using Web Search Techniques to Catch Copyright Violators | InSight

Scanning a copy of a popular cartoon from a newspaper or magazine and placing it on a Web page would most likely be a violation of the owner's copyright. Some cartoonists regularly search the Web using various search tools, looking for unauthorized copies of their work. They threaten or take legal action when they find Web sites that appear to violate their copyrights.

Fair Use and Plagiarism

The U.S. copyright law allows people to use copyrighted works if their use is a fair use. The **fair use** of a copyrighted work includes copying it for use in criticism, comment, news reporting, teaching, scholarship, or research. The law's definition of fair use is intentionally broad and can be difficult to interpret.

There have been many court cases on the fair use issue. These cases usually turn on two considerations: how the copyrighted material was used and the amount of the copyrighted material that was used. Uses that might generate revenue or deprive the copyright owner of revenue are least likely to be held as fair use. Uses of content from published works are more likely to be determined fair use than uses of content from unpublished works because the copyright owner of a published work has had a chance to benefit from the work through sales, publicity, increased reputation, or other means. The smaller the amount of the work that is used, the more likely the use will be considered fair use. However, using even a small amount of the work can be a violation if it is the heart of the work. This is especially true with musical compositions. The use of even a small portion of a song can be a violation. Again, there is no hard-and-fast rule that determines fair use. If a copyright holder disputes your use, the matter will be settled by the subjective assessment of a judge or jury.

Fair use of a copyrighted work requires a citation to the original work. If you are unsure whether your use is indeed fair use, the safest course of action is to contact the copyright owner and ask for permission to use the work. Acknowledging a source can be especially important when you use public domain material in papers, reports, or other school projects. Failure to cite the source of material that you use (whether it is in the public domain or it is protected by copyright) is called **plagiarism** and can be a serious violation of your school's academic honesty policy. The Internet makes it easy to copy someone else's work and commit plagiarism. A number of companies have created sites that teachers can use to identify plagiarism in papers that students submit. One of these sites, Turnitin.com, offers tips for students who want to avoid committing plagiarism unintentionally on its Research Resources page, which appears in Figure 4-20. The page also includes a link to another Turnitin.com site, Plagiarism.org, that offers additional information about the subject.

Figure 4-20 ▶ Turnitin.com Research Resources page

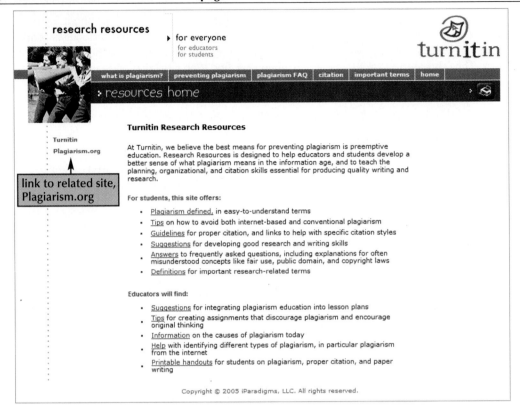

InSight | Using Free Content

Some Web sites offer text and other types of files free as samples and offer other files for sale. The free files often carry a restriction against selling or redistributing them, even though you may be able to use them without cost on your own personal Web page. You should carefully examine any site from which you download such files to determine what usage limitations apply. If you cannot find a clear statement of copyright terms or a statement that the files are in the public domain, you should not use them on your Web page or anywhere else.

The Online Companion page for Tutorial 4 contains a number of links to Web sites with further information about adhering to Web copyrights in the Additional Information section under the Copyright Information Resources heading. One of the most useful of these sites is the Stanford University Copyright & Fair Use site, shown in Figure 4-21.

Figure 4-21

Images and Graphics on the Web

The Web is an excellent source of images and graphics, but you should keep in mind what you learned earlier in this tutorial about respecting the copyright interests of the owners of these types of files. In this section, you will learn about graphics file formats and how to find images and graphics on the Web.

Graphics File Formats

Most images on the Web are in one of two file formats, GIF or JPEG. **GIF**, an acronym for **Graphics Interchange Format**, is an older format that does a very good job of compressing small- or medium-sized files. Most GIF files you find on the Web have a .gif extension. This file format can store only up to 256 different colors. The GIF format is widely used on the Internet for images that have only a few distinct colors, such as line drawings, cartoons, simple icons, and screen objects. Some of the more interesting screen objects on the Web are animated GIF files. An **animated GIF** file combines several images into a single GIF file.

When a Web browser that recognizes the animated GIF file type loads this type of file, it cycles through the images in the file and gives the appearance of cartoon-like animation. The size and color-depth limitations of the GIF file format prevent animated GIFs from delivering high-quality video, however.

JPEG, an acronym for **Joint Photographic Experts Group**, is a newer file format that stores many more colors than the GIF format—more than 16 million more, in fact—and more colors yields a higher-quality image. The JPEG format is particularly useful for photographs and continuous-tone art (images that do not have sharp edges). Most JPEG files that you find on the Web have a .jpg file extension.

Both of these formats offer file compression, which is important on the Web. Uncompressed graphics files containing images of significant size or complexity are too large to transmit efficiently. JPEG file compression is "lossy." A **lossy compression** procedure erases some elements of the graphic so that when it is displayed, it will not be as clear as the original image. The greater the level of compression, the more graphic detail is lost.

Although most graphic images on the Web are in either the JPEG or GIF formats, you might encounter images that use other file formats, including Windows bitmap file format (.bmp), Tagged Image File Format (or TIFF) format (.tif), PC Paintbrush format (.pcx), and the Portable Network Graphics (or PNG) format (.png). The Windows bitmap, TIFF, and PC Paintbrush formats are all uncompressed graphics formats. Web page designers usually avoid these formats because a Web browser takes too long to download them. The PNG format is a new format that the World Wide Web Consortium has approved as a standard. Although its promoters hope that it will become the prevailing Web standard, it is not yet widely used.

Finding Graphics and Images on the Web

The Additional Information section of the Online Companion page for this tutorial contains links to Web pages that offer photographs and images in the Photographs and Images section. Several sites permit downloading of at least some of the files for personal or commercial use.

One of the best Web resources for the fine arts is the WebMuseum site, which occasionally features special exhibitions. The WebMuseum's mainstay is its Famous Paintings collection, which includes images of artwork from around the world. Susan wants you to see the museum's self-portraits of Vincent van Gogh so you can gain experience using and searching for graphics files at a museum Web site.

To view Vincent van Gogh's self-portraits at the WebMuseum site:

▶ 1. Return to the Online Companion page for Session 4.2, and click the **WebMuseum** link.

▶ 2. Click the **Famous Artworks** collections hyperlink.

▶ 3. Click the **Artist Index** hyperlink.

▶ 4. Scroll down the list of artists to find the **Gogh, Vincent van** hyperlink, and then click it.

▶ 5. Click the **Self-Portraits** hyperlink to open the page shown in Figure 4-22.

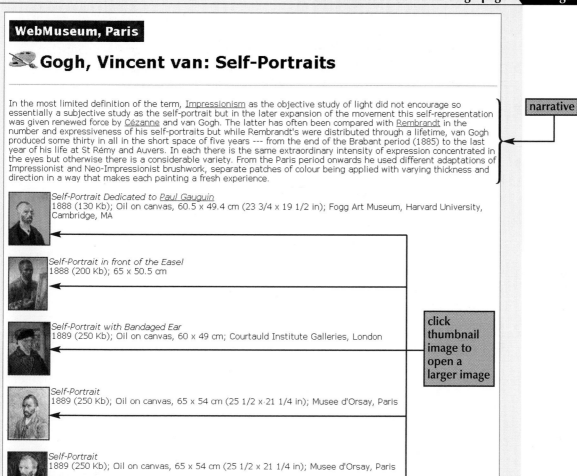

This page, devoted to van Gogh's self-portraits, includes a narrative about these works; the title, date created, file size, media, and size of the original; and information about the work's owner (if it is a public institution). You can click any of the small (or thumbnail) images to view a larger version of the image.

Some of the images included in the WebMuseum collection are in the public domain, especially those that are older. Other images are still protected by copyright. Remember, just because you see them on the WebMuseum site does not mean that you can copy them and use them without the permission of the copyright holder. Always track down the source of the image (in the case of WebMuseum exhibits, you would go to the museum or other organization that owns the artwork) and request permission to use it.

The robots that gather information for search engines cannot read graphics files to identify their attributes. Earlier search engines relied on HTML image tags that Web page builders include in their HTML documents; the tags contain terms that describe the image. This situation made finding image files on the Web difficult. Today, however, many search engine and Web directory sites have improved their image classification databases and provide separate search functions that are dedicated to finding Web pages with graphics content. A list of search engines that include image search features is included in the Online Companion Additional Information section under the heading Search Engines with Image Search Features.

Marti would like you to find some graphics and photos that include jazz-related subject matter.

To find jazz-related graphics and photos:

▶ **1.** Return to the Online Companion page for Session 4.2, and then find the list of **Search Engines with Image Search Features**.

▶ **2.** Choose one of the search engines and type **jazz** as the search term in the appropriate location on the page, and then click the site's **Search** (or similar) button to start the search.

▶ **3.** When you have found several images or photos related to jazz, examine the Web page on which they are located and attempt to determine whether the images are protected by copyright.

▶ **4.** Close your Web browser.

The results page of a Google Images search on the term "jazz" is shown in Figure 4-23. Each of the small images is a link to a page with a larger image. That page, in turn, is linked to the source of the image on the Web.

| Figure 4-23 | Results of a Google Images search on the term "jazz" |

You can send the URLs of the pages you found that contain jazz images to Marti in an email message, along with a note about any copyright restrictions you found.

In addition to images, you can find sounds and movies on the Web. You will learn about this next.

Multimedia on the Web

Multimedia is a general term that includes audio, video, and moving images (such as the graphics in a computer game). In the early days of the Web, the only multimedia form available was the animated GIF file. The animated GIF format has a limited ability to present moving graphics and cannot store any audio information. Today, Web site designers can include sound or video clips to enhance the information on their pages. To play any type of audio files (or the audio element of a video clip), your computer must be equipped with a sound card and either a speaker or earphones.

The use of multimedia elements on Web sites has greatly improved the functionality and usefulness of the Web. News sites can provide video of unfolding events as they happen, audio clips let customers listen to parts of songs before they buy them, and do-it-yourself help sites can provide video that shows demonstrations, such as a master plumber installing a new sink.

Tip

The computers in your school's lab or in your employer's offices might not have a sound card installed; if this is the case, you will not be able to listen to sounds on those computers.

Multimedia File Formats

Unlike graphics files, sound and video files appear on the Web in many different formats and can require that your Web browser have additional software extensions installed. These software extensions, or **plug-ins**, are usually available as free downloads. The firms that offer media players as free downloads earn their profits by selling encoding software to developers who want to include audio and video files in that format on their Web sites. Each firm that creates a format has an incentive to promote its use, so a variety of audio and video formats are used on the Web today.

Audio File Formats

One of the first widely used audio file formats on the Web was the **Wave (WAV) format**, which was jointly developed by Microsoft and IBM. WAV files store digitized audio and can be played on any Windows computer that supports sound. WAV files can be recorded at different quality levels, which results in different size files (higher quality means a larger file). In fact, music CDs are recorded in the WAV format at a very high quality level. A standard CD has a capacity of about 650 MB and can hold about 74 minutes of high-quality stereo music. You can recognize a WAV file on the Web by its .wav file extension.

Another commonly used Web file format is the MIDI format. The **MIDI (Musical Instrument Digital Interface)** format is a standard adopted by the music industry for controlling devices that create and read musical information. The MIDI format does not digitize the sound waveform; instead, it digitally records information about each element of the sound, including its pitch, length, and volume. Most keyboard synthesizers and other electronic instruments use MIDI so that music recorded on one instrument can be played on other instruments. MIDI files can also be played on computers that have a MIDI interface or software. It is much easier to edit music recorded in the MIDI format than music recorded in the WAV format because you can manipulate the individual characteristics of the sound with precision. MIDI files are much smaller than WAV files and are used in applications where storage space is at a premium. Most mobile phone ringtones, for example, are in the MIDI format. Usually, MIDI files have either a .midi or .mid file extension.

Because much of the Internet was originally constructed on computers running the UNIX operating system, the system's audio file format still appears on the Web, although very few new audio files are created in this format today. Most Web browsers can read this audio UNIX format, which is known as the AU format. AU format files usually have a file extension of .au. The AU format can store sound at various quality levels, and the resulting files are approximately the same size as WAV files recorded at similar quality levels.

Video File Formats

As you learned earlier in this tutorial, your computer needs a sound card and some way to play the sound (speaker or headphones) for you to hear audio files. Video files do not need any special hardware. Of course, if the video file has an audio track, you will need the sound card and the speaker or headphones to hear it. High-quality audio files and video files of any significant length can be very large. A popular technique for transferring large multimedia (both sound and video) files on the Web is called streaming transmission. In a **streaming transmission**, the Web server sends the first part of the file to the Web browser, which begins playing the file. While the browser is playing the file, the server is sending the next segment of the file. Streaming transmission allows you to access large audio or video files in less time than the download-then-play procedure, because the streamed file begins playing before it finishes downloading. RealNetworks, Inc. pioneered this technology and developed the RealAudio format for audio files and the RealVideo format for video files. The RealNetworks formats are compressed to further increase the efficiency with which they can be transferred over the Internet. For example, a 1-megabyte WAV file can be compressed into a 30-kilobyte RealAudio file.

Another streaming video format that has become popular is Adobe's Flash format. Playing Flash video files requires that your Web browser have the Adobe Flash Player software plug-in installed. Flash files can include video, high-resolution moving graphics, and graphic elements that interact with the user's mouse movements. Flash files usually have an .swf extension. Figure 4-24 shows the Adobe Flash Player High-Quality Video Demo page, which illustrates improvement in image quality from a previous version of Flash.

Tip

To play RealAudio files, which you can recognize by their .ra, .ram, or .rmj file extensions, you must download and install one of the Real file player plug-ins from the firm's Web site.

| Figure 4-24 | Adobe's Flash Player High-Quality Video Demo page |

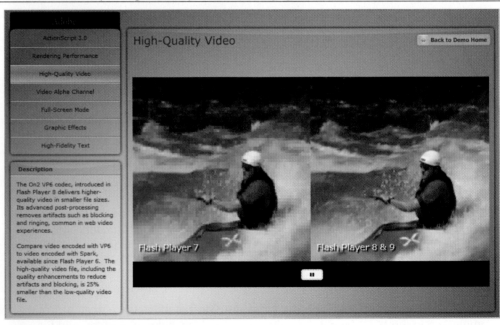

Video files can be very large, so the International Standards Organization's **Moving Picture Experts Group (MPEG)** has created a series of standards for compressed file formats. The compressed files in this format usually have a file extension that identifies the version of the MPEG standard with which they were encoded. For example, a video file that uses MPEG Level 2 compression would normally have an .mp2 file extension, although you will see alternative file extensions such as .mpe, .mpeg, .mpv2, or .mpg in use on the Web. The latest release of the MPEG standard is MPEG 4, which provides DVD-quality video when it is played.

Video files are also available in older formats on the Web. Most Web browsers can play Microsoft's **AVI (Audio Video Interleaved) format** files and, with the proper software plug-in downloaded and installed, also can play Apple's **QuickTime format** files. One minute of video and sound recorded in either of these formats results in a file that is about 6 MB. AVI files usually have an .avi extension, and Apple QuickTime files usually have an .mov extension.

When you tell Marti what you have learned about online video and copyright issues, she is intrigued. She asks you to find an online video that discusses the fair use exception in the U.S. copyright laws.

Tip
MPEG compression is similar to JPEG compression for graphics files in that it deletes information from the file and can thus reduce the quality of the video.

Finding Video Clips Online | Reference Window

- Open a video search site in your Web browser.
- Enter a search expression that includes the name or type of video you want to find.
- Run the search, and then examine the search results.
- Consider repeating the search with alternative search expressions to find a wider variety of videos that might meet your needs.

To search for videos that include a discussion of the fair use exception to U.S. copyright laws:

▶ 1. Return to the Online Companion page for Session 4.2, choose one of the tools in the Video Search Engines section to use in your search, and then click the link to the site you have chosen to open its video search page.

▶ 2. Enter the search expression **copyright fair use** in the search box, and then press the **Search** (or similar) button.

▶ 3. Examine your search results and click the links to any videos that look like they might satisfy Marti's request.

   Trouble? Your computer must have a sound card and either headphones or a speaker for you to hear the audio portion of any video you play.

▶ 4. Make a note of the URL of the best two videos you find so you can email them to Marti.

Audio from Video: The MP3 File Format

The audio portion of the MPEG file format was responsible for the greatest revolution in online music that has occurred in the history of the Web. The MPEG format's audio track, called **MPEG Audio Layer 3 (MP3)** became wildly popular in the late 1990s as disk storage on personal computers dropped in price and CD writers (also called CD burners) became affordable for home use. Files in the MP3 format are somewhat lower in quality than WAV format files, but they are 90 percent smaller. Thus, a CD that might hold 15 popular songs in high-quality WAV format (about 40 megabytes per song) could instead hold 150 popular songs in MP3 format (about 4 megabytes per song). The MP3 file format is the most popular for music on the Web today.

Ethical and Legal Concerns: Sharing Audio Files

The smaller size of MP3 files made it easy to send them from one person to another through the Internet, and file-sharing Web sites, such as Napster and Kazaa, became popular. People began copying music from CDs that they had purchased and converting that music into MP3 files, which they then exchanged with others on the Internet through the sites. This file-sharing activity is unethical because it deprives the creators of the audio works of their rights to control distribution and to profit from their work. It is also illegal in many countries, including the United States.

Companies in the recording industry and the recording artists themselves were not very happy with the large number of MP3 files that were being transmitted on these file-sharing networks. Recording companies and artists filed suits against Napster and other file-sharing sponsors for violating copyright laws. The recording companies were generally successful in obtaining court orders or out-of-court settlements that prevent further copyright violations in most of these suits. The case against Napster resulted in the company going out of business (the Napster of today is operated by a different company that bought the name from the failed company and sells music legally). In some of these cases, the recording companies have won hundreds of thousands of dollars in damages from individuals who illegally copied and shared music online. Many individuals, however, still violate the law and share MP3 files that contain copyrighted works.

Legal MP3 File Distribution

Since the popularity of the MP3 format became established, a number of Web sites have been created to sell digital music in MP3 and other formats. These sites, which include Napster under new management, have obtained the legal right to distribute the musical works they offer for sale. Advances in flash memory technology have made it possible to create portable digital music players (such as Apple's iPod) that can store thousands of songs downloaded from music Web sites.

Web sites such as eMusic, Rhapsody.com, and Apple's iTunes Store offer music for download in MP3 and other, lesser known, formats. Some of these sites charge per song, while others charge a monthly fee that allows subscribers to download as many songs as they wish. A small but growing group of recording artists has begun to distribute recordings that are available only as downloads from their own Web sites. Most of the sites that sell downloadable music place restrictions on the number of copies you can make of each song. Some of the sites restrict you from converting downloaded song files into other formats, or they restrict the types of devices on which you are permitted to play the song. The restrictions are implemented in the files themselves, using systems of encoding called **digital rights management (DRM)**. Because different online music vendors use different DRM systems, their files are often not compatible with each other.

Because of these differing DRM systems and because you can incur legal liability by using or copying downloaded files (even those you have purchased) in ways that the vendor prohibits, you should always check the site carefully for details about file formats and copying restrictions before you buy songs or sign up for a subscription.

Because Cosby Promotions represents a number of music artists, Marti is interested in learning more about how bands are selling their music on the Web. She asks you to do some research by finding the music of a band you like that is for sale on the Web and determining what format the music is sold in and if there are any limitations (DRM or contractual) attached to the use of the files once you buy them.

Tip

Make sure that the files from a particular site are compatible with your portable music player before you sign up for a download subscription.

To search for music to purchase online:

▶ 1. Return to the Online Companion page for Session 4.2, choose one of the links in the Online Music Stores section, and then click the link to the site you have chosen to open its home page.

▶ 2. The exact procedure you will use for your search will depend on which music store you chose. Use your chosen site's search function to find a band name or type of music.

   Trouble? If the online music store you chose does not offer music by your favorite band, you can search for another band or try a different site. Not all bands sell their music online, so you might not be able to find your first choice in any online music store.

   Trouble? Some online music stores require you to sign up for a trial membership before you can search for music. Many of these trial memberships are free. If you do not want to sign up for membership, try another music store.

▶ 3. Once you find the band or type of music you want, explore the site to determine what type of files the store sells (so you will know what types of portable music devices can play the file) and to determine what (if any) restrictions the store places on the copying or use of the files.

▶ 4. Make a note of the online music store name, the type of files it sells, and any restrictions on copying or use of the files so you can send this information to Marti in an email.

You can use the list of online music stores in the Online Companion to search for music files that you can use on your computer or on any personal music device you happen to own. The continuing developments in portable data storage technology and increasing bandwidth should ensure that digital music grows for many years.

Future of Electronic Publishing

One of the key changes that the Internet and the Web have brought to the world is that information can now be disseminated more rapidly than ever and in large quantities, but with a low required investment. The impact of this change is that firms in the public relations business—which spend great amounts of time and money trying to present their clients through the major media in the best possible light—might be facing a significantly changed business environment. Many industry analysts believe that the ease of publishing electronically on the Web might help reduce the concentration of media control that has been developing over the past three decades as newspapers and publishing companies merged with each other and, along with radio and television stations, were purchased by large media companies.

E-Zines

To be successful in print media publishing (such as publishing a monthly magazine), a publisher must have a large subscription or newsstand distribution. The publisher can earn a profit only if the high fixed costs of composing and creating the magazine are offset by large numbers of paid subscriptions or large numbers of readers that advertisers will pay to reach (or a combination of the two). The costs of publishing a Web page are very low compared to those for printing magazines or newspapers. Therefore, the subscription market required for a Web publication to survive can be very small or even nonexistent. If a Web-based magazine, or an **e-zine**, can attract advertisers, it can be financially successful with no subscribers and a relatively small number of readers. Because e-zines do not require a large readership, they can focus on specialized, narrow interests. Many e-zines publish new fiction and poetry, for example. The Additional Information section of the Online Companion page for this tutorial includes links to several e-zine Web sites under the heading E-zines.

Blogs (Web Logs) and Wikis

Most e-zines follow the general model used by print magazines for their layout, design, and structure. Also, like print magazines, e-zines are usually managed by an editor who solicits manuscripts from other writers and then publishes some of those manuscripts after editing them. However, the Web has enabled an entirely new type of individual publication. Earlier in this tutorial, you learned about blogs (short for "Web logs"). Blogs are usually written by a single person (called the blogger) who wishes to express a particular point of view. Some blogs allow others to add comments or reactions to the blogger's statements, which may be edited or deleted by the blogger. Although blogs exist on a wide variety of topics, most blogs focus on political, religious, or other issues about which people have strong opinions.

Blogs are usually run by one individual who writes the main commentary and decides which comments posted by readers will be included in the blog. Thus, the content and direction of the blog are controlled by its owner. Another form of interactive online writing is the wiki. A **wiki** is a Web site that is designed to allow multiple users to contribute content and edit existing content. Wiki is a Hawaiian word that means "fast," and wikis are set up to allow many different users to add and edit content quickly and easily. Most wikis are focused on facts or collaborative work. This contrasts with blogs, which are usually focused on the opinions of the blogger who controls the site. The home page of Wikitravel, a wiki that invites travelers to share their experiences in a collaborative world travel guide, is shown in Figure 4-25.

Figure 4-25	Wikitravel home page

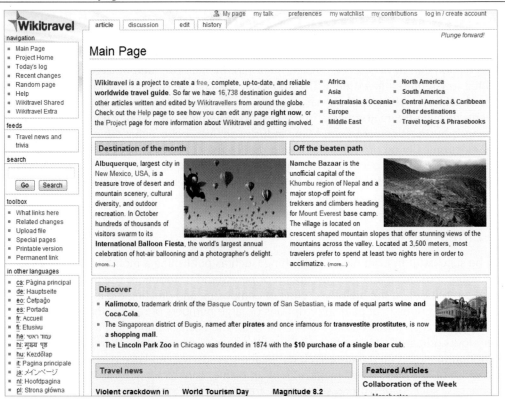

Marti appreciates your help with travel planning and gathering information regarding clients and planned promotion ideas. When you need to use the Web to find information for your classes or your job, remember to return to the Additional Information section of the Online Companion page for Tutorial 4 for a comprehensive list of Web information resources.

Session 4.2 Quick Check | Review

1. Explain why it can be important to determine a Web page author's identity and credentials when you plan to use the page's information as a research resource.
2. What information about Web page authors can help you assess their objectivity with respect to the contents of their Web pages?
3. Briefly describe two ways that libraries use the Web.
4. What are the advantages of using online reference works, such as dictionaries or encyclopedias, instead of print editions?
5. For how long is a work copyrighted?
6. Briefly explain the concept of "fair use."
7. True or False: Music stored in a WAV file format would be of lower quality and would result in a smaller file than the same music stored in an MP3-formatted file.
8. Briefly explain the differences between a blog and a wiki.

Tutorial Summary | Review

In this tutorial, you learned how to find current news stories, weather information, maps, and information about travel destinations on the Web by using specialized search engines and Web directories. Online library resources and other research and reference resources are also available on the Web.

You learned some basic facts about copyright protection, fair use, and avoiding plagiarism in the use of text, images, and multimedia files that you find on the Internet. You also learned how to access many of the graphics and multimedia resources on the Internet, and you learned which image, sound, and video file formats are common on the Web.

Key Terms

animated GIF file
AVI (Audio Video Interleaved) format
digital object identifier (DOI)
digital rights management (DRM)
e-zine
fair use
Graphics Interchange Format (GIF)
intellectual property

Joint Photographic Experts Group (JPEG)
lossy compression
MIDI (Musical Instrument Digital Interface) format
Moving Picture Experts Group (MPEG)
MPEG Audio Layer 3 (MP3)
multimedia
news search engine
plagiarism

plug-ins
public domain
QuickTime format
streaming transmission
Wave (WAV) format
Web logs (Weblogs or blogs)
white pages directory
wiki
wire service
yellow pages directory

| Practice | **Review Assignments** |

Get hands-on practice of the skills you learned in the tutorial using the same case scenario.

There are no Data Files needed for these Review Assignments.

Marti is preparing to visit a new techno band in Chicago, Illinois that she would like to sign. While in Chicago, she would like to visit several clubs that feature blues artists.

1. Start your Web browser, go to www.course.com/oc/np/internet7 to open the Online Companion page, log on to your account, click the Tutorial 4 link, and then click the Review Assignments link.
2. Obtain weather forecasts for the Chicago area from two of the weather sites included in the list of links for this assignment (or use weather sites with which you are familiar). Print the forecasts from each site.
3. The band is renting practice space in a warehouse near the corner of West 35th Street and South Morgan Street in Chicago's South Side. Print two maps from one of the map Web sites included in the list of links for this assignment. Include at least one street-level map and one higher-level map that show the surrounding area in Chicago.
4. Use one of the links to a travel destination guide site to locate information about restaurants in the Chicago area. Prepare a report that lists three restaurants you would recommend to Marti for entertaining clients while in Chicago.
5. Use one of the travel destination guide sites to locate at least two blues clubs that Marti can visit while she is in Chicago.
6. Use one or more of the links to News Search Engines in the Online Companion to find an article in a Chicago area newspaper that discusses a local band or an area club that features live music. Summarize the article in a short memo to Marti and include a citation to the article in the memo.
7. When you are finished, close your Web browser.

| Apply | **Case Problem 1** |

Apply the skills you learned in this tutorial to produce a map, driving directions, and list of prospective sales clients for a business trip.

There are no Data Files needed for this Case Problem.

Portland Concrete Mixers, Inc. You are a sales representative for Portland Concrete Mixers, Inc., a company that makes replacement parts for concrete mixing equipment. This equipment is mounted on trucks that deliver ready-mixed concrete to buildings and other job sites. You have been transferred to the Seattle area and would like to plan your first sales trip there. Because you plan to drive to Seattle, you need information about the best route as well as a map of Seattle. You hope to generate some new customers on this trip and, therefore, need to identify sales-lead prospects in the area. Companies that manufacture concrete are good prospects for you.

1. Start your Web browser, go to www.course.com/oc/np/internet7 to open the Online Companion page, log on to your account, click the Tutorial 4 link, and then click the Case Problem 1 link.
2. Choose one of the map sites from the list provided in the Online Companion.
3. Obtain driving directions from the site you have chosen. Your starting address is Portland, OR, and your destination address is Seattle, WA.
4. Obtain a map of Seattle from the site you have chosen. You can adjust the map to the level of detail you desire.

⊕ EXPLORE

5. To identify sales prospects in Seattle, return to the Online Companion page for Case Problem 1 in Tutorial 4, and use one or more of the directories listed under the Yellow Pages Directories heading to search for businesses in the Seattle area that sell concrete. The results pages for your searches should include contact information for a number of companies in the concrete business in Seattle. Copy the names and addresses of at least three sales prospects to a document that you will carry with you on your trip.

6. When you are finished, close your Web browser.

Research	**Case Problem 2**

Research specific types of MIDI files. Examine information about copyright restrictions.

There are no Data Files needed for this Case Problem.

Midland Elementary School Music Classes You are a third-grade language skills teacher at Midland Elementary School. The school has closed its music program because the state has cut the budget severely over the past several years. Although the school no longer has any music teachers on staff, you believe that it is important to expose your students to the music of the great composers, such as Beethoven and Mozart. You do not have a budget for buying CDs, but you do have a computer with an Internet connection in the classroom. You would like to find some music files to play on the computer, but you want to make sure that any use of these files complies with U.S. copyright law. You have heard that single musical instruments, particularly pianos, sound realistic when synthesized in the MIDI format and you would, therefore, like to find some music in this format to begin your collection for the class.

1. Start your Web browser, go to www.course.com/oc/np/internet7 to open the Online Companion page, log on to your account, click the Tutorial 4 link, and then click the Case Problem 2 link.

2. Click one or more of the MIDI music links provided for this Case Problem.

⊕ EXPLORE

3. Evaluate the files offered on these Web pages or the pages to which they lead. Write a short report summarizing your experience. In your report, describe any copyright restrictions that apply to the files that you would like to use. (*Hint*: The copyright restrictions might not be on the page from which you download the files, so be sure to look for links to pages such as "Terms and Conditions" on the site's home page.)

4. When you are finished, close your Web browser.

Create	**Case Problem 3**

Research pending legislation about child care, evaluate a child care information Web site, and create two reports.

There are no Data Files needed for this Case Problem.

Toddle Inn Headquartered in Minneapolis, Minnesota, Toddle Inn is a chain of day-care centers operating in several Midwestern states. The directors are interested in undertaking a national expansion program that will require outside financing and an effective public relations program that integrates with their strategic marketing plans. You are an intern in the office of Joan Caruso, a public relations consultant who does work for Toddle Inn. Joan has asked you to help her with some background research as she creates a proposal for Toddle Inn to integrate a Web site into its public relations program.

1. Start your Web browser, go to www.course.com/oc/np/internet7 to open the Online Companion page, log on to your account, click the Tutorial 4 link, and then click the Case Problem 3 link.

2. Follow the links provided there to one or more of the news search engines and directories to find at least three current (within the past three or four months) news reports about the child-care industry. Write a memo to Joan that summarizes the major issues identified in these reports.

3. Joan would like you to conduct an evaluation of the Child Care Parent/Provider Information Network Web site. Prepare an evaluation of the site that considers the author's or publisher's identity and objectivity as well as the site's content, form, and appearance.

⊕ **EXPLORE**

4. One issue that any public relations campaign must consider is the impact of pending legislation. Joan asks you to find out whether any bills are pending in the U.S. Congress that will affect the child-care industry. Return to the Online Companion page for Case Problem 3 in Tutorial 4, open the Thomas Legislative Information Web site, type "child care" (without quotation marks) in the Word/Phrase text box, and then click the Search button. Read one of the bills listed and prepare a one-paragraph summary for Joan of the bill's likely effects on the child-care industry in general and the Toddle Inn specifically.

5. When you are finished, close your Web browser.

| Create | **Case Problem 4** |

Identify Web sites that present arguments for and against prison privatization and create a report that summarizes findings.

There are no Data Files needed for this Case Problem.

Arnaud for Senate Campaign You work for the campaign team of Lisa Arnaud, who is running for a seat in the state senate. One issue that promises to play a prominent role in the upcoming election campaign is privatization of the state prison system. It is important for Lisa to establish a clear position on the issue early in the campaign, and she has asked you to prepare a briefing document for her to consider. Lisa tells you that she has no particular preference on the issue and that she wants you to obtain a balanced set of arguments for each side. Once the campaign takes a position, however, she will need to defend it. Therefore, Lisa wants to determine the quality of the information you gather. You decide to do part of your research on the Web.

1. Start your Web browser, go to www.course.com/oc/np/internet7 to open the Online Companion page, log on to your account, click the Tutorial 4 link, and then click the Case Problem 4 link.

2. Choose one of the listed search tools to conduct a search for "privatization prisons" (without the quotation marks).

⊕ **EXPLORE**

3. Examine your search results for authoritative sites that include positions on the issue. (*Hint*: You might need to follow a number of results page hyperlinks to find suitable Web pages. In general, you should avoid current news items that appear in the results list.)

4. Find one Web page that states a clear position in favor of privatization and another that states a clear position against privatization. Print a copy of each.

5. Prepare a three-paragraph report that summarizes the content of the Web pages you chose. Include full citations for the pages along with a one or two sentence evaluation of the quality of each page.

6. When you are finished, close your Web browser.

Research | **Case Problem 5**

Find images that meet a particular need and determine the copyright limitations on their use.

There are no Data Files needed for this Case Problem.

Kim's Travel and Cruises You are an assistant to Kim Phong, the owner of Kim's Travel and Cruises. The Web site for the firm includes pages that describe many of the destinations featured in the cruises she books for her clients. Kim would like to include images of flags that correspond to the country of each destination. She would also like to have a local artist create replicas of the flags as gifts for her regular clients. She would like you to find images of the flags from which the artist can create the replicas. You decide to do your research on the Web.

1. Start your Web browser, go to www.course.com/oc/np/internet7 to open the Online Companion page, log on to your account, click the Tutorial 4 link, and then click the Case Problem 5 link.
2. Select one of the sites listed for this problem and use it to conduct a search for images of flags for Thailand, Singapore, Malaysia, the People's Republic of China, South Korea, and Japan.
3. Repeat the search using another search engine.
4. Examine your list of search results for suitable flag images. You might need to follow a number of results page hyperlinks to find images that meet your needs.

⊕ EXPLORE

5. When you find a Web page or pages with suitable images, examine the Web site to determine what copyright or other restrictions exist regarding your use of the images. (*Hint*: Remember that you need to look for restrictions that could prevent the artist from creating replicas of the images you find; these restrictions might be different from restrictions on online use of the images.)
6. Prepare a one-paragraph report for each flag that describes the source you plan to use. Include the URL of the site where you found the flag image and a summary of the restrictions on Kim's use of the image. If the Web site does not include any description of restrictions, refer to the text and state your opinion regarding what restrictions might exist on Kim's use of the image.
7. Close your Web browser.

Review | **Quick Check Answers**

Session 4.1

1. a major wire service (or press agency or news service) based in Great Britain
2. when you want to find information that has been released recently but might not have been published in a newspaper or magazine
3. Different meteorologists often predict different weather conditions for the same location; gathering several forecasts provides a range of likely weather conditions.
4. You can change the map's scale, and you can email the map or save it to a hand-held computing device such as a personal digital assistant (PDA).
5. any three of: recommendations and reviews of restaurants, entertainment (or night-life), sports, shopping, landmarks, and other visitor information
6. False
7. yellow pages directory
8. white pages directory

Session 4.2

1. Author identity and credentials help establish the credibility of Web page content.
2. their employment or other professional affiliations
3. by adding online resources to their collections and by making their collections accessible to remote users and other libraries
4. available 24 hours a day, seven days a week; can be easier and faster to search
5. A work is copyrighted for the life of the author plus 70 years; works copyrighted by corporations or not-for-profit organizations are protected for 95 years from the date of publication or 120 years from the date of creation, whichever is earlier.
6. You can copy small parts of a work for use in criticism, comment, news reporting, teaching, scholarship, or research.
7. False
8. A blog is usually written by one person who uses the Web to express personal opinions on a particular subject; a wiki usually provides a place for a number of contributors to collect facts or work collaboratively on a project.

Objectives

Session 5.1
- Learn what FTP is and how it works
- Explore how to use a Web browser to transfer files
- Navigate an FTP site using a Web browser
- Learn about checking downloaded files for viruses and other threats

Session 5.2
- Learn about types of download software
- Evaluate download software for appropriateness and quality
- Download an FTP client program using a Web browser
- Download a compression program using an FTP client program
- Learn how to compress and decompress files
- Explore storage options on the Internet

Downloading and Storing Data

Using FTP and Other Services to Share and Store Data

Case | Sound Effects, Inc.

After graduating from the University of Southern California with a degree in business administration, Milt Spangler started Sound Effects, Inc., a company that produces sounds and voiceovers for local advertising agencies and other businesses that use digitally produced and created sounds. Milt hires professional actors to do voiceover work and other speaking roles, such as recording characters' voices in electronic games and educational programs for children.

Sound Effects operates with only a few permanent employees in the Los Angeles area. Many of the actors who provide voiceover work live elsewhere in the United States and Canada. These actors record their material for Milt in studios near their homes. Because their work is produced digitally, Milt needs a way to transfer files from studios in the actors' hometowns to the Los Angeles office, where he can edit and finalize the files for clients. The large sizes of digitally produced files and the high cost of sending files prohibit Milt from relying on email attachments and overnight delivery services as options for transporting files. He asks you to help him find ways to send, manage, and store large files using other methods.

Milt also needs a way to collaborate on documents that are used by multiple actors as scripts are developed and edited for production. Currently, the actors are sending documents via email attachments, but they are finding that having multiple copies of the document as it is passed to a group of people is becoming confusing and time consuming. Milt asks you to investigate some options for simplifying the process of storing and collaborating on documents.

Starting Data Files

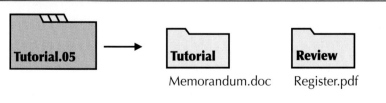

Tutorial.05 → Tutorial — Memorandum.doc

Review — Register.pdf

Cases
p_51642.jpg
p_57495.jpg
p_75436.jpg
p_78456.jpg
p_87462.jpg
p_88462.jpg

Session 5.1

Understanding File Transfer Protocol

You already know that you can use email attachments to send files over the Internet. Email is often a good way of transporting a file from one location to another, or even to yourself. For example, if you are working on a report in the university computer lab and forget to bring your disk or USB drive, you can attach the report to an email message you send to yourself; when you get home and download your email messages, you'll receive the file on your home computer. This method works for sending files to other people as well. However, many email servers limit the sizes of files you can attach to a single email message. Email servers might also limit the types of files you can send. For example, some servers will not accept file attachments that can execute programs in order to protect the email server from viruses that might be hidden in those files.

To address storage issues and issues related to transmitting large files from one location to another and between multiple users, you can use FTP. **FTP**, or **File Transfer Protocol**, is the Internet protocol that transfers files between computers that are connected to the Internet. The site to which you are sending files and from which you are receiving files is called an **FTP site**, **FTP server**, **remote computer**, or a **remote site**; when it is connected to an FTP site, your computer is called the **local computer** or the **local site**. You can use a Web browser to transfer files between computers, or you can use an **FTP client program**, which is a separate program that transfers files between computers.

When you send a file using FTP, you use a Web browser or an FTP client program to **upload** the file to send it from your computer to the remote site. When you receive a file, you use a Web browser or FTP client program to **download** the file from the remote site to your computer. In either case—uploading or downloading—you connect to a remote site and request it to transfer files to or from your computer. The FTP server receives file transfer requests and then manages the details of transferring files between the local and remote sites, even when the sites are running different operating systems. Most FTP client programs display the contents of the local and remote sites in different panes and have menu bars or toolbars to help you execute commands. Figure 5-1 shows a popular FTP client program, Core FTP LE, which is communicating with a remote site located at ftp.coreftp.com.

Tip

SFTP (Secure File Transfer Protocol) is a network protocol used to transfer files over a secure connection. FTP client programs and FTP servers at many colleges and universities use this protocol to encrypt files sent between computers.

FTP client program ◀ Figure 5-1

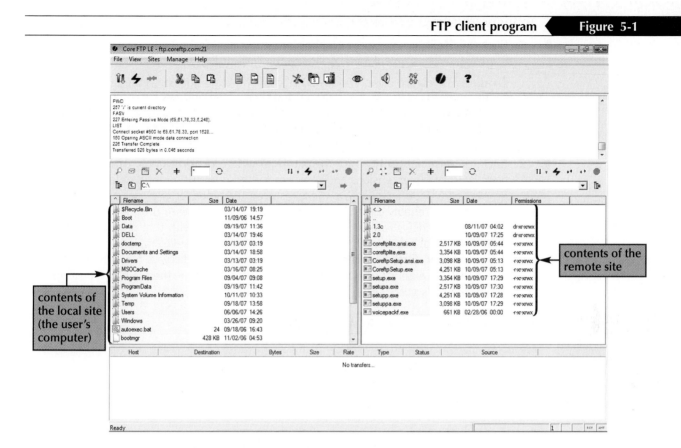

contents of the local site (the user's computer)

contents of the remote site

Most FTP client programs transfer files between computers in one of two formats. The most common data transfer format is **ASCII**, which contains symbols typed from the keyboard but does not include any nonprintable, binary codes. Many files, including Web pages and email messages, consist of ASCII (plain) text. Other files, such as pictures, movies, sound files, and graphics, are **binary**. Any file created by a word-processing program or containing character formatting, such as bold or italics, is binary. Most FTP client programs and Web browsers choose the file transfer mode automatically, sometimes based on the file's contents, so you don't need to know which data transfer format to use. However, if you download a file and then open it and see only codes, you can suspect that the file was transferred in the wrong mode. Simply execute the FTP operation again using the correct transfer mode.

File Types and Extensions

Programs such as Excel, Word, and Internet Explorer determine a file's type by the file extension. It is helpful to understand the relationship between a file's extension and programs that use that file type so you can determine a file's general use and assess your ability to read the file before you download it.

File extensions are added automatically by the program that created them based on a widely agreed-upon convention for associating files with programs. Your computer's operating system (Windows, for example) keeps track of most file extension associations and maintains a list of file extensions and programs that can open files with those file extensions. You can use Windows Explorer to learn about the file extension associations on your computer.

To view Windows file extension associations:

▶ **1.** Click the **Start** button on the taskbar, and then click **Default Programs** on the Start menu. The Control Panel opens to the Default Programs page.

   Trouble? If you are using Windows XP, click the Start button on the taskbar, point to All Programs, point to Accessories, and then click Windows Explorer to start the program. Click Tools on the menu bar, and then click Folder Options to open the Folder Options dialog box. Click the File Types tab, and then skip to Step 3. Your dialog box will look different than the one shown in Figure 5-2.

▶ **2.** Click the **Associate a file type or protocol with a program** link. After a few seconds, a list of file extensions and their associated descriptions and default programs opens. Figure 5-2 shows the registered file types for one user's computer; your list will probably differ. When you install a new software program on your computer, Windows registers the file type(s) associated with that program. Therefore, your list of registered file types depends on which programs are installed on your computer. Clicking a registered file type in the list displays more information about that file extension, including the program that opens the file and a description of the file's purpose.

| Figure 5-2 | Viewing registered file types in Windows Vista |

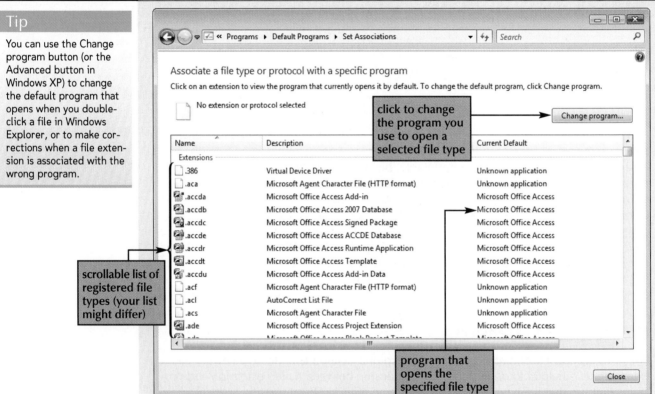

▶ **3.** Scroll down the list and click some of the registered file types, and then click the **Close** button to close the dialog box without making any changes.

Trouble? If you are using Windows XP, click the Cancel button to close the Folder Options dialog box.

▶ **4.** Click the **Close** button to close the Control Panel.

Trouble? If you are using Windows XP, click the Close button to close Windows Explorer.

Figure 5-3 describes some common file extensions that you might encounter on the Internet. Don't worry about remembering all the different file extensions; in practice, you might encounter only a few of them. Most often, you will see files on the Internet with extensions of .doc, .docx, .exe, .html, .txt, .pdf, or .zip.

Common file extensions ◀ **Figure 5-3**

Extension	Description
.accdb	Microsoft Access 2007 database
.bmp	Bitmap picture file
.doc	Microsoft Word version 2003 or earlier document
.docx	Microsoft Word 2007 document
.exe	Executable file
.gif	GIF picture file
.htm or .html	HTML document (Web page)
.jpg or .jpeg	Joint Photographic Experts Group picture file
.mdb	Microsoft Access 2003 or earlier database
.mpg	MPEG digitally compressed file
.pdf	Portable Document Format
.ppt	Microsoft PowerPoint 2003 or earlier presentation
.pptx	Microsoft PowerPoint 2007 presentation
.txt	Text file
.xls	Microsoft Excel 2003 or earlier workbook
.xlsx	Microsoft 2007 Excel workbook
.zip	Compressed file

Logging on to an FTP Site Using a Web Browser

To use a Web browser to transfer files between your computer and a remote site, you must first establish a connection to the remote site. Most Web browsers, including Microsoft Internet Explorer and Mozilla Firefox, support FTP, but they have limited functionality when compared to FTP client programs. You can use a Web browser to upload and download files from FTP sites, but if you are transferring a large number of files, you might find that it is difficult to use a browser because it doesn't provide some of the features included in an FTP client program, such as file resume and reconnection features. Figure 5-4 shows how Milt might use Firefox to make a connection to an FTP site that includes sound files organized into categories. To upload a file, he must drag it from his desktop or Windows Explorer and drop it in the correct location in the browser window. Downloading a file poses no problem because he only needs to select the file to download and tell the browser where to save it on his computer. Using a Web browser occasionally for uploading and downloading files is fine, but if Milt transfers a large number of files, he might prefer the features of an FTP client program.

Figure 5-4 ▶ **FTP connection using Firefox**

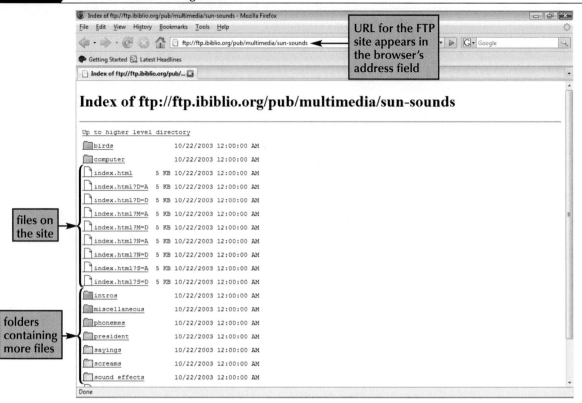

To use a remote site, regardless of how you access it, you must identify yourself, or **log on**, by supplying your user name and a password. Some FTP sites provide public access, which means anyone can connect to the FTP site. When you connect to a public FTP site, your access is restricted to only those files and folders designated for access by public users. Many software companies provide public FTP sites so users can download evaluation versions of their software and data to support their use of the program. Other FTP sites provide a combination of public and restricted access; some sites are completely restricted and do not allow public visitors. To access restricted FTP sites, you must have an account with the FTP site's owner or sponsor.

Anonymous FTP

Logging on to one of the many publicly accessible, remote computers connected to the Internet is known as an **anonymous login** because you use *anonymous* as your user name. You do not need a password to access a public computer; however, some users enter their full email address when prompted for a password. That way, the hosting organization can identify who is accessing the public areas of its FTP site. When you download or upload files using an anonymous login, you are participating in an **anonymous FTP session**. Figure 5-5 shows how Milt might use Internet Explorer to make an anonymous login to a public FTP site. When you connect to a public FTP site using a Web browser, the browser might automatically supply the user name "anonymous" and an appropriate password to access the site. If the site requires you to enter a user name and password, the browser will prompt you for these items.

FTP connection using Internet Explorer　　Figure 5-5

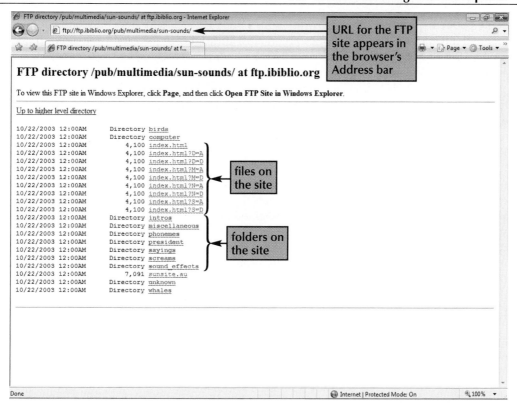

You can use many of the anonymous FTP sites connected to the Internet to download files to your computer. In most cases, public FTP sites impose limits on uploading files or provide only one publicly accessible directory to which you can upload files. Public FTP sites also limit your access to selected directories and files on their systems. People using FTP sites with anonymous logins usually cannot open and view all the directories and files on the site. You can determine which directories you have access to by experimenting. If you attempt to open directories or examine files that are not accessible to anonymous users, you will receive an error or warning message indicating that you do not have access to the requested file or directory. Experimenting with your access is allowable, but you should obey all rules and regulations regarding anonymous access. You can usually find information about the site's acceptable use rules and policies in the readme.txt file in the pub (public) directory. If you find a file by that or a similar name, be sure to read it carefully. Remember that you are using another person's or organization's FTP site at no cost to download files for your use.

Full-Privilege FTP

When you need to access an FTP site that is not public, such as one for your school or employer, you will use **full-privilege FTP**, where you are given access to its content with a user name and password. Even though you might have an account on a particular FTP site, your access might be limited to transferring files in a specific directory. When you log on to an FTP site with your user name and password, the system might automatically direct you to a particular directory on that FTP site in which you have been given rights to upload and download files. When you have an account on an FTP site, you can usually store files for longer periods than you can on a public FTP site.

Using a Public Directory

Some public FTP sites allow users with anonymous FTP access to view only one directory and any files or other directories it contains. This directory is usually named *pub* (for public). Besides permitting download access by anonymous users, the site's manager, also called the **Webmaster**, might allow users to upload files, making them available to anyone who connects to the site. Frequently, public directories provide a temporary location for users to upload and share data or programs that they think others might find useful. Most FTP sites place time limits, such as a few days or weeks, on how long anonymous users can store files in the public directory. The Webmaster determines how long files can remain in the public directory.

One potential problem of sites that permit users to upload files is that the Webmaster must monitor the files uploaded to a public directory on a regular basis. In addition to checking for viruses and other security threats that might be hidden in uploaded files, the Webmaster must find and delete any copyrighted files that were illegally uploaded to the site for public use. For example, uploading a licensed copy of a program to a public directory is a clear copyright violation because the license agreement most likely prohibits you from sharing the program with other users. Many FTP sites have specific policies that require you to acknowledge, before uploading any files, that you are the owner of the material or that its transfer to the FTP site will not violate any copyright or intellectual property restrictions.

Be sure to read the site's readme files to learn any rules about acceptable use when you enter an FTP site. Figure 5-6 shows the readme.txt file for Microsoft. Notice that the language in this document indicates that information on the site is provided "as is" and that Microsoft makes no warranties about the material on the site.

| Figure 5-6 | Readme file on Microsoft's FTP site |

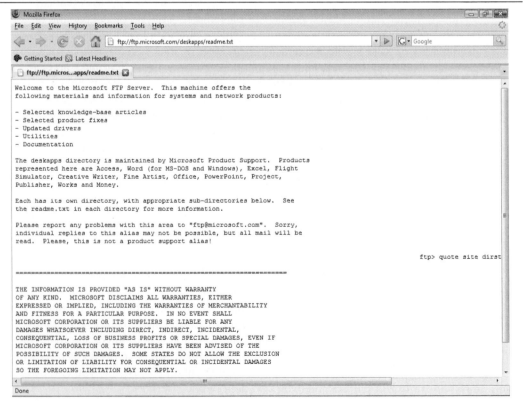

Now that you have reviewed some basic facts about FTP, Milt asks you to show him how to use a Web browser to navigate an FTP site. Sometimes Milt needs to obtain files of common sounds, such as a person laughing or a door closing, for use in the children's games that he produces. You will show Milt the FTP site at ibiblio.org, a library on the Internet that stores an archive of sound files, to introduce him to this resource and also to show him how to navigate an FTP site. Navigating an FTP site with a Web browser is very similar to using Windows Explorer to navigate the contents of a drive or folder on your computer.

Using a Web Browser to Navigate an FTP Site

Because most Internet users are adept at using a Web browser and know how hyperlinks work, they will have no difficulty navigating an FTP site in search of files. If you need to upload or download files to a site requiring full-privilege FTP access rights, the browser will prompt you for your user name and password.

When you visit an FTP site, your first goal should be to become familiar with its organization. FTP sites are organized hierarchically, much like the folders and files on a computer's hard drive. When you access an FTP site, you usually enter at the site's **root directory**, which contains other directories that contain files and other directories, such as those shown in Figure 5-7. Most sites prevent users with anonymous logins from accessing some files and directories in the root directory. When you enter a root directory for the first time, a message might appear indicating which file contains important information about navigating the site.

FTP site's hierarchical structure Figure 5-7

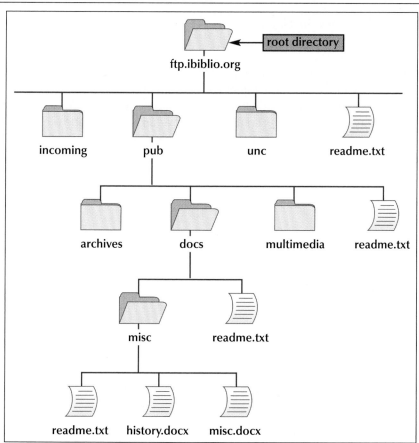

An FTP site usually stores two types of items—directories (folders) and files. Most Web browsers display directory and file links in different ways so you can distinguish directories from files. In Figure 5-8, which shows an FTP connection in Internet Explorer, the word "Directory" indicates a folder that you can open by clicking the link name next to the word "Directory." Individual files appear as hyperlinks, with their file size to the left of the link name. The link name includes the full filename, including the file extension. Clicking a link to a directory opens the folder and displays its contents; clicking the link to a filename opens the file and displays its contents. To download a file to your computer, right-click the filename to open the shortcut menu, click Save Target As, navigate to the drive and folder in which to save the file, and then click the Save button. To move up (or back) one directory, click the browser's Back button or the Up to higher level directory link.

| Figure 5-8 | **FTP site in Internet Explorer** |

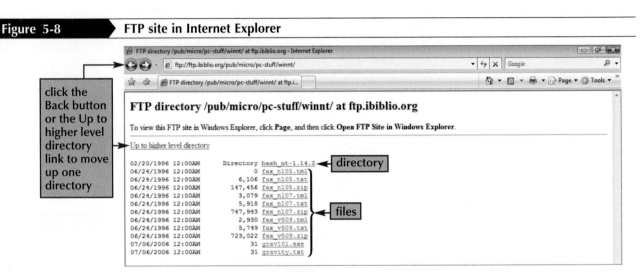

In Figure 5-9, which shows an FTP connection in Firefox, directories and files also both appear as hyperlinks. A yellow folder icon usually indicates a directory and a white page icon usually indicates a file. Clicking a link to a file opens the file; clicking a folder opens the directory and displays its contents. To move up (or back) one directory, click the browser's Back button or the Up to higher level directory link.

FTP site in Firefox Figure 5-9

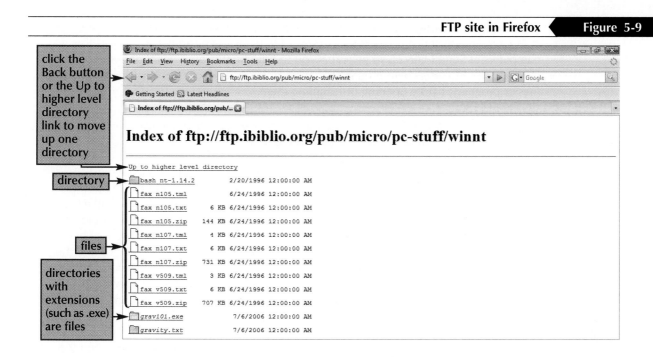

Milt asks you to show him how to use a Web browser to open and navigate an FTP site.

To open and navigate an FTP site using a Web browser:

▶ 1. Start your Web browser, open the Online Companion page at **www.course.com/oc/np/internet7** and log on to your account, click the **Tutorial 5** link, and then click the **Session 5.1** link. Click the **ibiblio.org** link and wait while your browser connects to the FTP site.

▶ 2. Click the **pub** folder (or link) to open it. The pub (public) directory opens and displays several directories. If necessary, use the scroll bar to view the contents of this directory.

When you are viewing files posted at an FTP site, the browser might open and display the contents of some files, such as text files (with the .txt file extension), and download other files, such as programs (files with the .exe file extension).

▶ 3. Click any folder to open it, and then examine the folder's contents.

Trouble? If you try to open a folder that does not permit anonymous users, the browser will display an error message. Close the dialog box, and then try another folder until you open one successfully.

▶ 4. Explore several directories at this FTP site until you find a file named **readme.txt** (or **readme**) or **index.html** (or **index**), and then click the file to open it. Sometimes you might find site information in the readme.txt, about.txt, or welcome.txt file. You might encounter other names, but they all serve the same function; that is, to provide an overview of the site's structure and file locations.

▶ 5. Click your browser's **Back** button to close the file that you opened, and then click the link to move to a higher level directory until you reach the root directory at ftp://ftp.ibiblio.org.

▶ 6. Close your browser.

Before you open or install any file or program that you downloaded from another computer, you must first check it for viruses. Milt wants to ensure the security of the computers at Sound Effects, so he wants you to help him locate several options for checking its computers before he starts transferring files and for checking downloaded files or programs before opening or installing them.

Checking Files for Viruses

For everyone using the Internet, computer viruses pose a real and potentially costly threat. Computer viruses are programs that "infect" your computer and cause harm to your disk or programs. People create viruses by coding programs that hide by attaching themselves to other programs on a computer. Some viruses simply display an annoying or silly message on your screen and then go away, whereas others can cause real harm by reformatting your hard drive, changing all of your computer's file extensions and their associations, or sending a copy of the virus to everyone in your email program's address book. You must know how to detect and eradicate viruses if you plan to download anything, including data, programs, instant messages, or email attachments, from any Internet server.

Software that only detects viruses and eliminates them is called an **antivirus program**. The category of software that detects viruses and other common security threats on the Internet is called **Internet security software**. This software usually includes tools that eradicate specific Internet threats, including viruses. Internet security software and antivirus programs start automatically when you start the computer and regularly scan the files on your computer and the files being downloaded to your computer and compare them to a signature that known viruses carry. A **virus signature** (also called a **virus pattern** or a **virus definition**) is a sequence (string) of characters that is always present in a particular virus. An antivirus program can scan a single file or folder or your entire computer to search for infected files. When the antivirus program finds a virus signature, it warns you. You can either delete the file containing the virus or ask the antivirus program to remove the virus. Most antivirus programs can clean infected files by removing the virus. If your computer does not have an antivirus program or security suite installed on it, you can follow the links in the Internet Security Software section of the Online Companion page for Tutorial 5 to find resources for obtaining and using Internet security and antivirus programs.

Tip

An antivirus program might be part of an Internet security suite of programs that also scans files for other security threats, such as spyware, and does other things such as blocking unwanted pop-up ads.

Using Antivirus Software Effectively | InSight

Dell Inc., Hewlett Packard, Apple, and other computer manufacturers preload most new computers with an antivirus program or Internet security suite. Three popular choices for protecting computers are produced by Symantec (Norton), McAfee, and ZoneAlarm. Security and antivirus programs protect your computer from viruses, but only when they are turned on, properly configured, and include current virus patterns. When you first start your antivirus program, it will ask you to make a connection to its server, from which the program will download the most recent virus patterns. You must regularly download virus patterns from the server to keep your computer safe. Some programs include features that automatically download the patterns for you on a weekly or bi-weekly basis; other programs require you to connect to the server and initiate the download. When you purchase and install an antivirus program, you usually receive a free trial subscription—usually up to 12 months—for downloading current virus patterns. After this initial period ends, you must pay the software producer a fee to continue downloading current virus patterns. In either case, your antivirus software can protect you only from viruses that it recognizes. If you install an antivirus program and do not regularly download new patterns, your computer isn't protected from dozens of new virus threats each month. In addition, if your antivirus software isn't turned on or set to scan downloaded files, it cannot protect your computer.

And, finally, as you use FTP and other methods to obtain files, keep in mind that you usually have to open or execute a file to unleash any virus it contains. By regularly scanning your computer for viruses, keeping your virus patterns current, configuring your antivirus program to work automatically, and scanning all downloaded files, you can protect your computer from viruses.

Figure 5-10 shows the configuration screen for Norton Internet Security, a program by Symantec that provides antivirus protection and other components that protect the user's computer against other types of common Internet threats, such as spyware. Notice that the user's system is set to auto-protect, meaning that the antivirus software starts automatically when Windows starts. This screen also indicates that the important features provided by Norton Internet Security are turned on and protecting the user's computer. Automatic LiveUpdate is a feature that, when enabled, automatically connects to the Symantec Web site and checks for and downloads new virus patterns and other program updates on a timetable set by the user. The options shown in this window are global, and you usually need to set them only once.

Figure 5-10 Configuring Norton Internet Security

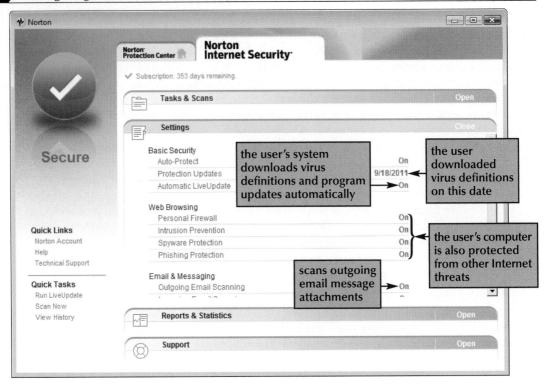

Because any file that you download from the Internet can contain a virus, it is important to use your antivirus software as directed. Before downloading any file, make sure that your antivirus software is turned on, enabled, and uses current virus patterns. After downloading the file, use the antivirus software to scan it for viruses. Most antivirus programs let you select which types of files to scan; the safest course is to scan all files. Most antivirus programs let you initiate a scan by right-clicking a file and then choosing an option on the shortcut menu to scan the file. If the file is free of known viruses, a dialog box will open and tell you that no viruses were found. In addition, you might be able to request a full system scan, in which all of the files on your computer are scanned and checked for viruses; many antivirus software programs also allow you to set up a schedule for automatically performing full system scans on a regular basis. If the program finds a virus, it will present you with options for handling the file. Figure 5-11 shows the virus and spyware protection options for Norton Internet Security.

Virus and Spyware Protection Options in Norton Internet Security ◀ Figure 5-11

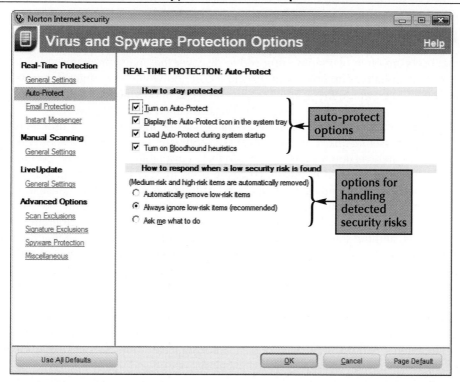

In addition to installing updated antivirus software and virus patterns, another way to protect your computer from viruses is to be careful about which files you download and the sources you use to get those files. If Milt wants to download the newest version of a program, he might discover that many Web sites include a link to download the executable file that installs it. Milt can download and install the file from any of these Web sites, but a better choice is to download it directly from the software's producer. Not only is he assured of a valid copy of the program, but he can make sure that he is downloading its most recent version. Because the software comes directly from its producer, the likelihood of a virus is low.

Milt now has a clear understanding of FTP and the tools he needs to transfer files using FTP. In Session 5.2, you will use the Internet to find reviews of and download an FTP client program that Milt and his contractors can use to transfer files between the Los Angeles studio and different areas of the United States and Canada. You will also download a file compression program and explore some options for collaborating and storing files on the Internet.

Session 5.1 Quick Check | Review

1. What two types of programs are commonly used to transfer files on the Internet?
2. What user name do you enter to connect to an FTP site anonymously?
3. What is the usual name of the directory on a FTP site that allows anonymous users?
4. What two types of items might you find in the root directory of an FTP site?
5. What would you type in your browser's address field to open the FTP site at zdnet.com?
6. What is an Internet security suite?

Session 5.2

Types of Download Software

Internet users are often pleasantly surprised to discover that many programs are available for download at little or no cost, or at the same cost you would encounter if you went to a retail outlet to purchase them. The four general types of downloaded software are freeware, shareware, limited edition, and licensed (also called a full version).

Developers often make their software available for free in exchange for user feedback. After collecting user feedback and improving the software, many developers provide an upgrade of the free version for a fee. Software that is available to users at no cost and with no restrictions is called **freeware**. Freeware users must accept the implicit or explicit warning that the software might contain errors, called **bugs**, which could cause the program to halt or malfunction or even damage the user's computer. The main risk associated with using freeware is that its limited testing sometimes results in a program that contains bugs, and the software's developer is rarely liable for any damage that the freeware program might cause. On the other hand, many good-quality commercial software programs started as freeware. To see what kinds of successes and problems users have reported, you should use an Internet search engine to locate reviews before you download, install, virus check, and use any freeware program.

Shareware is similar to freeware, but it is usually available for free only for a short evaluation period. After the evaluation period expires—usually after a specified number of days or a specific number of uses—shareware stops functioning. Shareware users are expected to stop using the shareware after the specified initial trial period and uninstall it from their computers. Otherwise, anyone who likes the program and wants to continue using it can purchase a license. Shareware developers use three popular methods to turn trial users into paying customers. The first way is to build a counter into the program that keeps track of the number of times they have used a program. After users have reached a usage limit, the software is disabled. The second way inserts an internal date checker that causes the shareware to stop working after a specific time period from the installation date has elapsed, such as 30 days. Third, many shareware developers use a "nag" screen that appears each time you start the program to encourage those users who do not purchase a license to stop using the shareware, although the program might continue to work. The screen usually displays a message with the developer's name and Web address and asks users to abide by the licensing agreement and to submit payment for the shareware version of the product.

Shareware is usually more reliable than freeware because the shareware developer is sometimes willing to accept responsibility for the program's operation. Usually, shareware developers have an established process for users to report any bugs and receive free or low-cost software upgrades and patches.

Some developers distribute restricted versions of their software for free to let people use it without cost. A restricted version of a program is called a **limited edition** (often abbreviated as LE) or an **evaluation version**, and it provides most of the functionality of the full version that is available for purchase. However, limited edition software sometimes omits one or more useful features of the full version. You can sometimes download a limited edition version and use it for free. If you like the limited edition, you can purchase the full version. The limited edition usually performs standard FTP tasks but disables or omits some of the advanced features that make the full product especially attractive. Because the complete versions of limited edition software are inexpensive, most users of the limited edition will upgrade by purchasing the comprehensive version so they can use its additional capabilities.

Regardless of which type of software you use to evaluate a product, most developers provide you with a means of contacting them to purchase a license to use the full version of the evaluation copy. Purchasing a license usually involves paying a fee to get a code to unlock the software and render it fully functional.

Evaluating Download Software

Because Milt will need to upload and download files, he is most interested in obtaining an FTP client program that can handle both transactions. To help Milt make his decision about an FTP client program, your first goal is to make sure that the software you will download and install is reliable. Perhaps equally important is how various software tools compare to each other, so you need to find some sort of ratings system that will guide you in making good decisions about which software to choose. Finally, cost is a consideration because Milt will need to provide this software to employees in his studio and ask his contractors to obtain it.

Evaluating Features of an FTP Client Program | InSight

Although you can use a Web browser or an FTP client program to upload and download files, FTP client programs include options that make file transfers easier or more efficient. The features provided by an FTP client program vary from one program to another. When selecting an FTP client program, choose one that supports all or most of the following desirable features:

- Provides a multipane display so you can see both the local and remote sites simultaneously.
- Allows you to transfer multiple files in one FTP session. Some FTP clients restrict the number of files you can transfer at one time. If you need to transfer many files, this restriction can significantly increase the amount of time it will need take to transfer the files.
- Permits drag-and-drop file transfers so you can use the mouse to drag and drop files between the local and remote sites.
- Lets you create and delete directories on the local and remote sites, and rename files and directories on the local and remote sites.
- Allows you to set up scheduled file transfers at a future date and time so you can transfer selected files unattended.
- Recovers interrupted file transfers by continuing the transfer process from the point where the connection was lost or interrupted.
- Reconnects automatically to sites that disconnect a transfer when your connection exceeds the maximum allotted time.

A good way to locate software on the Internet is to use one or more Internet search engines. If you are searching for FTP client programs, you can look for reviews or comparisons of the software by users or vendors. For example, several popular computer magazines feature articles that compare and rate programs used for specific purposes. The criteria these sites use to judge which program is best might be different from your own criteria. However, it never hurts to review the ratings when you can.

Computer magazines frequently use their software testing laboratories to review software, conduct product comparisons, and report the results. They should not have a vested interest in the outcome, but always view the results with a critical eye to identify any biases. The Program Reviews and Download Sites section of the Online Companion page for Tutorial 5 contains links to publishers of software and hardware product reviews and sites that provide downloads of popular programs.

After hearing positive feedback about it, Milt asks you to conduct research about FileZilla, an FTP client program that is part of an open source project and therefore is free to its users. You'll begin your research by searching for information about this program.

Tip

The source code in an open source project is licensed so that it is possible for other programmers to use, modify, improve, and redistribute the program with the goal of improving it for all users.

To learn more about FileZilla from reviews:

▶ **1.** Start your Web browser, open the Online Companion Web page at **www.course.com/oc/np/internet7** and log on to your account, click the **Tutorial 5** link, and then click the **Session 5.2** link.

▶ **2.** Click one of the links in the Evaluating Download Software section, and then wait for your browser to load the home page for the site you selected.

▶ **3.** Locate the search text box on the site, and then enter the search term **FileZilla** in the text box and press the **Enter** key.

   Trouble? If you don't find any links to FileZilla on the site you selected in Step 2, return to the Online Companion page for Session 5.2, choose another site, and then repeat Step 3.

▶ **4.** Evaluate the resources returned by your search to find one that contains information that evaluates or reviews the FileZilla Client program, and then click the link. (*Note:* You should not download the FileZilla program at this time.) As you are evaluating the FileZilla review, note whether the program has any of the desirable features of a FTP client program, and whether it would meet the needs of Sound Effects contractors for transferring files.

▶ **5.** Return to the Online Companion page for Session 5.2, and then choose another link in the Evaluating Download Software section.

▶ **6.** Repeat Steps 3 and 4 to evaluate the resources at the second site.

▶ **7.** Return to the Online Companion page for Session 5.2.

After discussing your findings with Milt, he asks you to download, install, and use this program for several weeks to determine its usefulness for Sound Effects. To make sure that you download the latest version of FileZilla, you will use a Web browser to download it directly from the FileZilla Web site.

Using a Web Browser to Download an FTP Client Program

Based on your research, Milt has decided that the FileZilla FTP client program is the best choice for Sound Effects. You will use a browser to download the FileZilla program next.

Reference Window | Using a Browser to Download a File

- Start your Web browser, and then open the Web site from which you will download the file.
- Navigate to the page that contains the file you want to download, and then click the link to the file.
- In Internet Explorer, click the Save button in the File Download dialog box, click the Browse Folders link (if necessary), navigate to the drive or folder in which to store the file, and then click the Save button. If necessary, click the Close button to close the dialog box.
- In Firefox, click the Save File button to download the file. If your browser gives you the option to select the location in which to save the file, click the Save it to disk option button (if necessary), and then click the OK button. Navigate to the drive or folder in which to store the file, and then click the Save button. If necessary, click the Close button to close the dialog box. If the file is downloaded automatically to an existing folder or to the desktop, click the Close button to close the Downloads dialog box, locate the file, and then cut and paste it to the drive and folder in which to store the file.

To use a browser to download the FileZilla program:

▶ **1.** On the Online Companion page for Session 5.2, click the **FileZilla** link and wait while your Web browser opens the FileZilla Web site. See Figure 5-12.

FileZilla Web site ◀ **Figure 5-12**

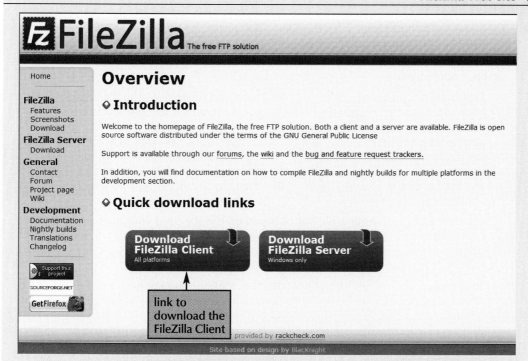

▶ **2.** Find the link to download the FileZilla Client and click it. A page opens with options for downloading the program in various formats.

Trouble? If you don't have the starting Data Files for this tutorial, you need to get them before you can proceed. Your instructor will either give you the Data Files or ask you to obtain them from a specified location (such as a network drive). In either case, make a backup copy of the Data Files before you start so that you will have the orginal files available in case you need to start over. If you have any questions about the Data Files, see your instructor or technical support person for assistance.

▶ **3.** Find the link to download the Windows version (or the version you need for your operating system) of the FileZilla setup (.exe) file.

Trouble? The FileZilla Web site might change over time. If you cannot find the link to download the FileZilla setup (.exe) file, return to the Online Companion page for Session 5.2, click the FileZilla Client download link, and use the instructions at this Web site to download the FileZilla Client program.

▶ **4.** Click the link to download the Windows FileZilla setup (.exe) file. A Web page opens and indicates that the download should start automatically. You will download this file to the Tutorial.05\Tutorial folder. (*Note:* If you are using Internet Explorer, read the following Trouble and continue to the next step. If you are using Firefox, go to Step 6.)

Trouble? If you are using Internet Explorer, your security settings might cause the Information Bar dialog box to open and the Information Bar to display a message that the browser blocked the site from downloading a file to your computer. Click the Close button in the Information Bar dialog box, click the Information Bar to open a shortcut menu, and then click Download File.

▶ **5.** If you are using Internet Explorer, click the **Save** button in the File Download – Security Warning dialog box, navigate to the **Tutorial.05\Tutorial** folder included with your Data Files, and then click the **Save** button. When the download is complete, the Download complete dialog box will close.

Trouble? If the Download complete dialog box does not close automatically, click the Close button.

Tip

To change the default download location in Firefox or to set Firefox to always prompt you where to save files, click Tools on the menu bar, click Options, click the Main icon in the Options dialog box, and then change the settings in the Downloads section.

▶ **6.** If you are using Firefox, click the **Save File** button, navigate to the **Tutorial.05\Tutorial** folder with your Data Files, and then click the **Save** button. If necessary, click the **Close** button to close the Downloads dialog box after the file has been downloaded.

Trouble? If the Downloads dialog box opens and downloads the file without asking you for a location, note the default location to which all downloads are saved at the bottom of the dialog box (the location will be to the right of the "All files downloaded to" text). Click the location to open it, use Windows Explorer to move the file from the default download location to the Tutorial.05\Tutorial folder included with your Data Files, click the Close button to close Windows Explorer, and then click the Close button to close the Downloads dialog box.

The time it takes to transfer a file varies based on the speed of your Internet connection and the file's size. If you are on a local area network (LAN) with a T1 Internet connection, then the transfer time is a few seconds. If you are using a modem and a dial-up connection, then the transfer time could take several minutes. Another factor in the download time is the amount of traffic at the site. Many simultaneous users can result in delayed downloads. If you encounter problems while downloading a file, stop the process by clicking the Cancel button and try again later.

After downloading anything from the Internet—even files from reputable sources—your first priority is to scan the file for security threats. You can download many high-quality security suites from the Internet and install and use them for a limited time to determine their appropriateness for your own security needs. Because most security programs are large in size, you won't download one in this tutorial, but you can click the links in the Internet Security Software section of the Online Companion page for Tutorial 5 to download trial versions of different security programs for your operating system.

You must install the FileZilla program on your computer to use it. You can use Windows Explorer to check the Tutorial.05\Tutorial folder to make sure that it contains the FileZilla setup file.

Note: If your instructor or technical support person permits you to install and use the program, complete the next set of steps to install the program. If your lab policy prohibits you from installing programs, read the following steps so you know how to install the program, but do *not* complete the steps at the computer.

To install FileZilla on your computer:

▶ **1.** Start Windows Explorer, and then navigate to the **Tutorial.05\Tutorial** folder included with your Data Files.

Trouble? If required to do so by your instructor, follow the instructions provided to scan the FileZilla setup file that you downloaded for security threats before proceeding to Step 2.

▶ **2.** Double-click the **FileZilla** setup file to start the installation process. A Setup dialog box opens and displays the license agreement for installing and using the program. See Figure 5-13.

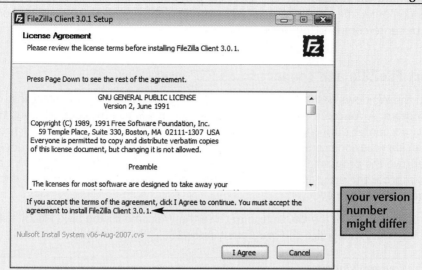

Trouble? If an Open File - Security Warning dialog box opens, click the Run button.

Trouble? If a User Account Control dialog box opens, click the Allow link.

▶ **3.** Use the scroll bar to read the license agreement, and then click the **I Agree** button.

▶ **4.** In the next dialog box, choose the option button to make the program available to any user who uses the computer, and then click the **Next** button.

Trouble? If the installation instructions for FileZilla differ from those shown in the steps, follow the on-screen instructions.

▶ **5.** In the next dialog box, make sure that the following components will be installed, as indicated by check marks in the check boxes to the left of their names: **FileZilla Client**, **Language files**, **Shell Extension**, and **Desktop Icon**.

▶ **6.** Click the **Next** button, change the default destination folder if asked to do so by your instructor, and then click the **Next** button.

▶ **7.** In the final dialog box, click the **Install** button. When the installation is complete, you will see a dialog box that indicates that FileZilla has been installed on your computer. Click the **Finish** button to continue.

Tip

After installing a program, you can delete the downloaded file from your computer, or you can keep it in case you need to reinstall the program. Some programs automatically delete downloaded files to save space on your computer.

After installing the program, you can use it to transfer files.

Using an FTP Client Program to Download WinZip

Milt is very interested in compressing files to decrease the amount of storage space they require and also to decrease the time it takes to upload and download files. Many file compression programs available on the Internet are reliable and easy to use. One popular program is WinZip, which is available for free during its evaluation period. WinZip has been downloaded by millions of users and has received many awards from computer magazines and other sources.

To test the FTP client program that you downloaded for Milt earlier, you will use it to connect to the WinZip FTP site so you can download an evaluation copy of the program. When you establish a connection to an FTP site, you can save the site's address and your user name and password so you can easily return to the site later. Milt already learned that the FTP site for WinZip is ftp.winzip.com. You will enter this information and connect to the FTP site using an anonymous login.

Tip

You can usually find the FTP address for an FTP site by replacing the "www" in a site's Web address with "ftp." Some companies include hyperlinks on their Web sites to their FTP sites.

Note: In the following steps, you will use the FileZilla program to download the Win-Zip program. If you do not have an FTP client program or cannot install one on your school's computer, then read the steps without completing them at the computer or use a Web browser to complete the steps.

To start FileZilla and connect to an FTP site:

▶ **1.** On the Windows desktop, double-click the **FileZilla Client** icon to start the program. A Welcome dialog box might open and ask you to report all bugs that you encounter during your use of the software. As part of an open source project, FileZilla relies on users to report problems and, in many cases, to write code to improve the program. Your license agreement doesn't require you to report bugs or improve the program, but your cooperation to improve the program is encouraged and welcomed.

▶ **2.** If necessary, click the **OK** button to close the Welcome dialog box. FileZilla starts. If necessary, maximize the program window. See Figure 5-14.

Figure 5-14 ▶ **FileZilla program window**

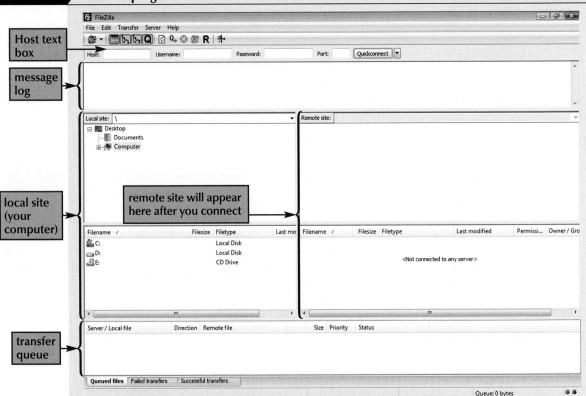

Trouble? Because it is an open source program, the FileZilla program window might change over time, so your screen might look different. The basic features of the program should stay the same, so any differences should not affect your work.

▶ **3.** With the insertion point in the Host text box, type the address of the FTP site for WinZip, **ftp.winzip.com**.

4. Press the **Tab** key to move to the Username text box, and then type **anonymous**. Because you are making an anonymous connection to the WinZip FTP site, you do not need to supply a password. Some users change the default password to their email address to identify their use of the site, but this custom is not required.

5. Click the **Quickconnect** button. FileZilla connects to the FTP site and enters a password for you in the Password text box. The message log displays the commands issued by FileZilla, the FTP server's responses, and the status of your connection. You will know that you made a connection when the message log displays the status "Directory listing successful" and the contents of the FTP site are displayed in the Remote site pane. See Figure 5-15.

Connection made to WinZip FTP site | **Figure 5-15**

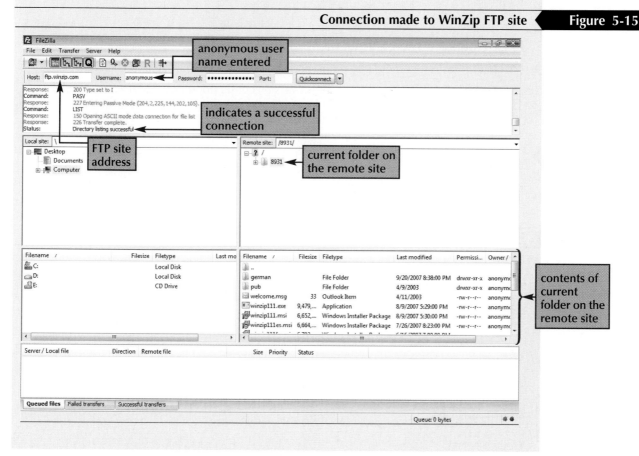

Now that you have connected to the FTP site, you can locate and download the WinZip program.

Downloading a File Using an FTP Client Program | Reference Window

- Log on to the remote site by supplying its URL, your user name or anonymous, and your password (if necessary).
- Navigate to the file you want to download.
- Click the filename on the remote site to select it.
- Navigate to the drive or folder on your computer to which to download the file.
- Drag the file from the remote site to the drive or folder on your computer.
- End the FTP session by disconnecting from the remote site.

FileZilla refers to your local drive as a "local site" and to the FTP site as the "remote site." To download a file from the FTP server, you need to find it in the Remote site pane. Then you use the directory tree in the Local site pane to navigate to the drive and folder to which you want to download the file. To download the file, drag it from the Remote site pane to the Local site pane.

The file that you will download is stored in the FTP site's root directory, so you won't need to navigate through the site's folders to find it. If you needed to navigate the FTP site to find a file, double-clicking a folder in the top Remote site pane on opens it and displays its contents in the bottom Remote site pane. Clicking the folder icon at the top of the Remote site pane (with two dots to its right) moves up to the higher level directory at the site.

To download a file to your computer:

▶ **1.** In the bottom Remote site pane, find the **winzip111.exe** file and click it.

Trouble? WinZip releases updated versions of its popular program on a regular basis. If the winzip file that you locate contains a different number, then a new version is available. Click that file in Step 1, making sure that it contains the .exe file extension, and continue with Step 2.

▶ **2.** In the Local site pane on the top left, navigate to the drive and folder containing your Data Files, and then open the **Tutorial.05\Tutorial** folder. Figure 5-16 shows the contents of the Tutorial folder in the Local site pane and the selected winzip111.exe file in the Remote site pane.

Figure 5-16 ▶ **File selected on the remote site for download**

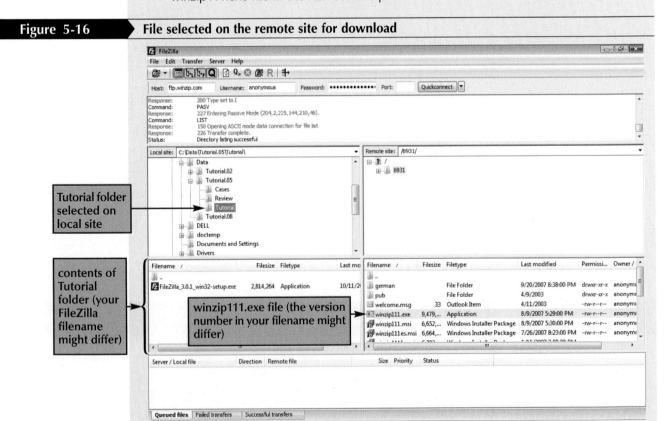

To transfer the file from the Remote site to the Tutorial folder, you drag it from the Remote site pane to the Local site pane. FileZilla will issue the commands to transfer the file.

3. Click the **winzip111.exe** file in the Remote site pane, and then drag it to the **Tutorial** folder in the bottom Local site pane. The message log will display the commands used to transfer the file, and the transfer queue will display the download progress. Depending on your Internet connection, it might take anywhere from a few seconds to several minutes or more to download the file. The download is complete when the message log displays the message "File transfer successful," as shown in Figure 5-17, and the transfer queue at the bottom of the window shows one successful transfer.

File after downloading to local site ◀ Figure 5-17

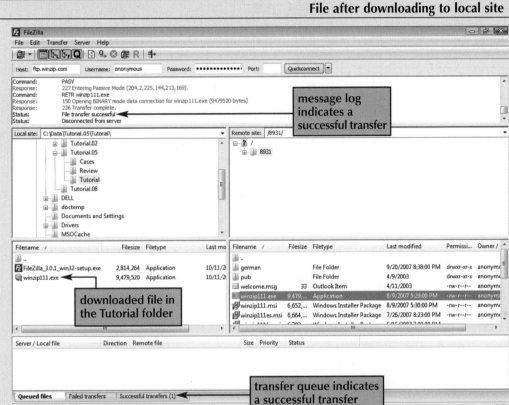

Trouble? The WinZip server might disconnect you automatically from the server when the download is complete. This causes no problems.

4. Click **File** on the menu bar, and then click **Exit** to log off the WinZip FTP site and to close the FileZilla program.

5. If you have permission from your instructor or lab manager to install the WinZip program, open Windows Explorer, navigate to the **Tutorial.05\Tutorial** folder included with your Data Files, scan the downloaded file for security threats, double-click **winzip111.exe**, and then follow the on-screen instructions, including reading and accepting the terms in the license agreement.

Trouble? If you downloaded a more recent version of WinZip, the filename that you double-click might be different from the one in Step 5. This difference causes no problems.

Trouble? If a User Account Control dialog box opens, click the Continue button.

Trouble? If a dialog box opens and asks if you want to learn more about another program, click the No, please continue installing WinZip option button to continue.

6. When prompted to select a start interface, make sure that the **Start with the WinZip Wizard** option button is selected.

▶ **7.** In the final dialog box, make sure that the **Launch WinZip 11.1** check box contains a check mark, and then click the **Finish** button. WinZip starts and displays the evaluation version dialog box shown in Figure 5-18.

Figure 5-18 ▶ **WinZip evaluation version startup screen**

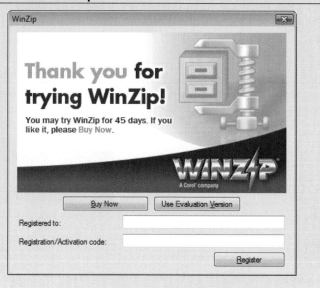

The WinZip program that you downloaded and installed is an evaluation version that you can use for 45 days to evaluate the software at no charge. Each time you start the program, it will remind you about your use of an evaluation copy that has not yet been registered. If you continue using the software, you can click a button in the reminder screen to purchase a license to use the full version. Milt will use WinZip frequently to compress the sound files he produces, so he wants to use the program during the evaluation period to see how it works.

Compressing and Decompressing Files

Internet files of all types are frequently stored in compressed form. **Compressed files** use less space when stored and they take less time to be transferred from one computer to another. Some files are compressed automatically in their native file formats, such as JPEG and MPEG files. For files that are not compressed automatically, you can use a program to reduce the file size and thereby significantly decrease the transmission time. Compression will be especially important to Milt, because many of his contractors live in areas that do not have broadband service and must connect to the Internet using connections with slow upload and download times. In addition, by compressing sound files, they will require less space on the Internet site he selects to store the files.

You can use a **file compression program** to decrease the original size of most files. After you download a compressed file, you must use a program to restore the file to its original state before you can open or use it. The process of restoring a compressed file to its original state is called **file decompression**, **file expansion**, or **file extraction**. FTP recognizes most compressed files by their extensions. The most common extension is .zip, which is why some people refer to compressed files as **zip files** or a **zip archive**.

Milt wants you to use WinZip to compress and decompress some files so he can evaluate the software.

To use WinZip to compress files:

1. In the WinZip dialog box, click the **Use Evaluation Version** button to close the dialog box and start WinZip. WinZip starts the WinZip Wizard, a series of dialog boxes that will prompt you for the activity that you want to perform. You can also start WinZip in WinZip Classic mode, where you use the program's menu bar and toolbar to execute commands. Both methods accomplish the same tasks.

2. Click the **Next** button, click the **Quick Search (faster)** option button, and then click the **Next** button.

   Trouble? The steps you encounter when you run the WinZip Wizard might be different, depending on the WinZip version you installed. Follow the steps as closely as possible if you encounter any differences.

3. Click the **Create a new Zip file** option button in the WinZip Wizard – Select Activity dialog box, and then click the **Next** button. The WinZip Wizard – Choose Zip Name dialog box opens. You can type a filename in the File name text box to save the file in the default folder or use the Browse button to locate a specific folder in which to store the zip file.

4. Click the **Browse** button to open the New Archive dialog box, navigate to the **Tutorial.05** folder included with your Data Files, type **zipfile.zip** in the File name text box, and then click the **OK** button.

5. Click the **Next** button. The WinZip Wizard – Select Files [zipfile.zip] dialog box opens and prompts you for the location from which to add files to the zip file you just created.

6. Click the **Add folders** button, select the **Tutorial** folder in the Tutorial.05 folder included with your Data Files, click the **OK** button, and then click the **Zip Now** button. WinZip searches for the files you selected, creates a zip file named zipfile.zip, and displays the dialog box shown in Figure 5-19 when the zip operation is complete.

WinZip Wizard – Zip Complete [zipfile.zip] dialog box　　　**Figure 5-19**

7. Click the **Finish** button to close the WinZip Wizard. The file zipfile.zip appears in Windows Explorer in the Tutorial.05 folder.

Internet Tutorial 5 Downloading and Storing Data

The WinZip Wizard made it easy to compress files. After you become more familiar with WinZip, you might want to use the WinZip Classic setting to compress and decompress files. To compress files using the WinZip Classic interface, follow these steps:

1. In Windows Explorer, select the folders and/or files that you want to compress.
2. Right-click the selected items to compress, point to WinZip on the shortcut menu, click Add to Zip file, and then if necessary, click the Use Evaluation Version button.
3. In the Add dialog box, type the location in which to save the compressed file in the Add to archive text box. Make sure to include the drive letter, folder, and filename of the compressed file. Figure 5-20 shows the Add dialog box after the user selected a folder to compress in a file named zipfile.zip in the Tutorial.05 folder on drive C.

Figure 5-20 ▶ **Add dialog box**

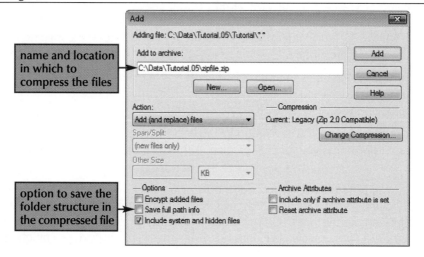

4. Click the Save full path info check box to save the files with the original folder structure that you have on your computer. To save the files without any folder structure, clear this check box.
5. Click the Add button. WinZip compresses the files.
6. Close WinZip.

When you want to decompress a zipped file, you can double-click it to start the WinZip Wizard, which guides you through the process of selecting the location in which to decompress the files. Another way of decompressing the files is to right-click the zip file and use the shortcut menu to select an option.

To decompress the file:

▶ 1. With the contents of the Tutorial.05 folder open in Windows Explorer, right-click the **zipfile.zip** file, and then point to **WinZip** on the shortcut menu. Figure 5-21 shows the available options for decompressing the file.

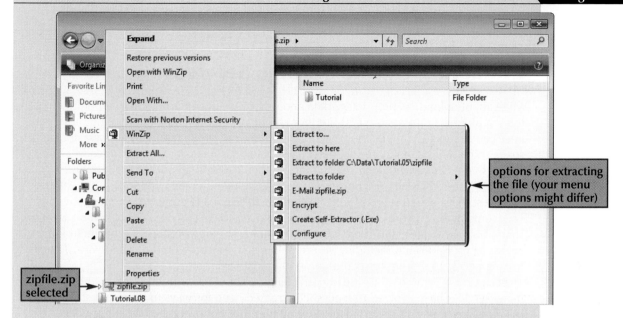

Using the shortcut menu to extract a file | Figure 5-21

The options for decompressing the file might differ based on your WinZip version and operating system, but some common options are to extract it to a location you choose (Extract to), extract it to the same folder where the .zip file is stored (Extract to here), extract to a new folder in the same folder where the .zip file is stored and using the name of the .zip file (Extract to folder ... where ... is the path), extract to a recent location (Extract to folder, with a submenu that opens and lists the recently used locations), email the .zip file to a recipient you select (Email ... where ... is the .zip filename), change the security settings of the .zip file to protect it with a password (Encrypt), create a self-extracting file (Create Self-Extractor (.Exe), or configure the .zip file with advanced options (Configure).

You will choose the option to extract the .zip file to a folder with the same name.

> **2.** On the shortcut menu, click **Extract to folder** (this option will also contain the path to your Data Files).

> **3.** In the WinZip dialog box, click the **Use Evaluation Version** button. WinZip unzips the zipfile.zip file to a folder named zipfile in the Tutorial.05 folder included with your Data Files, and displays the updated file listing for your Data Files in Windows Explorer.

> **4.** Click the **Close** button to close Windows Explorer.

Tip

If you see a "Scan with Norton Internet Security" option or something similar on the shortcut menu, clicking this option scans the selected file for viruses and other threats.

In addition to its utility in transferring files between computers, FTP is an excellent way to share files with other users and to store files temporarily or permanently. The File Compression Programs section of the Online Companion page for Tutorial 5 contains links to other file compression programs that you can download and examine at no cost during the program's evaluation period.

Now that Milt has used an FTP client program and understands how to compress files to decrease their file size, he asks you to investigate the online storage services available on the Internet so he has a place to store files used by his company and to collaborate on documents.

Evaluating Online Storage Services

Milt cannot upload his proprietary data and other sensitive information to a public directory on a publicly accessible FTP site, nor can he ask his contractors to do the same. Milt needs access to a site that is both secure and password protected, with enough storage space so that files can remain on the site for as long as necessary. He also needs to provide his contractors with access to this site so they can upload and download files.

When you use an ISP for your Internet connection and email account, you might also receive some space to store a Web site or files. This space is useful to you because your user name and password control access to the site. However, you probably won't want to share this space with other users, because by doing so you will need to give them full access to your account, including your email messages. You would have no way of controlling access to the site or securing important data from other users.

Because FTP is an easy-to-use and efficient way of transferring files across the Internet, many services have evolved to meet the increased need for ways to store and share files. FTP sites are one way of sharing and storing files, but not everyone has full-privilege access to an FTP server. To meet this need, a new business model was formed, where ISPs and other entities provide storage space on their servers, either for free or for a small monthly fee, with an option to purchase additional storage space later. Users access the online storage space using an FTP client program, a program or other interface provided by the provider, or a Web browser. The space is secured with an account name and password and permits the sharing of files by many users. Many individuals use these online storage services to store backup files, sound files, personal Web sites, pictures, and other data. In addition, the proliferation of large data files moving across the Internet has the potential to overload many networks and mail servers when these files are attached to email messages, so online storage providers offer an alternative to consuming a company's network resources. These sites have become so popular that many now provide easy interfaces for uploading and downloading files that don't require the use of any separate FTP client programs, and instead use simple Web page interfaces.

As more registered users started using these services, and as those users started storing large files and increasing the number of daily transfers, many sites experienced conflicts with users competing for the company's resources. As a result of bandwidth problems, many online storage providers changed their policies to limit the number of transfers and amount of space provided, to charge a small monthly fee for use of the space, or a combination of both. Most providers of free services offer an option to purchase additional space and transfers for a fee.

Using an online storage provider might be a good opportunity for Milt. As he reviews his requirements, he decides that he needs at least two gigabytes of space and the capability to allow restricted and full access, depending on the user. Because the cost of maintaining his own FTP server might be an impediment to his overall operating budget, Milt is willing to pay a monthly fee for use of whichever provider best meets his needs. In addition, because Milt works with only a few contractors at a time, his space will not have a high number of transfers each day. Milt and his contractors will upload and download files, so they will need to use an FTP client program or an easy-to-use Web page interface to execute the transfers. Being able to use any FTP client program or a Web browser to log on to the site will make it easier for Milt and his contractors to access and use the site. Finally, Milt wants to make sure that the provider will protect the security of his data from unauthorized use.

Like other free services found on the Internet, online storage providers come and go on a regular basis. For this reason, most individuals and businesses that rely on these types of services are careful to back up important files and keep a copy of them locally in case the provider experiences a technical problem or suddenly ceases operations. In addition, some businesses rely on two online storage providers to store their files, so they have a primary and secondary set of files in case of a problem.

Xdrive, which in 2005 became a service of AOL (America Online), provides users with five gigabytes of secure online storage space for free, with an option to upgrade to additional space for a fee. Many individuals use Xdrive to store and share large files and large collections of files, such as music, videos, and pictures. Xdrive is also a simple way for people employed in satellite and home offices to transfer files to people working in corporate offices.

Another online storage provider is Box.net, which provides a variety of storage options for individuals, businesses, and large organizations. All accounts include storage, a Web page interface that requires no additional software downloads, and access to the service using any computer or mobile device. Figure 5-22 shows the flexibility of Box.net's plans.

Box.net home page | Figure 5-22

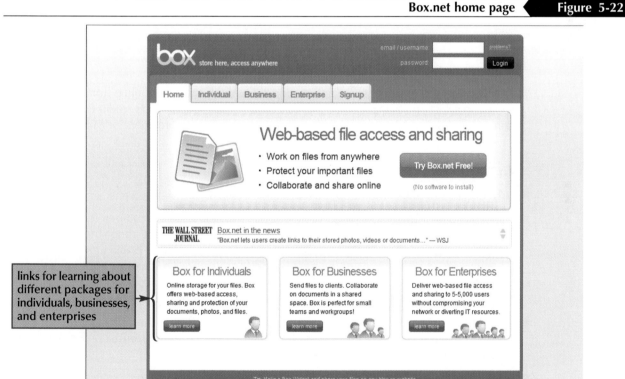

links for learning about different packages for individuals, businesses, and enterprises

Milt also likes the integration of Box.net with Zoho, a provider of online document editing, which makes document collaboration possible for Sound Effects contractors. Zoho lets users open a compatible document, workbook, presentation, database, or other file type using a browser and edit it using only the browser. This means that a user can use Box.net to store a file and use Zoho to open a Word document or Excel workbook, for example, using a browser, make changes, and save it directly on the Box.net server, without having to download the file, save it on the computer, make changes, and then upload the new version of the file to Box.net. Figure 5-23 shows a sample Word document open in the browser window, which Milt is editing using Zoho. After making his change, Milt can save the document back to Box.net.

Figure 5-23   **Word document opened using a browser and Zoho**

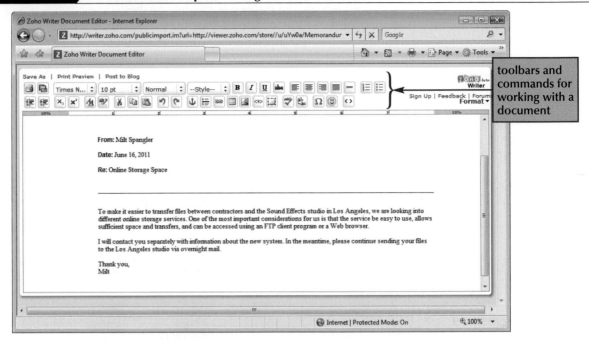

Milt wants you to gather some information about these and other online storage providers so he can select one to manage file transfers between the Sound Effects studio and its contractors. You'll explore the Web sites of three online storage providers for Milt next.

To learn more about online storage providers:

▶ **1.** Return to the Online Companion page for Session 5.2.

▶ **2.** Click one of the links in the Online Storage Providers section to open its home page, and then use the links on the home page to learn more about the services the company offers. As you explore the site, pay attention to pricing options, file storage limits (in terms of file sizes, transfer restrictions and limits, and the amount of time you can store files), and any trial offers the service provides. (*Note:* Do not sign up for an account with any online storage provider at this time.)

▶ **3.** Return to the Online Companion page for Session 5.2, and then click another link and explore the services, pricing, file storage options, and potential trial periods for another online storage provider.

▶ **4.** Return to the Online Companion page for Session 5.2, and then explore the Web site and options for your final online storage provider.

▶ **5.** Close your Web browser.

Milt is pleased with the information that you have provided. His goal of finding the perfect online storage provider will be much easier now that he has resources he can evaluate. He is confident that he will be able to find a suitable provider for his company.

Session 5.2 Quick Check | Review

1. What is freeware, shareware, and limited edition software?
2. After downloading a program from the Internet, what should you do prior to installing it?
3. What are the three most important considerations when using antivirus software to ensure that a virus does not infect your computer?
4. How might an online storage provider help a company reduce its network activity and increase its productivity?
5. True or False: Some online storage providers offer free storage for registered users.

Tutorial Summary | Review

In this tutorial, you learned how to use a Web browser and an FTP client program to transfer files on the Internet. You also learned how to evaluate freeware, shareware, limited edition, and licensed programs. Finally, you learned how to use online storage providers to store files that you can share with other users.

You might already have many needs for file storage on the Web—perhaps you have a large collection of picture files that you want to share with your friends or you need to set up a Web site to use as a central point for collaboration with a study group to prepare a term project. In any case, using the skills you learned in this tutorial will prepare you to evaluate and download the best online storage provider for your needs; set up an account to store the files; and use your computer to upload, download, and manage your files.

Key Terms

anonymous FTP session	File Transfer Protocol (FTP)	root directory
anonymous login	freeware	Secure File Transfer Proto-
antivirus program	FTP client program	col (SFTP)
ASCII	FTP server	shareware
binary	FTP site	upload
bug	full-privilege FTP	virus definition
compressed file	Internet security software	virus pattern
download	limited edition	virus signature
evaluation version	local computer	Webmaster
file compression program	local site	zip archive
file decompression	log on	zip file
file expansion	remote computer	
file extraction	remote site	

| Practice | **Review Assignments** |

Practice the skills you learned in the tutorial using the same case scenario.

Data File needed for the Review Assignments: Register.pdf

Milt just received an email message with an attachment saved with a .pdf file extension, and he needs to install a program to read it. Portable Document Format (PDF), developed by Adobe Corporation, provides a convenient, self-contained package for delivering and displaying documents containing text, graphics, charts, and other objects. To create a PDF file, you need to purchase and learn how to use a program called Adobe Acrobat. When you download a PDF file, you do not need the same program as the file's creator to display, browse, and print the document; you can use the free Adobe Reader program to view the document. For example, if you download a PDF file that was created from a Microsoft Word document, you can use Adobe Reader to view the document, even if you don't have Word installed on your computer. Adobe Reader is a free, simple-to-install program. You will download Adobe Reader so Milt can read the PDF file he received.

Note: Be sure that the device to which you are downloading the Adobe Reader program has sufficient space for the program's size (over 22 megabytes). Your instructor might ask you to download the program to your hard drive or to simply read the following steps without actually downloading the file.

1. Start your Web browser, open the Online Companion page at www.course.com/oc/np/internet7 and log on to your account, click the Tutorial 5 link, and then click the Review Assignments link. Click the Adobe link and wait while the browser opens the home page for the Adobe Web site.
2. Explore the Adobe home page and click the link to learn more about products in the Acrobat family. Then read about Adobe Reader and Adobe Acrobat so you understand how both programs are used.
3. Find the link to download the free Adobe Reader program, and then click it. Read the instructions provided and download the Adobe Reader program for your operating system. Save the file in the Tutorial.05\Review folder included with your Data Files.
4. When the download is complete, follow the on-screen instructions to install Adobe Reader, and then close your browser. (*Note:* Check with your instructor or technical support person before installing any program on your computer.)
5. Open Windows Explorer, and then locate and double-click the **Register.pdf** file in the Tutorial.05\Review folder. Adobe Reader starts and opens the file.
6. Print the document. (*Hint:* Use the Print button on the Adobe Reader toolbar.)
7. Close Adobe Reader and Windows Explorer.

| Apply | **Case Problem 1** |

Practice using WinZip to compress and decompress files.

Data Files needed for this Case Problem: p_51642.jpg, p_57495.jpg, p_75436.jpg, p_78456.jpg, p_87462.jpg, and p_88462.jpg

Montgomery Real Estate   Al Montgomery has been a real estate broker in Atlanta, Georgia for more than 20 years. Over the years, many of his clients have bought second homes in nearby Myrtle Beach, South Carolina, where they enjoy golf and other activities during the spring and summer months. Al recently started listing and buying properties in Myrtle Beach for many of his long-time clients from Atlanta. As a result, he travels between the two cities frequently and uses his digital camera to take pictures of houses of interest. He then sends the pictures back to his office as email attachments.

Most of the time, Al's pictures have small file sizes, but recently, he purchased an 8 megapixel digital camera, which takes pictures that have file sizes of more than one megabyte each. His ISP is rejecting messages with large attachments. He plans to explore other options for transferring files, but in the meantime, you decide to teach him how to use a file compression program to compress the files to decrease their file size so he can continue to email them to his office.

1. Start Windows Explorer and navigate to the **Tutorial.05\Cases** folder included with your Data Files.

2. Select the following files as a group: **p_51642.jpg**, **p_57495.jpg**, **p_75436.jpg**, **p_78456.jpg**, **p_87462.jpg**, and **p_88462.jpg**.

3. Use the WinZip shortcut menu for the selected files to compress them in the Tutorial.05 folder as a file named **Pictures.zip**. (*Note:* If you do not have WinZip installed on your computer, start your Web browser, open the Online Companion page at www.course.com/oc/np/internet7 and log on to your account, click the Tutorial 5 link, and then click the Case Problem 1 link. Click the WinZip link to open the WinZip home page and download the program. If you need help installing the program, review the steps in Session 5.2. Be sure to check with your instructor or lab manager before installing this or any other software on a public computer.)

4. Extract the **Pictures.zip** file to a location on another drive or in another folder.

5. Delete the files that you extracted in Step 4.

⊕ **EXPLORE**
6. Start WinZip and click the button that lets you buy the program, and then explore the options for purchasing WinZip. Use your browser to print the page that provides the pricing options for a single-user license. Then find and print a page that explains how to install the license and unlock the software.

7. Close your browser and Windows Explorer.

Research | Case Problem 2

Use the Internet to locate reviews of programs that provide a way to manage password data.

There are no Data Files needed for this Case Problem.

Allison Sapphire, CPA Allison Sapphire is a Certified Public Accountant (CPA) who operates her business as a sole proprietor. She specializes in accounting and tax return preparation for self-employed individuals and not-for-profit organizations. Until now, Allison has stored login and password information for different secure Internet sites that she accesses in a Word document on her computer's hard drive. However, she knows that this method is not secure. She asks you to recommend a password manager program that she can use to store all of her logins and passwords in a protected way on her computer. Because she is trying this kind of software for the first time, she wants a program that is simple to use and that has a free trial period so she can evaluate the program and decide if she wants to purchase it later. She also wants to make sure that the program you recommend is compatible with Windows Vista.

You will complete the following steps to research the different password manager programs available, and then you will recommend one for Allison and download the program.

1. Start your Web browser, open the Online Companion page at www.course.com/oc/np/internet7 and log on to your account, click the Tutorial 5 link, and then click the Case Problem 2 link.

2. Visit one of the sites listed in the Case Problem 2 section to search for information about password managers. You can use the links of software organized by category to search for password manager software, or you can use the search feature at the Web site to search for programs that include a password feature.

⊕ EXPLORE

3. Explore the links to learn more about the programs you can download. If the site includes program reviews, read them to evaluate the programs for Allison. When you find a program that Allison should consider, use your browser's Print dialog box to print the first page.

⊕ EXPLORE

4. Return to the Online Companion page for Case Problem 2. Use another link in the Case Problem 2 section to open another download site, and then search again for password manager software. Use the reviews to understand the programs available at this second site, identify a program for Allison, and then use your browser's Print dialog box to print the first page of the review.

5. Based on your research, determine which of the two programs you reviewed to recommend for Allison to help her protect her passwords as described in the case problem description.

6. If you have permission to do so, download to the Tutorial.05\Cases folder included with your Data Files the password manager program you are recommending. (*Note:* Check with your instructor before downloading any files from the Internet. Before downloading the file, make sure that you have enough disk space to save it in the location you specify.)

7. If you are able to do so, scan the file you downloaded for viruses.

8. Close your browser.

9. Write a short memo to Allison that explains why you have chosen the program you selected and list some advantages it has over other programs you evaluated during your research.

Create | **Case Problem 3**

Use the Internet to locate information about online storage providers so you can recommend the best one for a small business.

There are no Data Files needed for this Case Problem.

Biehle Clipping Service   When Blake Biehle was in college, he completed a brief internship at an advertising agency and soon discovered a need for a clipping service that would record televised commercials so companies could monitor the marketing campaigns prepared by their competitors. The advertising agency had a staff member who tried to assimilate marketing information from estimating the number of 30-second commercials purchased by businesses in certain industries, such as grocery stores, and using that data to estimate the cost of the commercials. This system worked well but it suffered because most of the data was estimated.

After Blake completed his internship and during his last year of college, he approached the largest grocery store and department store in the area and offered to use a video recorder to record all three local television networks, 24 hours a day. He proposed that he could provide these businesses with exact information about their competitors' marketing campaigns. Both businesses accepted Blake's proposal, and other businesses in other areas soon hired him for the same role. After graduating from college, he expanded his business to news clipping and recording radio broadcast services and hired several monitors and editors to help him collect and process the data.

Blake needs a way to store the marketing data he prepares in PDF format for his clients. He has a Web site but the host doesn't provide any online storage space. He asks you to do some research on online storage providers and prepare a report of your findings, with a recommendation for which provider to use.

1. Start your Web browser, open the Online Companion page at www.course.com/oc/np/internet7 and log on to your account, click the Tutorial 5 link, and then click the Case Problem 3 link.

⊕ EXPLORE
2. Visit four sites listed in this section. When you are exploring each site, try to find answers to questions that Blake might ask, such as why using an online storage provider is better than using email attachments, how to create and log in to an account, how to share files with other users, how much space is provided and at what cost, security features, and ease of use. For each site that you visit, print one page that contains answers to some of these questions. (*Note:* Do not sign up for an account at any of these sites.)

3. Close your browser.

4. Write a memo to Blake that identifies the online storage providers you examined and explains the pros and cons of using each one. In the final paragraph, recommend one provider for Blake and give the reasons for your selection and why the provider you are recommending would work well for Blake's clipping service.

Challenge | Case Problem 4

Explore resources on the Internet that provide online document collaboration services.

There are no Data Files needed for this Case Problem.

Big Lake Youth Association   The Big Lake Youth Association organizes recreational sports teams of basketball, soccer, and lacrosse for boys and girls ages 4 to 17 in the Big Lake area. The association just added girls' volleyball to its list of sports. Because this is a new sport for the association, it wants to prepare a document that describes all of the rules and regulations for the sport. The local middle schools offer volleyball as part of their athletics programs, so it is important to have feedback not only from the volunteer volleyball coaches in the league but also from the coaches at area middle schools to make sure that the rules are consistent with what the players will encounter if they advance from the recreational league to the school programs. As the volleyball commissioner, you want to find a way for the coaches and other people to collaborate on the creation and management of this document, and also find an easy way to update it.

1. Start your Web browser, open the Online Companion page at www.course.com/oc/np/internet7 and log on to your account, click the Tutorial 5 link, and then click the Case Problem 4 link.

⊕ EXPLORE
2. Use the links in the Case Problem 4 section to learn more about online collaboration services. You might find links to videos or other resources that will walk you through the steps required to use the service. You might also see links to try the service by viewing and editing one or more sample documents. Use these links and other information at each site to learn more about the services and what is required to use them. (*Note:* You do not need to create an account to explore the features of each service—limit your exploration to what you can find at each site without creating an account or logging in to an account.)

⊕ EXPLORE   3. Answer the following questions using information you found during your research.
  a.   Which service do you recommend for the Big Lake Youth Association and why?
  b.   What are some of the features provided by each service that the association would benefit from? What difficulties do you foresee?
  c.   What problems are these types of services designed to solve?
  d.   In your opinion, do you think that these services provide a good solution? Why or why not?
4. Close your browser.

Research | **Case Problem 5**

Locate and review information on the Internal Revenue Service Web site and download a publication.

There are no Data Files needed for this Case Problem.

Marisa Montoyo   Marisa Montoyo just finished her third year of college. This past summer, she worked part-time as a lifeguard at the local community pool. She earned almost $4,600 at her job, and this was the only income she earned during the year. She also has income from a college account that her grandmother set up for her and that she owns since turning 21 years of age. In the past, Marisa has not filed a federal income tax return. This year, however, she thinks that she might need to do so. She asks for your help to research the filing requirements. Because you know that going to the correct source is important, you will research the publications for specific filings at the Internal Revenue Service Web site. After locating the correct one, you'll download it for Marisa, so she can review it and determine whether she needs to file a return.

1. Start your Web browser, open the Online Companion page at www.course.com/oc/np/internet7 and log on to your account, click the Tutorial 5 link, and then click the Case Problem 5 link. Click the Internal Revenue Service link and wait while the browser opens the Web site for the Internal Revenue Service.

⊕ EXPLORE   2. Use the links at the site or the search feature to find information about filing requirements for dependents. When you find a publication that you believe will answer Marisa's question, open it using your browser and make sure that it contains the information Marisa needs. Then save the PDF file to the Tutorial.05\Cases folder included with your Data Files. (*Hint:* Use the File menu for Adobe Reader or your browser and the Save a Copy or Save Page As command to save it in the Tutorial.05\Cases folder.)

⊕ EXPLORE   3. Open the PDF file for the publication that you downloaded to the Tutorial.05\Cases folder. (*Hint:* Double-click the file in Windows Explorer to open it.) Marisa is single, not blind, and her parents claim her as a dependent on their federal income tax return. She has $4,600 of earned income and $1,200 of unearned income. Does she need to file a tax return? Use Adobe Reader to print the page that you used to determine the answer to this question.

4. Close Adobe Reader, and then close your browser.

| Reinforce | Lab Assignments |

Student Edition Labs

The interactive Student Edition Lab on **Keeping Your Computer Virus Free** is designed to help you master some of the key concepts and skills presented in this tutorial, including:

- using FTP and a browser to download files
- using an FTP client program to download files
- using a file compression program to compress and decompress files

This lab is available online and can be accessed from the Tutorial 5 Web page on the Online Companion at www.course.com/oc/np/internet7.

| Review | Quick Check Answers |

Session 5.1

1. FTP client program and Web browser
2. anonymous
3. pub
4. directories (folders) and files
5. ftp://ftp.zdnet.com
6. The category of software that detects viruses and other common security threats on the Internet

Session 5.2

1. Freeware is free software that has no restrictions on its use or guarantees for its performance; shareware is free or for-fee software that usually is operable for a limited time period; limited edition software is a limited version of a complete program that either functions for a limited time or includes only core features.
2. Scan it for viruses
3. Make sure that the antivirus software program is turned on, configured properly to scan all downloaded files, and that it uses current virus definitions
4. A company can reduce its network activity by encouraging its employees to use an online storage provider instead of email attachments to transport large files. A company can increase its productivity by offering online storage for traveling employees or those employees in satellite offices.
5. True

Reality Check

Consider a topic that you would like to research, such as a medical condition that you have or that a family member or close friend has, a degree that you would like to pursue, or a career or hobby that interests you. Use search engines on the Internet and a download site to gather information about your chosen topic.

Note: Please be sure *not* to include any personal information of a sensitive nature in the documents you create to be submitted to your instructor for this exercise. Later on, you can update the documents with such information for your own personal use.

1. Start your browser and use the search engine of your choice to find three Web sites related to your chosen topic.

2. Evaluate each site that you find to make sure that it meets the criteria discussed in this book for evaluating Web site content. Note the URL of each Web site's home page and the page that contains information about the site's sponsor. Be sure to use the criteria identified in this book to evaluate the sites.

3. If applicable, use a download site to investigate software or online storage sites that might help you with your chosen topic. (*Note:* Do not download anything from the site.) If you find something that might help you with your chosen topic, note the URL of the page that contains the content you found.

4. In an email message addressed to your instructor, identify the topic you chose, the sites that you selected to learn more about your topic, the software or online storage site that you may have selected if it relates to your chosen topic, and any other information that you found to help you understand your chosen topic. Explain why you chose these sites and provide details about the site's credentials and why you believe that the information on these sites is valid.

5. Send the email message to your instructor and close your browser.

Objectives

- Discover uses for the Internet
- Learn about computer networks and connectivity
- Explore the history of the Internet and the Web

The Internet and the World Wide Web

History, Structure, and Technologies

The Internet and the World Wide Web: Amazing Developments

The Internet—a large collection of computers all over the world that are connected to one another in various ways—is one of the most amazing technological developments of the 20th century. Using the Internet you can communicate with other people around the world through electronic mail (or email) or instant messaging software; read online versions of newspapers, magazines, academic journals, and books; join discussions on almost any conceivable topic; participate in games and simulations; and obtain computer software. In recent years, the Internet has allowed companies to connect with customers and each other. Today, all kinds of businesses provide information about their products and services on the Internet. Many of these businesses use the Internet to market and sell their products and services. The part of the Internet known as the World Wide Web (or the Web), is a subset of the computers on the Internet that are connected to each other in a specific way that makes those computers and their contents easily accessible to all computers in that subset. The Web has helped to make Internet resources available to people who are not computer experts.

Starting Data Files

There are no starting Data Files needed for this appendix.

Uses for the Internet

The Internet and the Web give people around the world a convenient and instantaneous way to communicate with each other, obtain information, conduct business transactions, and find entertainment.

New Ways to Communicate

In the 1970s, email and other messaging systems were developed within large companies and government organizations. These systems let people within an organization send messages to other people in that organization. Very few organizations allowed their computers to be connected to the computers in other organizations, and many different messaging systems were used, most of which were not compatible with each other.

The Internet provided a common set of rules for email interchange and allowed persons in different organizations (and even persons who were not in any organization at all) to send messages to each other, regardless of the messaging system each person was using. In addition to email, the Web offers other ways to communicate. Electronic discussions are hosted on many Web sites, and many people use instant messaging software to chat with each other over the Internet.

Information Resources

The amount of information that is available online today is staggering. Millions of Web sites, which are collections of HTML documents stored on computers that are connected to the Internet, offer an amazing variety of useful information on almost any imaginable topic. Online versions of newspapers, magazines, government documents, research reports, and books offer a wealth of information greater than the holdings of any library.

Some sites are like encyclopedias; they offer a wide range of information on many different topics. Figure A-1 shows a small part of one such site, which is named "How Stuff Works." The site includes explanations of how all kinds of things operate.

How Stuff Works Web site ◀ **Figure A-1**

Other Web sites specialize in specific types of information. For example, you can find Web sites that offer DVD player reviews, recipes for Mexican food, or instructions for growing houseplants. Many of the first resources to appear on the Internet were collections of computer software. This is not surprising, because many of the earliest users of the Internet were computer enthusiasts. Today, many Web sites offer software you can download and install on your computer. Some of these software products are free; others are trial or demo versions (versions that you can use for a limited amount of time or without all of the features of the full versions) that allow you to try the software for a period of time before buying a license that allows you to continue using the software. Figure A-2 shows one Web site, Tucows, that offers downloads of free software, trial version software, and demo version software.

Figure A-2   Tucows Web site

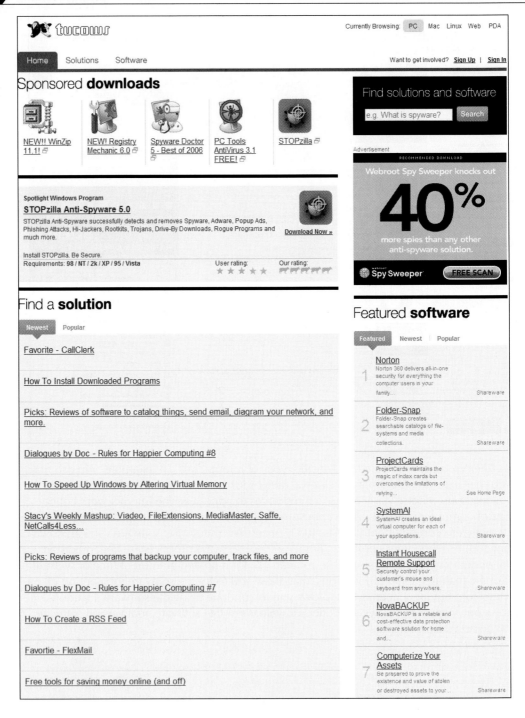

Doing Business Online

The Web can make buying and selling products and services easier for companies and their customers. The first major business activity conducted on the Internet was done by large companies who started using the Internet in the mid-1990s to handle the paperwork on purchases and sales of industrial goods. Soon thereafter, individual consumers began buying items such as books, music CDs, and clothing on the Web. Today, billions of dollars in business and consumer transactions occur each year on the Web. Some companies, such as Amazon.com, exist only on the Web. Other companies, such as Coldwater Creek, maintain a Web site to supplement sales in their physical stores. Electronic storefronts, such as the Coldwater Creek site shown in Figure A-3, sell everything that you would expect to find in their mall stores and more.

Coldwater Creek Web site ◄ **Figure A-3**

In addition to buying and selling activities, companies use the Internet to coordinate their operations throughout the world, managing supplies, inventories, and factory production operations from thousands of miles away. An increasing number of companies use the Web to recruit employees and find other companies that are potential partners in opening new markets or finding new sources of supplies.

Entertainment

Many Web sites offer reviews of restaurants, movies, theater, musical events, and books. You can download music or play interactive games with people around the world using the Internet.

The Web provides a good way to follow your favorite sports teams, too. All of the major sports organizations have Web sites with current information about the teams in their leagues. In fact, the Web gives you a way to follow sports teams around the world in a variety of languages. The Web has also promoted the growth of fantasy sports gaming by making it easier to collect the statistical results of player performance in real sporting contests and facilitating communication between fantasy gamers as they play their games online.

Computer Networks

As you know, computers that are connected to each other form a network. Each computer on a network has a network interface card installed inside it. A **network interface card** (often called a **NIC** or simply a network card) is a circuit board card or other device used to connect a computer to a network of other computers. Many newer personal computers have a network interface device built into them, so that it is not necessary to add a separate NIC to make the computer networkable. These cards are connected to cables that are, in turn, connected to the company's main computer, called a server. A **server** is a general term for any computer that accepts requests from other computers that are connected to it and shares some or all of its resources, such as printers, files, or programs, with those computers.

Client/Server Local Area Networks

The server runs software that coordinates the information flow among the other computers in the network, which are called **clients**. The software that runs on the server computer is called a **network operating system**. Connecting computers this way, in which one server computer shares its resources with multiple client computers, is called a **client/server network**. Client/server networks commonly are used to connect LANs (the local area networks you learned about in Tutorial 1). Figure A-4 shows a typical client/server LAN.

Client/server LAN   Figure A-4

Each computer, printer, or other device attached to a network is called a **node** or **network node**. The server can be a powerful personal computer (PC) or a larger, more expensive computer. Most of these larger computers use are called "servers" to distinguish them from desktop or notebook computers. Companies that need large amounts of computing power often connect hundreds or even thousands of large PCs together to act as servers.

Like any personal computer, servers have operating systems; however, they also can run network operating systems software. Although network operating systems software can be more expensive than the operating system software for a standalone computer, having computers connected in a client/server network can provide cost savings. For example, by connecting each client computer to the server, all of the computers can share the server-installed network printer and tape drive for backups.

Most personal computer operating systems, including current versions of Microsoft Windows and Macintosh operating systems, have built-in networking capabilities. Also, some personal computer operating systems that can serve as network operating systems, such as Linux, are available on the Internet and can be downloaded and used at no cost.

Connecting Computers to a Network

Not all LANs use the same kind of cables to connect their computers. The oldest cable type is called **twisted-pair cable**, which telephone companies have used for years to wire residences and businesses. Twisted-pair cable has two or more insulated copper wires that are twisted around each other and enclosed in another layer of plastic insulation. A wire that carries an electric current generates an electromagnetic field around itself. This electromagnetic field can induce a small flow of electricity in nearby objects, including other wires. This induced flow of unwanted electricity is called **electrical interference**. In twisted-pair wiring, the wires are twisted because wrapping the two wires around each other reduces the amount of electrical interference that each wire in the pair might pick up from other nearby current-carrying wires. The type of twisted-pair cable that telephone companies have used for years to transmit voice signals is called **Category 1 cable**. Category 1 cable transmits information more slowly than the other cable types, but it is also much less expensive.

Coaxial cable is an insulated copper wire encased in a metal shield that is enclosed with plastic insulation. The signal-carrying wire is completely surrounded by the metal shield, so it resists electrical interference much better than twisted-pair cable. Coaxial cable also carries signals about 20 times faster than Category 1 twisted-pair; however, it is considerably more expensive. Because coaxial cable is thicker and less flexible than twisted-pair, it is harder for installation workers to handle and thus is more expensive to install. You probably have seen coaxial cable because it is used for most cable television connections. You might hear this type of cable called "coax" (koh-axe) by network technicians.

In the past 20 years, cable manufacturers have developed better versions of twisted-pair cable. The current standards for twisted-pair cable used in computer networks are Category 5, Category 5e, and Category 6 cable. **Category 5 cable** carries signals between 10 and 100 times faster than coaxial cable and is just as easy to install as Category 1 cable. **Category 5e cable** (the "e" stands for "enhanced") and **Category 6 cable** are two newer versions of twisted-pair cable that look exactly like regular Category 5 cable, but that are constructed of higher quality materials so they can carry more signals even faster—up to 10 times faster. Many businesses and schools have Category 5 cable installed, but they are replacing it with Category 5e or Category 6 cable as they upgrade their network hardware to handle the highest LAN speeds available today. You might hear these cable types called "Cat-5" or "Cat-6" cable by network technicians.

The most expensive cable type is fiber-optic cable, which does not use an electrical signal at all. **Fiber-optic cable** (also called simply fiber) transmits information by using lasers to pulse beams of light through very thin strands of glass. Fiber-optic cable transmits signals much faster than either coaxial cable or any category of twisted-pair cable. Because it does not use electricity, fiber-optic cable is completely immune to electrical interference. Fiber-optic cable is lighter and more durable than coaxial cable, but it is harder to work with and more expensive than either coaxial cable or Category 5 twisted-pair cable. The price of fiber-optic cable and the laser sending and receiving equipment needed at each end of the cable has dropped dramatically in recent years. Thus, companies are using fiber-optic cable in more and more networks as the cost becomes more affordable; however, its main use today remains connecting networks to each other rather than as part of the networks themselves. Figure A-5 shows these three types of cable.

Figure A-5 ▷ **Twisted-pair, coaxial, and fiber-optic cables**

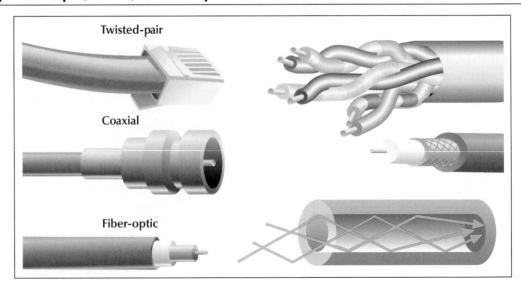

Twisted-pair

Coaxial

Fiber-optic

Perhaps the most liberating way to connect computers in a LAN is to avoid cable completely. **Wireless networks** are becoming more common as the cost of the wireless transmitters and receivers that plug into or replace network cards continues to drop. Wireless LANs are especially welcome in organizations that occupy old buildings. Many cities have structures that were built before electricity and telephones were widely available. These buildings have no provision for running wires through walls or between floors, so a wireless network can be the best option for connecting resources.

Wireless connections are also popular with companies whose employees use laptop computers and take them from meeting to meeting. A wireless network can help workers be more effective and productive in flexible team environments. Many schools have added wireless access points to their networks so that students can use their wireless-equipped laptop computers in classrooms, in libraries, and in study lounges. Some schools have even placed network access points on the outside edges of their buildings so that students can use their computers in patios and other outdoor areas, such as parking lots. The cost of wireless networks is dropping, and many people have installed them in their homes. Figure A-6 shows the physical layout of a small wireless network that might be useful in a small office or a home. The wireless network includes two desktop PCs, two laptop PCs, a shared printer, and no connecting network cables.

A small wireless network | **Figure A-6**

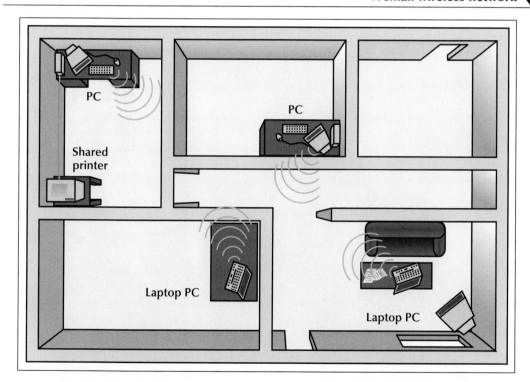

All of these connection types—twisted-pair, Category 1, coaxial, Category 5, Category 5e, Category 6, fiber-optic, and wireless—are options for creating LANs. These LANs can, in turn, be connected to the Internet or to other, larger networks, such as those discussed in the next section.

Origins of the Internet

In the early 1960s, the U.S. Department of Defense undertook a major research project. Because this was a military project and was authorized as a part of national security, the true motivations are not known with certainty, but most people close to the project believe it arose from the government's concerns about the possible effects of nuclear attack on military computing facilities. The Department of Defense realized that the weapons of the future would require powerful computers for coordination and control. The powerful computers of that time were all large mainframe computers, so the Department of Defense began examining ways to connect these computers to each other and to weapons installations that were distributed all over the world.

The agency charged with this task was the **Advanced Research Projects Agency (ARPA)**. (During its lifetime, this agency has used two acronyms, ARPA and DARPA; this book uses its current acronym, **DARPA**, for **Defense Advanced Research Projects Agency**.) DARPA hired many of the best communications technology researchers and for many years funded research at leading universities and institutes to explore the task of creating a worldwide network of computers. A photo of these dedicated computer networking pioneers appears in Figure A-7.

Figure A-7   **ARPANET scientists**

©1969, BBN Technologies

Courtesy of BBN Technologies

DARPA researchers soon became concerned about computer networks' vulnerability to attack, because networks at that time relied on a single, central control function. If the network's central control point were damaged or attacked, the network would be unusable. Consequently, they worked hard to devise ways to eliminate the need for network communications to rely on a central control function.

Connectivity: Circuit Switching vs. Packet Switching

One of the first networking-related topics to be researched by the DARPA scientists was connectivity, or methods of sending messages over networks. The first computer networks were created in the 1950s. The models for those early networks were the telephone companies, because most early wide area networks (WANs) used leased telephone company lines to connect computers to each other. In telephone company systems of that time, a telephone call established a single connection between sender and receiver. Once the connection was established, all data then traveled along that single path. The telephone company's central switching system selected specific telephone lines, or circuits, that would be connected to create the single path. This centrally controlled, single-connection method is called **circuit switching**. Most local telephone traffic today is still handled using circuit-switching technologies.

Although circuit switching is efficient and economical, it relies on a central point of control and a series of connections that form a single path. This makes circuit-switched communications vulnerable to the destruction of the central control point or any link in the series of connections that make up the single path that carries the signal.

Packet switching is an alternative means for sending messages. In a packet-switching network, files and messages are broken down into packets that are labeled electronically with codes for their origin and destination. The packets travel from computer to computer along the network until they reach their destination. The destination computer collects the packets and reassembles the original data from the pieces in each packet. Each computer that an individual packet encounters on its trip through the network determines the best way to move the packet forward to its destination. Computers and other devices that perform this function on networks are often called routing computers, or **routers**, and the programs they use to determine the best path for packets are called **routing algorithms**. Thus, packet-switched networks are inherently more reliable than circuit-switched networks because they rely on multiple routers instead of a central point of control and because each router can send individual packets along different paths if parts of the network are not operating.

By 1967, DARPA researchers had published their plan for a packet-switching network, and in 1969, they connected the first computer switches at four locations: the University of California at Los Angeles, SRI International, the University of California at Santa Barbara, and the University of Utah. This experimental WAN was called the **ARPANET**. Figure A-8 shows a famous hand-drawn sketch of the Internet as it existed in 1969.

Figure A-8   The Internet's humble beginning as the ARPANET, 1969

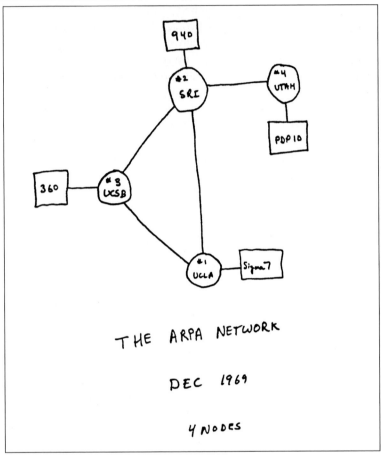

Computer History Museum

The ARPANET grew over the next three years to include more than 20 computers. The ARPANET used the **Network Control Protocol (NCP)** to enable each of those computers to communicate with other computers on the network. A **protocol** is a collection of rules for formatting, ordering, and error-checking data sent across a network.

Open Architecture Philosophy

As more researchers connected their computers and computer networks to the ARPANET, interest in the network grew in the academic community. One reason for increased interest in the project was its adherence to an **open architecture** philosophy; that is, each network could continue using its own protocols and data-transmission methods internally. The open architecture philosophy includes four key points:

- Independent networks should not require any internal changes to be connected to the Internet.
- Packets that do not arrive at their destinations must be retransmitted from their source network.
- Router computers do not retain information about the packets they handle.
- No global control will exist over the network.

This open architecture philosophy was revolutionary at the time. Most companies that built computer networking products at that time, including IBM and Digital Equipment Corporation, put considerable effort into making their networks incompatible with other networks. These manufacturers believed that they could lock out competitors by not making their products easy to connect with products made by other companies. The shift to an open architecture approach is what made the Internet of today possible.

In the early 1970s, Vinton Cerf and Robert Kahn developed a set of protocols that implemented the open architecture philosophy better than the NCP. These new protocols were the **Transmission Control Protocol** and the **Internet Protocol**, which usually are referred to by their combined acronym, **TCP/IP**. TCP includes rules that computers on a network use to establish and break connections; IP includes rules for routing of individual data packets. TCP/IP continues to be used today in LANs and on the Internet. The term "Internet" was first used in a 1974 article about the TCP protocol written by Cerf and Kahn. The importance of the TCP/IP protocol in the history of the Internet is so great that many people consider Vinton Cerf to be the father of the Internet.

A number of TCP/IP-based networks—independent of the ARPANET—were created in the late 1970s and early 1980s. The National Science Foundation (NSF) funded the **Computer Science Network (CSNET)** for educational and research institutions that did not have access to the ARPANET. The City University of New York started a network of IBM mainframes at universities, called the **Because It's Time** (originally, "Because It's There") **Network (BITNET)**.

Birth of Email: A New Use for Networks

Although the goals of ARPANET were still to control weapons systems and transfer research files, other uses for this vast network began to appear in the early 1970s. In 1972, an ARPANET researcher named Ray Tomlinson wrote a program that could send and receive messages over the network. Email had been born and rapidly became widely used in the computer research community. In 1976, the Queen of England sent an email message over the ARPANET. The ARPANET continued to develop faster and more effective network technologies; for example, ARPANET began sending packets by satellite in 1976.

More New Uses for Networks Emerge

By 1981, the ARPANET had expanded to include more than 200 networks. The number of individuals in the military and education research communities that used the network continued to grow. Many of these new participants used the networking technology to transfer files and access computers remotely. The TCP/IP suite included two tools for performing these tasks, which you learned about in Tutorial 1. File Transfer Protocol (FTP) enabled users to transfer files between computers, and Telnet let users log in to their computer accounts from remote sites. Both FTP and Telnet still are widely used on the Internet today for file transfers and remote logins, even though more advanced techniques facilitate multimedia transmissions such as real-time audio and video clips. The first email mailing lists also appeared on these networks. A **mailing list** is an email address that takes any message it receives and forwards it to any user who has subscribed to the list.

Although file transfer and remote login were attractive features of these new TCP/IP networks, their improved email and other communications facilities attracted many users in the education and research communities. Mailing lists (such as BITNET's **LISTSERV**), information posting areas (such as the **User's News Network**, or **Usenet**, **newsgroups**), and adventure games were among the new applications appearing on the ARPANET.

Although the people using these networks were developing many creative applications, relatively few people had access to the networks. Most of these people were members of the research and academic communities. From 1979 to 1989, these new and interesting network applications were improved and tested with an increasing number of users. TCP/IP became more widely used as academic and research institutions realized the benefits of having a common communications network. The explosion of PC use during that time also helped more people become comfortable with computing.

Interconnecting the Networks

The early 1980s saw continued growth in the ARPANET and other networks. The **Joint Academic Network (Janet)** was established in the United Kingdom to link universities there. Traffic increased on all of these networks, and in 1984, the Department of Defense split the ARPANET into two specialized networks: ARPANET would continue its advanced research activities, and **MILNET** (for **Military Network**) would be reserved for military uses that required greater security.

By 1987, congestion on the ARPANET caused by a rapidly increasing number of users on the limited-capacity leased telephone lines was becoming severe. To reduce the traffic load on the ARPANET, a network run by the National Science Foundation, called NSFnet, merged with another NSF network, called CSNet, and with BITNET to form one network that could carry much of the network traffic that had been carried by the ARPANET. The resulting NSFnet awarded a contract to Merit Network, Inc., IBM, Sprint, and the state of Michigan to upgrade and operate the main NSFnet backbone. A **network backbone** includes the long-distance lines and supporting technology that transport large amounts of data between major network nodes. By the late 1980s, many other TCP/IP networks had merged or established interconnections. Figure A-9 summarizes how the individual networks described in this section combined to become the Internet as it is known today.

| Figure A-9 | Networks that became the Internet |

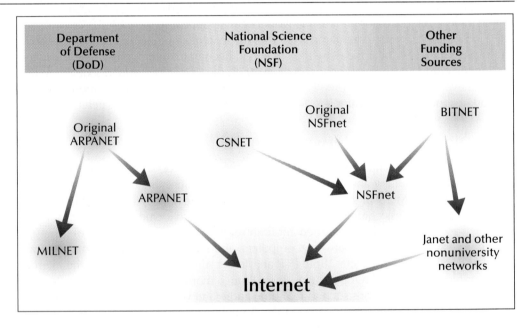

Commercial Interest Increases

As PCs became more powerful, affordable, and readily available during the 1980s, companies increasingly used them to construct LANs. Although these LANs included email software that employees could use to send messages to each other, businesses wanted their employees to be able to communicate with people outside their corporate LANs. The National Science Foundation (NSF) prohibited commercial network traffic on the networks it funded, so businesses turned to commercial email services. Larger firms built their own TCP/IP-based WANs that used leased telephone lines to connect field offices to corporate headquarters. Today, people use the term **intranet** to describe LANs or WANs that use the TCP/IP protocol but do not connect to sites outside a single organization. Although most companies allow only their employees to use the company intranet, some companies give specific outsiders, such as customers, vendors, or business partners, access to their intranets. These outside parties agree to respect the confidentiality of the information on the network. An intranet that allows selected outside parties to connect is often called an **extranet**.

In 1989, the NSF permitted two commercial email services, MCI Mail and CompuServe, to establish limited connections to the Internet that allowed their commercial subscribers to exchange email messages with the members of the academic and research communities who were connected to the Internet. These connections allowed commercial enterprises to send email directly to Internet addresses and allowed members of the research and education communities on the Internet to send email directly to MCI Mail and CompuServe addresses. The NSF justified this limited commercial use of the Internet as a service that would primarily benefit the Internet's noncommercial users.

People from all walks of life—not just scientists or academic researchers—started thinking of these networks as a global resource that we now know as the Internet. Information systems professionals began to form volunteer groups such as the **Internet Engineering Task Force (IETF)**, which first met in 1986. The IETF is a self-organized group that makes technical contributions to the engineering of the Internet and its technologies. IETF is the main body that develops new Internet standards.

Internet Threats

Just as the world was coming to realize the value of these interconnected networks, however, it also became aware of the threats to privacy and computer security posed by these networks. In 1988, Robert Morris, Jr., a graduate student in computer science at Cornell University, launched a program called the **Internet Worm** that used weaknesses in email programs and operating systems to distribute itself to more than 6,000 of the 60,000 computers that were then connected to the Internet. The Worm program created multiple copies of itself on the computers it infected. The large number of program copies consumed the processing power of each infected computer and prevented it from running other programs. This event brought international attention and concern to the Internet. Unfortunately, worms and other malicious programs such as viruses still appear regularly on the Internet today; these incidents do considerable damage to individual computers and networks and cost companies millions of dollars in lost productivity.

The Internet is a powerful communications tool for bringing people together over wide distances. Unfortunately, a tool such as the Internet, which can do so much good, can also be used for evil. In addition to causing damage through malicious programs, the Internet makes it easy for criminals and terrorists all over the world to work together more efficiently and effectively.

Although the network of networks that is now known as the Internet had grown from four computers on the ARPANET in 1969 to more than 300,000 computers on many interconnected networks by 1990, the greatest growth in the Internet was yet to come.

Growth of the Internet

A formal definition of Internet, which was adopted in 1995 by the Federal Networking Council (FNC), appears in Figure A-10.

| Figure A-10 | The FNC's October 1995 resolution to define the term Internet |

RESOLUTION: The Federal Networking Council (FNC) agrees that the following language reflects our definition of the term Internet. Internet refers to the global information system that

(i) is logically linked together by a globally unique address space based on the Internet Protocol (IP) or its subsequent extensions/follow-ons;

(ii) is able to support communications using the Transmission Control Protocol/Internet Protocol (TCP/IP) suite or its subsequent extensions/follow-ons, and/or other IP-compatible protocols; and

(iii) provides, uses or makes accessible, either publicly or privately, high level services layered on the communications and related infrastructure described herein.

Source: http://www.nitrd.gov/fnc/Internet_res.html

The researchers who had been so involved in the creation and growth of the Internet accepted it as part of their working environment, but people outside the research community were largely unaware of the potential offered by a large interconnected set of computer networks until the 1990s.

From Research Project to Information Infrastructure

Realizing that the Internet was becoming much more than a scientific research project, the U.S. Department of Defense finally closed the research portion of its network, the ARPANET, in 1995. The NSF also wanted to turn over the Internet to others so it could return its attention and funds to other research projects.

The process of shutting down the ARPANET and privatizing the Internet began in 1991, when the NSF eased its restrictions on Internet commercial activity. Businesses and individuals continued to connect to the Internet in ever-increasing numbers. Although nobody really knows how big the Internet is, one commonly used measure is the number of Internet hosts. An **Internet host** is a computer that connects a LAN or a WAN to the Internet. Each Internet host might have any number of computers connected to it. Figure A-11 shows the rapid growth in the number of Internet host computers. As you can see, the growth has been dramatic.

Growth in the number of Internet hosts | Figure A-11

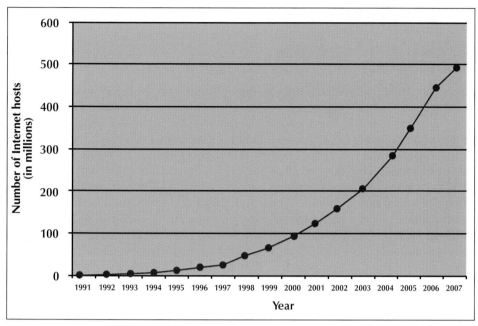

Source: Adapted from Internet Systems Consortium (http://www.isc.org/) and other sources

The numbers in the figure probably understate the true growth of the Internet in recent years for two reasons. First, the number of hosts connected to the Internet includes only those computers that are directly connected to the Internet. In other words, if a LAN with 100 PCs is connected to the Internet through only one host computer, those 100 computers appear as one host in the count. Because the number and size of LANs have increased in recent years, the host count probably understates the growth in the number of all computers that have access to the Internet. Second, the number of computers is only one measure of growth. Internet traffic now carries more files that contain graphics, sound, and video, so Internet files have become larger. A given number of users sending video clips will use much more of the Internet's capacity than the same number of users will use by sending email messages or text files.

The Internet has no central management or coordination, and the routing computers do not retain copies of the packets they handle. Some companies and research organizations estimate the number of regular users of the Internet today to be more than a billion, but no one knows how many individual email messages or files travel on the Internet, and no one really knows how many people use the Internet today.

New Structure for the Internet

As NSFnet converted the main traffic-carrying backbone portion of its network to private firms, it organized the network around four **network access points (NAPs)**, which were operated by four different telecommunications companies. These four companies and their successors sell access to the Internet through their NAPs to organizations and businesses. The NSFnet still exists for government and research use, but it uses these same NAPs for long-range data transmission.

With nearly 500 million connected Internet host computers and more than a billion worldwide Internet users, the Internet faces some challenges. The firms that sell network access continue to invest in the network architecture because they can recoup their investments by selling improved services to existing customers and also attract new Internet users.

So the infrastructure of the Internet should continue to be expanded; however, the TCP/IP numbering system that identifies computers and other devices connected to the Internet is running short of numbers. This numbering system is discussed in the next section.

IP Addressing

Each computer on the Internet has a unique identification number, called an **IP (Internet Protocol) address**. IP addressing is a way of identifying each unique computer on the Web, just like your home address is a way of identifying your home in a city. The IP addressing system currently in use on the Internet is **IP version 4 (IPv4)**. IPv4 uses a 32-bit number to label each address on the Internet. The 32-bit IP address is usually written in four 8-bit parts. In most computer applications, an 8-bit number is called a **byte**; however, in networking applications, an 8-bit number is often called an **octet**. In the binary (base 2) numbering system, an octet can have values from 00000000 to 11111111; the decimal equivalents of these binary numbers are 0 and 255, respectively. Each part of a 32-bit IP address is separated from the previous part by a period, such as 106.29.242.17. You might hear a person pronounce this address as "one hundred six dot twenty-nine dot two four two dot seventeen." This notation is often called **dotted decimal notation**. The combination of these four parts provides 4.2 billion possible addresses (256 × 256 × 256 × 256). Because each of the four parts of a dotted decimal number can range from 0 to 255, IP addresses range from 0.0.0.0 (which would be written in binary as 32 zeros) to 255.255.255.255 (which would be written in binary as 32 ones). Although many people find dotted decimal notation to be somewhat confusing at first, most do agree that writing, reading, and remembering a computer address as 216.115.108.245 is easier than 11011000011100110110110011110101 or its full decimal equivalent, which is 3,631,443,189.

In the mid-1990s, the accelerating growth of the Internet created concern that the world could run out of IP addresses within a few years. In the early days of the Internet, the 4 billion addresses provided by the IPv4 rules certainly seemed to be more addresses than an experimental research network would ever need. However, about 2 billion of those addresses today are either in use or unavailable for use because of the way blocks of addresses were assigned to organizations. New kinds of devices that can access the Internet's many networks, such as wireless personal digital assistants and mobile phones, keep the demand for IP addresses high.

Network engineers have devised a number of stop-gap techniques, such as **subnetting**, which is the use of reserved private IP addresses within LANs and WANs to provide additional address space. **Private IP addresses** are series of IP numbers that have been set aside for subnet use and are not permitted on packets that travel on the Internet. In subnetting, a computer called a **network address translation (NAT) device** converts those private IP addresses into normal IP addresses when the packets move from the LAN or WAN onto the Internet.

The IETF worked on several new protocols that could solve the limited addressing capacity of IPv4 and, in 1997, approved **IP version 6 (IPv6)** as the protocol that would replace IPv4. The new IP version is being implemented gradually over a 20-year period because the two protocols are not directly compatible. However, network engineers have devised ways to run both protocols together on interconnected networks. The major advantage of IPv6 is that the number of addresses is more than a billion times larger than the four billion addresses available in IPv4. IPv6 also changes the format of the packet itself.

Improvements in networking technologies over the past 20 years have made many of the fields in the IPv4 packet unnecessary. IPv6 eliminates those fields and adds new fields for security and other optional information.

In just over 30 years, the Internet has become one of the most impressive technological and social accomplishments of the century. Millions of people use a complex, interconnected network of computers that run thousands of different software packages. The computers are located in almost every country in the world. Billions of dollars change hands every year over the Internet in exchange for all kinds of products and services. All of the Internet's activity occurs with no central coordination point or control. Even more interesting is that the Internet began as a way for the military to maintain control while under attack.

The opening of the Internet to business enterprise helped increase its growth dramatically; however, another development worked hand in hand with the commercialization of the Internet to spur its growth. That development was the technological advance known as the World Wide Web.

World Wide Web

The World Wide Web (Web) is more a way of thinking about information storage and retrieval than it is a technology. Many people use "the Web" and "the Internet" terms interchangeably, but they are not the same thing. As you will learn in this section, the Web is software that runs on many of the computers that are connected to each other through the Internet. Two important innovations played key roles in making the Internet easier to use and more accessible to people who were not research scientists: hypertext and graphical user interfaces (GUIs).

Origins of Hypertext

In 1945, Vannevar Bush, who was director of the U.S. Office of Scientific Research and Development, wrote an *Atlantic Monthly* article about ways that scientists could apply to peacetime activities the skills they learned during World War II. The article included a number of visionary ideas about future uses of technology to organize and facilitate efficient access to information. Bush speculated that engineers eventually would build a machine that he called the **Memex**, a memory extension device that would store all of a person's books, records, letters, and research results on microfilm. Bush's Memex would include mechanical aids to help users consult their collected knowledge fast and in a wide variety of ways. In the 1960s, Ted Nelson described a similar system in which text on one page links to text on other pages. Nelson called his page-linking system **hypertext**. Douglas Engelbart, who also invented the computer mouse, created the first experimental hypertext system on one of the large computers of the 1960s. In 1976, Nelson published a book, *Dream Machines*, in which he outlined project Xanadu, a global system for online hypertext publishing and commerce. Figure A-12 includes photos of Bush, Nelson, and Engelbart, three forward-looking thinkers whose ideas laid the foundation for the Web.

Left to right: Vannevar Bush, Ted Nelson, and Douglas Engelbart   Figure A-12

MIT Museum

Courtesy of Ted Nelson/Project Xanadu

Courtesy of the Bootstrap Institute

Hypertext and the World Wide Web Come to the Internet

In 1989, Tim Berners-Lee and Robert Calliau were working at CERN—the European Laboratory for Particle Physics. (The acronym, CERN, comes from the French of the original name of the laboratory, the *Conseil Européen pour la Recherche Nucléaire*.) Berners-Lee and Calliau were trying to improve the laboratory's research document-handling procedures. CERN had been using the Internet for two years to circulate its scientific papers and data among the high-energy physics research community throughout the world; however, the Internet did not help the agency display the complex graphics that were important parts of its theoretical models. Independently, Berners-Lee and Calliau each proposed a hypertext development project to improve CERN's document-handling capabilities.

Over the next two years, Berners-Lee developed the code for a hypertext server program and made it available on the Internet. A **hypertext server** is a computer that stores files written in the hypertext markup language and lets other computers connect to it and read the files. Berners-Lee, who was familiar with **Standard Generalized Markup Language (SGML)**, a set of rules that organizations have used for many years to manage large document-filing systems, began developing a subset of SGML that he called Hypertext Markup Language (HTML). HTML, like all markup languages, includes a set of codes (or tags) attached to text. These codes describe the relationships among text elements. For example, HTML includes tags that indicate which text is part of a header element, which text is part of a paragraph element, and which text is part of a numbered list element. One important type of tag is the hypertext link tag. A hypertext link, or hyperlink, points to another location in the same or another HTML document. HTML documents can also include links to other types of files, such as word-processing documents, spreadsheets, graphics, audio clips, and video clips.

An HTML document differs from a word-processing document because it does not specify *how* a particular text element will appear. For example, you might use word-processing software to create a document heading by setting the heading text font to Arial, its font size to 14 points, and its position to centered. The document displays and prints these exact settings whenever you open the document in the word processor. In contrast, an HTML document surrounds the text with a pair of **heading tags** to indicate that the text should be considered a heading. Many programs can read HTML documents. The programs recognize the heading tags and display the text in whatever manner that program normally displays headings. Different programs might display the heading text differently.

Like the Internet itself, standards for HTML are not controlled by any central managing organization. Standards for technologies that are used on the Web (including HTML) are developed and promulgated by the World Wide Web Consortium (W3C), an international organization formed in 1994 and sponsored by universities and businesses from around the world. Berners-Lee was appointed director of the W3C when it was formed and continues in that position today.

Web Browsers and Graphical User Interfaces

Several different types of software can read HTML documents, but most people use a Web browser such as Mozilla Firefox or Microsoft Internet Explorer to read HTML documents that are part of the Web. A Web browser is software that lets users read (or browse) HTML documents and move from one HTML document to another through the text formatted with hypertext link tags in each file. If the HTML documents are on computers connected to the Internet, you can use a Web browser to move from an HTML document on one computer to an HTML document on any other computer on the Internet.

The first Web browsers were text-based and lacked the graphical elements, such as buttons, that make today's browsers so easy to use. Figure A-13 shows a Web page displayed in Lynx, a text-based browser that was commonly used in the early days of the Web. As you can see, it does not look very much like the Web pages we are all used to seeing in Web browsers today.

Web page rendered in a text-based browser | **Figure A-13**

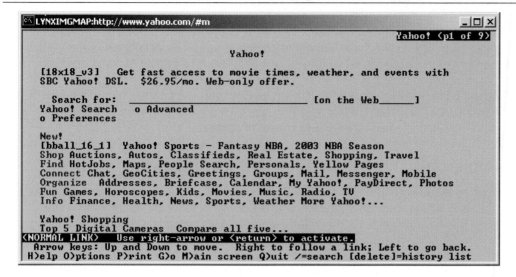

In 1993, a group of students led by Marc Andreessen at the University of Illinois wrote Mosaic, the first GUI program that could read HTML and use HTML documents' hyperlinks to navigate from page to page on computers anywhere on the Internet. Mosaic was the first Web browser that became widely available for PCs. Figure A-14 shows a 1993 Web page displayed in an early version of the Mosaic Web browser.

Mosaic, the first widely available Web browser | **Figure A-14**

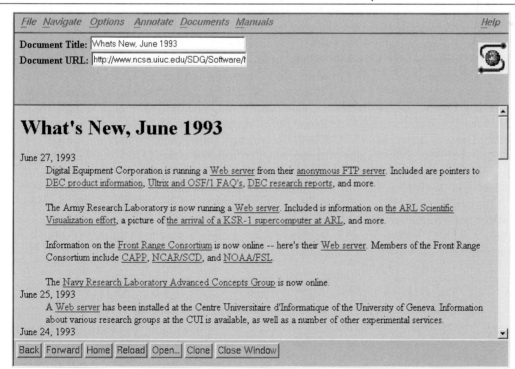

Source: http://www.dejavu.org/emulator.htm

A Web browser presents an HTML document in an easy-to-read format in its graphical user interface. A **graphical user interface** (**GUI**, pronounced "gooey") is a way of presenting program output using pictures, icons, and other graphical elements instead of just displaying text. Almost all PCs today use a GUI such as Microsoft Windows or the Macintosh user interface. Researchers have found that computer users—especially new users—learn new programs more quickly when they have a GUI interface instead of a text interface. Because each Web page has its own set of controls (hyperlinks, buttons to click, and blank text boxes in which to type text), every person who visits a Web site for the first time becomes a "new user" of that site. Thus, the GUI presented in Web browsers has been an important element in the rapid growth of the Web.

Commercialization of the Web and the Internet

Programmers quickly realized that a functional system of pages connected by hyperlinks would provide many new Internet users with an easy way to locate information on the Internet. Businesses quickly recognized the profit-making potential offered by a worldwide network of easy-to-use computers. In 1994, Andreessen and other members of the University of Illinois Mosaic team joined with James Clark of Silicon Graphics to found Netscape Communications. The university was not too happy when the team decided to leave the school and develop a commercial product. The university refused to allow the team to use the name "Mosaic." Netscape's first browser was, therefore, called the "Mosaic Killer" or "Mozilla." Shortly after its release, the product was renamed Netscape Navigator. The program was an instant success. Netscape became one of the fastest growing software companies ever.

Microsoft created its Internet Explorer Web browser and entered the market soon after Netscape's success became apparent. Microsoft offered its browser at no cost to computer owners who used its Windows operating system. Within a few years, most users had switched to Internet Explorer, and Netscape was unable to earn enough money to stay in business. Microsoft was accused of wielding its monopoly power to drive Netscape out of business; these accusations led to the trial of Microsoft on charges that it violated U.S. antitrust laws. These charges were settled in a consent decree, but other violations by Microsoft led to a second trial in which the company was found guilty. Parts of Netscape were sold to America Online, but the Netscape Navigator browser became open-source software. **Open-source software** is created and maintained by volunteer programmers, often hundreds of them, who work together using the Internet to build and refine a program. The program is made available to users at no charge. The current open-source release of this browser is called Mozilla, which recalls the name of the original Netscape product. In an interesting turn of Web history, the Netscape Navigator browser that is available today is based on the Mozilla open-source software.

The proliferation of tools to make the Internet more usable led to an explosion in the amount of information being stored online. The number of Web sites has grown even more rapidly than the Internet itself. Figure A-15 shows the growth in the Web during its lifetime.

Growth of the World Wide Web | **Figure A-15**

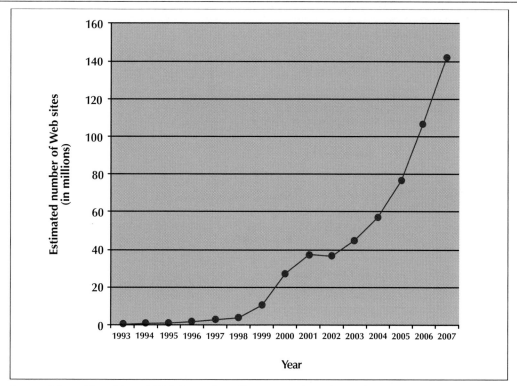

Source: Adapted from Netcraft Web Survey (http://www.netcraft.com/survey/Reports)

After a brief dip between 2001 and 2002, growth in the number of Web sites resumed at its former rapid rate. As individual Web sites become larger, they each include many more pages. Most experts agree that the number of pages available on the Web today is greater than 1 billion, and that number is increasing faster than ever. As more people obtain access to the Web, commercial uses of the Web and the variety of nonbusiness uses will continue to increase.

Business of Providing Internet Access

The NAPs (network access points) that maintain the core operations and long-haul backbone of the Internet do not offer direct connections to individuals or small businesses. Instead, they offer connections to large organizations and businesses that, in turn, provide Internet access to other businesses and individuals. These firms are called **Internet access providers (IAPs)** or **Internet service providers (ISPs)**. Most of these firms call themselves ISPs because they offer more than just access to the Internet. ISPs usually provide their customers with the software they need to connect to the ISP, browse the Web, send and receive email messages, and perform other Internet-related functions such as file transfer and remote login to other computers. ISPs often provide network consulting services to their customers and help them design Web pages. Some ISPs have developed a full range of services that include network management, training, and marketing advice. Large ISPs that sell Internet access along with other services to businesses are often called **commerce service providers (CSPs)** because they help businesses conduct business activities (or commerce) on the Internet. The larger ISPs also sell Internet access to smaller ISPs, which in turn sell access and services to their own business and individual customers. This hierarchy of Internet service providers appears in Figure A-16.

Figure A-16   **Hierarchy of Internet service providers**

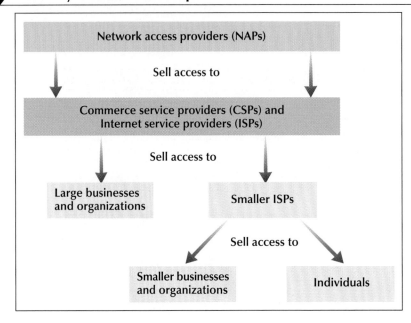

Connection Bandwidth

Of the differences that exist among different levels of Internet service providers, one of the most important is the connection bandwidth that an ISP can offer. **Bandwidth** is the amount of data that can travel through a communications circuit in one second. The bandwidth that an ISP can deliver depends on the type of connection it has to the Internet and the kind of connection you have to the ISP.

The available bandwidth for any type of network connection between two points is limited to the narrowest bandwidth that exists in any part of the network. For example, if you connect to an ISP through a regular telephone line, your bandwidth is limited to the bandwidth of that telephone line, regardless of the bandwidth connection that the ISP has to the Internet. Bandwidth for Internet connections is measured the same way as bandwidth for connections within networks, in multiples of **bits per second (bps)**. Discussions of bandwidth often use the terms **kilobits per second (Kbps)**, which is 1,024 bps; **megabits per second (Mbps)**, which is 1,048,576 bps; and **gigabits per second (Gbps)**, which is 1,073,741,824 bps.

Sometimes computer users become confused by the use of bits to measure bandwidth, because file sizes are measured in bytes. As explained earlier in this appendix, a byte is eight bits; it is abbreviated using an uppercase "B." Thus, a **kilobyte (KB)** is 1,024 bytes, or 8,192 bits. Similarly, a **megabyte (MB)** is 1,048,576 bytes (or 8,388,608 bits) and a **gigabyte (GB)** is 1,073,741,824 bytes (or 8,589,934,592 bits).

Most LANs today run either Fast Ethernet, which operates at 100 Mbps, or Gigabit Ethernet, which operates at 1 Gbps. Some older LANs still use an earlier version of Ethernet that operates at about 10 Mbps. The effective bandwidth of wireless LANs depends on the distance between computers and what types of barriers the wireless signals must pass through (for example, wireless signals travel more easily through glass than steel). Most wireless LANs achieve an operating bandwidth of between 2 Mbps and 10 Mbps, although newer wireless devices that can achieve more than 100 Mbps are now available. Figure A-17 shows some examples of typical times required to send different types of files over different types of LANs.

Typical file transmission times for various types of LANs ◄ **Figure A-17**

Type of File	Typical File Size	Wireless (7 Mbps)	Ethernet (10 Mbps)	Fast Ethernet (100 Mbps)	Gigabit Ethernet (1 Gbps)
One-paragraph text message	5 KB	Less than .1 second	Less than .1 second	Less than .1 second	Less than .1 second
Word processing document, 20 pages	100 KB	.1 second	Less than .1 second	Less than .1 second	Less than .1 second
Web page containing several small graphics	200 KB	.2 second	.2 second	Less than .1 second	Less than .1 second
Presentation file with 20 slides and several large graphics	800 KB	1 second	.7 second	Less than .1 second	Less than .1 second
Color brochure, five pages with several color photos	2 MB	3 seconds	2 seconds	.2 second	Less than .1 second
Compressed music file (MP3 format) containing a four-minute song	5 MB	6 seconds	4 seconds	.4 second	Less than .1 second
Uncompressed music file containing a four-minute song	60 MB	1 minute	50 seconds	5 seconds	.5 second
Compressed video file containing a 10-minute interview	200 MB	4 minutes	4 minutes	17 seconds	2 seconds
Compressed video file containing a feature-length film	4 GB	1.5 hours	1 hour	6 minutes	35 seconds

When you extend your network beyond a local area, either through a WAN or by connecting to the Internet, the speed of the connection depends on what type of connection you use. One way to connect computers or networks over longer distances is to use regular telephone service (sometimes referred to as **dial-up**, **POTS**, or **plain old telephone service**). Regular telephone service to most U.S. residential and business customers provides a maximum bandwidth of between 28.8 Kbps and 56 Kbps. These rates vary because the United States has a number of different telephone companies that do not all use the same technology. When you connect your computer, which communicates using digital signals, to another computer through a telephone line, which uses analog signals, you must convert the signals from one form to the other. The device that performs this signal conversion is called a **modem**, which is short for modulator-demodulator. Converting a digital signal to an analog signal is called **modulation**; converting that analog signal back into digital form is called **demodulation**. A modem performs both functions; that is, it acts as a modulator and demodulator.

Some telephone companies offer a higher grade of service that uses one of a series of protocols called **Digital Subscriber Line (DSL)** or **Digital Subscriber Loop (DSL)**. The first technology that was developed using a DSL protocol is called **Integrated Services Digital Network (ISDN)**. ISDN service has been available in various parts of the United States since 1984. Although considerably more expensive than regular telephone service, ISDN offers bandwidths of up to 256 Kbps. ISDN is much more widely available in Australia, France, Germany, Japan, and Singapore than in the United States because the regulatory structure of the telecommunications industries in those countries encouraged rapid deployment of this new technology.

All technologies based on the DSL protocol require the implementing telephone company to install new equipment at its switching stations, which can be very expensive. New technologies that use the DSL protocol are currently being implemented around the world. One of those, **Asymmetric Digital Subscriber Line** (**ADSL**, also abbreviated **DSL**), offers transmission speeds ranging from 16 to 640 Kbps from the user to the telephone company and from 1.5 to 9 Mbps from the telephone company to the user.

Businesses and large organizations often obtain their connection to the Internet by connecting to an ISP using higher-bandwidth telephone company connections called **T1** (1.544 Mbps) and **T3** (44.736 Mbps) connections. (The names T1 and T3 were originally acronyms for Telephone 1 and Telephone 3, respectively, but very few people use these terms any longer.) Companies with operations in multiple locations sometimes lease T1 and T3 lines from telephone companies to create their own WANs that connect their locations to each other.

T1 and T3 connections are much more expensive than POTS or ISDN connections; however, organizations that must link hundreds or thousands of individual users to WANs or to the Internet require the greater bandwidth of T1 and T3 connections. Smaller firms can save money by renting access to a partial T1 connection from a telephone company. In a partial T1 rental, the connection is shared with other companies.

The NAPs operate the Internet backbone using a variety of connections. In addition to T1 and T3 lines, the NAPs use newer connections that have bandwidths of more than 1 Gbps—in some cases exceeding 10 Gbps. These new connection options use fiber-optic cables, and they are referred to as OC3, OC12, and so forth. **OC** is short for **optical carrier**. NAPs also use high-bandwidth satellite and radio communications links to transfer data over long distances.

A group of research universities and the National Science Foundation (NSF) now operates a network called **Internet2** that has backbone bandwidths greater than 10 Gbps. The Internet2 project continues the tradition of the DARPA scientists by sponsoring research at the frontiers of network technologies.

A connection option that is increasingly available in the United States and some other countries is to connect to the Internet through a cable television company. The cable company transmits data in the same cables it uses to provide television service. Cable can deliver up to 10 Mbps to an individual user and can accept up to 768 Kbps from an individual user. In practice, cable connections usually deliver speeds between 500 Kbps and 3 Mbps, although some cable companies offer guarantees of higher speeds (for higher monthly fees, of course). These speeds far exceed those of existing POTS and ISDN connections and are comparable to speeds provided by the ADSL technologies currently being implemented by telephone companies and other companies that rent facilities from the telephone companies.

An option that is particularly appealing to users in remote areas is connecting by satellite. Using a satellite-dish receiver, you can download at a bandwidth of approximately 400 Kbps. In the early days of satellite Internet access, you could not send information to the Internet using a satellite-dish antenna, so you needed to also have an ISP account to send files or email. Today, most satellite ISPs install transmitters on the dish antenna. This allows two-way satellite connections to the Internet.

The actual bandwidth provided by all these Internet connection methods varies from provider to provider and with the amount of traffic on the Internet. During peak operating hours, traffic on the Internet can become congested, resulting in slower data transmission. The bandwidth achieved is limited to the lowest amount of bandwidth available at any point in the network. To picture this, think of water flowing through a set of pipes with varying diameters, or traffic moving through a section of highway with a lane closure. The water (or traffic) slows to the speed it can maintain through the narrowest part of its pathway.

Figure A-18 shows typical file transmission times for various types of Internet connection options. The speeds shown are examples of what a user can expect on average during download operations. Any Internet connection that is faster than POTS is generally called a **broadband** connection.

Typical file transmission times for various types of Internet connections ◀ **Figure A-18**

Type of File	Typical File Size	POTS (25 Kbps)	ISDN or Satellite (100 Kbps)	Residential Cable or DSL (300 Kbps)	Business Leased T-1 (1.4 Mbps)
One-paragraph text message	5 KB	2 seconds	.4 second	.2 second	Less than .1 second
Word processing document, 20 pages	100 KB	33 seconds	8 seconds	3 seconds	Less than .1 second
Web page containing several small graphics	200 KB	1 minute	16 seconds	6 seconds	Less than .1 second
Presentation file with 20 slides and several large graphics	800 KB	4 minutes	1 minute	22 seconds	Less than .1 second
Color brochure, five pages with several color photos	2 MB	11 minutes	3 minutes	1 minute	Less than .1 second
Compressed music file (MP3 format) containing a four-minute song	5 MB	28 minutes	7 minutes	2 minutes	Less than .1 second
Uncompressed music file containing a four-minute song	60 MB	6 hours	1.5 hours	28 minutes	.4 second
Compressed video file containing a 10-minute interview	200 MB	19 hours	5 hours	2 hours	1 second
Compressed video file containing a feature-length film	4 GB	16 days	4 days	30 hours	25 seconds

Of course, faster Internet connections cost significantly more money than slower connections. Figure A-19 summarizes the bandwidths, costs, and typical uses for the most common types of connections currently in use on the Internet. Some companies offer **fixed-point wireless** connections, which use technology similar to wireless LANs. These offerings are available only in limited areas, and prices are still highly variable.

Figure A-19   **Types of Internet connections**

Service	Upstream Speed (Kbps)	Downstream Speed (Kbps)	Capacity (Number of Simultaneous Users)	One-time Startup Costs	Continuing Monthly Costs
Residential-Small Business Services					
POTS	28–56	28–56	1	$0–$20	$9–$20
ISDN	128–256	128–256	1–3	$60–$300	$50–$90
ADSL	100–640	500–9,000	1–4	$50–$100	$40–$200
Cable	300–1,500	500–10,000	1–4	$0–$100	$40–$100
Satellite	125–150	400–500	1–3	$0–$800	$40–$100
Business Services					
Leased digital line (DS0)	64	64	1–10	$50–$200	$40–$150
Fractional T1 leased line	128–1,544	128–1,544	5–180	$50–$800	$100–$1,000
T1 leased line	1,544	1,544	100–200	$100–$2,000	$600–$1,600
T3 leased line	44,700	44,700	1,000–10,000	$1,000–$9,000	$5,000–$12,000
Large Business, ISP, NAP, and Internet2 Services					
OC3 leased line	156,000	156,000	1,000–50,000	$3,000–$12,000	$9,000–$22,000
OC12 leased line	622,000	622,000	Backbone	Negotiated	$25,000–$100,000
OC48 leased line	2,500,000	2,500,000	Backbone	Negotiated	Negotiated
OC192 leased line	10,000,000	10,000,000	Backbone	Negotiated	Negotiated

Appendix Summary | Review

In this appendix, you learned that the Internet is a remarkable technological and social development. From its birth as a scientific research project to its current role as a global communications network that links more than a billion persons, businesses, organizations, and governments, the Internet has made information available on a scale never before imagined. You learned how client/server networks work when they are interconnected. You also learned about the people who played important roles in the development of the technologies and philosophies that underlie the success of the Internet.

The Internet grew rapidly, especially after the Web became available as a new way of using the Internet. You learned about the business of providing Internet access and the various bandwidth and pricing choices available for connecting to the Internet.

Key Terms

Advanced Research Projects
    Agency (ARPA)
ARPANET
Asymmetric Digital
    Subscriber Line (ADSL
    or DSL)
bandwidth
Because It's Time Network
    (BITNET)
bits per second (bps)
broadband
byte
Category 1 cable
Category 5 cable
Category 5e cable
Category 6 cable
circuit switching
client
client/server network
coaxial cable
commerce service provider
    (CSP)
Computer Science Network
    (CSNET)

Defense Advanced
    Research Projects
    Agency (DARPA)
demodulation
dial-up
Digital Subscriber Line
    (DSL)
Digital Subscriber Loop
    (DSL)
dotted decimal notation
electrical interference
extranet
fiber-optic cable
fixed-point wireless
gigabits per second (Gbps)
gigabyte (GB)
graphical user interface
    (GUI)
heading tag
hypertext
hypertext server
Integrated Services Digital
    Network (ISDN)

Internet access provider
    (IAP)
Internet Engineering Task
    Force (IETF)
Internet host
Internet Protocol
Internet service provider
    (ISP)
Internet Worm
Internet2
intranet
IP (Internet Protocol)
    address
IP version 4 (IPv4)
IP version 6 (IPv6)
Joint Academic Network
    (Janet)
kilobits per second (Kbps)
kilobyte (KB)
LISTSERV
mailing list
megabits per second (Mbps)
megabyte (MB)

Memex
MILNET (Military Network)
modem
modulation
network access point (NAP)
network address translation
    (NAT) device
network backbone
Network Control Protocol
    (NCP)
network interface card
    (NIC)
network operating system

node (network node)
octet
open architecture
open-source software
optical carrier (OC)
packet switching
plain old telephone service
    (POTS)
private IP address
protocol
router
routing algorithm
server

Standard Generalized
    Markup Language
    (SGML)
subnetting
T1
T3
TCP/IP
Transmission Control
    Protocol
twisted-pair cable
User's News Network
    (Usenet) newsgroups
wireless network

Reinforce | Lab Assignments

Student Edition Labs

The interactive Student Edition Lab on **Connecting to the Internet** is designed to help you master some of the key concepts and skills presented in this appendix, including:

- establishing an Internet connection

- using dial-up connections

- installing ISP software

- creating connections manually

- disconnecting

This lab is available online and can be accessed from the Appendix Web page on the Online Companion at www.course.com/oc/np/internet7.

Objectives

- Use and expand the skills you learned in Tutorials 3 and 4
- Visit Web sites to find information about a disease or medical condition
- Evaluate the resources you find
- Examine the resources provided by a credentialing site to evaluate health care information on the Web

Locating and Evaluating Health Care Information on the Internet

Many Web sites provide information about medical care, prescription drugs, and related health topics. An increasing number of doctors and other health care professionals have concerns about the quality of medical and health resources available on the Internet because anyone can post anything on the Web—there are no requirements for or restrictions on giving medical advice in this manner. Thus, it is not surprising that recent surveys have shown that a significant number of health information Web sites include information that is incorrect.

When you need information about a specific disease or medical condition, you can use one of the many sites on the Internet to conduct your research. In some cases, you might visit sites with connections to research institutions, medical facilities, and universities. Sites in these categories include the Medical College of Wisconsin HealthLink, WebMD, and the Mayo Clinic. When you visit the sites of these organizations, you can read about the specific disease or medical condition that interests you, and often you will find links to other sites that provide more information. For example, if you are trying to learn about emphysema, a condition commonly associated with smoking cigarettes, one of these sites might provide information about the condition and links to other Web sites, such as the American Lung Association, where you can get more detailed information.

Just like any other Web site, it's up to you to evaluate the quality of the resources and information it provides. Sometimes you can make these determinations easily. For example, the American Lung Association is a well-known health organization that was founded in 1904 to fight tuberculosis and other lung diseases through donations and resources from public and private sources, foundations, and government agencies. Other resources, however, might be more difficult to evaluate because you might not be familiar with them. Fortunately, accrediting agencies that evaluate health information sites have Web sites that provide information about medical sites. Two of these sites are the Health on the Net (HON) Foundation and the URAC Health Web Site Accreditation. You can use the resources at these sites and other credentialing sites to evaluate health resources you find on the Internet. In some cases, the credentialing site might let you search its database to locate sites that it has already deemed credible using its own sets of rules, guidelines, and quality standards.

Starting Data Files

There are no starting Data Files needed for this assignment.

In this assignment, you will select a specific disease or medical condition that interests you (or your instructor might provide one for you to use), find information about it, and then use a credentialing site to evaluate its resources.

1. Visit at least two health information sites to obtain information about the disease or medical condition you selected. You can use your favorite search engine or directory to find the sites. Gather the information and evaluate the quality of the information and the quality of the Web site from which you obtained it.

2. Visit at least one credentialing or accreditation site and review its contents. Write a summary that describes how the site operates and evaluate whether the site accomplishes its goals.

3. Visit a site maintained by the U.S. government that offers health care information, such as the U.S. Centers for Disease Control and Prevention (CDC) or the U.S. National Institutes of Health MedlinePlus. Explore the site you selected and then write a review of the site in which you describe how the government-sponsored site is different from the privately operated sites you already visited.

Objectives

- Use and expand the skills you learned in Tutorials 3, 4, and 5
- Explore the content requirements and processes for published encyclopedia resources
- Examine the content of and quality controls for a collaborative encyclopedia Web site
- Evaluate encyclopedia resources available on the Web and their role in research

Evaluating Encyclopedia Resources on the Internet

In Tutorials 3 through 5, you learned that the Internet contains the largest collection of data on earth. You also learned techniques for evaluating the data you get from the Internet to ensure that it is complete, thorough, unbiased, and free from security threats such as viruses. As you search for information, you must assume responsibility for interpreting and analyzing the information you collect to make sure that it meets these criteria.

When you use Google or another search engine to search for information about a topic, chances are very good that your search results will include links to information that is posted on Wikipedia. Wikipedia, which began in 2001, is a much younger "encyclopedia" than its published counterparts, such as *World Book Encyclopedia* (which is more than 90 years old) or *Encyclopedia Britannica* (which is more than 235 years old). *World Book Encyclopedia* and *Encyclopedia Britannica* have set high standards for research and information for generations by relying on accredited and credentialed authors for content, subject matter experts for thorough reviews of that content, and editorial boards of experts in various fields to set standards for content. This established process of writing and reviewing greatly reduces problems related to bias or inaccuracies.

Wikipedia, on the other hand, does not apply these same types of standards to its content. The content that you find in Wikipedia might be written and reviewed by a casual user or an expert. According to the Wikipedia Web site, since its creation in 2001, over 75,000 people have actively contributed to over 8.7 million articles in more than 250 languages. As a result of this collaboration, Wikipedia is one of the largest resource sites on the Internet. This collaboration of individuals has resulted in an enormous accumulation of knowledge. However, because material is freely contributed by people who might *not* be subject matter experts, and edited and reviewed by people with their own unique perspectives and biases, Wikipedia's content is subject to different quality standards than you might find in other publications.

Starting Data Files

There are no starting Data Files needed for this assignment.

In this assignment, you will use the Internet to explore some of the pros and cons of using a collaborative site such as Wikipedia as a resource when conducting research.

1. Use your favorite search engine or directory to find the Web site for *World Book Encyclopedia*, and then use the "About Us," "Board," "Reviews," or other similarly named links on the publisher's Web site to learn about its contribution requirements and other quality assurance policies. (You might need to review other pages at each site to get a full picture of the encyclopedia's quality assurance standards.) Pay particular attention to author and reviewer credential requirements, review processes that ensure quality content, and any processes listed for making corrections to the published works.

2. Return to your search engine, and then find the Web site for *Encyclopedia Britannica*. Use the guidelines in Step 1 to evaluate this publisher's Web site for similar information.

3. Return to your searching engine, and then search using the term **Wikipedia quality issues** and explore the links to learn about some of controversies that have arisen as a result of Wikipedia's collaborative nature. Be sure to review material that details specific problems that have occurred and try to understand, what, if any, measures Wikipedia has taken to resolve these problems.

4. Referring back to the information you gathered in Steps 1 and 2 and the research you did in Step 3, what is your opinion of the use of traditional encyclopedias such as *World Book Enclyclopedia* or *Encyclopedia Britannica* when compared to an online collaborative project such as Wikipedia? What role does each encyclopedia play in the field of research? How would you use each of these sources when conducting research? What level of confidence do you place in each source, and why?

Additional Research Assignment 3

- Use and expand the skills you learned in Tutorials 3, 4, and 5
- Learn about the Mars Student Imaging Project
- Find distance learning programs at your school or in your area
- Consider ways that distance learning can enhance education

Advances in Distance Learning

The Internet has enhanced the way that students in grades kindergarten through 12 learn about and participate in scientific research. The National Aeronautics and Space Administration (NASA) began its historic Mars Exploration Rover Mission, which is a long-term robotic exploration of the planet Mars, in June, 2003 and successfully landed a rover on the planet surface in January, 2004. NASA teamed with the Mars Education Program at Arizona State University to offer students in the United States the opportunity to participate in the Mars Student Imaging Project (MSIP), in which students in grades 5 though college sophomore level work in teams with scientists on the Mars project and choose a site on the Mars planet that they would like to map (photograph) from an orbiting rover. Archived data is also available for students to use in research projects. Students participate in the project via distance learning, which is made possible through video conferencing, chats, and teleconferencing. Students complete their projects by writing and submitting a final scientific report for publication in the online MSIP Science Journal.

Starting Data Files

There are no starting Data Files needed for this assignment.

In this assignment, you will explore the Mars Student Imaging Project site and other distance learning sites that you find on the Internet. Then you will consider the future of using distance learning to enhance education of grade school and college students.

1. Use your favorite search engine or directory to locate the Mars Student Imaging Project Web site, and then spend some time exploring the site to become more familiar with the project. Which Internet technologies make this project possible for students located in the United States?

2. Use your search engine or directory to explore distance learning opportunities at your own school or at other colleges and universities in your area. How do these programs compare to the Mars Student Imaging Project? Which Internet technologies make these programs possible? Are all students able to participate in distance learning programs? Why or why not?

3. Based on your findings, determine other ways schools can use the Internet to enhance the education of grade school and college students. Are there technological impediments that prevent this method of learning? If so, what are they? What advantages do these types of programs offer students and educators?

Objectives

- Use and expand the skills you learned in Tutorials 1, 3, and 4
- Use a search tool to find Web sites with information about the Semantic Web
- Use the skills you learned in this book to evaluate the resources you find
- Draw conclusions about the future of the Semantic Web based on your research

The Future of the Semantic Web

Tim Berners-Lee, widely regarded as the founding father of the World Wide Web, has been active in promoting and developing a project that blends technologies and information to create a next-generation Web, which he calls the **Semantic Web**. Today, people are the primary users of the Web as a communication medium. An increasing portion of the traffic on the Internet, however, is computers communicating with other computers. The Semantic Web is intended to facilitate automated computer-to-computer communication that can support all types of human activity.

The Semantic Web project, as currently conceived, would result in words on Web pages being tagged with their meanings (the meanings of words are called **semantics**, thus the name "Semantic Web"). These tags would turn the Web into a huge computer-readable database. People could use intelligent programs called **software agents** to read the Web page tags to determine the meaning of the words in their contexts. For example, a software agent could be given an instruction to find an airline ticket with certain terms (such as a specific date, destination city, and a cost limit). The software agent would launch a search on the Web and return an electronic ticket that meets the criteria. Instead of a user having to visit several Web sites to gather information, compare prices and itineraries, and make a decision, the software agent would automatically do the searching, comparing, and purchasing.

The key elements that must be added to Web standards so that software agents can perform these functions (and thus create the Semantic Web) include a well-defined tagging system and a set of standards called an ontology. Many researchers working on the Semantic Web project believe that Extensible Markup Language (XML) could work as a tagging system. Unlike HTML, which has a common set of defined tags (for example, <h1> is the tag for a level-one heading), XML tags are defined by users. Different users can create different definitions for the same XML tag. If a group of users agrees on a common set of definitions, they can all use the same XML tags. For the Semantic Web to work, everyone must agree on a common set of XML tags that will be used on the Web. Semantic Web researchers call this common set of tag definitions a **resource description framework (RDF)**. An **ontology** is a set of standards that defines, in detail, the relationships among RDF standards and specific XML tags within a particular knowledge domain. For example, the ontology for cooking would include concepts such as ingredients, utensils, and ovens; however, it would also include rules and behavioral expectations, such as identifying ingredients that can be mixed using utensils, the resulting product that can be eaten

Starting Data Files

There are no starting Data Files needed for this assignment.

by people, and ovens that generate heat within a confined area. Ontologies and the RDF would provide the intelligence about the knowledge domain so that software agents could make decisions as humans would.

In this assignment, you will search for information about the Semantic Web and evaluate its potential for future use.

1. Use your favorite search engine or Web directory to find sites with information about the Semantic Web, XML, RDF, and the term "ontology" as it is used in this area of research (the term "ontology" is used in philosophy and other disciplines, so you will need to use some of the techniques you learned in Tutorial 3 to narrow your results). Prepare a report of about 800 words that summarizes your findings on each of the four topics. Include citations to at least two Web pages for each of the four topics in your report.

2. For each of the eight (or more) Web pages you cited in the report required by the previous step, evaluate the quality of the information you obtained and evaluate the overall quality of the Web site from which you obtained it. Summarize your evaluations in your report. Be sure to include the reasons for your evaluations and explain how you performed the evaluations.

3. Using the information you have gathered about the Semantic Web, evaluate the likelihood that it will become a useful part of the Web within the next ten years. Include a summary of your evaluation in your report and cite at least four Web sources that support your arguments.

Glossary/Index

Task Reference

TASK	PAGE #	RECOMMENDED METHOD	WHERE USED
FIREFOX TASKS			
Bookmark file, save to a disk	WEB 54	*See* Reference Window: Saving a Bookmark File to a Disk	Firefox
Bookmark, save in a folder	WEB 53	*See* Reference Window: Saving a Bookmark in a Bookmarks Folder	Firefox
Bookmarks folder, create	WEB 52	*See* Reference Window: Creating a New Bookmarks Folder	Firefox
Bookmarks Manager window, open	WEB 52	Click Bookmarks, click Organize Bookmarks	Firefox
Cookies, delete	WEB 62	Click Tools, click Options, click the Privacy icon, click the Show Cookies button, select a cookie, click the Remove Cookie button	Firefox
Cookies, manage	WEB 62	*See* Reference Window: Managing Cookies in Firefox	Firefox
File, download using a browser	WEB 290	*See* Reference Window: Using a Browser to Download a File	Firefox
Firefox, start	Web 46	Click the Start button, point to All Programs, point to Mozilla Firefox, click Mozilla Firefox	
Help, get	WEB 63	*See* Reference Window: Opening Firefox Help	Firefox
History list, open	WEB 55	Click History, click Show in Sidebar	Firefox
Home page, change default	WEB 56	*See* Reference Window: Changing the Default Home Page in Firefox	Firefox
Home page, return to	WEB 56	Click the Home button	Firefox
Page tabs, using for navigation	WEB 58	*See* Reference Window: Using Page Tabs to Navigate in Firefox	Firefox
Print settings, change	WEB 59	*See* Reference Window: Using Page Setup to Create a Custom Format for Printing a Web Page	Firefox
Start page, return to	WEB 56	Click the Home button	Firefox
URL, enter and go to	WEB 49	*See* Reference Window: Entering a URL in the Location Bar	Firefox
Web page graphic, save	WEB 68	*See* Reference Window: Saving an Image from a Web Page	Firefox
Web page navigation using hyperlinks and the mouse	WEB 50	*See* Reference Window: Navigating Between Web Pages Using Hyperlinks and the Mouse	Firefox
Web page text, copying to a WordPad document	WEB 66	*See* Reference Window: Copying Text from a Web Page to a WordPad Document	Firefox
Web page text, save	WEB 66	*See* Reference Window: Copying Text from a Web Page to a WordPad Document	Firefox
Web page, check security	WEB 60	Double-click the security indicator button	Firefox
Web page, move forward in history list	WEB 14	Click the Forward button	Firefox
Web page, print	WEB 58	*See* Reference Window: Printing the Current Web Page	Firefox
Web page, reload	WEB 14	Click the Reload button	Firefox
Web page, return to previous in history list	WEB 14	Click the Back button	Firefox
Web page, save	WEB 64	*See* Reference Window: Saving a Web Page	Firefox

TASK	PAGE #	RECOMMENDED METHOD	WHERE USED
Web page, set a custom format for printing	WEB 59	*See* Reference Window: Using Page Setup to Create a Custom Format for Printing a Web Page	Firefox
FTP, WINZIP, AND WINDOWS TASKS			
File extensions, view in Windows Explorer	WEB 276	Start Windows Explorer, click Tools, click Folder Options, click the File Types tab	Windows XP
File extensions, view in Windows Explorer	WEB 276	Click Start, click Default Programs, click Associate a file type or protocol with a program link	Windows Vista
File(s), compress using WinZip	WEB 299	Start WinZip, use the WinZip Wizard to enter the filename for the compressed file(s) and the location to save the file, select the folders and/or files to compress, click Zip Now, click Finish	WinZip
File(s), decompress using WinZip	WEB 300	Start Windows Explorer, right-click the .zip file, point to WinZip, click the desired option for extracting the file	WinZip
File, download using an FTP client program	WEB 295	*See* Reference Window: Downloading a File Using an FTP Client Program	FTP
MICROSOFT INTERNET EXPLORER TASKS			
Address book, open	WEB 119	Click the Addresses button	Outlook Express
Attached file, save	WEB 112	*See* Reference Window: Viewing and Saving an Attached File in Outlook Express	Outlook Express
Attached file, save	WEB 131	*See* Reference Window: Viewing and Saving an Attached File in Windows Mail	Windows Mail
Attached file, view	WEB 112	*See* Reference Window: Viewing and Saving an Attached File in Outlook Express	Outlook Express
Attached file, view	WEB 131	*See* Reference Window: Viewing and Saving an Attached File in Windows Mail	Windows Mail
Contact, add to address book	WEB 119	*See* Reference Window: Adding a Contact to the Outlook Express Address Book	Outlook Express
Contact, add to Windows Contacts	WEB 138	*See* Reference Window: Adding a Contact to Windows Contacts	Windows Mail
Cookies, delete all	WEB 40	*See* Reference Window: Deleting all Cookies in Internet Explorer	Internet Explorer
Cookies, setting placement options	WEB 40	*See* Reference Window: Set Internet Explorer Options that Control Placement of Cookies on Your Computer	Internet Explorer
Favorite, move to a new folder	WEB 31	*See* Reference Window: Moving an Existing Favorite into a New Folder	Internet Explorer
Favorites Center, open	WEB 29	Click the Favorites Center button	Internet Explorer
Favorites folder, create	WEB 30	*See* Reference Window: Creating a New Favorites Folder	Internet Explorer
File, attach in New Message window	WEB 109	Click the Attach button, locate and double-click the file	Outlook Express
File, attach in New Message window	WEB 128	Click the Attach File To Message button, locate and double-click the file	Windows Mail
File, download using a browser	WEB 290	*See* Reference Window: Using a Browser to Download a File	Internet Explorer
Full Screen, change to	WEB 24	Click the Tools button arrow, click Full Screen	Internet Explorer

TASK	PAGE #	RECOMMENDED METHOD	WHERE USED
Group of contacts, add to address book	WEB 121	*See* Reference Window: Adding a Group of Contacts to the Address Book	Outlook Express
Group of contacts, add to Windows Contacts	WEB 140	*See* Reference Window: Adding a Group of Contacts to Windows Contacts	Windows Mail
Help, get	WEB 41	*See* Reference Window: Opening Internet Explorer Help	Internet Explorer
History list, open	WEB 33	Click the Recent Pages button, click History	Internet Explorer
Home page, change default	WEB 34	*See* Reference Window: Changing the Default Home Page in Internet Explorer	Internet Explorer
Home page, return to	WEB 34	Click the Home button	Internet Explorer
Internet Explorer, start	WEB 21	Click the Start button, point to All Programs, click Internet Explorer	
Mail account, set up	WEB 106	Click Tools, click Accounts, click the Mail tab, click the Add button, follow steps in the Internet Connection Wizard	Outlook Express
Mail account, set up	WEB 125	Click Tools, click Accounts, click the Add button, click E-mail Account, click Next, follow the on-screen steps	Windows Mail
Mail folder, create	WEB 116, WEB 135	Right-click the folder in which to create the new folder, click New Folder, type the name of the folder, click OK	Outlook Express, Windows Mail
Mail folder, delete	WEB 118	*See* Reference Window: Deleting an Email Message or a Folder in Outlook Express	Outlook Express
Mail folder, delete	WEB 137	*See* Reference Window: Deleting an Email Message or a Folder in Windows Mail	Windows Mail
Mail, compose	WEB 108, WEB 127	Click the Create Mail button	Outlook Express, Windows Mail
Mail, delete	WEB 118	*See* Reference Window: Deleting an Email Message or a Folder in Outlook Express	Outlook Express
Mail, delete	WEB 137	*See* Reference Window: Deleting an Email Message or a Folder in Windows Mail	Windows Mail
Mail, delete permanently	WEB 118, WEB 137	Open the Deleted Items folder, click the message to delete, click the Delete button, click the Yes button	Outlook Express, Windows Mail
Mail, forward	WEB 116	*See* Reference Window: Forwarding an Email Message Using Outlook Express	Outlook Express
Mail, forward	WEB 135	*See* Reference Window: Forwarding an Email Message Using Windows Mail	Windows Mail
Mail, move to another folder	WEB 117, WEB 136	Drag the message from the message list to a folder in the Folders pane	Outlook Express, Windows Mail
Mail, print	WEB 117, WEB 136	Click the message in the Inbox, click the Print button, click the Print button again	Outlook Express, Windows Mail
Mail, read	WEB 111, WEB 130	Click the message summary	Outlook Express, Windows Mail
Mail, receive	WEB 110	*See* Reference Window: Using Outlook Express to Send and Receive Messages	Outlook Express
Mail, receive	WEB 130	*See* Reference Window: Using Windows Mail to Send and Receive Messages	Windows Mail

TASK	PAGE #	RECOMMENDED METHOD	WHERE USED
Mail, reply to	WEB 115	*See* Reference Window: Replying to a Message Using Outlook Express	Outlook Express
Mail, reply to	WEB 134	*See* Reference Window: Replying to a Message Using Windows Mail	Windows Mail
Mail, send	WEB 108	*See* Reference Window: Sending a Message Using Outlook Express	Outlook Express
Mail, send	WEB 127	*See* Reference Window: Sending a Message Using Windows Mail	Windows Mail
Mail, send and receive	WEB 110	*See* Reference Window: Using Outlook Express to Send and Receive Messages	Outlook Express
Mail, send and receive	WEB 130	*See* Reference Window: Using Windows Mail to Send and Receive Messages	Windows Mail
Mail, spell check in New Message window	WEB 110, WEB 129	Click the Spelling button	Outlook Express, Windows Mail
Outlook Express, start	WEB 106	Click the Start button, point to All Programs, click Outlook Express	
Page tabs, using for navigation	WEB 35	*See* Reference Window: Using Page Tabs to Navigate in Internet Explorer	Internet Explorer
Start page, return to	WEB 28	Click the Home button	Internet Explorer
Toolbar, customize	WEB 25	Click the Tools button arrow, click Toolbars, click Customize	Internet Explorer
Toolbar, hide or restore	WEB 25	See Reference Window: Hiding and Restoring Toolbars in Internet Explorer	Internet Explorer
URL, enter and go to	WEB 25	*See* Reference Window: Entering a URL in the Address Bar	Internet Explorer
Web page image, save	WEB 45	*See* Reference Window: Saving an Image from a Web Page	Internet Explorer
Web page navigation using hyperlinks and the mouse	WEB 27	*See* Reference Window: Navigating Between Web Pages Using Hyperlinks and the Mouse	Internet Explorer
Web page text, copying to a WordPad document	WEB 43	*See* Reference Window: Copying text from a Web Page to a WordPad Document	Internet Explorer
Web page text, save	WEB 43	*See* Reference Window: Copying Text from a Web Page to a WordPad Document	Internet Explorer
Web page, change print settings	WEB 37	Click the Print button arrow, click Page Setup	Internet Explorer
Web page, check security elements	WEB 38	Click the Page button arrow, click Security Report, click View certificates button	Internet Explorer
Web page, move forward in history list	WEB 14	Click the Forward button	Internet Explorer
Web page, preview	WEB 36	Click the Print button arrow, click Print Preview	Internet Explorer
Web page, print	WEB 36	*See* Reference Window: Printing the Current Web Page	Internet Explorer
Web page, refresh	WEB 14	Click the Refresh button	Internet Explorer
Web page, return to previous in history list	WEB 14	Click the Back button	Internet Explorer
Web page, save	WEB 42	*See* Reference Window: Saving a Web Page	Internet Explorer
Web pages, move between using hyperlinks and the mouse	WEB 27	*See* Reference Window: Navigating Between Web Pages Using Hyperlinks and the Mouse	Internet Explorer

TASK	PAGE #	RECOMMENDED METHOD	WHERE USED
Windows Contacts, open	WEB 139	Click the Contacts button	Windows Mail
Windows Mail, start	WEB 125	Click the Start button, click All Programs, click Windows Mail	
WEB TASKS			
Business listings, find	WEB 243	*See* Reference Window: Finding Business Listings on the Web	Web
Clustered search results using Clusty	WEB 209	*See* Reference Window: Obtaining Clustered Search Results Using Clusty	Web
Complex search using AltaVista	WEB 203	*See* Reference Window: Conducting a Complex Search Using AltaVista	AltaVista
Current news stories, search	WEB 233	*See* Reference Window: Searching Current News Stories	Web
Filtered search using Ask.com	WEB 205	*See* Reference Window: Conducting a Filtered Search Using Ask.com	Ask Jeeves
Filtered search using Google Advanced Search	WEB 207	*See* Reference Window: Conducting a Filtered Search Using Google Advanced Search	Google
Local area map, find a	WEB 239	*See* Reference Window: Finding a Local Area Map on the Web	Web
Metasearch engine, use	WEB 196	*See* Reference Window: Using a Metasearch Engine	Web
Travel destination information, find	WEB 241	*See* Reference Window: Obtaining Travel Destination Information	Web
Video Clips, find	WEB 263	*See* Reference Window: Finding Video Clips Online	Web
Weather forecast, find	WEB 236	*See* Reference Window: Finding a Weather Forecast	Web
Web research resource, evaluate	WEB 214	*See* Reference Window: Evaluating a Web Research Resource	Web
Web sites that have been modified recently, find	WEB 229	See Reference Window: Finding Web Sites that Have Been Modified Recently	Web
White pages listing, search	WEB 245	*See* Reference Window: Searching for Your White Pages Listing	Web
WINDOWS LIVE HOTMAIL TASKS			
Attached file, save	WEB 157	See Reference Window: Viewing and Saving an Attached File in Windows Live Hotmail	Windows Live Hotmail
Attached file, view	WEB 157	*See* Reference Window: Viewing and Saving an Attached File in Windows Live Hotmail	Windows Live Hotmail
Contact, add to Windows Live Contacts	WEB 163	*See* Reference Window: Adding a Contact to Windows Live Contacts	Windows Live Hotmail
File, attach	WEB 154	Click Attach, click File, click Browse if using Firefox, locate and double-click the file, click Open or OK	Windows Live Hotmail
Group, add to Windows Live Contacts	WEB 164	*See* Reference Window: Adding a Group to Windows Live Contacts	Windows Live Hotmail
Mail folder, create	WEB 161	Click the Mail page, click the Inbox, click New button arrow, click Folder, type the folder name, press Enter	Windows Live Hotmail
Mail folder, delete	WEB 162	*See* Reference Window: Deleting a Windows Live Hotmail Folder	Windows Live Hotmail
Mail, compose	WEB 153	Go to the Windows Live Hotmail home page, log on to your account, click New	Windows Live Hotmail

TASK	PAGE #	RECOMMENDED METHOD	WHERE USED
Mail, delete	WEB 162	*See* Reference Window: Deleting an Email Message Using Windows Live Hotmail	Windows Live Hotmail
Mail, delete permanently	WEB 162	*See* Reference Window: Deleting an Email Message Using Windows Live Hotmail	Windows Live Hotmail
Mail, forward	WEB 160	*See* Reference Window: Forwarding an Email Message Using Windows Live Hotmail	Windows Live Hotmail
Mail, print	WEB 161	Select the message, click Print, select your printer, click Print or OK	Windows Live Hotmail
Mail, read	WEB 156	Log on to your Windows Live Hotmail account, click the Mail page, click the sender's name for the message in the Inbox	Windows Live Hotmail
Mail, receive	WEB 156	Click the Inbox	Windows Live Hotmail
Mail, reply to all recipients	WEB 159	*See* Reference Window: Replying to a Message Using Windows Live Hotmail	Windows Live Hotmail
Mail, reply to sender	WEB 159	*See* Reference Window: Replying to a Message Using Windows Live Hotmail	Windows Live Hotmail
Mail, send	WEB 153	*See* Reference Window: Sending a Message Using Windows Live Hotmail	Windows Live Hotmail
Mail, spell check	WEB 155	Make sure the "Spell check on" button is enabled, right-click a word with a red, wavy underline, and either click the correct word in the list, ignore the error, add the word to the dictionary, or close the menu and edit the word	Windows Live Hotmail
Windows Live Contacts, open	WEB 163	Click the Contacts page	Windows Live Hotmail
Windows Live Hotmail account, set up	WEB 144	Start your browser, connect to the Internet, go to the Windows Live Hotmail home page, click Sign up, follow the on-screen steps	Windows Live Hotmail
Windows Live Hotmail, start	WEB 150	Go to the Windows Live Hotmail home page, log on to your account	Windows Live Hotmail